For Richard Petter
With best personal regards
Jean Marie Fabey

Washington DC
April 1984

The Spanish Civil War, 1936-39

American Hemispheric Perspectives

Edited by Mark Falcoff and Fredrick B. Pike

UNIVERSITY OF NEBRASKA PRESS
Lincoln and London

凹凹

Copyright 1982 by the University of Nebraska Press
All rights reserved
Manufactured in the United States of America

The paper in this book meets the guidelines for permanence and
durability of the Committee on Production Guidelines for Book
Longevity of the Council on Library Resources

Library of Congress Cataloging in Publication Data
Main entry under title:
The Spanish Civil War, 1936–39.

   Includes index.
   Contents: Annotated chronology / by Fredrick
B. Pike — Introduction: the background to the
Civil War in Spain . . . / by Fredrick B. Pike —
Mexico / by T. G. Powell — [etc.]
   1. Spain—History—Civil War, 1936–1939—
Foreign public opinion—Addresses, essays, lec-
tures.   2. Spain—History—Civil War, 1936–1939—
Influence and results—Addresses, essays, lectures.
3. Latin America—History—20th century—Addresses,
essays, lectures.   I. Falcoff, Mark, 1941–
II. Pike, Fredrick B.
DP269.8.P8S6   946.081   81–14644
ISBN 0–8032–1961–X   AACR2

Contents

Preface

Mark Falcoff

Today, forty years after its conclusion, the Spanish civil war has come to be recognized as one of the most critical events in the political history of the twentieth century. And it is becoming increasingly clear, as well, that it constitutes a major turning-point in the evolution of Western culture and thought. In an age in which all of the great crusades of the recent past have suffered from the closer inspection of revisionist historians or the cynicism of hindsight, to a remarkable degree the Spanish war remains "the last great cause," the one heroic undertaking of our troubled century still worthy of the commitment and sacrifice it exacted, not only from its participants but also from the politically engaged of many countries.

The most enduring capacity of the Spanish conflict to capture the imagination of the world will be found in any university library. There, where the ages of Spanish history march briskly along a few feet of shelving space, there is a sudden slowing of progress in 1931, a pause for the ill-fated Second Republic, and then, for three years commencing in 1936, a vast expansion of titles, not infrequently matching in number all that has gone before. In 1964, a leading scholar of the war cited the existence of more than five hundred books on the subject in various European languages. In the past fifteen years, that figure has probably doubled, due partly to the rising interest of a new generation of authors too young to remember the war itself, but also to a loosening of censorship in Spain, facilitating a new wave of publications, many by exiles who have finally returned to tell their own story.

In the Western democracies, particularly Great Britain, France, and the United States, much of the interest evoked by the Spanish war has been a response to the belief that it was a critical encounter between democracy and fascism, whose tragic outcome rendered the Second World War virtually inevitable. This line of interpretation holds that the failure of bourgeois democracy to—in the characteristically hyperbolic phrase—"stop fascism in its tracks in Spain" revealed a basic lack of resolve that encouraged Hitler and Mussolini to pursue their aggressive designs for world domination, at a human and cultural cost that is still being paid. But, as Professor Pike points out in the Introduction to this book, often the Spanish conflict was also viewed by the same commentators in a somewhat wider (and more fantastic) perspective: as the struggle of a more primitive, more rural, and presumably more "innocent" and authentic civilization against the corrupting forces of modern technology and its allegedly dehumanizing social institutions— the sharpest metaphor being the bombing of the Basque village of Guernica by the German Condor Legion in 1937. Whatever the ultimate validity of these "Western" views of the Spanish civil war (and contemporary scholarship is doing much to question them), they remain the operative myths that define the posture of left-wing intellectuals in Western Europe and the United States, today much as they did for their predecessors a generation or two ago.

In the fifteen republics of Spanish America, the war provoked a debate hardly less passionate, but one that turned on a quite different set of issues. There, a confrontation between "democracy" and "fascism" could hardly take place on any level other than the literary, for in no Spanish American country was fascism (understood as an authoritarian mass movement of the right) a serious threat to the established order, and democracy (at least as practiced in Western Europe, the United States, and even in the Spanish Republic) could be found almost nowhere. On the other hand, the peculiarly *Spanish* controversies that had ignited the war in the first place—land reform, the role of the military in public life, church-state relations, educational and cultural innovation—were fully familiar to Spanish Americans, since for the most part the very same issues (often in a somewhat different form) had long constituted the neuralgic points of their own public life. It was these issues that informed Spanish American discussion of the peninsular conflict, and their outcome in Spain did much to influence the course of Spanish American history. What those issues were, how they were interpreted, how they affected official relations with embattled Republican Spain, and how they shaped subsequent events in Spanish America is the subject of the present volume. The essays that follow are thus intended to contribute both to the history of the Spanish civil war and to that of six Spanish American republics during a particularly important period of political and cultural transition.

Unlike Americans or Western Europeans, Spanish Americans did not "discover" the criticality of Spanish issues in the summer of 1936. Although more than a hundred years had passed since these countries had formed part of the Spanish Empire, the severing of colonial ties had not diminished peninsular influence altogether. Indeed, in two countries —Cuba and Argentina—it had dramatically intensified as a consequence of massive immigration. When the Spanish American republics observed their centenary of independence in 1924, the Mother Country had long since lost her cultural supremacy over their elites to France and her control of the region's economy to Great Britain and the United States, but her imprint was still unmistakable in the language, in religious and social customs, in architecture and literary trends, in some political forms and military practices. This influence, moreover, was continually revivified (particularly after 1898) by the uninterrupted export to Spanish America of immigrants, university lecturers, books and their authors, clergymen, and a wide range of consumer goods.[1] Although Spanish statesmen and publicists always tended to exaggerate (sometimes wildly) the importance of these influences, and to minimize (often scandalously) the competing indigenous and non-Hispanic contributions to Latin American life, it is nonetheless true that, right up to the Second World War, Spanish American nations bore the unmistakable marks of their own parentage and regarded Spanish culture as part of their national patrimony.

The unique position of Spain in the constellation of foreign influences in Latin America entered a new and somewhat confusing phase after the fall of the monarchy in 1931, for the Second Republic, which shortly followed, shifted the cultural ground on which so many Spanish Americans had long assumed they stood. As I have remarked in my essay in this volume, the years 1931–36 in Spain were characterized by "a frontal attack on an entire series of national ills whose nature had been the subject of informed public discussion for more than a hundred years. . . . To many, the fall of the monarchy was the signal for the release of pent-up energies and forces, through whose actions Spain would presumably telescope in a few brief moments the centuries of European history that had passed her by since the Counter Reformation." The drama that unfolded in the Second Republic during the early thirties thus touched only superficially on Europe-wide questions of "fascism" and "democracy"; in reality, it turned on a far older theme in Spanish history—the confrontation between modernity and tradition, a tension always present (in a somewhat different form) in Spanish America as well.

What was wrenching about this process for Spanish Americans was the degree to which they were deprived, almost overnight, of what had once been an unambiguous point of cultural reference. Spain herself ceased to be a fixed, identifiable quantity, a home to which one could finally return after having sampled—and become disillusioned with— the glittering but ultimately unsatisfying products of other civilizations. Instead, taking a page from the book of her estranged children in the Americas, the Mother Country herself was now seen shopping for ideologies and agendas in the familiar marketplaces of Northern Europe and even the Soviet Union. Not all Spanish Americans were pleased; none viewed this development as a matter of mere academic interest.

In order to understand why this was so, it is necessary to review briefly the role that Spain had played in the forging of Spanish American identity. Since the early nineteenth century, to many Spanish Americans "Spain" represented a heritage that both attracted and repelled. For conservatives, it embodied what anthropologists like to call the Great Tradition, the quintessential expression of racial genius and the ultimate source of cultural identity. The fact that it also stood for a society dominated by a landed aristocracy, the church, and the military made it no less attractive to this class, for whom the first half of the nineteenth century was one long essay in the restoration of a social order sundered by the wars of independence. For Spanish American liberals, in contrast, Spain had been—in Bolívar's unforgettable phrase —"the stepmother," destroyer of noble Indian civilizations, oppressor of the mixed-blood populations that followed, and source of all those features that allegedly kept the Spanish American republics in a state of perpetual backwardness and humiliation. For these people, the Mother Country represented a long, dark medieval night perpetually threatening to descend once more, whether in the form of peninsular reconquest, conservative political hegemony, or home-grown clericalism.

This opposition, of course, oversimplifies matters somewhat. For example, after the defeat of Spain in Cuba by the United States in 1898, some Spanish American liberals favored rapprochement with the Mother Country in the light of the more pressing threat of United States expansion; some of these same commentators even tried to discern within the Spanish tradition certain liberal strains with which to identify—an enterprise that met with indifferent success. The point is, however, that for both Hispanophiles and Hispanophobes in the Western hemisphere, until 1931 "Spain" represented an unambiguous polar reference point by which they could pilot their own quest for national identity.

The coming of the Second Republic reversed the terms of debate: at first, at least, Spanish American liberals were delighted to find in the peninsula a vitality, an optimism, and a will for renewal far greater indeed than in any other Western European nation for the same period, whereas conservatives, disconcerted by the anti-clerical projects of the regime and the excesses of its followers, as well as its halting, if resolute, attacks on large landed property and the military caste, were overcome by a sense of anger and betrayal. When Spain split in two in 1936, this debate entered a new phase. Two Spains, presumably of equal authenticity, offered Spanish Americans a choice.

The conflict over which Spain was the real one—a debate that unsettled virtually every Spanish American republic—thus replicated, in an appropriately colonial fashion, the drama of the peninsula itself. As the essays that follow show, the terms of that conflict varied enormously from country to country, depending on its racial makeup and historical experience in the conquest and the wars of independence, the size of its Spanish community, the strength (or weakness) of liberal institutions, the countervailing powers of the clergy and military, and the general direction of its political life. The Spanish civil war thus constitutes an extremely useful measure with which to establish the comparative distance traveled by Spanish American republics since independence and to view, within the framework of ideology and foreign policy, the peculiar social and ideological tensions of the nineteen-thirties.

"Nineteen-thirties" is itself a key term of critical significance here, for much of the interest of these essays rests on the fact that they explore the great questions of Spain and Spanish America at the very point when the spirit of Victorian optimism, which had hitherto guided the development of these countries, suffered a definitive collapse. Far more than the First World War, the Great Depression of 1929–30 had exposed the inadequacies of liberal institutions in Spanish America and encouraged the search for alternatives. What the "crisis of 1930" revealed to Spanish Americans was, above all, that no single nineteenth-century panacea—civilian government, parliamentary representation,

xiv   THE SPANISH CIVIL WAR: AMERICAN HEMISPHERIC PERSPECTIVES

secularization of education, professionalization of the military—was as important in determining their fate as their role in the international division of labor. Moreover, the enormity of the crash exposed, supposedly for all time, the fundamental weakness of those nations (Great Britain, France, the United States) who in the past had served as developmental models. At the same time, it imparted to Fascist Italy and Nazi Germany (and, in a somewhat different fashion, the Soviet Union) a glitter of success that proved irresistible to many. Perhaps most important of all, since most of these countries were still ruled by traditional elites, the world crisis seemed to reveal that liberal institutions were no longer capable of managing the tensions generated by modernization—urbanization, secularization, the entry into the political scene of an organized and militant proletariat, the creation of an adversary intelligentsia, and so on.

What appealed to many Spanish Americans about European fascism was precisely its presumed capacity to integrate modernization within the framework of traditional social controls and values. To be sure, this came from a rather superficial reading of European events, but the point is valid nonetheless. It was to Italy, after all, that Chilean President Arturo Alessandri repaired after his overthrow by the military in 1924, and many a later Latin American leftist (including the present "red" Archbishop of Olinda and Recife, Brazil, Dom Helder Câmara) learned his first political lessons at the school of Salazar and Mussolini.

It is against this background that one can easily understand the widespread response to the Spanish war. To the Spanish American right, the Franco uprising suggested not only that traditional elements in peninsular society had lost none of their historic vitality but also that they possessed the capacity to generate a new, post-capitalist political system that "worked." For the left, however, the Spanish war likewise afforded grounds for hope and reasons for identification. Here, after all, was a society, long written off by its own liberals as irremediably backward and in need of "Europeanization" (no less!), moving to the very vanguard of Western European political and cultural life. The Anglo-Saxons and the French could debate democracy and fascism; to the Spanish Americans, the war represented a contest between two roads to modernization—one that would leave the institutions of the past fundamentally in place, adapting them to new uses and needs, and another that sought to supersede them altogether, partly by drawing on a supposedly primordial Iberian social order whose latterday expressions were anarchism, anarcho-syndicalism, and revolutionary socialism. At a time when Spanish Americans were throwing off the inherited cultural baggage of the previous hundred years and seeking new sources of authenticity and direction, developments in the peninsula could not fail to be of consuming interest, all the more so because the structure and values of Iberian society continued to parallel, in so many important respects, their own.

It remains to justify our selection of the countries to be studied. Mexico was an obvious choice because, apart from its regional importance, it had already experienced a revolution whose goals were, at least in theory, the same as those that actuated the Second Republic in Spain. It was also the only country to unambiguously rush to the aid of the Republic in wartime, and it received a larger number of refugees after 1939 than any other. The linkages between the Spanish war and a later social revolution made Cuba of especial interest, to which might be added the fact that for its size the island republic had the largest Spanish community of any Latin American nation. Colombia could not easily be omitted, since it was perhaps the classical land of "liberalism" and "conservatism" in the Spanish sense of those words, where church-state relations and a debate between corporatists and individualists have dominated political discourse since independence.

Peru, the quintessential "Indian" country of South America, cast in exaggerated relief some of the issues of national identity that any controversy involving Spain would naturally engender. The lively, vivid political life of Chile—in some ways, closer to that of the Spanish Republic than any other—assumed additional importance in the context of a Popular Front government, the only such regime in the Spanish world apart from that in the peninsula itself. Argentina, the leading Spanish American nation of the period, was also the one whose Spanish community was the most prosperous, the most active, and, in absolute numbers, the largest; further, the controversies of the day—particularly the role of the military in politics—made it a unique mirror in which to view reflections of events in the peninsula both before and after the war. The chapter on Spain and the United States reminds us that, from the Spanish American point of view, these two have been (and remain) the polar points of reference within which practically all discussions concerning tradition and modernity, order and progress, equality and hierarchy, have been carried on. In addition, the illusions that the United States has harbored about the peninsula have on occasion influenced U.S. policy in Spanish America as well.

Some countries have been omitted because the principal issues they raised are covered to some extent in existing chapters (Peru for

Bolivia, Argentina for Uruguay); others, like Ecuador, Venezuela, or the Central American republics, were left out simply for lack of space. And Brazil, here as elsewhere, requires a treatment apart, as accords with its cultural, geographical, and linguistic uniqueness. What would be required in any case would be a study of the effect of Salazar rather than Franco on Brazilian political thought and action. The editors and contributors cannot but hope that such a work may yet appear; if it were to owe any inspiration to the present volume, they would feel more than rewarded for the labors they have just completed.

Note

1. On this point one could hardly do better than to consult the masterly (and pioneering) work of my co-editor, Fredrick B. Pike, *Hispanismo, 1898–1936: Spanish Liberals and Conservatives and Their Relations with Spanish America* (Notre Dame, 1971).

Annotated Chronology

Fredrick B. Pike

The Background in Spain

1868   Queen Isabella II is overthrown, and subsequent endeavors to install a foreign prince on the Spanish throne end in failure.

1873   The First Republic is proclaimed, but extreme regionalism threatens to dismember the nation.

1875–1902   Restoration of the monarchy is accomplished as Alfonso XII, son of Isabella II, rules 1875–85. During the regency of María Cristina (1885–1902), Spain goes to war with the United States, and in consequence of its defeat *(el desastre)* loses Cuba, Puerto Rico, and the Philippines. Following 1898, the year of *el desastre,* Spain attempts to recoup her losses by intensifying efforts to maintain a cultural presence, and even to establish a spiritual leadership, in Spanish America while at the same time strengthening economic ties with the former colonies. Hispanismo, as this program is called, is directed toward containing the rising tide of the United States cultural and economic penetration. Through the years, Hispanismo will enjoy only spotty success, rising to heights of literary frenzy in the years when Spanish American relations with the "Colossus of the North" are especially troubled, only to decline to well-nigh total insignificance in eras of North-South rapprochement, as in the late 1930s with the growing success of the Good Neighbor policy.

1902   Alfonso XIII attains his majority and ascends the Spanish throne.

1914–18   Spain maintains neutrality in World War I, but Restoration compromises and accommodations begin to disintegrate before a rising tide of social discontent.

1919–23   Waves of strikes and violence engulf the country, as failures in the unpopular Moroccan War are highlighted by the 1921 disaster at Annual.

The 1920s in Spain and Spanish America: Firm-Handed Politics and Signs of Economic Development

Spain   The dictatorship of General Miguel Primo de Rivera, Marqués de Estella (1923–30), produces bungled attempts to restructure the socio-economic system along corporatist lines. Despite difficulties, many economic and social indices rise, but intellectuals grow increasingly intransigent and anarchists more militant in their opposition.

Mexico   General Plutarco Elías Calles, as president and strong man, begins to bring order to Mexico (1924–34), convulsed by revolutionary conflict since 1910.

Cuba   General Gerardo Machado rules as dictator (1925–33) against an initial background of sugar-based prosperity and an orgy of corruption.

Colombia   The Conservative Party, in power since 1909, rides a coffee boom that contributes to stability.

Peru   The eleven-year modernizing civilian dictatorship of Augusto B. Leguía (1919–30), a period known as the *oncenio,* benefits from an expanding export economy and the availability of foreign credit.

Chile   Military intervention occurs in 1924—for the first time in more than thirty years—when President Arturo Alessandri, elected in 1920, proves unable to deliver on promises of renovation. After an initial period of confusion, Lieutenant-Colonel Carlos Ibáñez del Campo assumes power as a reformist-moderate military dictator (1925–31).

Argentina   An increasingly divided Radical party, which had turned a Conservative "oligarchy" out of office in 1916 on the promise of extensive reforms, suffers from a lack of direction and from corruption on a more extensive scale than ever before. Elected for a second presidential term in 1928, Radical leader Hipólito Yrigoyen is unable to heal divisions within the party or to meet rising demands for basic transformations.

From 1930 to 1939: Highlights in Spain and the American Hemisphere

1930   Primo de Rivera resigns as Spain's prime minister in January, and political turmoil mounts.
Enrique Olaya Herrera is elected president of Colombia for a four-year term, marking the return of the Liberal party to power. Liberals will shortly exult over the establishment of a Republic in Spain, recognizing the *madre patria's* Republicans as brothers-in-arms in the struggle against conservative obscurantism. Leguía is overthrown in Peru, as the military assumes a tenuous control. Undermined—like Primo de Rivera, Colombian Conservatives, and Leguía—by the effects of the Great Depression, President Yrigoyen is ousted in Argentina by General José F. Uriburu, who launches an attempt to impose corporatist structures under military supervision.

1931   After elections in the larger municipalities produce Republican majorities, Alfonso XIII abdicates and departs Spain in April. The Second Republic is proclaimed. The anti-clerical initiatives of the government of Manuel Azaña, accompanied by widespread convent burnings and terrorism, begin to polarize the nation. Azaña moves further left in October, shunting aside the centrist Radicals and relying more heavily on the Socialists.
Luis Sánchez Cerro is elected president of Peru, defeating the leftist challenge of the *Alianza Popular Revolucionaria Americana* (APRA). Peruvian defenders of the embattled establishment begin to compare Apristas to the extremists among Spanish Republicans, ready to label both as Communists.
Ibáñez is overthrown as an economic crisis grips Chile. The political situation grows increasingly chaotic as Socialists of various beliefs, encouraged by events in Spain, prepare an all-out bid for power.
Uriburu faces increasing difficulties within Argentina as the Conservatives and other traditional right-of-center forces join with proscribed Radicals to oppose a corporatist restructuring of the political system.

1932   Spanish parliamentary elections in November result in a rightist victory. Alejandro Lerroux of the Radical Party forms a government with the support, but not yet the direct participation, of the Confederación de Derechas Autónomas (CEDA), presided over by José María Gil Robles, whom leftists accuse of Fascist leanings. Arturo Alessandri is elected, for the second time, president of Chile, in December. The inception of his six-year rule brings an end to the period of military intervention initiated in 1924. Pursuing a conservative law-and-order approach, Alessandri is sympathetic to the Spanish right.

Uriburu is forced to step down in Argentina in favor of his rival within the army, General Agustín P. Justo, who is elected (through fraudulent balloting) to a six-year term, beginning a period of Conservative-Radical collaboration known as the Concordancia. Primarily concerned—like Alessandri—with a return to "business as usual," the Concordancia's leaders are equally opposed to corporatist "regeneration" and leftism of any sort, whether in Argentina or Spain.

1933   Prophesying their country's move into fascism, Spanish leftists grow increasingly alienated from the moderate-conservative (but certifiably Republican) Lerroux government. Some Socialists, under Francisco Largo Caballero, assume a revolutionary (as opposed to a gradualist, social democratic) stance, but others, under Indalecio Prieto, pursue a moderate, collaborationist line. In many ways, the Socialist rift will never be healed.

Under pressure from the newly-inaugurated Franklin D. Roosevelt administration in the United States, Machado steps down in Cuba as a period of intense political unrest begins. A "Sergeants' Revolt," led by Fulgencio Batista, portends a new era of military-civilian collaboration, purportedly in line with New Deal reformism.

Sánchez Cerro is assassinated in Peru, and Marshal Oscar Benavides begins a moderate, reformist dictatorship against a background of virtual civil war as the APRA continues its struggle for power. Like Alessandri in Chile and Justo in Argentina, Benavides favors the Spanish right as the only viable alternative to chaos and communism.

1934   Lerroux in October permits participation of CEDA ministers in his government, which precipitates an unsuccessful Socialist insurrection in the Asturias and a separatist revolt in Catalonia. Government repression intensifies in the aftermath of these uprisings.

General Lázaro Cárdenas, elected to a six-year presidential term in Mexico, will gain increasing institutional control over the previously unfocused forces of the Revolution and initiate sweeping social reforms. At first, his position toward the Spanish Republic remains ambivalent, given the temporary ascendancy of conservative forces. Only after the Mexican president consolidates his own power in the aftermath of breaking with his patron, Calles, and after the Republic itself moves leftward in February 1936, will Cárdenas extend his enthusiastic blessings. Ruling through puppets, Batista begins to emerge as the dominant figure in Cuban politics, seeking to legitimate his power through social reforms and democratic posturings.

The Liberal party's Alfonso López Pumarejo is elected to a four-year term as president of Colombia and unveils a program of extensive reform dubbed *la revolución en marcha* (the revolution on the march).

1935   Spain is plagued by increasing ministerial instability as rightists disagree on the most effective means of maintaining the upper hand over their opponents.

The mood of isolation from Europe contributes to the ongoing efforts of the FDR administration to forge a solid basis of American hemisphere collaboration. Latin America, however, remains suspicious about U.S. intervention and reluctant to be drawn into trade patterns that diminish ties to Europe.

1936   Spain's February parliamentary elections produce a narrow victory for the Popular Front, a coalition of Socialists, Communists, anarchists, and left-to-moderate Republicans. The country is increasingly polarized as various conservative factions refuse to resign themselves to their electoral defeat. Intransigent rightist José Calvo Sotelo is assassinated in July by assault guards of the Republican government, an event that helps to trigger a military uprising against the Popular Front that benefits from Italian backing. As Nationalist armies advance on Madrid in the fall, the first Communist International Brigade arrives. Madrid's reenforced Loyalists repulse the Nationalist attack, thereby ensuring a protracted struggle rather than the easy victory that many enemies of the Republic had initially anticipated.

Pressured by the British government, desiring Italian friendship, and fearing a general European war, the Popular Front government of Léon Blum in France falls into line with a non-intervention policy that denies British-French aid to the Loyalists but is powerless to block Russian assistance to the Republic or Italo-German aid to the Nationalists. Given the leftward move of the Republic in February, the die is cast: the Peruvian, Chilean, and Argentine regimes, preoccupied by issues of domestic order, will sympathize with the Nationalists.

In contrast, the advent of the Popular Front in Spain assures the warmth of an embrace by Mexico's Cárdenas, anxious to be seen as more of a leftist than in truth he is. Similarly, Colombian Liberals and Cuba's Batista display overt sympathy for the Republic, either because of supposed ideological compatibilities or because Loyalist partisanship is deemed a useful ploy in proving the sincerity of local reformist pronouncements. In short, and not surprisingly, Spanish-American responses to the civil war in Spain grow largely out of expediency defined in terms of the local political context. Nor does the United States prove an exception to this pattern. President Roosevelt and Secretary of State Cordell Hull intensify efforts to forge a united Latin American bloc favorably disposed to Washington's economic interests and international policies. In line with this, Washington moves further than ever before toward renouncing intervention in hemispheric affairs. Partly because of a desire not to offend partisans of either Republicans or Nationalists in Spanish America, Washington is disposed to follow the general lines of Anglo-French non-interventionist policies. Thereby the administration gains broad support from its own electorate, little inclined at this point to take on foreign commitments. At the same time, however, the New Deal administration incurs heated denunciations from a domestic intellectual community overwhelmingly committed to Spain's Republican cause.

1937   Spain's Nationalist movement gradually solidifies its components (ranging from capitalist pragmatists to ideological Carlists and Falangists) and acquires increasing support from Italy and Germany, although bargaining with the latter country remains acrimonious. Loyalists are beset by factional divisiveness as Communists move to gain control over the disorganized Republic, causing anarchists to slacken their war efforts. Extending their purges to Spain, Stalin's agents solidify their control over the government of Prime Minister Juan Negrín, to the discomfiture of the Republic's old-line Socialists. The lingering hopes for British-French aid with which to counter Russian leverage remain unfulfilled.

1938   As Stalin begins to reassess his international position, Russian supplies to the Republic taper off and the Nationalists continue their march to conquest. From President Azaña on down, Republicans increasingly are gripped by defeatism. Following the British-German Munich accords in the fall, Stalin decides on a policy of friendship with Hitler and withdraws the International Brigades from Spain.

In the wake of an unsuccessful putsch by Chile's Nazi party, a Popular Front of Radicals, Socialists and Communists (considerably more moderate than its Spanish namesake had been on assuming power) elects Radical Pedro Aquirre Cerda to the presidency. Though clearly favorable to the Loyalists, Chile's new government recognizes that the Spanish Republic is doomed. Roberto M. Ortiz, positively inclined toward Washington's international policies, is elected president of Argentina. He moves to counter the rising forces of right-wing nationalism in his country, whose representatives are ideologically sympathetic to the Spanish Nationalists as well as to German national socialism and Italian fascism. For a brief period, Argentina abandons its opposition to U.S. efforts to align the hemisphere in an unequivocal stance against international fascism.

1939 Loyalists in Madrid make a belated move against Communist domination but fail in peace negotiations with the Nationalists, who insist on unconditional surrender. On April 1, Generalissimo Franco announces the end of the war. In all, it has claimed an estimated 600,000 lives—authorities continue to argue heatedly over the exact number of casualties.
On April 5, Chile's Popular Front becomes the last Latin American regime—apart from Mexico, which never extended recognition—to establish relations with the Franco government.

1940 and Beyond

With the exception of Argentina, Latin America moves into line with Washington's hemispheric policies and grows increasingly committed to the Allied cause. Opposition mounts throughout the region to ideologies associated with Franco and the Axis. The Argentines, however, follow a path of their own, falling under radical-rightist and nationalist influences that help to prepare the way for the rise of Colonel Juan Perón.
Spain's endeavors to lure Spanish America away from Washington's leadership through the ideology of Hispanidad, stressing common ties of religion and cultural traditions that are fundamentally anti-liberal, are rebuffed. Outside of Argentina, authoritarian hopes have peaked by some time prior to 1940, and the counter-tide of gradualist, secular reform, drawing on economic concessions to reduce social tensions within a relatively liberal

political framework, and buoyed by hopes of massive post–World War II infusions of private and public U.S. development capital, begins to gather strength.

The cautious, pro-business presidencies of Manuel Avila Camacho in Mexico (1940–46), Batista in Cuba (1940–44), and Manuel Prado in Peru (1939–45), as well as the disintegration of Chile's Popular Front and the stuffily moderate presidency of Radical Juan Antonio Ríos (1942–46), all point to the prevailing concern for not rocking the boat or in any way jeopardizing capitalist development.

Only in later years, as disillusionment with liberal, reformist gradualism surfaces once more both in the United States and Spanish America, do the utopian might-have-beens of the Spanish civil war begin to fire the imagination of a new generation of seekers after the ideal society.

The Background to the Civil War in Spain and the U.S. Response to the War

Fredrick B. Pike

The Background in Europe and Spain: Dissenters from Modernity

In a fascination born of envy and scorn, European intellectuals turned their attention in the late nineteenth century to "primitive" Spain, struck by the differences that separated it from "progressive" nations. Composers reflected this trend. Among those who tried their hands at depicting Spain and its puzzling national character, or who found inspiration in Spanish sources, were—in addition to a distinguished group of Russians headed by Rimski-Korsakov—Georges Bizet, Emmanuel Chabrier, Claude Debussy, Edouard Lalo, Jules Massanet, Maurice Ravel, Gustav Mahler, Moritz Moskowski, Richard Strauss, Hugo Wolf, and Giuseppe Verdi. Spaniards also discerned the differences that excited both approbation and disdain among foreigners. Those who were proud of the differences talked of Spain's destiny in terms of *españolizar:* strengthening its "Spanishness." Those perceiving their distinctiveness as a badge of inferiority harped on the need to *europeizar* or Europeanize their land. In Spanish America a similar debate raged, but there contention often revolved about whether to spurn or emulate the United States. Thus the Hispanic world was rent by an identity dilemma—and the agonies of this dilemma would peak at the time of the Spanish civil war. To understand the broader background out of which this culminating struggle in the quest of identity emerged, and at the same time to comprehend the reaction of the outside world to Spain's civil war, it is necessary to cast a brief glance at Europe in the late nineteenth century. By then, many of the problems that brought dissension to the explosive stage among Spanish-speaking peoples in the 1930s had already been in evidence for a considerable time.

The processes of modernization that lay behind the bourgeois revolutions of Western Europe had left in their wake a great deal of human carnage and misery. Throughout much of the second half of the nineteenth century old aristocracies and new capitalist classes had, in fact, fretted over the danger of social uprisings from below or, more likely, of mass-supported revolutionary movements led from above by those who, because they had been victimized by ongoing change, spewed forth antimodernist anathemas.[1] By 1900, though, it seemed that bourgeois Europe (bourgeois is used to denote elites of power, wealth, and prestige, as well as their hangers-on) was learning to finesse the victims of modernization as the old, free-wheeling ways of liberal individualism gave way to social and economic planning.

The rationalization of capitalism already under way at the turn of the century not only accelerated the pace of cartelization but also brought about an interpenetration of economics and politics in which representatives of corporate giants acquired political clout while at the same time government bureaucracy took on economic roles aimed at controlling markets and allocating goods and resources. Corporate business groups, with the cooperation and sometimes the friendly nudging of government, took to dealing amicably, even paternalistically, with organized labor. Both in business and government circles confidence grew that rationalized corporations could produce sufficient wealth to placate labor through monetary rewards—a process that came to be known as economism. Society seemed about to surmount old adversary relationships between capital and labor as various forms of social insurance began to be perceived as perhaps even more beneficial to the privileged than to the lower classes.

In ways that differed from country to country, bourgeois Europe, as Charles Maier describes the development, was recast into a corporatist mold. Whether the process was carried out more by business itself as in Germany, or more by government as in Italy, or in a unique, combined approach as in France, the results were strikingly similar: parliaments became more and more irrelevant as each country found a new and precarious equilibrium "based upon new interest-group compromises or new forms of coercion."[2] By the late 1920s the trend had advanced so far that "increasingly the legislative processes tended only to register rather than to shape the results of bargaining between economic competitors or independent bureaucratic agencies.... Fragmented parliamentary majorities yielded to ministerial bureaucracies, or sometimes directly to party councils, where interest-group representatives could more easily work out social burdens and rewards."[3] Out of this corporatist equilibrium came at least a brief moment of conflict resolution that the old system could not have provided. Success depended on constant brokerage between interest groups as carried out not in parliament by elected representatives but in government ministries by bureaucrats beholden to leaders of business and finance rather than to an electorate..

Still, the victims of continuing modernization proved too numerous to be easily silenced. They included small businessmen and artisans, unorganized and without access to the evolving corporate mechanisms and unable to resist the centralization of expanding big business that drove them to the wall. Facing the prospect of proletarianization, these groups grew all the more hateful toward the proletariat. "They refused to make accord either with socialists, or with parties representing successful businessmen," as they sullenly awaited deliverance from other sources. The years of European inflation, culminating in 1923, witnessed the discomfiture of an increasing number of persons who once had considered themselves rather well off, including middle-class pensioners and shopkeepers. To their discontent was added that of farmers "bewildered to find themselves sinking into debt while others grew rich."[4] United with discomfited and *déclassé* middle sectors as well as farmers in condemning the course of events was a broad array of Europe's most articulate intellectuals. For many of them the quarrel with the existing order was basic and irreconcilable: it lay with the vital processes of modernization as heretofore carried out.

Directed toward maximizing material resources and using an ever-expanding potential for the enlargement and improvement of material life, modernization rests on the "long-term transformation of societies by industrialization, urbanization, bureaucratization, and the extension of social mobility and political participation."[5] It is equated, then, with technology, democracy, secularism, with individualism and progress;[6] its criteria derive from rationalism, empiricism, science, and the scientific method. It can, in fact, be defined as both the capacity to accept progressively the fruits of modern sciences and technology and the societal changes wrought by that process.[7] "During the past four centuries," writes Sheldon Wolin, " 'modernity' has become a summary expression for the material promises which the combined power of science, technology, and capitalist industrial organization would realize in ever-increasing increments."[8]

Within modern society, legitimacy for governing classes depends on their ability to satisfy the rising material expectations of the citizenry. Society's essential prerequisite thus becomes endless growth, as accomplished through science, technology, and management that can quantitatively demonstrate efficiency. From such a society the traditional sources of legitimacy, including magic and the sacred, the mystical and the mythical, together with all intuitive, suprarational approaches to knowledge and understanding, are banished in derision.

Antimodernist utopian intellectuals of the early twentieth century tended to claim supremacy in creative imagination, in the suprarational and suprasensatory realms of human existence. They contended that creativity as well as understanding of the human condition spring from the myth-haunted imagination. Science, they affirmed, concerned exclusively with the material, quantifiable aspects of existence, is incapable of the holistic vision of a world in which the sum is somehow greater than its measurable parts. On their claims to deal with the human condition in its entirety and to be able to provide ultimate meaning to life through the mystical, intuitive vision, intellectuals—many of whom stand as heirs to a neo-Platonic tradition—justified their demands for hierarchical preeminence in society, a preeminence akin to that granted the priesthood in most early societies.

Customarily uneasy about the claims of science in providing new and meaningful insights and put off by its demythologizing, desacralizing effects, poets, painters, and humanists felt more than ever threatened with obsolescence by the "second scientific revolution" under way in the early twentieth century. With Einstein as its most visible symbol, the second revolution seemed about to set scientists still farther apart from ordinary mortals and to confer on them a uniquely exalted status.

Who would mediate between scientists, standing apart with their secrets and speaking a recondite language comprehensible only to other scientists, and the commonality of mankind? Given the prevailing power structure of the early twentieth century, it seemed only too obvious that the politically entrenched, symbiotically united business-and-bureaucratic class would assume this function. Thus the very people whom intellectuals condemned as insensitive barbarians threatening to exterminate what was highest and noblest in humanity seemed about to strengthen their grip on power by providing linkage between a new breed of scientists and ordinary citizens. Dismayed by this prospect, intellectuals grew obsessed with changing the present order so that they might become the mediators and the political masters, or at the very least the favored allies, of the scientists. Thereby they could, ostensibly, direct new scientific discoveries and technology toward objectives that transcended mere material affluence.[9] Unless culturally-sensitive elites changed the current drift of civilization, the prevailing business-bureaucratic hierarchy, aided by technology, would develop means for buying the complacency of the masses through ever greater material rewards, all the while snuffing out the spiritual spark within them and transforming them into brutes, with the intellectuals shunted aside as superfluous beings.

The intellectuals' inability to find anything worthwhile in the existing order was reflected in the final volume of Marcel Proust's *Remembrance of Things Past,* published in 1927 and shortly referred to by Edmund Wilson as the history "of the Heartbreak House of capitalist culture." As a whole, however, intellectuals did not abandon themselves to heartbreak. They dreamed of a better future, even though it might be no more than the ephemeral one prophesied for Germany by Oswald Spengler in his apocalyptic second volume of *Decline of the West* (1922): the fleeting triumph of the heroic over the mercenary before ultimate tragedy overcame the West. Any number of intellectuals were more optimistic about long-term prospects. With psychiatrist Carl G. Jung[10] and philosopher José Ortega y Gasset,[11] with painters such as Max Pechstein and Paul Klee (who observed, "The world in its present shape is not the only possible world"[12]), and composers such as Gustav Mahler and Arnold Schönberg, they saw themselves as prophets who would forge not only a new science of intangibles and the unconscious, a new literature, art, and music, but beyond this a new world.[13]

The world depression caused utopianist prophets to take heart, for with it the demise of the old order seemed at hand. Bearing the brunt of the economic collapse, European youth emerged as the source of despair for defenders of the old ways but as the basis of hope for those obsessed with dreams of an altogether different tomorrow. With their "vigor, impatience, thwarted idealism, [and] conviction there must be a way out,"[14] alienated youth were hailed by intellectuals as the instrument for ending bourgeois materialism and imposing on the malleable men of science a new and more spiritual master class blessed with a holistic view of existence.

By the time of the depression, a certain commonality had emerged in bourgeois life throughout Europe. Similarly, a commonality in opposition to bourgeois life had appeared. Spain, because of its delayed modernization, had developed more slowly than other countries the commonality of bourgeois culture. By 1930, however, the dislocating effects of modernization and incipient *embourgeoisement* had impinged adversely on so many Spaniards that the same forces of opposition to capitalist modernity evident elsewhere in Europe had begun to burst forth. Thus, although the Spanish civil war was in many ways a home-grown phenomenon, it was also a reflection of the struggle between the defenders and critics of modernity, which, having originated in the late nineteenth century, threatened during the 1920s and 1930s to destabilize all of Europe.

With the onset of the depression, many Spanish utopianists could believe their ideal order was nearer at hand than in the advanced countries of Europe precisely because the bourgeoisie was of more recent origin and more tenuous in its existence. Thus the revolutionary rightist José Antonio Primo de Rivera proclaimed, "Spain, blessed be your backwardness,"[15] while on the left "even the hitherto reformist socialist party seemed to have become convinced that the millennium was at hand."[16]

Showing a naiveté that matched their impatience, Spain's proliferating millennialists, bent on extermination of the bourgeois threat, exhibited a glowing optimism about their country's natural wealth—even as most "Third World" radicals in the post-World War II era. Their country seemed a paradise of resources whose potential had remained unfulfilled because of institutions vitiated by sin and error.[17] Like their counterparts in developed Europe, Spain's prophets of a new day both excoriated and placed their hopes in science. They believed that science, once placed in the service of the people by virtuous leaders, "could bring the good life and happiness to all labouring mankind"[18] by turning natural potential into actual abundance.

The sanguine intellectuals, though, were not preoccupied with material abundance. Reflecting the neo-Platonic beliefs both of the European middle ages and the period between the two world wars, Spain's would-be shapers of a new order professed that the outer, material world was only part, and the least important part at that, of human existence. Typical of Spain's "Generation of 1927," Andalusian poet Vicente Aleixandre (winner of the Nobel Prize for literature in 1977) proclaimed his belief in the interior world of the unconscious, a world that was just as real and potentially far nobler than the sordid exterior world of business exchange and stock markets. He and his companions, at least vaguely aware of the Vienna school of psychiatry, regarded themselves as intellectual frontiersmen, exploring the long-neglected realms of inwardness. Beyond this, they had a mission that was by no means just inner-directed. Many of them, at least, were excited by the prospects of uplifting the masses. By resocializing marginal citizens, intellectuals hoped to transform them into beings concerned not so much with material as with nonmaterial gratifications. Once resocialized, their docility would be guaranteed by their ability to recognize the moral superiority of the philosopher-artist princes who by their creativity added to the common fund of spiritual treasure that would ultimately enrich the lives of underlings.

Spain and Modernization

Basically, the social-political ills that Spain's intellectuals felt called upon to cure in the early decades of the twentieth century can be traced to the incipient modernization that had brought in its wake the usual variety of discontents. Modern capitalism had been late in appearing in the Iberian peninsula. When it finally came, it tended to fall under the control of foreigners, particularly in the case of utilities, transport, and mining. Foreigners thus provided a convenient scapegoat for nationalistic and xenophobic critics of the economic-social order. The foreign presence and high visibility exacerbated traditional anticapitalist prejudices once directed primarily against Jews.[19] Meantime, persistent habits of savers and investors in seeking security in land and politics impeded the type of domestic capital formation that might have gone to create an industrial base. One consequence was that by the latter part of the century an overbuilt railroad system remained underutilized.[20] All the while, politically dominant Castile kept the portals tightly closed against the entry of capitalist institutions. Confined largely to Catalonia, the Asturias, and the Basque provinces, Spanish capitalism proved "unable to impose its values on Spanish society, [and] incapable of founding a broadly significant movement among the Spanish masses." Although remaining "something of a pariah among vested institutions of Spain,"[21] capitalism nevertheless slowly expanded its foothold in the late nineteenth and early twentieth centuries.

Even the tentative emergence of Spanish capitalism, and with it a cautious spirit of economic and even parliamentary liberalism, aroused opposition from various conservatives and helped to produce between 1899 and 1909 projects for corporative suffrage and an antimodernist "revolution from above." This in turn goaded the Liberal party toward increasingly progressive postitions embracing democratic reshaping of the upper house of the Cortes, or national assembly, and separation of church and state. Thus, by the years immediately preceding World War I, the consensus politics initiated in Restoration Spain by Cánovas del Castillo on the collapse of the First Republic (1875) had disintegrated. The internal political disarray in Spain raises doubt, as Thomas H. Baker points out, about the system's "potential to evolve into a genuine parliamentary democracy."[22]

Throughout developed Europe, by the end of the nineteenth century, governments were forming links to the proletariat by means of interventionist policies; they were, in fact, anticipating discontents that would otherwise have sustained or created the demand for political change. But in Spain it was different: the slow pace of development did not provide government with the wherewithal to placate the masses, even in the unlikely event that politicians could have agreed on the proper interventionist formulas.[23] By 1917 economic inadequacy had combined with political disputes, especially between clericals and secularists, to render the hopeful social legislation of the early twentieth century a dead letter.

Social problems intensified in the course of World War I, during which Spain remained neutral. The commercial advantages of neutrality swelled many private fortunes, creating a more highly visible body of plutocrats who, if anything, exhibited a lower level of ethics, discretion, and social responsibility than the families of old wealth. If for Russia the dislocations of war helped trigger a social revolution, for Spain the ostentatious success of a privileged few nourished by neutrality had very nearly the same consequence. Only the left's divisiveness and failure to coordinate the 1917 working-class uprisings with the 1918-20 agrarian insurrections granted a reprieve to the old order.[24]

By 1923 parliamentarism was held in lower esteem in Spain than in the rest of Europe, where, as already noted, it was giving way to de facto corporatism. Troubled by persisting social unrest, by a seemingly endless African war, and by a thoroughly splintered, ineffective, and discredited political system, King Alfonso XIII accepted military dictator Miguel Primo de Rivera as a savior.

The Great Depression brought a precipitous halt to the economic progress through which Primo de Rivera managed, for a time, to justify his presence at the helm. Forced into exile in 1930, he was shortly joined by Alfonso XIII as Spain embarked on its second experiment with republican rule[25] and elevated the moderate Niceto Alcalá Zamora, who had previously been a liberal monarchist, to the presidency—a position he would hold until the triumph of the Popular Front in April of 1936.

Seldom has an experiment with a new form of government been undertaken by a country so divided and factionalized as Spain in the 1930s. Contributing to a fundamental polarization was disagreement over the role that leaders should assume vis-à-vis the masses. One assortment of elites feared the masses above all else and thought only of how to keep them quiescent and politically marginal. Another assortment believed they could attain political power only by mobilizing mass support. This second group, as it turned out, forced the hand of the first, goading its members to respond to the mobilization efforts of their adversaries by turning their own hands to populist and incendiary politics. Tugged and pulled from different directions by uncompromising leaders in wild disagreement among themselves, the masses, though remaining pawns, were about to become politicized to a degree never before conceived of in Spain and scarcely matched even by Europe's most developed countries.

Spain's age of "the crowd," of the unleashed unconscious, as the crowd was described by influential French writer Gustave Le Bon,[26] had begun. But if the social unconscious had evolved into prominence just as its psychic counterpart was being projected into importance by Freud, Jung, and Adler, most self-styled "thinking" Spaniards remained persuaded that the unconscious needed a new kind of control and direction, a whole new set of norms, suited to the needs of a changing world order. But they could not agree on the nature of the new control, direction, and norms.

The Second Republic: The Left and the Ideological Labyrinth

The Moderate Left and Liberal Modernization vs. Corporatist Factions. Along with political participation of the masses and the religious question, the latter to be discussed under a separate heading, modernization was a principal issue in dividing Spaniards of the Second Republic. Indeed, the role of the masses and the religious question were largely subsumed under the modernization issue. In the ideological labyrinth resulting from the multitude of approaches to modernization, only one leftist faction advocated the classical, individualistic, free-enterprise capitalism approach. This faction of Republicans made up one sector of the moderate left.

Manuel Azaña provides the most striking example of a moderate left proponent of liberal modernization.[27] At different times minister of war, prime minister, and eventually president of the Second Republic, Azaña's attitudes led one observer to label him a political romantic: "For his approach to Spanish politics was predicated on the existence of a modern, economically developed, politically advanced Spain, a Spain in which a large, alert middle class stood as the guarantor of civil liberty and parliamentary democracy."[28]

Even more romantic was Azaña's view that the Spanish economy would rapidly develop the means to placate the masses through increased material rewards. In this, he and his school parted company with the great bulk of intellectuals and with many political figures. Spanish thinkers in the aggregate had long been persuaded that liberal-style modernization led inexorably to all-pervasive materialism that removed hierarchies of values along with gradations of social rank and thus encouraged what Ortega y Gasset graphically described as the vertical invasion of the barbarians. More than ever before, Spanish elites and would-be elites aspired during the Second Republic to a type of modernization that would leave hierarchies at the very core of social-political organization. Like Georges Sorel, who had a considerable following in Spain, they agreed on the importance of myth and magic as utilized by a new secular priesthood who, by drawing on their mastery over the realm of the mystical, could mobilize the masses in the service of a transcendent ideal.

Virtually all of those Spanish thinkers who rejected capitalism's leveling materialism and democracy's rationalistic pragmatism in their quest for moral certitude based on transcendent sources of cognition embraced one form or another of corporatism. A variety of reasons account for this, and the most important of them revolve about the issue of modernization.

Writing in *The Public Interest* (Summer 1976), Peter Berger attributes the durability of the Socialist theory to its promise to synthesize features of modernity and premodernity. According to its theory, socialism will bring about development without destroying the sense of community preserved in the Middle Ages and cherished among virtually all primitive societies. Even as it accomplishes prodigies of progress, socialism allegedly will nourish fraternity, persuading people to happily subordinate their personal desires to group interests and to the decisions of group and national leaders. Surely the subordination of the individual ego, potentially opening the way for the domination of the many by the few, is one of the most attractive features that elites (confident that they can avoid having their autonomy blunted by the herd instinct) have found in socialism.

Just as much as socialism, corporatism promises to weave the warp of modernity with the woof of traditionalism to produce a new social fabric. Believers in this theory foresee a society in which socially disruptive competitive individualism is tamed by the obligations of group belongingness, and in which the good life comes about, not through the operation of the unseen hand, but through the management and control of sensitive, intuitive leaders who understand how to control science and technology in the interest of objectives that surmount material gratification.

Within as well as without Spain, the cult of the "organic folk," much harped on by European intellectuals beginning around the middle of the nineteenth century, was based on a desire for solidarity and the end of emergent class conflict.[29] In Germany, among other European countries, this desire had surfaced sooner than in Spain owing to the earlier appearance and more thoroughgoing transformations of modern-

ization. But as modernization stole into Spain, so did a longing for a
return to a mythological community of the past that had not known
social tensions. Often it was virtually impossible to discern whether
lost-community mythology was socialist or corporatist, leftist or rightist.

To say that Spanish elites, would-be and actual, inclined more
generally in the 1930s toward corporatism than capitalism is, admittedly, to say very little, for there are any number of varieties of corporatism.[30] They range, in fact, from fascism on the right to
anarcho-syndicalism on the left. One of the essential points that distin-
guishes various types of corporatism is the degree of importance assigned to the moderating power. Its function being to coordinate and
synthesize the different corporate entities to society (whether functional, regional, or local) and to resolve inter- and intra-corporate-group
disputes, the moderating power is omnipresent and omnipotent in a
highly centralized system such as fascism, and virtually nonexistent in
the decentralized political culture that ostensibly is the objective of
anarchism.

Spanish leftists could, in general, sympathize with corporatism's
goal of encouraging collective rather than individual consciousness in
society. And many leftist programs seemed, at least for the short term,
as markedly corporatist as those of the right. But, aside from the constituency that labeled itself moderate, most leftists purported to see no
need for a perpetual or even a long-term moderating power of genuine
strength. Thus they were more cautious in their corporatism than rightists. The latter recognized hierarchical authority as a permanent, imperi-
ous need arising basically out of human nature itself and so were more
comfortable with the concept of moderating power, less ambiguous and
often less disengenuous about its role. Insofar as corporatism could
appeal to both left and right, it did so fundamentally on the basis of its
promise to provide the fruits of modernity without liberal-type transformations that heretofore had accompanied modernization.

The Corporatist Moderate Left. In its intellectual roots, the corporatist moderate left of the Second Republic drew inspiration principally
from a variant of nineteenth-century liberalism known as Krausism,
and especially from the Krausist-influenced intellectual Joaquín Costa
(1846-1911).[31] One of Spain's most prescient turn-of-the-century intellectuals, Costa, whose influence grew throughout the Spanish-speaking
world after his death, was concerned with devising the means for adding
a superstructure of modernity onto a foundation of social traditionalism. In particular, he urged restoration of the communal properties that
most rural towns had held prior to the onslaught of liberal reforms that

got under way in Spain in 1836. Costa believed that the rural masses, if provided with security in collectivized property ownership, would not intrude into the process of development, over which an urban, capitalist, and individualistic bourgeoisie would preside. It was his hope to combine the strong points of capitalism and socialism while eliminating the undesirable features of both.

Building on foundations laid by Costa, Spanish moderate (and some not-so-moderate) leftists fell into line with various English and European intellectuals in the common endeavor to synthesize patterns of socialism with those of corporatism. What Joseph Featherstone writes about certain developments in political ideology outside the Iberian peninsula is equally applicable to Spanish trends in the 1920s and 1930s. Surveying his field during the period between the turn of the century and World War II, Featherstone notes that the defense of communal values "and face-to-face community are part of political beliefs that are . . . by no means clearly of the right or of the left." Socialism, in fact, came to include a defense of the "communal emphases and values and perspectives that had mostly, in the nineteenth century, been the possession of the right." In this development, socialism embraced the ideal of an organic culture, "which was in origin a line of elite criticism of industrial society resting on values of an idealized medieval culture."[32] Although they often substituted an internationalist obsession for the nationalism of the right, the Socialists shared with their antagonists a thoroughgoing detestation of liberal modernity, an idealized vision of the past, and a utopian dream of a future that could be fulfilled through decisive, cataclysmic action rather than the gradualist reforms in which Darwinian progressives trusted. In discussing the perceived need for an apocalyptic upheaval, though, we are leaving the turf of the moderates and entering that of the extreme left.

The Far Left and the Farthest Left. Ideologically the Spanish Communists can be grouped on the far left, but they generally acted with moderation during the Second Republic. In their analysis they stressed Spain's backwardness and poverty and its continuing feudalism. Accordingly, a two-stage revolution was prescribed: first, the bourgeois-democratic revolution; then, at a later stage, a "grow over" into a genuine Socialist revolution.[33] As early as 1873 Friedrich Engels had provided the analysis from which Communists scarcely deviated in the 1930s: "Spain is so backward a country industrially, that *immediate*, complete emancipation of the working class is entirely out of the question. Before it gets that far, Spain must pass through various preliminary stages of development and clear away quite a number of obstacles."[34]

Once the civil war got under way in July of 1936 the Communists steadily maintained their moderation,[35] if anything drifting farther to the right as they sought to discipline the disparate forces of the Republic and to attract support from the Western democratic powers. It may well be that Moscow's interest lay, as David T. Cattell argues in *Communism and the Spanish Civil War* (1955), not in actually winning the war, recognized even in 1937 as impossible, but merely in keeping Germany and Italy pinned down in Spain as long as possible. As Spanish Communists came to suspect this strategy, they defected increasingly from the party.

Meantime, from 1932 onward, Spain's non-Communist Marxian Socialists had been moving farther leftward, convinced that utopia was at hand now and required for its attainment only one revolution rather than a protracted two-stage procedure. In their view, private industrialists, bankers, and merchants could be eliminated at once. Just as much as the Communists, the Marxian Socialists tended to be elitist; they envisioned a society that for the foreseeable future would be under the control of combined technocratic and humanist elites who would dominate the masses in the latter's best interests, gradually awakening their consciousness and rewarding them with a combination of material and nonmaterial gratifications.

Farther to the left among Spain's Second Republic corporatists, in that their belief in human perfectability led them to reject altogether the need for a centralized moderating power, stood the anarchists. Often the most exploited victims of Spain's incipient urbanization-industrialization, anarchists (who existed in many varieties and guises, from the exalted idealist to the common gangster) looked back to a romanticized communitarian period in the nation's past and ahead to a collectivized future free from the competitive struggle dictated by possessive individualism. Anticipating contentment from a minimum of material goods and believing that in the light of scientific-technological advances this minimum could be produced through only a few hours of labor each day, anarchists—at least the idealists among them—looked forward to devoting most of their time to the leisurely pursuit of full human development, thereby overcoming the alienation that liberal capitalism's pursuit of material progress had imposed on its victims. In the ideal society, mutual aid would replace the Darwinian struggle, and the distinction between workers and owners would disappear. Organized in collectivities, workers would become owners of the means of production, relying on the collective rather than the managerial bureaucrats to apply the maxim "from each according to ability, to each according to need" (some dissidents insisted on changing the second part to read "to each according to productive labor"). Ultimately, coercion would cease to be necessary, for traditional ethics, positing a conflict between duty and inclination, were dismissed as the specious product of state-induced false consciousness.[36]

Much of the thrust of Spanish anarchism, like that of peasant upheavals in early twentieth-century Russia, was directed toward "restoring the traditional peasant world order under better economic conditions, not at transforming the peasants into a modern social class forced to compete in a pluralistic society."[37] Thus Spanish anarchists included many figures who, even as the extreme-right Carlists, responded to a mythological urge that Jung would describe as an archetype. Theirs was the longing to return to a stage of blessedness and communal security such as had existed before the kind of catastrophe that in Christian mythology is described as the Fall.[38] For anarchist freethinkers, the onslaught of modernization substituted for the Fall.

The Second Republic: The Right and the Ideological Labyrinth

The Capitalist Right. The Spanish right during the Second Republic could muster a counterpart to the moderate leftists who accepted the classical liberal tenets of capitalism as the preferred model for modernization. In distinction to their leftist counterparts, however, rightist capitalists usually cherished the traditional myths of monarchism and Catholicism as essential for preserving social order. In their view, economism (the process of securing social harmony through steadily increasing material rewards) was an inadequate long-term guarantee of stability. Not even in the short term could Spain, given its underdevelopment, rely on economism as an antidote to revolution.

Unlike the Azaña-type capitalists of the left, capitalist rightists could not always claim the label of moderates. Moreover, they were more open to corporatism than many of the leftist advocates of bourgeois capitalism. José Calvo Sotelo provides an example. This man, who urged the need to combine capitalism with Catholicism and monarchy, was an admirer of Charles Maurras and Action Française.[39] And he sang the glories of the totalitarian state, organized along corporatist lines with a strong moderating power evidently intended to exercise its prerogatives more in the disciplining of labor than the checking of private capital.

Through the Bloque Nacional that he organized, Calvo Sotelo hoped to enlist Spanish rightists in a crusade to save the capitalist society. To lessen the danger of revolution against bourgeois capitalism he urged a highly centralized, state-administered system of social justice calculated to win the gratitude and assure the dependence of working classes. He insisted, though, that before Spain could bring about redistribution it had to produce more wealth. His implication was that the state should collaborate principally with the capitalists who knew how to produce, giving workers just enough in the way of protection and services to tame their revolutionary impulses. At the same time he recognized the value of Catholicism in keeping labor in line during the critical period. "Skeptical positivism" and Masonry purportedly placed too great a stress on material gratification and did not encourage heroic sacrifice. Therefore Calvo Sotelo and his partisans demanded the formation of a Catholic state that would refuse absolutely to accommodate any man or group desirous of limiting the church's temporal influence. The desacralized society in his view was the revolutionary society.[40] In seeking a synthesis of bourgeois capitalism and Catholicism, this Galician conservative was attempting to fuse two forces and value systems that many Spaniards had long considered mutually exclusive.

The Anticapitalist, Corporatist Right. Prominent among those rejecting Calvo Sotelo's modernization formulas as providing too great an opening to liberal capitalism was José María Gil Robles, founder of the CEDA (Confederación Española de Derechas Autónomas).[41] Dubious about the long-range political acumen of businessmen and fearful of the social consequences of giving them too free a rein, Gil Robles favored a type of corporatism that would restrain rather than enhance capitalist autonomy—though in the waging of practical politics he was driven to making so many compromises with capitalists as virtually to nullify his professed ideology.

The CEDA failed to live up to its name of Confederation of Rightists. Numerous Spanish conservatives rejected Gil Robles's organization because of its refusal to make an unequivocal commitment to monarchism. And Catholic leaders grew suspicious because the confederation's program did not make clear whether the paternalism intended to perpetuate worker dependence would be controlled by a state apparatus or by the church. To the former possibility they offered implacable opposition, on the grounds that state bureaucrats had already been so thoroughly infused with liberal, "Jewish and Masonic" materialism that they could think only of placating the masses through economism and would thus ignore the spiritual safeguards that alone, in the final analysis, were capable of preventing leveling revolution.

The Revolutionary Corporatist Right. Founded by José Antonio Primo de Rivera (he who exulted, "Spain, blessed be your backwardness"), son of dictator Miguel Primo de Rivera, the Spanish Falange is often held up as the closest approximation of a Fascist movement in Spain. Whether or not the movement is correctly labeled Fascist is largely a matter of definition. Like Fascist movements outside of Spain, the Falange attracted people fearful of losing status to the newly-emerging tycoons of industrial and financial capitalism, and struggling to avoid descent into proletarian ranks. Also in line with patterns of fascism elsewhere, Falangistas glorified the past, preached a heady nationalism, denigrated scientific methodology as they extolled myth and animating ideals, urged the corporative structure of society in their rejection of parliamentary democracy, pitched their main appeal to youth as they called for revolutionary action, and remained ambiguous about the place of religion in the future state. And, if one accepts the widely-held view that fascism is basically revolutionary in approach, then the Falange may be accurately placed under this rubric.[42]

On the most important of all ideological considerations, its antimaterialism, the Falange qualifies as a Fascist movement. According to the penetrating and persuasive analysis of Alan Cassels,

> Socialism began and remains quintessentially anticapitalist no matter how many maximalist and minimalist programs proliferate. Similarly, fascism everywhere in Europe between the wars constituted a reaction against the dominant materialist culture; this is why all *fascisms* were sworn and consistent foes of both bourgeois liberalism and dialectical materialism. How this antimaterialism was expressed—by a flight from modernity or into new forms of modernism, for example—varied according to national circumstances, but did not change the basic thrust and identity of fascism at large.[43]

Falangists criticized materialistic capitalism from a number of perspectives. Perhaps their favorite charge was that its huge, anonymous corporations dehumanized workers and deprived them of a sense of individual dignity. According to José Antonio, capitalism, guided and shaped by a heartless bourgeois plutocracy (which, in contrast to genuine elites, was incapable of charitable instincts), led inevitably to communism. Therefore, in order to block communism in Spain it would be necessary to do away with capitalism. Only with bourgeois capitalism swept aside by violent revolution would it be possible to forge a paternalistic, organic state capable of withstanding all future threats from atheistic materialism.

If superimposed on the existing capitalist-bourgeois structure, the corporate state, José Antonio affirmed, would simply contribute to perpetuating the dominance of capital over labor. To Spain's nonrevolutionary rightists, he charged, the corporate state signified the organization of capitalists into one group and laborers into another, with the state always intervening to aid the capitalists. In contrast, he and his followers advocated revolutionary corporatism, preceded by the destruction of the capitalist system as it had heretofore existed.[44]

The ideal national syndicalist corporate structure portrayed by Falangists required the forming of joint capital-labor syndicates. Within these syndicates, distinctions between capital and labor would little by little pass away as the two functions came to be combined in the same men. This would be accomplished through profit-sharing devices resulting in the distribution to workers not just of money but of shares in each enterprise. In this way private property and capitalism as they had previously existed would disappear.[45] Hierarchy would remain, however, for the moderating power at the national level would be exercised by select elites. These elites would devise and protect a corpus of unifying national myths in harmony both with past traditions and the needs of the new social order. New myths were essential, for Catholicism, which has once bound Spaniards together in a common cause transcending individual interests, no longer commanded the zealous commitment of the majority.

The Farthest Right. On the far right of Spain's ideological spectrum Carlism provided in some ways a mirror image of anarchism on the extreme left. Like many anarchists, many Carlists rejected the goals customarily associated with modernity: scientific methodology, empiricism, industrialization, urbanization, secularism, materialism, capitalism, and centralization. In their profound reverence for the Catholic faith, Carlists parted company with anarchists. But in the 1930s they tended to reject the Christianity of resignation to which the official church remained committed. Carlism harked back to the revolutionary optimism of early Christianity and to the various millenarian protests that through the centuries oppressed people had instigated in the name of Christianity. The kingdom of God could be built on this earth, Carlists of the 1930s believed, if only the corrupting forces of modernizing materialism, in which category capitalism and communism stood together as diabolical elements, were exorcised.[46]

Born in the 1830s, Carlism a century later continued to represent the protest against modernization by Spaniards, especially in the northern farming communities, who had been disadvantaged by the introduction of modern ways. Like many other protest movements originating in dislocations occasioned by the first incursions of modernity, Carlism did not reject science and modern technology in toto. These and other features of modernity they accepted as the necessary means that, if properly controlled and utilized by elites remaining uncontaminated by bourgeois values, could usher in the kingdom of justice on earth—now!

To this day, students of the Spanish Republic puzzle over the ability of right and left to hammer their conflicting constituencies into reasonably cohesive armies. And they can find it equally perplexing to account for the alignment of some elements with Franco's Nationalists rather than the Republic's Loyalists—and vice versa. Though by no means explaining all enigmas, attitudes toward monarchism as opposed to republicanism and, far more important than this, toward religion as opposed to desacralization help account for the manner in which Spaniards deployed themselves in their titanic civil struggle.

The Religious Issue

In the eyes of orthodox Catholicism's apologists, freedom of conscience, quite apart from its theological implications, heralded the ultimate demise of social and political order. Stability in temporal society, according to the defenders of orthodoxy, demanded acceptance by the vast majority of dependence on leadership elites; and such temporal dependence in turn necessitated religious beliefs in which people accepted their dependence for salvation on the ministrations of a priestly class set apart from ordinary men. Once people became religiously individualistic and inclined to regard salvation as the work of the individual conscience, then patterns of deference would yield to the chaos of atomistic individualism in the temporal realm. Just as much as in the Middle Ages, the Catholic orthodox view in nineteenth- and twentieth-century Spain was that the religious and the temporal are symbiotically connected, and thus that attitudes about the supernatural must inescapably determine the political environment. Once individualistic chaos, based on freedom of conscience, came to prevail in matters of supernatural faith, social-political anarchy could not be far behind. And, in the 1930s, the still-unresolved issue of toleration, of freedom of conscience, lay at the heart of the religious question in Spain.

In the opinion of the eminent Spanish conservative thinker Pedro Sáinz Rodríguez, the real turmoil of modernization appeared in Spain when the worldwide revolution in religion finally penetrated the peninsula. In the early nineteenth century Spain was at last called upon to meet squarely two intimately connected questions: Is religious faith a matter to be determined by the nation-state or is it a matter of the individual conscience? Should national policy be one of insisting on religious unity, even if this must be attained through Inquisition-like means, or should it be one of tolerance? As Sáinz Rodríguez explained it: "The struggles of the nineteenth century in Spain are really religious struggles of the type that had surged in other European countries at the time of the Renaissance, in which the root question is the one of tolerance, of individual vs. collective or national faith." His analysis, written in 1928, concluded on a prophetic note: "The religious question is still a hypersensitive one in Spain, because the wars over it have been so recent; in this fact one finds the possibility of a new civil war."[47]

In his penetrating study *The Secularization of the European Mind in the Nineteenth Century* (Cambridge, England, 1975), Owen Chadwick maintains that secularization was not a movement against religion but rather a quest for a Christianity that fulfilled the promise of personal freedom. In his view, the attack against orthodoxy arose less from the decline of religion than from the love of liberty. Perhaps this was true also of Azaña-type moderate left liberals in Spain: they could not perceive how liberty and all of its ostensible rewards, including modernization, could possibly be achieved in anything other than a secular environment. As Azaña and like-minded liberals eyed the Spanish church in the 1930s, they could well have described their feelings with the words that Condorcet directed to Turgot in 1774: "The colossus is half destroyed, but we must liquidate it. . . . It is still doing great harm. Most of the ills that afflict us are the work of the monster and can only be abolished when it is abolished."[48]

Spain's orthodox apologists could reply, as Balzac had replied to French freethinkers, that attacks against religious hierarchy led inexorably to removal of social restraints, and that only the cherished myths of religion gave meaning to life and made social cohesiveness possible. But Spain in the 1920s and 1930s was, like the rest of Europe, inhabited by intellectuals convinced that fresh, more vital myths, uncompromised by association with a discredited past, could usher in a new and utopian order, awakening people from torpor, from false consciousness and spurious consent to outworn beliefs counterproductive to the realization of human potential. The Catholic church in Spain thus faced the simultaneous assault of libertarians and of those who would dominate the masses in new ways by purported control over updated kinds of magic and suprarational, mystical insights.

Divisiveness grew more bitter as Spain in the early depression years moved toward becoming a mass society—a society, that is, in which huge and functionally undifferentiated segments of the population were accessible to would-be manipulators of the mind and engineers of the soul. Unemployment was one of the factors facilitating the holding of mass political rallies, and for indoctrination purposes these became as important as morality and mystery plays had been in the Middle Ages. In the months immediately preceding the civil war the number of unemployed reached about seven hundred thousand out of a total labor force of between eight and nine million. The huge number of unemployed, together with masses of underemployed, "was probably one of the main reasons for the war."[49] Perhaps, moreover, the prevalence of youth among the unemployed and underemployed accounted for the success of political activists in stirring up the frenzy of the masses. And in the mass politicization under way, the religious debate remained one of the most emotion-fraught issues. Essentially, professional definers of needs and the would-be concocters of new myths were struggling with the perpetuators of the old myth over the "regimentation of leisure"[50] among the masses. Against this background, the die for the Spanish tragedy was cast when in 1931 the Republican Cortes decreed the separation of church and state along with religious liberty, nationalized certain ecclesiastical holdings, and declared religious orders subject to special limiting laws and permanently debarred them from industry, commerce, and teaching.[51]

Ever since the liberal onslaught began in the nineteenth century, the church had used every means at its disposal to effect the reconquest of Spanish society. After 1931 it confronted grievances that made those of the past fade into insignificance. In the struggle ahead it would neither grant nor could it reasonably expect quarter. More than any other single factor, it was the religious question that polarized Spain into two camps and made it possible to distinguish splintered rightists from faction-ridden leftists.[52] The Church's significance in Spain's bloody convulsion resulted from its being in the eye of the storm brewing over the issue of how to modernize.

The United States and Spanish Civil War: The Religious Issue

An anonymous *Harper's Magazine* correspondent, writing in the 1890s on the horrors of clerical domination of the state, concluded: "Every Roman Catholic nation of the world has always gone from bad to worse."[53] And Ray Allen Billington in his classic study *The Protestant Crusade* (New York, 1938) shows that during a good part of the nineteenth century "genuine" Americans often were raised to hate Catholics and Romanism. Some of this prejudice extended on into the 1930s and helped influence American attitudes toward the Spanish civil war. Influential also were prevailing "civil religion" attitudes.

The value system of the civil religion posits that politicians should manifest religion but that they should, like Socrates, try to make their companions "moderate about gods" (Xenophon, *Memorabilia*, IV, 3). Religion for them should be vague and amorphous, consisting of a set of principles dimly associated with the Judaeo-Christian faith and above all related to the vaguely-defined "American way of life." To many Americans reared in the values of the civil religion, it appeared that the harassments directed against the church by Spanish Republicans constituted a well-deserved punishment that the clergy had earned by dint of its attempt to stamp a narrow ecclesiastical mold on civil life. Therefore the onslaught against the church, even when it degenerated into plunder and violence, was perceived as the beginning of the Americanization of Spain. Once religious liberty was achieved there could follow political and economic freedom. Only the country that revered this trinity of liberties could avoid going from bad to worse.[54]

In his perceptive study of American responses to the Spanish civil war, Allen Guttmann notes: "To most in the United States, Republic meant 'popular government,' 'freedom of worship and separation of church and state,' and our 'own traditions of education for democracy.' "[55] Little wonder that in signing a declaration in defense of the Republic, clergymen of the Baptist, Congregational, Episcopal, Lutheran, Methodist, and Presbyterian churches attached paramount importance to the fact that "the Republic established complete religious freedom in Spain for the first time in the country's history."[56]

Many—though, as we shall see, by no means all—American Catholics found it as easy as most orthodox Protestants and civil religion deists to choose sides in the Spanish struggle. The Catholics, though, came down on the side of the Nationalists. Two developments strengthened the general impression that virtually all American Catholics favored the Franco-led "crusade."[57] To begin with, the Catholic hierarchy in the United States did line up solidly behind the Nationalists. Beyond this, Catholics who spoke out publicly on the Spanish issue were nearly unanimous in backing the Nationalists—or "Rebels," as their adversaries dubbed them.

The Spanish civil war touched the still-sensitive nerve of religious prejudice in the United States. By assailing Franco and the Catholic crusade in Spain, many Protestants were actually assailing Catholics in their own land. Responding to this attack, some Catholics felt driven to justify Franco on the grounds of American democratic principles, maintaining that the Nationalists were combating such un-American menaces as communism and anarchism while at the same time spearheading reforms that would prepare the way for democracy.[58] For others, proof of having joined mainstream Americanism almost necessitated support of the Republic. But Catholics of this inclination hesitated to reveal their preferences, fearful they could not remain in their church's embrace if they openly challenged the hierarchy's line on any issue, including the Spanish civil war. Given the spirit of the times, many Catholics (30 percent of them, according to opinion polls) took a portentous step as they attached their sympathies not to Franco but rather to the Republic; indeed, only four out of every ten American Catholics favored Franco, and 30 percent expressed no opinion.[59] (Among Protestants, Franco enjoyed only 9 percent support, and a mere 2 percent of Jews favored his cause, certainly understandable in view of the overt antisemitism proclaimed by many Nationalists.)

Although American Catholics might side with the Republic, they dared not, with very few exceptions,[60] do so publicly. The times scarcely permitted this. Chronologically, Catholics stood closer to the repressive atmosphere occasioned by the Americanism "heresy" of the turn of the century[61] than to the unforeseeable "voluntarism" of the 1970s. In a way, their willingness to cast their private sympathies with the Republic can be seen as the first glimmering of the dawn of American Catholicism's voluntarism.[62]

The United States and the Spanish Civil War: The Fascism Issue

"Ultimately, of course," John Diggins writes, "it was the Spanish Civil War that brought the overwhelming majority of literary intellectuals into an unequivocal anti-Fascist front."[63] The reason for this was that the Nationalist side from the outset of the war came to be identified with fascism. A number of factors are involved in this identification, most obviously the assistance that Italy and Germany quickly extended to Franco's armies.[64] Also there was the fact that, depending on how one defined the term, there were Nationalists who could be described as Fascists or, in far more numerous instances, as Fascist types—even though Mussolini complained about the lack of Spanish Fascists and did not view his intervention as a means of spreading fascism but rather as a means of blocking Spain's alignment with Bolshevism, which he feared would produce adverse effects in Italy. Another and highly important reason for the tendency of Americans to associate the Nationalist cause with fascism must be traced to the effectiveness of Marxist propaganda.

In 1925, 1930, or even 1933, association with fascism would not have been the kiss of death for Nationalists that it had become by 1936. Initially, many in the United States had hailed Mussolini as a heroic figure engaged in the Americanization of Italy, introducing the pragmatic spirit, getting things done, and blocking the spread of revolutionary socialism. Some business groups in the 1920s sympathized with fascism as one possible road toward the new sort of industrial corporatism that Secretary of Commerce and later President Herbert Hoover seemed intent on fostering in the United States. As late as 1934, *Fortune* came out with an entire edition in praise of the corporate state. According to Diggins, this "was perhaps Fascism's greatest public relations coup among America's more sophisticated publications."[65]

Many Americans outside the business community, moreover, showed an early leaning toward Italy's Fascist experiment. It appealed to antimodernists as an attempt to respiritualize civilization by fostering devotion to national grandeur and other great ideals, as an endeavor to replace individualistic competitiveness with a sense of community instilled by membership in functional guilds. Although many Americans were troubled by the authoritarianism of fascism, they nonetheless viewed it as an appropriate system for achieving development in retarded countries. In their appraisal, development must result ultimately in the same happy consequences it had produced in the United States, namely "political liberation and moral uplift."[66]

Clearly, fascism meant different things to different Americans, and many liked what they perceived in it. Had the Generals' Revolt against the Republic occurred, say, in 1932 and been linked to fascism, Spain's military rebels might actually have derived advantage among Americans from this linkage—even though the dour Franco could never have matched Mussolini's charisma or comic qualities. But the Generals' Revolt occurred in 1936, and by then opinion had shifted decidedly against fascism. For one thing, the business community had begun to have second thoughts. During the early years of the depression, fascism might still have appeared as a justifiable effort "to rationalize the economy through a wholesome marriage of government and industry"; so long as this was the impression, business could look on with equanimity. When, however, it became clear that the New Deal's corporatism "meant a regulatory state rather than self-government by corporate wealth, business reacted against Roosevelt and Mussolini with equal vehemence."[67]

By 1936 a few persons, it is true, might still applaud Fascists and Spain's Nationalists as defenders "of the economy of the farm, the village, the small town against the megalopolitan civilization of giant cities."[68] But by that year the overwhelming majority of American opponents of modernity, those persons who hoped to see a simple, primitive, virtuous, close-to-the-soil way of life triumph over the threat of centralized, highly coordinated capitalist efficiency in Spain, had come to view fascism as the enemy. The 1935 Italian war against Ethiopia, and the coverage that Ernest Hemingway provided, help to explain this development.

Depicting the Ethiopians as living in a society of primitive virtue,

Hemingway described the brutal intrusion among them of mechanized modern culture, symbolized by that diabolical instrument of modern technology, the dive bomber. His accounts of the struggle of men close to nature against machine-age brutality created a vivid impression among many Americans. And, almost at the inception of the Spanish civil war, the Italian bombers put in their appearance on the side of the Nationalists. Hemingway and a good part of the American public (among them Blacks who, denied a chance to fight in Ethiopia, grasped at the means to strike a blow at the Italians by enlisting in the Abraham Lincoln Battalion) found in the Spanish Republicans the symbol of the heroic underdog. Republicans became the embodiment of premodern innocence; they were defending the spontaneity and freedom of the organic community against the regimentation and tyranny of the twentieth century as served now by Fascist planes, the harbinger of mechanized doom as they meted out "impersonal deaths to peasant guerrillas."[69]

By the outbreak of the civil war, fascism had been further sullied by its association with Germany's abhorrent national socialism. What is more, Americans ranging from highly-placed public officials to yellow-press journalists had become convinced of the existence of an international Fascist conspiracy, already gripping in its tentacles not only Italy and Germany but Austria, Portugal, and Japan, and threatening soon to envelop all Latin America. From Madrid, U.S. Ambassador Claude Bowers reported that Spain, once converted into a fascist state, would be used as an entering wedge in South and Central America.[70] Given the commitment of the State Department under Cordell Hull to free trade,[71] the specter of fascism's steady expansion, carried out in line with a dark international conspiracy, could only arouse profound disquiet.[72]

Operating at the time was a form of the domino theory that assumed, incorrectly, an essentially close bond between Spain and Latin America. As Spain went, so also, according to many influential persons in addition to Bowers, Latin America would go. The issue, then, was perceived as either a Republican victory or the envelopment not only of Spain but of Latin America as well by the fascist international, thereby dooming the entire set of commercial expectations that inspired much of the Good Neighbor Policy's thrust.[73]

Even the Hollywood cinema of the period revealed a fear of Fascist incursions in Latin America. Thus the 1939 movie on the life of Benito Juárez, starring Paul Muni, was made in such a way as to have Emperor Maximilian symbolize for the 1860s the kind of European intervention that fascist states threatened in the late 1930s.[74] And desire to combat the real or imagined Fascist International helped motivate many Abraham Lincoln Battalion recruits,[75] though whether the purpose in fighting fascism was to defend democracy and Americanism or to strengthen communism is not always clear.

Finally, the success of Communists and leftist sympathizers in propagating the Moscow definition of fascism had, by 1936, solidified opposition in the United States to any movement that appeared even remotely fascistic. According to the Communist line, fascism was a capitalist conspiracy conceived by the threatened bourgeoisie. Its purpose was to put down the proletariat challenge and in the process to strengthen bourgeois domination over the weaker middle sectors. To virtually no avail did academicians such as Talcott Parsons point out that the bonds between business and fascism were tenuous and that much of the emotional drive behind the ideology was anticapitalist. In the ranks of organized labor, where "there was never any doubt that Fascism was a capitalist conspiracy pure and simple,"[76] and in other sectors of popular opinion, it was a basic assumption by 1936 that fascism represented a devious shoring up of capitalism. In the light of capitalism's low esteem in the depression-ridden United States, especially among intellectuals but also among much of the public at large, it is little wonder that fascism became a term of opprobrium and that the Spanish civil war, because of its timing (and often, too, because of its religious implications), crystallized opinion against fascism.

The United States "General Public" and the Spanish Civil War

The Spanish civil war was the event in foreign affairs that most clearly awakened American emotions during the 1930s—at least up to 1939, when Hitler went on the warpath.[77] Numerous opinion polls conducted during the decade leave no doubt about this.[78] As already noted, American sympathies lay on the whole with the Republic, although various business groups sided with the Nationalists and the Hearst newspapers quickly labeled the Republicans "Reds" and unleashed a stream of diatribes against them. Often leftist or Communist leanings lay behind Republican partisanship, all the more so as Russian assistance became by October of 1936 the vital element in staving off victory by Franco. But by far the most important consideration in swaying majority opinion toward the Republic was the conviction that the virtues of Americanism lay with this side—an attitude previously noted in discussion of the religious issue. Ever enthused by prospects of converting an expanding sphere of the world to democratic republicanism, Americans now saw a unique opportunity in Spain.

As might have been expected in the light of his dabbling in the founding-fathers period of United States history, Ambassador Bowers placed the Spanish situation in the context of a confrontation between Hamiltonians and Jeffersonians: the richest and most powerful elements, including aristocrats, landlords, the clergy, and the military, were out to defeat the writers, professional men, intellectuals, peasants, and workers who supported middle-class democracy.[79] And Allen Guttmann convincingly contends that Americans identified the Republic with the struggle for liberal, democratic values, including free speech, a free press, the right of assembly, and respect for protection of minorities within a system of political pluralism.[80] Dante Puzzo also summarizes well the prevailing American attitudes toward the government of the Republic in 1936: "it was certainly not communistic; nor even moderately socialistic; it was Azañan. Its spirit was not that of Stalin and the Dictatorship of the Proletariat but rather of Roosevelt and the New Deal."[81]

Although disagreeing himself with prevailing American attitudes on the struggle in Spain, based as they were on naive and simplistic half-truths, Carlton Hayes depicted most accurately the general view of his countrymen. To the typical American,

> the republic represented an earnest effort of forward-looking, peace-loving, democratic Spaniards to reform their country and bring it abreast of other Western democracies, both socially and politically; to free the masses from poverty, illiteracy, and superstition, and to substitute for irresponsible monarchy or military dictatorship a government of the people, by the people, and for the people. This fine effort had the support of the vast majority of Spaniards, but from the first to last it was opposed by the plottings and machinations of a reactionary oligarchy, consisting of army chiefs, landlords, and Catholic clergy. These were not strong enough, of themselves, to destroy the Republic, but they [tried to do so] with the help of Moorish troops and the military might of Hitler and Mussolini.[82]

Owing in part to the success of Communist propaganda,[83] abetted by the public's naiveté, which caused non-Marxist observers to see in the Republic only what they hoped to find, most Americans who paid any attention to Spain were unaware of the presence of wild-eyed revolutionary Socialists and anarchists among the defenders of middle-class, liberal, democratic, capitalist values. Nor did they comprehend that the middle-class liberals within the Loyalist coalition were so weak and disorganized, so beleaguered by utopian radicals, that the only pro-Republic group whose discipline and tough-minded steadfastness of purpose gave it a good chance of gaining control over the anti-Franco forces was the Spanish Communist party. In spite of this reality, the Buffalo *Evening News* expressed the widespread feeling among American sympathizers with the Republic when it editorialized on February 21, 1936, that Spanish anarchists, Socialists, and Bolsheviks would pose no more than a passing embarrassment to Azaña's liberalism.

Although the Spanish civil war stirred the emotions of Americans more than any other foreign event of the period, it still left a broad sector of the citizenry uninvolved and uninterested. Gallup polls showed that those with "no opinion" on the war ranged from 24 to 34 percent of respondents.[84] Helping to account for this is the fact that from the birth of their republic Americans have tended to believe that Spain suffered from a particularly virulent form of Old World evils. Thus, it was difficult for many to believe that issues of Americanism could really be involved in the struggle that Spaniards were waging. Senator Key Pittman manifested this public mood when he spoke out against intervention of any sort in the Spanish conflict. With far greater accuracy than many of the interventionists, he tartly observed that both sides in Spain represented "foreign theories of government."[85]

The prejudices of Americanism led in the 1930s, even as in bygone decades, to the conclusion that Mediterranean people could not respond to enlightened efforts on their behalf and were therefore best left alone. Randolph Churchill's description of English attitudes toward the Spanish Civil War applied equally to a broad segment of American opinion: "They [the English public] don't care a damn who's right ór who ought to win. A few excitable Catholics and ardent Socialists think this war matters, but for the general public it's just a lot of bloody dagoes killing each other."[86]

United States Government Responses to the Civil War

Like the general public, official America as represented by policy-makers in Washington remained suspicious about crusading for the regeneration of Spain.[87] The foreign policy establishment had been burned, and recently at that. Attempts as close to home as in Haiti, the Dominican Republic, Cuba, and Nicaragua to uplift wayward people had ended in failure while at the same time inciting ill will throughout Latin America. Disillusionment about the possibility of exporting U.S. values helped shape the noninterventionist approach of the Good Neighbor Policy in dealing with Latin America. And nonintervention seemed the only feasible policy to pursue with Spain, all the more so as intervention there could conceivably lead to involvement in a struggle that might expand into a general European war.

Behind the nonintervention predilections of the Franklin D. Roosevelt administration lay not only disillusionment and a desire to avoid European entanglements but also an approach that was "openly libertarian." Within the United States, Roosevelt "did not argue with urban ethnic life-styles, and Southern whites were allowed to treat Southern blacks as they wished." So far as domestic politics was concerned, Waspish tendencies (which Robert Kelley [88] finds primarily as the badge of the Republican Party in the late nineteenth and early twentieth centuries), focusing on assimilation of people not yet regarded as fully American, gave way to a live-and-let-live approach. And this carried over into foreign affairs, diluting the concern for reform abroad that has sporadically influenced the conduct of external relations. Believers in the international assimilationist process might want to help Spaniards transform themselves in line with Americanism; but administration figures, beset by doubt and uncertainty as they desperately sought expedients that would somehow enable America to muddle through, were in a hands-off mood. Though critics might condemn them as morally insensitive, it would be just as sensible to praise them for their enlightened pluralism and sense of limitations as to what U.S. pressure could accomplish.

Widely rumored to be sympathetic to the Republic,[89] President Roosevelt clearly recognized the many political pitfalls in overt commitment. So, in December of 1936, he urged American firms not to attempt to send goods to either side in Spain and looked on approvingly, the following month, as Congress, through a joint resolution later enacted into federal law, established a Spanish embargo. The vote in the House approving the resolution was 406–1, and in the Senate 81–0.[90]

Among the potential political pitfalls contributing to FDR's reluctance to demonstrate overt support for the Republic—assuming he actually felt so inclined—there loomed, in addition to the general mood of noninvolvement, the Catholic issue. Perhaps mistaking the unanimous position of the hierarchy for solid Catholic rank-and-file backing of the Nationalists, FDR hesitated to give offense to a voting bloc that had become one of the bastions of Democratic strength. Moreover, just as the general public was sorely divided over the Spanish issue, thus making any overt administration stance politically risky, the State Department itself was torn by dissension. And this lent additional justification for the president's general inclination to remain ambiguous on issues insofar as possible so as to avoid rocking the boat.

State Department divisions, which have never received the careful research they warrant, presaged the savage infighting that would later accompany Cold War diplomacy. Many officials, among them Lawrence Duggan, strongly endorsed the Republic and looked approvingly on the steady stream of dispatches arriving from Ambassador Bowers urging support for the Loyalists. Increasingly this State Department group expressed alarm over the Fascist menace in Latin America, real and imagined, fearing that an international conspiracy was at work and that a Nationalist victory in Spain would work toward bringing Latin America into the Fascist fold. Others in the department worried more about the imminence of a Communist threat. Sounding very much like Henry Stimson in the 1920s when he blamed troublesome developments in Nicaragua and Mexico on Communist activity, and also like Sumner Welles and Jefferson Caffrey, who liked to attribute difficulties in Cuba at the outset of the Roosevelt administration to Communist infiltration, the New Deal's Secretary of State Cordell Hull looked to Bolshevik influence to explain the Spanish Republic's sometimes threatening attitudes toward U.S. business.[91] Worried that the Republic's drift leftward heralded the coming of a genuine social revolution, and perturbed that in July of 1936 the Madrid government had begun to distribute "large quantities of arms and ammunition into the hands of irresponsible members of the left-wing political organizations,"[92] Hull shared a view widely held in the British Foreign Office: that the revolutionary-utopianist elements linked to the Republic would facilitate an eventual takeover by the Communists, the only organized and disciplined faction.

All the while, Washington officials tended to see a link between Spain and Latin America. The $80 million invested in Spain seemed trifling in comparison to the nearly $3 billion invested in Latin America as of 1936. A move toward leftist economic nationalism in Spain would, officials feared, jeopardize United States holdings in Latin America. By 1937 American oil interests were experiencing grave difficulties in Mexico and Bolivia and milder ones in Venezuela and Peru, and Ecuador was threatening the expropriation of a gold-mining company. An anticapitalist plague seemed to be spreading in the Spanish-speaking world, and if Washington did not contain it in Spain (where Franco was widely perceived as more likely than the Republicans to safeguard foreign investment), then it threatened to assume epidemic proportions among the economically hard-pressed governments of Latin America. Because of the connection between Spanish and Latin American developments, which existed more in the minds of a few U.S. observers than in reality, it seemed to behoove Washington to treat the Second Republic with extreme caution.

Additional advantages in Latin America, as an area of paramount economic and security concern to the United States, seemed obtainable by maintaining a hands-off policy with economically and strategically less important Spain. Latin American electorates—those of the Spanish-speaking republics more so than Brazil's—were sorely divided over the Spanish issue. Although the vast number of politically-marginal citizens had little concern for and may not even have heard of the civil war, among literate Spanish Americans one could scarcely find the "no opinion" types discovered in abundance by Gallup pollsters in the United States. More so than among Americans, Spanish America's politically-aware citizens found the issues in Spain vitally relevant to their own republics.

If neutrality was useful to the FDR administration in avoiding offense to certain domestic sectors committed to one side or the other in the Spanish struggle, it was altogether indispensable if Washington was to avoid outraging equally- or more-committed Spanish American segments that in the light of American national interest, had to be finessed into friendly relations. Also, by pursuing a neutral role Washington could keep its options open and maintain credibility as it worked to undermine and to play off against each other the two un-American menaces that concerned it in Latin America: fascism and communism.

With between one-fourth and one-third of the American public remaining indifferent to the Spanish civil war, the U.S. government found a large constituency to provide at least tacit support for the neutrality policy toward Spain. But neutrality incurred the outraged condemnation of a very vocal minority in the United States, the intellectuals. Overwhelmingly, American intellectuals flocked to the Republic's banner.[93] And when they wrote about the fervent response of Americans to the war they were actually writing about themselves, confusing, as is their wont, their feelings with those of all Americans as they assumed the right to speak for "the people."

United States Intellectuals and the Spanish Civil War

To a degree not fully grasped by the public at large, American intellectuals of the 1930s had closed ranks with European counterparts and rejected many features of the liberal mythology of evolutionary progress spearheaded by the capitalist bourgeoisie. Nor was the intellectuals' indictment of bourgeois culture a recent phenomenon, arising mainly in response to the depression's unprecedented shattering of confidence. One need think only of Brooks and Henry Adams to appreciate this fact. But the Adamses had many companions, men who in their criticism of the industrial society that atomized human relations harked back in some ways to John C. Calhoun and even to the Transcendentalist revolt against materialism that William R. Hutchison has described so well.[94] Indeed, as Michael Kammen has demonstrated, the paradoxes of American culture were already firmly rooted in colonial times, and among these was the concept of "collective individualism." "What dualism in the American experience," Kammen inquires, "is more central to an understanding of our nature?"[95]

Reformers of the 1890s, it has been argued, wanted by and large just to extend to the lower classes the wonders of the materially affluent society previously reserved for middle classes.[96] But between that decade and the 1920s, intellectuals increasingly confessed abandonment of hope in the liberal dream.[97] Warning that the American masses could never attain adequate security within the framework of the old individualistic, competitive liberalism, they saw the likelihood of an ultimate revolution from below unless the directing business classes could be prevented from reaping the fruits of their own folly.

The twenties were rife with indications of intellectual alienation: "Hardly any writer of the time accepted at its face value the arrogant commercialism which touted itself as the new civilization." Invariably, manifestation of alienation converged upon an anti-industrial, anti-machine, anti-capitalist bias."[98] The depression years only lent emphasis to an alienation already well established and helped spread its discontents among broader sectors of the populace. During the 1930s even the "desperate comedy" of Hollywood movies propagated searing condemnations of the liberal order.[99]

Uninterested in saving the existing order, the evils of which they delighted in describing and exaggerating, intellectuals tended in the 1930s to wax rhapsodic about the wonders of the new society that lay just beyond the horizon. James Gilbert captures their mood: "Standing, as they thought, on the brink of a new social order, intellectuals needed and used metaphors of colossal change. . . . The more flaws they discovered in the classical order of laissez-faire, the more that old theory fell apart and the more compelling reform Darwinism came to be."[100] Reform Darwinism in this era carried implications not of competition but rather of collectivist collaboration, rationally designed so as to result in a balance between human activity and environmental resources. In short, what seemed necessary was an intensified interpenetration of those two ingredients of American dualism, collectivism and individualism—a resolving of opposites in harmony so as to produce a sudden surge of national energy. Abandoning faith in gradual progress, America's intellectuals had begun to flirt with regeneration mythology, which, as with the alchemists and in fact all seekers of the perfect psychic and the ideal social equilibrium, has always hinged on the reconciliation of opposites. Even as in Spain and Europe as a whole, disillusionment with modernity's individualism had awakened the desire to achieve a perfect synthesis between it and the collectivism ascribed to an idealized past. Americans might not describe the envisioned society as corporatist, but the name applied to the future utopia scarcely matters. In essence, Spaniards and Americans had both set off in quest of the archetypal utopia in which tensions and strife would be resolved in symbiotic union.

The new society was indeed wonderful to contemplate. Poverty, of course, would no longer exist. John Dewey's was only one voice in a veritable chorus as he exclaimed "the hope of abolishing poverty is not Utopian."[101] In this conviction Dewey and his fellow thinkers reinforced the optimistic notions that Social Gospelers had been dispensing for some time. And Lewis Mumford spoke for many intellectuals when he predicted the emergence of "a neotechnic civilization. . . . clean, decentralized, functional, and automated."[102] The new civilization could release energies for leisure and self-expression and stimulate a broader concern with the development of the more exalted spiritual, intellectual, and artistic facets of human nature.

No mere economic reforms, it went without saying, could bring about America's rebirth.[103] Regeneration would have to be achieved under the control of men who understood the tasks of spiritual reeducation—in short, the intellectuals. Poets and artists would have to collaborate in creating new ideals for Americans and presiding over the resocialization of the crowd, which would produce improved men and women attuned to the wonders of spiritual-artistic pleasures and indifferent to the crassness of material rewards. Whether gradually or suddenly, the crowd would be weaned from the leadership of discredited businessmen, whose promises to provide ever-expanding material gratifications had proved false, and trained to welcome the command of those whose right to lead derived from their ability to satisfy higher needs. Political disintegration and class, ethnic, religious, and economic conflict would disappear as Americans, "completely loyal to their political and *intellectual leaders,*"[104] consented freely and enthusiastically to serve the men responsible not just for their material security but for their aesthetic enrichment as well. Understandably, such theorists of elitism as Vilfredo Pareto and Gaetano Mosca, to say nothing of Lenin, enjoyed cult status among America's would-be forgers of the new society, convinced as they were that only "an intellectual vanguard. . . . could articulate the half-hidden laws of social development."[105]

Communism, with its Leninist stress on the importance of intellectual workers as the vanguard of the social revolution, whose task it was to form the consciousness of the masses, delighted many intellectuals. Indeed, it represented the best available rationalization for their desire to claim domination over the masses and at the same time become the masters of businessman and scientists. Communism offered an alternative to the type of leveling that culturati feared would result from continuation of the liberal system; and, in its Leninist guise, it held forth the promise that intellectuals could assert their leadership now, not awaiting the slow working out of historical processes.

Beyond this, communism promised warm collective relationships and a surcease to the loneliness of the atomistic liberal order about which so many writers poignantly complained. Vivian Gornick in *The Romance of American Communism* (New York, 1977) quotes Paul Levinson, who joined the Communist party in a Bronx housing cooperative: "It was life, the only life I ever knew, and it was *alive*. Intense, absorbing, filled with a kind of comradeship I never again expected to know." Whereas some hoped to turn collectivism into the opportunity to dominate those who were newly assembled in groups, others sought through "belongingness" simply to escape from freedom and to satisfy what Gornick terms "the hunger for submission." Indeed, among the "People of Paradox" the quest for individual autonomy has never been free from the counterpoint of the hunger for submission. However, only in certain periods perceived as times of transition, of personal or social regeneration, can the American male, without fear of renouncing masculinity, admit to the need for submission—as Bob Dylan did in his prize-winning song of 1979, "Gotta Serve Somebody."

Perhaps above all else the attraction of Soviet experiments to a generation of American intellectuals convinced they had reached the threshhold of tommorow lay in what Russia stood for psychologically and culturally. According to Richard Pells, "The image of death and rebirth, of the old world decaying as the new emerged in all its youthful strength, ran through most descriptions of Soviet life. Even the hardships in Russia imparted a sense of spirit and energy to writers whose own country was floundering without purpose or direction."[106] Accounting also for the rise of communism was the ability of the movement to direct its appeal not just toward alienated intellectuals but also toward Americans still immersed in the ideological mainstream and hoping the old American dream might yet be realized. To the latter, the leadership of Earl Browder proved enormously attractive, helping to propel membership in the American Communist party (CPUSA) from seven thousand in 1930 to about a hundred thousand by the early 1940s

—a figure by no means reflecting the full extent of communism's popularity.[107] Browder enjoyed stunning success in convincing audiences that "Communism is Twentieth-Century Americanism" as he evolved toward an independent, unorthodox Marxist polycentrism that would ultimately lead, in 1945, to his ouster as head of the CPUSA.[108]

Like technocrats who dreamed of replacing incumbent elites and exercising a moderating power in a new kind of society, Communists and Communist sympathizers in the United States accepted science, industry, urbanization, and many other features of modernity. They rejected, though, the modernity of liberal capitalism. In this they had much in common not only with Spanish Communists but with a broad grouping of other sectors in Spain, deployed on both the Republican and the Nationalist sides. American rightists also found much in common with aspirations expressed by Spaniards of both sides. Particularly striking is the bond of common values shared by Southern Agrarians, that group of intellectuals clustered about Vanderbilt University and including John Crowe Ransom, Allen Tate, and Robert Penn Warren, and Spain's Carlists—except for the latter's rabid Catholicism.

Like northern Abolitionists, decribed by David Donald as a "displaced elite" protesting against the new industrial system and angered by their inability to adjust to urban society,[109] Southern Agrarians made a frontal attack on the evils of capitalist modernity. Holding out for a "southern way of life," as opposed to what they called the American or prevailing way, they resembled in many ways the New Humanist school of Irving Babbitt and Paul Elmer More, but with an important exception. Unlike the Humanists, the Agrarians insisted that religious orthodoxy of some sort was essential. Given the American religious milieu, most Agrarians remained obscure or silent as to just what type of orthodoxy they had in mind.[110]

It is tempting to dismiss the Agrarians and persons of their persuasion as hopelessly romantic reactionaries. But they were not altogether devoid of an element of postmodernism that can, if emphasized to the exclusion of other traits, qualify them as minor prophets rather than antiquarians. Objecting to the school that saw progress in terms of unlimited physical growth while totally ignoring ecological costs, the Agrarians proclaimed the need for humans to respect their symbiotic connection with nature and to seek spiritual fulfillment within the confines of a no-growth society. In their own way, they were involved in the archetypal search for the perfect society in which the claims of the individual may be reconciled with the claims of the community— whether a social or an environmental community. In this way, the one and the many would be fused.

Like so many other American intellectuals, the Agrarians found much to admire in the Spain of the 1930s, though there could be considerable doubt as to whether what they liked inhered more on the Nationalist or on the Republican side. Just as much as Carlists, after all, anarchists clung to an agrarian myth. In any event, the Agrarians and numerous Americans representing different streams of thought would have agreed with Franz Borkenau on the attraction of Spain in the 1930s:

> There, life is not yet efficient; that means that it is not yet mechanized; that beauty is still more important. . . . than practical use; sentiment more important than action; honour very often more important than success; love and friendship more important than one's job. In other words, it is the lure of a civilization near to ourselves,. . . but which has not yet participated in our later developments toward mechanism, the adoration of quantity, and of the utilitarian aspect of things. In this lure. . . is implied the concession. . . that after all something seems wrong with our own . . . civilization.[111]

Virtually all American intellectuals could find something they liked in Spain—or, what is just as important, could imagine they found it there. And this, ultimately, explains their fascination with the civil war, for they were able to externalize their longings and aspirations for America into identification with participants in the Spanish civil war, hoping that somehow the victory of the cause they backed would start a groundswell that would ultimately lead to the triumph of that cause throughout the world. First Spain, then America, then the world.

Essentially, it was the timing of the civil war that assured the passionate interest of U.S. intellectuals in quest of an ideal society. Had the struggle erupted, say, in the late 1940s or the 1950s, it would have found the vast majority of America's intellectuals cured of their utopianism and co-opted in one way or another into a shored-up and modified version of the old American system. In the 1930s, though, America's self-proclaimed saviors of higher values were, in large numbers, disaffected from the system[112]—even as were their descendents in the 1960s, when the Spanish civil war would have been a sensation among counter-culture gurus. They had become a part of the widespread opposition throughout the Western World to a bourgeois society. In their antibourgeois mood, American and European culturati of the 1920s and 1930s spearheaded an "introspective revolution":[113] they hoped to expand consciousness, not through empirical perception and rational analysis of the outside world, but rather by opening a window onto the inside world of the unconscious, so as to refresh themselves in the spontaneity and creative impulses of unrepressed, primordial psychic energy. For the introspective revolution, Freud and especially Jung, with his concept of the collective unconscious, helped provide an aura of scientific justification for a concern with what moderns contemptuously dismissed as the occult.

Projecting outward into the social world the desire to be remade psychically, regenerationists thought of establishing symbiotic fusions with primitives, with the "folk," with all those persons customarily stereotyped as spontaneous, unreflective, unrepressed "id" people. American regenerationists joined in the primitivist folk cult through interest in their own country's Indians and Blacks, suddenly transformed from benighted, inferior peoples into noble savages.[114] The hope now was not to uplift wayward wild men but to be reborn by coming together with uncorrupted sources of primordial vitality, thus fusing in harmony the opposites of rationality and instinct. Affective attachment to id types as projections of the internal unconscious extended overseas as well, and American intellectuals grasped in rhetorical embrace the Indians and mixed bloods of South America and the simple, pure folk of Spain, joining José Antonio in blessing Spaniards for their backwardness. Because they had not yet confined instinctual energy and creativity to the iron cages of rational control and sublimation in pursuit of material progress,[115] Spaniards and other primitives became essential sources of wholeness for Americans in quest of rebirth—both psychic and social.

The triumph of Franco smashed the hopes that American intellectuals had placed in Spain. The very image of a Latin Calvin Coolidge, Franco epitomized the cold, calculating, rational spirit of control and repression imposed over all that was spontaneous, instinctual, fanciful, symbolic, and mythological. For having dashed the naive regenerationist hopes of intellectuals and artists about a Dionysian crusade that would originate in Spain and then envelop the world, Spaniards and their Caudillo could not be forgiven. Rather than the contrived explanation of fascism that could not fool very many of those who really knew Franco's Spain, it was the unabashed materialism, the bourgeois vulgarity, the alliance between technocrats and business entrepreneurs and military, and the attempts to stifle the impetuous, the mystical, and the imaginative that rendered the Caudillo's regime anathema to those who had dreamed of Spain's restoration to the paradisal state antedating business monotony and capitalist alienation. Franco became a latter-day incarnation of the sixteenth-century symbol of repression and suppression, Philip II.

An American artist provides one of the best insights into the mood of despair that gripped American culturati as they contemplated Spain in the aftermath of the civil war. In the series of black and white abstractions entitled "Elegy to the Spanish Republic" that he painted in the early 1940s, Robert Motherwell filled his canvases with symbols of repression, constriction, and rigidity. "Nearly overwhelming in the anguish they imply,"[116] the "Elegies" captured for their age the despondency that post-civil war Spain evoked in the hearts of seekers after wholeness, after psychic and social rebirth.[117]

More widely known and more accessible in its symbolism, Picasso's "Guernica" stands also as—to paraphrase Edmund Wilson on Marcel Proust—the heartbreak house of *anti*capitalist culture. At the top of the painting, slightly left of center, glares the symbol of modernity that has triumphed and in its triumph wreaked havoc on Spain: the blink-on electric light. Farther to the right a woman's hand clutches a lighted candle. Here is the symbol of the female principle united to the male principle so as to resolve in androgynous wholeness the conflict between opposites—the classic vision of salvation. The regenerationists had hoped to merge the eternal feminine, stereotyped through the ages as the spirit of tranquility, repose, and selfless surrender to group interests, with the male principle of assertiveness, enterprise, and striving ego autonomy. But the hope of restoring the unity of a paradisal state when introversion and extroversion, collectivism and individualism, Yin and Yang had been perfectly fused succumbed to the naked, glaring power of alienating modernity. Thus ended one of the most convulsive moments of twentieth-century regenerationist hopes.

Notes

1. See, for example, Shulamit Volkov, *The Rise of Popular Antimodernism in Germany: The Urban Master Artisans, 1873–1896* (Princeton, 1978). An altogether admirable survey of Europe in transition is Jan Romein, *The Watershed of Two Eras: Europe in 1900* (Middletown, Conn., 1978).

2. Charles Maier, *Recasting Bourgeois Europe: Stabilization in France, Germany, and Italy in the Decade After World War I* (Princeton, 1975), p. 4.

3. Ibid., p. 353.

4. Raymond J. Sontag, *A Broken World, 1919–1939* (New York, 1971), p. 178.

5. Edward R. Tannenbaum, *1900: The Generation before the Great War* (Garden City, N.J., 1976), p. 1.

6. Robert A. Nisbet, *Social Change and History: Aspects of the Western Theory of Development* (New York, 1969), p. 191. See also Marc Raeff, "The Well-Ordered Police State and the Development of Modernity in Seventeenth- and Eighteenth-Century Europe: An Attempt at a Comparative Approach," *American Historical Review* 80 (1975): 1222: "I would suggest the following as

conveying the essence of what we call 'modern,' as opposed to earlier, 'traditional'. . . patterns of culture: . . . society's conscious desire to maximize all its resources and to use this new potential dynamically for the enlargement and improvement of its way of life." Likewise useful is Joseph R. Gusfield, "Tradition and Modernity: Misplaced Polarities in the Study of Social Change," *American Journal of Sociology* 72 (1967): 351–62.

7. See the introduction to Cyril E. Black, et al., *The Modernization of Japan and Russia: A Comparative Study* (New York, 1975).

8. Wolin, "The State of the Union," *New York Review of Books* (May 18, 1978): 30.

9. An example of this approach is afforded by the Bauhaus, founded in Germany in 1919. Its members were revolutionaries with utopian ideals, intent on throwing out the past in favor of an imagined future in which science and technology, in alliance with architecture and art, would transform the world. Primarily, the Bauhaus saw a new architecture as the means to regenerate the human condition.

10. Especially effective in depicting Jung as a key figure in the age of transition is Peter Homans, *Jung in Context: Modernity and the Making of a Psychology* (Chicago, 1979).

11. Outstanding on Ortega is Robert Wohl, *The Generation of 1914* (Cambridge, Mass., 1979), chapter 5, "Spain: The Theme of Our Time."

12. Quoted by Peter Selz, *Art in a Troubled Era: German and Austrian Expressionism* (Chicago, 1978), p. 26.

13. A brilliant depiction of the spirit of these times is provided by Carl E. Schorske, *Fin-de-Siècle Vienna* (New York, 1980). See also Peter Gay, *Freud, Jews and Other Germans: Masters and Victims in Modernist Culture* (New York, 1978), and Frederic V. Grunfeld, *Prophets without Honour: A Background to Freud, Kafka, Einstein and Their World* (New York, 1979).

14. Sontag, *Broken World,* p. 168.

15. José Antonio Primo de Rivera, *Obras de. . . ., edición cronológico,* compiled by Agustín del Río Cisneros (Madrid, 1966, 4th ed.), p. 787.

16. Hugh Thomas, "Reflection and Reinterpretation," in Philip Toynbee, ed., *The Distant Drum: Reflections on the Spanish Civil War* (London, 1976), p. 32.

17. A similar optimism infused early Italian fascism. See F. L. Carsten, *The Rise of Fascism* (Berkeley, 1971), p. 17.

18. Claude Cockburn, "Reflection and Reinterpretation," in Toynbee, ed., *Distant Drum,* p. 47.

19. For background material essential to understanding how anti-Semitism and anti-Masonry became lumped together with aversion to bourgeois liberal capitalism, see Joseph Katz, *Jews and Freemasons in Europe 1723–1939,* trans. Leonard Oschry (Cambridge, Mass., 1970), and Leon Poliakov, *The Aryan Myth: A History of Fascist and Nationalistic Ideas in Europe* (New York, 1974).

20. See David Ringrose, *Transportation and Economic Stagnation in Spain, 1750–1850* (Durham, N.C., 1970), and Nicolás Sánchez-Albornoz, *Jalones en la modernización de España* (Barcelona, 1975).

21. Dante Puzzo, *Spain and the Great Powers, 1936–1941* (New York, 1962), pp. 16–17.

22. Baker, "From Consensus to Polarization: 1898, Conservative Regeneration and Restoration Party Politics," paper presented at the March 1977

meeting of the Society for Spanish and Portuguese Historical Studies, Lexington, Ky., mimeo. See also María Carmen García Nieto, Javier M. Donezar, and Luis López Puerta, *Crisis del sistema Canovista, 1898–1923* (Madrid, 1972). The background to this period is handled skillfully by Earl R. Beck, *A Time of Triumph and of Sorrow: Spanish Politics during the Reign of Alfonso XII, 1874–1885* (Carbondale, Ill., 1979).

23. On economic development in general and some of the accompanying social problems, see J. E. Casariego, *El Marqués de Sargadelos o los comienzos del industrialismo capitalista en España* (Oviedo, 1974); Carlo M. Cipolla, ed., *The Emergence of Industrial Societies,* vol. 4, part 2, of *The Fontana Economic History of Europe* (New York, 1977); Antonio Elorza and María del Carmen Iglesias, *Burgueses y proletarios: Clase obrera y reforma social en la Restauración* (Barcelona, 1974); Luis García San Miguel, *De la sociedad aristocrática a la sociedad industrial en la España del siglo XIX* (Madrid, 1973); José M. Maravall, *El desarrollo económico y la clase obrera: Un estudio sociológico de los conflictos obreros en España* (Barcelona, 1970); Miguel Martínez Cuadrado, *La burguesía conservadora, 1874–1931,* vol. 6 of *Historia de España Alfaguara* (Madrid, 1973); Jordi Nadal, *El fracaso de la revolución industrial en España, 1814–1931* (Barcelona, 1975); Santiago Roldán, et al., *Consolidación del capitalismo en España, 1914–1920,* 2 vols. (Madrid, 1974); Nicolás Sánchez-Albornoz, *España hace un siglo: Una economía dual,* 2d ed. (Madrid, 1977); Gabriel Tortella Cásares, *Los orígenes del capitalismo en España: Banca, industria y ferrocarriles en el siglo XIX* (Madrid, 1973); Manuel Túñon de Lara, *La España del siglo XX, 1914–1939,* 2d ed. (Paris, 1973); Jaime Vicens Vives, ed. *Burguesía, industrialización, obrerismo,* vol. 5 of *Historia social y económica de España y América* (Barcelona, 1959); and Pedro Voltes Bou, *Historia de la economía española en los siglos XIX y XX,* 2 vols. (Madrid, 1974).

24. See Gerald H. Meaker, *The Revolutionary Left in Spain, 1914–1923* (Stanford, 1974), esp. pp. 62–188.

25. See Shlomo Ben-Ami, *The Origins of the Second Republic in Spain* (New York, 1978), and Duque de Maura and Melchor Fernández Almagro, *Por qué cayó Alfonso XIII: Evolución y disolución de los partidos históricos durante su reinado* (Madrid, 1948). For general accounts of the Second Republic, see Joaquín Arraras, *Historia de la Segunda República española* (Madrid, 1965); Ricardo de la Cierva, *Antecedentes: Monarquía y República 1898–1936,* vol. 1 of *Historia de la Guerra Civil Española* (Madrid, 1969); Santiago Galindo Herrera, *Historia de los partidos monárquicos bajo la Segunda República* (Madrid, 1954), Ramón Tamames, *La República, la era de Franco* (Madrid, 1973), and Manuel Túñon de Lara, *La II República: Estudio de historia contemporánea,* 2 vols. (Madrid, 1976). Despite leftist partisanship, the best survey of the Republic in English is Gabriel Jackson, *The Spanish Republic and the Civil War, 1931–1939* (Princeton, 1965). On the immediate background to the collapse of order see Juan J. Linz, "From Great Hopes to Civil War: The Breakdown of Democracy in Spain," in Linz and Alfred C. Stepan, eds., *The Breakdown of Democratic Regimes* (Baltimore, 1978), and Paul Preston, *The Coming of the Spanish Civil War: Reform, Reaction, and Revolution in the Second Republic, 1931–1936* (New York, 1978). The finest English-language coverage of the war itself is Hugh Thomas's massive *The Spanish Civil War* (New York, 1977), a thoroughly revised and much expanded edition of a classic first published in 1961. Useful also is Raymond Carr, ed., *The Republic and the Civil War in Spain* (New York, 1971). Spanish-language sources are absolutely staggering in number and proliferating on a monthly, even a weekly, basis. A

good work with which to begin is Vicente Palacio Atard, Ricardo de la Cierva, and Ramón Salas Larrazábal, *Aproximación a la guerra española, 1936–1939* (Madrid, 1970). Excellent in its approach is Georges Soria, *Guerre et revolution en Espagne, 1936–1939*, 5 vols. (Paris, 1977), a lavishly illustrated account enhanced by valuable interview material. Even better in its stunning use of interview sources is Ronald Fraser, *Blood of Spain: An Oral History of the Spanish Civil War* (New York, 1979). Abounding in rich insights into the attitudes of foreign poets involved in one way or another in the struggle is Valentine Cunningham, ed., *The Penguin Book of Spanish Civil War Verse* (Harmondsworth, Middlesex, Eng., 1980). By no means universally committed to the Republic, the poets display a complexity of attitudes that mirrors the complexity of the civil war itself.

26. See Le Bon, *The Crowd: A Study of the Popular Mind* (London, 1952), esp. pp. 6, 10, 118. Originally published in 1896, this work influenced Mussolini and was widely quoted by Spanish intellectuals.

27. A remarkably revealing source is Azaña, *Obras completas*, ed. by Juan Marichal, 4 vols. (Mexico City, 1974). See also Frank Sedwick, *The Tragedy of Manuel Azaña and the Fate of the Spanish Republic* (Columbus, 1963).

28. Puzzo, *Spain and the Great Powers*, p. 25.

29. See Henry Hatfield, "The Myth of Nazism," in Henry A. Murray, ed., *Myth and Mythmaking* (Boston, 1960), pp. 214–5.

30. See Philippe C. Schmitter, "Still the Century of Corporatism?" in F. B. Pike and T. J. Stritch, eds., *The New Corporatism: Social-Political Structures in the Iberian World* (Notre Dame, 1974), pp. 85–131. An abundance of rich comparative material is found in Howard J. Wiarda, *Corporatism and Development: The Portuguese Experience* (Amherst, 1977).

31. On Krausism see my "Making the Hispanic World Safe from Democracy: Spanish Liberals and Hispanismo," *The Review of Politics* 33 (1971): 307–22; Elías Díaz, *La filosofía social del Krausismo español* (Madrid, 1973); Juan José Gil Cremades, *Krausistas y liberales* (Madrid, 1975); and Antoni Jutglar, *Ideologías y clases en España contemporánea: Aproximación a la historia social de las ideas*, 2 vols. (Madrid, 1973). On Costa see my "Capitalism and Consumerism in Spain of the 1890s," *Inter-American Economic Affairs* 26 (1973): 19–47, and G. J. G. Cheyne, *A Bibliographical Study of the Writings of Joaquín Costa* (London, 1971).

32. Joseph Featherstone, "Rousseau and Modernity," *Daedalus* (Summer, 1978): 184.

33. See Kermit McKenzie, *Comintern and World Revolution, 1928–1943: The Shaping of Doctrine* (New York, 1963).

34. Karl Marx and Frederick Engels, *Revolution in Spain*, edited and translated anonymously (New York, 1939), p. 14.

35. See Thomas, "Reflection and Reinterpretation," p. 40. Also indispensable is Burnett Bolloten, *The Spanish Revolution: The Left and the Struggle for Power during the Civil War* (Chapel Hill, 1978).

36. The classic study of Spanish rural anarchism is Juan Díaz del Moral, *Historia de las agitaciones campesinas andaluzas* (Madrid, 1929). See also James Joll, *The Anarchists*, 2d ed. (Cambridge, Mass., 1980), and Robert W. Kern, *Red Years, Black Years: A Political History of Spanish Anarchism, 1911–1937* (Philadelphia, 1978). Rich in background material are Gerald Brenan, *The Spanish Labyrinth* (Cambridge, Eng., 1943); Raymond Carr, *Spain, 1808–1939* (Oxford,

Eng., 1966); Edward Malefakis, *Agrarian Reform and Peasant Revolution in Spain: Origins of the Civil War* (New Haven, 1970); and Michael R. Weisser, *The Peasants of the Montes: The Roots of Rural Rebellion in Spain* (Chicago, 1977). In her revisionist *Anarchists of Andalusia, 1868–1903* (Princeton, 1977) Temma Kaplan stresses the practical, pragmatic thrust of anarchism in northern Cádiz province, downplaying the millennialism stressed by most accounts. However, the base of her study appears too narrow to justify her generalizations.

37. Tannenbaum, *1900*, p. 67.

38. See Mircea Eliade, "The Yearning for Paradise in Primitive Tradition," in Murray, ed., *Myth*, pp. 62–66.

39. Useful for placing the Calvo Sotelo position in its broader context is Ernest Nolde, *Three Faces of Fascism: Action Française, Italian Fascism, National Socialism*, trans. Leila Vennewitz (New York, 1966). See also Paul Mazgaj, *The Action Française and Revolutionary Syndicalism* (Chapel Hill, N.C., 1979), tracing the interaction between the syndicalist left and the royalist right in an analysis that in some of its ramifications is applicable to Spain.

40. See my *Hispanismo, 1898–1936: Spanish Conservatives and Liberals and Their Relations with Spanish America* (Notre Dame, 1971), esp. pp. 279–80, and Francis G. Wilson, *Political Thought in National Spain* (Urbana, 1967). For comparative background material see Hans Rogger and Eugen Weber, eds., *The European Right: A Historical Profile* (Berkeley, 1966).

41. See Gil Robles, *No fue posible la paz* (Barcelona, 1968); Barbara Schmoll Mahoney, "José María Gil Robles: The Catholic Politician in the Second Republic," Ph.D. dissertation, St. Louis University (1975); and Richard A. H. Robinson, *The Origins of Franco's Spain: The Right, the Republic and Revolution, 1931–1936* (Pittsburgh, 1970), a study that concentrates on Gil Robles and the CEDA.

42. Michael A. Ledeen, *The First Duce: D'Anunzio at Fiume* (Baltimore, 1978), finds in the Italian adventure at Fiume (1919–20) many features that were associated—though not exclusively—with the advancing shadow of fascism, including: youth calling for elimination of the old and corrupt political leadership; artists suggesting that aesthetics should constitute the basis for political decisions; poets insisting on a beautiful world instead of a utilitarian one; and women and minorities of all types clamoring for their fair share of political power. Luigi Barzini, reviewing the book (*New York Review of Books* [June 15, 1978]: 24) adds that Ledeen might have included certain additional features, including: "the widespread use of drugs, uninhibited sex, the occasional flaunting of homosexual proclivities, nudism, the bizarre hairdos and whiskers intended to show disdain for bourgeois conventions." Perhaps this lends support to the thesis of A. James Gregor in *The Fascist Persuasion in Radical Politics* (Princeton, 1974) that radicalism of the 1970s owed more to "paradigmatic" fascism than to Marxism. See also Gregor, *Young Mussolini and the Intellectual Origins of Fascism* (Berkeley, 1979). On the radicalism of fascism's origins see also Renzo de Felice, *Fascism: An Informal Introduction to Its Theory and Practice* (New Brunswick, N.J., 1976) and *Interpretations of Fascism* (Cambridge, Mass., 1977); David D. Roberts, *The Syndicalist Tradition and Italian Fascism* (Chapel Hill, N.C., 1979); and Roland Sarti, "Fascist Modernization in Italy: Traditional or Revolutionary?" *American Historical Review* 75 (1970): 1029–45. Frequently applicable to Spain are the analyses of Gino Germani in *Authoritarianism, Fascism, and National Populism* (New Brunswick, 1978).

43. Cassels, "Communication," *American Historical Review* 84 (1979): 1232. On the antimaterialist, antibourgeois prejudices of the Falange, see my *Hispanismo,* esp. pp. 283–93. If the Falange demonstrated many features of the paradigmatic Fascist model, it was still a home-grown form of fascism lacking direct ties to the Italian movement.

44. Clearly, the Falange conforms to the description often made of paradigmatic fascism as a movement against liberal-style modernization and at the same time an episode in the modernization of late-developing countries. Further, like most Fascist movements the Falange contained an agrarian streak directed against financiers and industrialists, a glorification of poetic, artistic vision, and a willingness to use violence to usher in a new order in which select beings would instruct the masses in such a manner as to persuade them ultimately to welcome the role of obedience that unimaginative bourgeois society forced on them through material inducements and repression. See A. F. K. Organski, "Fascism and Modernization," in S. J. Woolf, ed., *The Nature of Fascism* (New York, 1968), esp. pp. 19, 30.

45. See José Luis de Arrese, *La revolución social del nacional sindicalismo* (Madrid, 1940), p. 223.

46. See the fine study by Martin Blinkhorn, *Carlism and Crisis in Spain, 1931–1939* (Cambridge, Eng., 1975), delivering more than the title indicates with an extensive study of the origins and nineteenth-century history of Carlism.

47. Pedro Sáinz Rodríguez, "Interpretación histórica de la España contemporánea," *Revista de las Españas* 22–23 (1928): 247–49. For the fascinating memoirs of this important rightist thinker and political personage who staunchly defended monarchism and thus looked askance at Franco, see note 64.

48. Quoted in Georges Sorel, *The Illusions of Progress,* trans. John and Charlotte Stanley (Berkeley, 1969), pp. 102–3.

49. Thomas, "Reflection and Reinterpretation," p. 35.

50. These are the apt terms used by Maier, *Recasting Bourgeois Europe,* pp. 585–86, in connection with the rise of Italian fascism.

51. See Fernando de Meer, *La cuestión religiosa en la Cortes Constituyente de la II República española* (Pamplona, 1975). For a masterful synthesis of the background to the explosion, see Stanley G. Payne, *The Spanish Revolution: A Study of the Social and Political Tensions that Culminated in the Civil War in Spain* (New York, 1970). Also indispensable are Payne's *Falange: A History of Spanish Fascism* (Stanford, 1961), and *Politics and the Military in Modern Spain* (Stanford, 1967).

52. Admittedly, there are exceptions to this statement, the most noteworthy being the pro-Republic position of the devoutly Catholic Basque provinces, adopted largely in the desire for regional autonomy. See Stanley G. Payne, *Basque Nationalism* (Reno, 1975).

53. Quoted by J. Alberich in *Bulletin of Hispanic Studies* 51 (1974): 185.

54. Belief in the organic interconnectedness of the three sacred liberties was manifested by John Q. Adams, who hoped to begin the Americanization of Latin America by pressuring the newly-independent republics to adopt religious freedom. In its wake, ostensibly, would come political and economic liberty. See Wilkins B. Winn, "The Efforts of the United States to Secure Religious Liberty in a Commercial Treaty with Mexico, 1825–1831," *The Americas* 27 (1972): 311–32.

55. Guttmann, *The Wound in the Heart: America and the Spanish Civil War* (New York, 1962), p. 81.

56. Ibid., p. 94. See also Pedro Manuel Arambide, "The Reactions of the Protestant and Catholic Churches in the U.S.A. to the Spanish Civil War," Ph.D. dissertation, Memphis State University (1976).

57. See George Q. Flynn, *Roosevelt and Romanism: Catholics and American Diplomacy, 1937–1945* (Westport, Conn., 1976), esp. pp. 29–52, and J. David Valaik, "American Catholics and the Second Spanish Republic," *Journal of Church and State* 10 (1968), pp. 13–28.

58. John F. Diggins, *Mussolini and Fascism: The View from America* (Princeton, 1972), pp. 190, 192.

59. Ibid. pp. 5–65, and Flynn, *Roosevelt*, pp. 52–62.

60. *The Catholic Worker*, guided by Dorothy Day and Peter Maurin, and *Commonweal*, under the editorship of George Shuster, were the only two national Catholic publications daring to take a public stand critical of Franco and therefore in opposition to the American episcopacy. See Mary C. Segers, "Equality and Christian Anarchism: The Political and Social Ideas of the Catholic Worker Movement," *The Review of Politics* 40 (1978), esp. pp. 201–2.

61. See Thomas T. McAvoy, *The Great Crisis in American Catholic History, 1895–1900* (Chicago, 1957).

62. On voluntarism in American Catholicism of the 1960s and 70s see Andrew Greeley, *The American Catholic: A Social Portrait* (New York, 1977).

63. Diggins, *Mussolini*, p. 249. See also D. E. J. Spooner, "The Response of Some British and American Writers to the Spanish Civil War," Ph.D. dissertation, Bristol University (1968), and K. W. Watkins, *Britain Divided* (London, 1963).

64. Sáinz Rodríguez, *Testimonio y recuerdos* (Barcelona, 1977), provides significant insights into attempts of the anti-Republican right to obtain backing from Italy for the projected Generals' Rebellion. On the broader aspects of the topic see John F. Coverdale, *Italian Intervention in the Spanish Civil War* (Princeton, 1975), perhaps the best study in English on the subject of international intervention in the war. On Russian intervention see David Cattell, *Communism and the Spanish Civil War* (Berkeley, 1955) and *Soviet Diplomacy and the Spanish Civil War* (Berkeley, 1957). Other useful works on international diplomacy and the Spanish struggle include Jill Edwards, *The British Government and the Spanish Civil War, 1936–1939* (London, 1979); Norman J. Padelford, *International Law and Diplomacy in the Spanish Civil War* (New York, 1939); P. A. M. Van der Esch, *Prelude to War: The International Repercussions of the Spanish Civil War, 1936–1939* (The Hague, 1951); Angel Viñas, *El Oro de Moscú: Alfa y omega de un mito franquista* (Barcelona, 1979); and William E. Watters, *An International Affair: Non-intervention in the Spanish Civil War, 1936–1939* (New York, 1971). An essential reference source is James W. Cortada, comp., *A Bibliographic Guide to Spanish Diplomatic History, 1460–1977* (Westport, Conn., 1977), esp. pp. 291–323.

65. Diggins, *Mussolini*, p. 26. See also John A. Garraty, "The New Deal, National Socialism, and the Great Depression," *American Historical Review* 74 (1974): 914.

66. Diggins, *Mussolini*, p. 60.

67. Ibid., p. 165.

68. This was how the Nationalist cause impressed Englishman Arnold

Lunn. See his *Spanish Rehearsal* (New York, 1937), p. vii. Some Americans shared his view, most notably Seward Collins. Editor of the *American Review,* Collins found in fascism the small person's revolt against the titans of financial capitalism. In this he unwittingly grasped the essence of José Antonio's Falange far better than most of its American critics.

69. See José Luis Castillo-Puche, *Hemingway in Spain* (New York, 1974); Scott Donaldson, *By Force of Will: The Life and Art of Ernest Hemingway* (New York, 1977), chapter 5; and Richard H. Pells, *Radical Visions and American Dreams: Culture and Social Thought in the Depression Years* (New York, 1973), pp. 210–13. One of the most notorious incidents of the civil war, propagandized relentlessly and resulting in widespread revulsion against the Nationalists, was the destruction of the small Vizcayan town of Guernica on April 26, 1937— undoubtedly by German bombers, although the issue remains contested by some. See Herbert R. Southworth, *Guernica! Guernica!* (Berkeley, 1977), and Gordon Thomas and Max Morgan Witts, *Guernica* (New York, 1976), for accounts occasionally marred by anti-Nationalist animus.

70. Bowers, *My Mission to Spain* (New York, 1954), pp. 411–12.

71. Charles P. Kindleberger, "U.S. Foreign Economic Policy, 1776–1976," *Foreign Affairs* 55 (1977): 404, observes that Hull had a "fanatical preoccupation with foreign trade."

72. See Michael A. Ledeen, *Universal Fascism: The Theory and Practice of the Fascist International, 1928–1936* (New York, 1972).

73. On this subject see Kenneth J. Grieb, "The Fascist Mirage in Central America: Guatemalan-United States Relations and the Yankee Fear of Fascism, 1936–1944," in Jules Davis, ed., *Perspectives in American Diplomacy* (New York, 1976); Michael Grow, "The United States, Nazi Germany, and Corporatism in the River Plate Basin, 1939–1945," Ph.D. dissertation, George Washington University (1975); and S. J. Woolf, "Did a Fascist Economic System Exist?" in Woolf, ed., *Nature of Fascism,* esp. pp. 132–42. There was a tremendous outpouring of journalistic accounts of the Fascist menace in Latin America during the late 1930s and early 1940s. The myth of Latin America's ineluctable drift into fascism helped sell shoddy books just as effectively as the myth of the 1960s on the hemisphere's coming explosion and its inexorable move toward communism. Heading the list of serious scholarly studies on the German threat are Alton Frye, *Nazi Germany and the American Hemisphere, 1933–1941* (New Haven, 1967), and Arnold Ebel, *Das Dritte Reich und Argentinien* (Koln, 1971).

74. See Paul J. Vanderwood, "American Cinema and Mexican Heroes: The Cases of Juárez and Zapata," paper presented at the 1976 sessions of the Conference on Latin American History of the American Historical Association and summarized in *Hispanic American Historical Review* 57 (1977): 399–400.

75. See Arthur H. Landis, *The Abraham Lincoln Brigade* (New York, 1967), esp. pp. xi–xiii. Other works of the extensive literature on this subject include Alvah Bessie, *Men in Battle* (New York, 1939); Edwin Rolfe, *The Lincoln Battalion* (New York, 1939); and Robert Rosenstone, *Crusade on the Left: The Abraham Lincoln Battalion in the Spanish Civil War* (New York, 1969).

76. Diggins, *Mussolini,* p. 176.

77. The civil war also passionately divided those who reported on it and resulted in coverage that was outstanding for its partiality. See Philip Knightley, *The First Casualty: From the Crimea to Vietnam, the War Correspondent as Hero, Propagandist and Myth Maker* (New York, 1975). According to Knightley the

first casualty in Spanish civil war coverage, as in previous and subsequent international struggles, was truth in reporting. The French press provides a microcosm of this phenomenon: see David Wingeate Pike, *Conjecture, Propaganda, and Deceit and the Spanish Civil War: The International Crisis over Spain, 1936–1939, as Seen in the French Press* (Stanford, 1968), printed under the auspices of the California Institute of International Studies.

78. See Hadley Cantril and Mildred Strunk, *Public Opinion, 1936–1946* (Princeton, 1951), pp. 807–9.

79. Bowers, *My Mission to Spain,* pp. 49–50.

80. Guttmann, *Wound in the Heart,* pp. 4–5.

81. Puzzo, *Spain and the Great Powers,* p. 35.

82. Hayes, *The United States and Spain: An Interpretation* (New York, 1951), pp. 83–84. Understanding of the American mindset vis-à-vis the civil war may be enhanced by reading Cornad Furay, *The Grass Roots Mind in America: The American Sense of Absolutes* (New York, 1977).

83. See Burnett Bolloten, *The Grand Camouflage: The Spanish Civil War and the Revolution 1936–1939* (New York, 1961). An updating of this work with a considerable expansion of footnotes and the addition of nearly seventy pages of text on revolutionary Catalonia and the crucial Barcelona events of May 1937 is *La révolution espagnole,* I, *La gauche et la lutte pour le pouvoir* (Paris, 1977).

84. See note 78.

85. Fred L. Israel, *Nevada's Key Pittman* (Lincoln, 1963), p. 149.

86. Quoted in Arnold Lunn, *Spanish Rehearsal,* p. 20. There was also a nobler side to Americans' noninterventionist preferences. Like Herbert Hoover, many thoughtful persons feared individual freedom at home would ultimately be jeopardized by liberal crusading types who, by overextending U.S. foreign commitments, would make inevitable the creation of a centralizing military-industrial complex that would not only erode time-honored liberties but also weaken middle-class security by abetting inflation. See Joan Hoff Wilson's probing, controversial *Herbert Hoover: Forgotten Progressive* (Boston, 1975). For a study of these attitudes projected into the Cold War era see Ronald Radosh, *Prophets on the Right: Conservative Critics of American Globalism* (New York, 1977).

87. For valuable overviews, see James W. Cortada, *Two Nations over Time: Spain and the United States, 1776–1977* (Westport, Conn., 1978), chapter 12; Robert Dallek, *Franklin D. Roosevelt and American Foreign Policy, 1932–1945* (New York, 1979); G. W. C. Fee, "The Course of the United States Government Policy toward the Spanish Civil War, 1936–1939," B. Litt. dissertation, Cambridge University (1955); and Richard P. Traina, *American Diplomacy and the Spanish Civil War* (Bloomington, Ind., 1969).

88. Robert Kelley, "Ideology and Political Culture from Jefferson to Nixon," *American Historical Review* 82 (1977), esp. p. 552.

89. If FDR was circumspect about revealing his civil war sympathies, his wife threw discretion to the winds. Her rabidly pro-Republic stance she justified by the common stereotypes of democracy's struggle with totalitarianism. In her mind, there was no question that morality inhered in the Loyalists, vice in the Rebels. See Joseph P. Lash, *Eleanor and Franklin* (New York, 1971), p. 737–41.

90. Flynn, *Roosevelt,* p. 30. See also Puzzo, *Spain and the Great Powers,* p. 156 and note 84. For a succinct analysis of the consequences of the neutrality

policy pursued by the democracies, see Alistair Hennessy's review of Raymond Carr's fine study *The Spanish Tragedy* (London, 1977), in *The New Statesman* (August 12, 1977), p. 216.

91. See James W. Cortada, ed., *Spain in the Twentieth Century World: Essays on Spanish Diplomacy, 1898–1978* (Westport, Conn., 1980), and "United States Relations with Spain's Second Republic, 1931–1936," paper presented at the March 1977 meeting of the Society for Spanish and Portuguese Historical Studies, Lexington, Ky., mimeo, and Douglas J. Little, "Malevolent Neutrality: The United States, Great Britain, and the Spanish Revolution, 1931–1936," Ph.D. dissertation, Cornell University (1978).

92. Cordell Hull, *The Memoirs of . . .*, 2 vols. (New York, 1948), I, 475.

93. See Stanley Weintraub, *The Last Great Cause: The Intellectuals and the Spanish Civil War* (New York, 1968).

94. On the lingering influence of Calhoun's critique of rampant individualism, see Mark E. Neely, Jr., "The Organic Theory of State in America, 1838–1918," Ph.D. dissertation, Yale University (1973). For intellectual criticism of America's turn-of-the-century prevailing order, see Daniel Aaron, *Writers on the Left* (New York, 1969); Paul A. Carter, *The Spiritual Crisis of the Gilded Age* (De Kalb., Ill., 1971); James B. Gilbert, *Work Without Salvation: America's Intellectuals and Industrial Alienation, 1880–1910* (Baltimore, 1977); Christopher Lasch, *New Radicalism in America, 1889–1963* (New York, 1965); Howard Mumford Jones, *The Age of Energy: Varieties of American Experience, 1865–1915* (Cambridge, Mass., 1971); Wilson C. McWilliams, *The Idea of Fraternity in America* (Berkeley, 1974); and Robert H. Wiebe, *The Search for Order, 1877–1920* (New York, 1967). For a fascinating and provocative study of how women and clergymen combined to combat the capitalist ethic of aggressive, individualistic, ego-maximizing qualities, stereotyped as masculine, see Ann Douglas, *The Feminization of American Culture* (New York, 1977).

95. Michael Kammen, *People of Paradox: An Inquiry Concerning the Origins of American Civilization* (New York, 1973), p. 269.

96. See, for example, Peter Frederick, *Knights of the Golden Rule: The Intellectual as Christian Social Reformer in the 1890s* (Lexington, Ky., 1976).

97. See Arthur A. Ekirch, Jr., *Progressivism in America: A Study of the Era from Theodore Roosevelt to Woodrow Wilson* (New York, 1975).

98. Alexander Karanikas, *Tillers of a Myth: Southern Agrarians as Social and Literary Critics* (Madison, 1969), pp. 6,8. See also Stuart I. Rochester, *American Liberal Disillusionment in the Wake of World War I* (University Park, Pa., 1977). In some ways the new mood in America displayed symptoms of the "Great Awakenings" that seem to recur cyclically. See William G. McLoughlin, *Revivals, Awakenings, and Reform: An Essay on Religion and Social Change in America, 1607–1977* (Chicago, 1978). Useful for placing this period in perspective in Alfred Braunthal, *Salvation and the Perfect Society: The Eternal Quest* (Amherst, 1979).

99. See Andrew Bergman, *We're in the Money: Depression America and Its Films* (New York, 1971), p. 41.

100. James Gilbert, *Designing the Industrial State: The Intellectual Pursuit of Collectivism in America, 1880–1940* (Chicago, 1972), p. 43. Also valuable is Charles R. Hearn, *The American Dream in the Great Depression* (Westport, Conn., 1977). Hearn shows that prior to the depression serious writers had already evidenced disillusionment in the American dream of success, equated with

business triumphs, while popular literature continued to glorify this dream. In the 1930s the serious writers grew still more disillusioned, and popular literature began to reveal doubt and disenchantment. Providing useful perspectives on intellectuals and the American dream during the 1930s and early 1940s is Otis L. Graham, *An Encore for Reform: The Old Progressives and the New Deal* (New York, 1967).

101. Gilbert, *Designing,* p. 24.

102. Pells, *Radical Visions,* pp. 108–10. On the optimism of the period see J. Warren Wagar, *Good Tidings: The Belief in Progress from Darwin to Marcuse* (Bloomington, Ind., 1972).

103. Under challenge by alienated intellectuals was the traditional gospel of material growth as described in Chester L. Cooper, ed., *Growth in America* (Westport, Conn., 1976) and Richard M. Huber, *The American Idea of Success* (New York, 1971).

104. Thomas Krueger and William Glidden, "The New Deal Intellectual Elite," in F. C. Jaher, ed., *The Rich, the Well Born, and the Powerful* (Urbana, 1973), p. 365. The emphasis is mine.

105. Gilbert, *Designing,* p. 66.

106. Pells, *Radical Visions,* p. 65.

107. See Daniel Bell, *Marxian Socialism in the United States* (Princeton, 1967); Theodore Draper, *American Communism and Soviet Russia: The Formative Period* (New York, 1960); and Philip J. Jaffe, *Rise and Fall of American Communism* (New York, 1975). Two provocative essays provide comparative analysis for this period: James Weinstein, "The Fortunes of the Old Left Compared to the Fortunes of the New Left," in John H. M. Laslett and Seymour Martin Lipset, eds., *Failure of a Dream? Essays in the History of American Socialism* (New York, 1974), pp. 677–712, and Howard Zinn, "A Comparison of the Militant Left of the Thirties and Sixties," in Morton J. Frisch and Martin Diamond, eds., *The Thirties: A Reconsideration in the Light of the American Political Tradition* (De Kalb, Ill., 1968), pp. 27–43. In *Up from Communism: Conservative Odysseys in American Intellectual History* (New York, 1975), John Diggins maintains that it is primarily "continuity in disdain for liberalism" that binds the critics of the Lockean society in the 1930s, most of whom were located on the far left, with those former Communists who in later decades formed a hard core of the conservative right. See also George H. Nash, *The Conservative Intellectual Movement in America since 1945* (New York, 1976), especially his section on conservative thinkers who have turned against their earlier Marxism.

108. See James Gilbert Ryan, "The Making of a Native Marxist: The Early Career of Earl Browder," *The Review of Politics* 39 (1977), esp. pp. 332–37.

109. David Donald, "The Abolitionists: The Displaced Elite," in Alfred F. Davis, ed., *Conflict and Consensus* (Lexington, Mass., 1972), pp. 329–44. Agrarians had something in common with northern writers like Melville and James and Henry Adams. See Patrick Gerster and Nicholas Cords, "The Northern Origins of Southern Mythology," *Journal of Southern History* 43 (1977), pp. 567–82.

110. Karanikas, *Tillers of a Myth,* provides a superb account of the Agrarians and also of the southern opposition to them that centered at the University of North Carolina in a group that advocated accommodation with liberalism. On the New Humanism challenge to liberal modernity see J. David

Hoeveler, Jr., *The New Humanism: A Critique of Modern America, 1900–1940* (Charlotte, 1977).

111. Borkenau, *The Spanish Cockpit* (Ann Arbor, 1963), pp. 299–300. The book appeared originally in 1937.

112. For interesting comparisons of United States attitudes toward the war in Vietnam in the 1960s and the Spanish Civil War in the 1930s, see Noam Chomsky, *American Power and the New Mandarins* (New York, 1969), pp. 23–157.

113. See Fred Weinstein and Gerald M. Platt, *The Wish To Be Free: Society, Psyche, and Value Change* (Berkeley, 1969), chapters 5 and 6. Insights into the "introspective revolution" as it existed in America abound in Malcolm Cowley, *The Dream of the Golden Mountains: Remembering the 1930s* (New York, 1980).

114. On new attitudes of intellectuals toward the American Indian in the 1920s, see Robert F. Berkhofer, Jr., *The White Man's Indian: Images of the American Indian from Columbus to the Present Day* (New York, 1978), esp. pp. 182–88, and Graham D. Taylor, *The New Deal and American Indian Tribalism: The Administration of the Indian Reorganization Act, 1934–1945* (Lincoln, 1980). Stunningly applicable to United States attitudes toward Indians are the findings of Henri Baudet in *Paradise on Earth: Some Thoughts on European Images of Non-European Man* (New Haven, 1965). On shifting attitudes of some American white intellectuals toward Blacks, see Wilson J. Moses, *The Golden Age of Black Nationalism, 1850–1925* (Hamden, Conn., 1978), esp. pp. 251–61. Richard King, *The Party of Eros: Radical Social Thought and the Realm of Freedom* (Chapel Hill, N.C., 1972), p. 23, notes the prevailing spirit of individual "release" and search for cultural rejuvenation. Rejecting the genteel middle-class culture, intellectuals turned to the "excluded and exploited segment of the society for an answer to its problems as well as their own. Some saw the workers as a source of salvation; . . . still others embraced the cause of the immigrant." On this and earlier cults of primitivism in America, see Richard Hofstadter, *Anti-Intellectualism in American Life* (New York, 1964). On the cult of primitivism as it focused on Spaniards, see my "Dabbling in Psycho-history: A Look at United States–Spanish Mutual Images from the 1920s to the 1970s," *Red River Valley Historical Journal* 4 (1980).

115. See Ronald T. Takaki's brilliant study *Iron Cages: Race and Culture in Nineteenth-Century America* (New York, 1979).

116. Edward B. Henning, *The Spirit of Surrealism* (Cleveland, 1979), p. 150.

117. Doomed to failure by their utopian dimensions, the dreams that evoked the Spanish civil war and were in turn evoked by it in foreign lands are startlingly similar to those of the counter culture of the 1960s. In describing the counter culture's "new mysticism," John Passmore, "Paradise Now," *Encounter* 34 (1970): 3–21, notes its objective was to abolish repression and establish an order of immediate gratification. The new mysticism he sees as another entry in the long history of "perfectabilism"—a view in which man is intrinsically good and salvation lies in communal rather than institutional forms, gratification rather than repression, exulting in being rather than sacrificing in the interests of becoming.

Mexico

T. G. Powell

Mexico experienced a modernization process in the nineteenth century that satisfied relatively few people. Begun by liberal politicians who dreamed of a secular capitalist society run by themselves in pseudo-democratic fashion, the process had been carried forward by General Porfirio Díaz, dictatorial ruler of the country from the 1870s until his overthrow in 1911. Several major flaws accounted for the unhappy outcome of Mexican modernization. Departure from time-honored Spanish social and economic traditions in favor of foreign development models destroyed Mexico's ever-precarious societal balance. New legislation and more efficient business practices by landowners deprived peasants of their lands and removed customary paternalistic protection from sharecroppers and laborers on large estates. Despite the appearances of a secure peace, maintained by army and police terror, the sufferings and hence revolutionary potential of rural Mexicans increased each year.[1]

As in various European countries, modernization in Mexico also victimized and alienated urban artisans, hard pressed by new economic conditions and unwilling to descend into Mexico's expanding industrial proletariat. This latter group itself began to show signs of organizational ability and militancy in the early 1900s when several major strikes against textile and mining companies had to be suppressed by massive government violence against the workers.[2] Many middle-sector Mexi-

This chapter is in part based upon T. G. Powell, *Mexico and the Spanish Civil War* (University of New Mexico Press, Albuquerque, 1981). The author thanks the University of New Mexico Press for permission to use this material.

cans had also chafed at President Díaz's formula for modernization, since its many concessions to foreign capitalists and corporations allowed them to take virtual control of the national economy. The dictator, moreover, kept his political circle restricted to a small clique, its members monopolizing fees, commissions, and bribes exacted from foreign investors. By the early 1900s bourgeois malcontents excluded from the system's benefits had found the courage to challenge it.[3] Finally, Mexico's church and many Catholics remained intransigent foes of modernization itself. Although coddled by Díaz, who astutely avoided the mistakes of his liberal predecessors by refusing to persecute Catholicism and to despoil ecclesiastical wealth, the Mexican church refused even to offer compromise on such issues as societal secularization and proscription of clerical incursions into politics.[4]

Mexico's Revolution of 1910 began ironically under the auspices of bourgeois liberal leadership in the person of Francisco Madero, a wealthy eccentric. Not the least of Madero's oddities was his belief that return to the pseudodemocracy of the 1850s would calm social tensions inflamed by modernization. Since modernizing liberals themselves had provoked a long period of constant domestic turbulence in Mexico, Madero's political vision had an especially quixotic character. Tragic events soon changed the Revolution's course. Lower-class victims of modernization joined the upheaval and trapped President Madero between themselves on the left and conservative, clerical defenders of Spanish colonial traditions on the right. Allied with the latter group were surviving supporters of Díaz. The incompetent Madero perished in February 1913, murdered during a military coup headed by rightist General Victoriano Huerta, the famous *cucaracha* (cockroach) that Revolutionaries immortalized in a popular song. General Huerta's coup immediately revived the Revolution, which came to be spearheaded by an uneasy coalition of liberals, led by gray-bearded Venustiano Carranza, and ragtag radical movements directed by two picturesque but controversial chieftans, Emiliano Zapata and Francisco "Pancho" Villa.[5]

Backed by U.S. President Woodrow Wilson, who did not like Huerta, the Revolutionaries toppled the hated tyrant in 1914. After Huerta's flight into exile, the rebels themselves split into warring factions. Carranza battled Zapata and Villa. By 1916 Carranza had triumphed, only to be robbed of his liberal victory by ideological reverses at the Revolutionary constituent congress of 1916–1917. Dominated by politicians who realized that Mexico's old modernization formula no longer had validity, the congress superimposed on basic liberal principles constitutional provisions exalting state power over virtually every facet of life. Subsequent Revolutionary regimes could then create a political system to deal effectively with such momentous problems as foreign imperialism, economic reconstruction, the cultural gap between Indians and other Mexicans, poverty and illiteracy, and continuing church resistance to modernity itself.[6]

Mexico's Constitution of 1917 did not, however, automatically provide practical solutions to these problems. President Alvaro Obregón (1920–24) made a modestly successful start at problem-solving, but his administration was followed by a largely destructive period of bigoted tyranny and corruption under General Plutarco E. Calles, president from 1924 to 1928 and "boss" of Mexico from 1929 to 1934.[7] Amid ongoing violence, President Lázaro Cárdenas (1934–40), another Revolutionary general, finally worked out a feasible plan for ruling Mexico and for making its socio-economic structure reasonably functional. Cárdenas's program, despite its employment of Marxist rhetoric, had a strongly traditional bias: it preserved the dominant-dependent, two-culture society of the Spanish colonial period and put an authoritarian corporatist stamp on Mexican politics and social relations.[8] Cardenista Mexico thus had much in common with General Franco's Nationalist government in Spain, a regime that the Mexican president despised and that he tried valiantly to defeat during the civil war by rendering unceasing aid to the Spanish Republic. Although he would have angrily denied it, Cárdenas himself even resembled Franco in presiding over what was essentially a military dictatorship.

Hispanism and Hispanophobia in Revolutionary Mexico

Popular attitudes in Mexico toward Spain and Spaniards in the 1930s ranged from admiring love to scornful hatred. Prominent among those Mexicans who venerated Spain were upper- and middle-class Catholics who looked back fondly on Mexico's colonial past and who resented the increasingly visible incursions of the Protestant United States into Mexican life. Generally despising the Revolution's programs and ideals, they had no desire to see Spain itself imitate Mexico politically and socially. They saw traditional Hispanic culture and values as bulwarks against American influence and also against the radicalism and anticlericalism that "threatened civilized life." For them, preservation of a vigorous Spanish culture in Mexico was one of the best defenses against the "imperialist" menace presented by the United States.[9]

Liberals and radicals could also be found among Mexican Hispanophiles. They loved plebeian as opposed to oligarchic Spain, and by 1931 far more Mexicans were aware of the "other Spain" than had been the case formerly. According to José Vasconcelos, this new awareness had been partly caused by periodic visits to Mexico in the 1920s by famous Spanish intellectuals and politicians of liberal or reformist persuasion: Marcelino Domingo, Ramón del Valle-Inclán, and Fernando de los Ríos. They won the hearts of many Mexicans and thus changed their attitudes toward Spain and Spaniards.[10] One of Mexico's most prominent liberal Hispanists was Alfonso Reyes. A son of General Bernardo Reyes, Alfonso had lived in Spain for many years following his father's violent death in the military uprising against President Madero in 1913. Reyes found his cultural roots in the peninsula. "I consider myself," he wrote in 1932, "a Spaniard with nuance. . . . When I turn my eyes to my land, I see it, and I understand it as such a natural prolongation of Spain! Going to Spain was for me entering more into Mexico. The two loves are fused within me and nothing will be able to separate them."[11] Well before 1931 Reyes had concluded that Spain's many problems could best be solved by the moderate left.[12]

Many other Mexicans found it easy to reconcile their Revolutionary affiliation with strong Hispanist sentiments. Some of them did this by pointing to an American imperialist plot that allegedly involved the "dehispanization" of Mexican culture as an essential step toward taking over the country. When an anonymous Hispanophobe produced a pamphlet in 1919 calling for the expulsion of Spaniards from Mexico and the confiscation of their property, two Revolutionaries with impeccable credentials, José Vasconcelos and Miguel Alessio Robles, responded with a vigorous defense of Hispanism.[13] Vasconcelos is generally remembered as one of Mexico's arch-conservatives. Prior to 1933, however, he had a consistently liberal-Revolutionary political and ideological record. Although challenging PNR leadership as an opposition candidate in the 1929 presidential election, he did so as a Revolutionary purist, promising to do away with military rule and corruption. Gradually, however, Vasconcelos became disillusioned with "leftism" and moved into reactionary ranks. Friendly attitudes of Spanish Republicans toward the Callista regime in Mexico influenced his political shift. If loyalty to the leftist cause required excusing what Vasconcelos regarded as the intolerable barbarism of Calles, then he would have nothing further to do with leftism or with the Republicans.[14]

Pervasive anti-Spanish sentiments, always evident among Mexicans, remained very much present in the 1920s and '30s. People manifested their Hispanophobic feelings in various ways: hostility toward members of the Spanish colony (pejoratively called *gachupines*); demands for the deportation of Spaniards and the seizure of their property; depreciation of Spain, Spanish culture, and the Spanish colonial record in public schools. Not even the Hispanist secretary of public education from 1920 to 1924, José Vasconcelos, had been able to remove such prejudices from the school system. Throughout the 1920s, required textbooks in primary schools consistently denigrated Spanish culture and contrasted Spain unfavorably with the "superior" Anglo-Saxon countries, England and the United States. Mary K. Vaughn's study of required primary school books, *History Textbooks in Mexico in the 1920s*, indicates that even some Catholic pedagogues had an anti-Spanish bias.[15]

From a Hispanist point of view, unfair treatment intensified during the 1930s as a Marxist-dominated Secretariat of Public Education stepped up attacks on the Spanish tradition. In 1935 public school teachers received examination books containing several questions that Mexican Hispanophiles and members of the Spanish colony regarded as deliberately insulting. One question stated that in forty years the Spaniards "assassinated" fifteen million Indians in Mexico, then asked students to calculate the average number of Indians killed each year. Another question required students to identify correct statements among the following possible answers: During their rule of Mexico, the Spaniards (a) encouraged drunkenness among Indians; (b) built roads to facilitate communications; (c) encouraged robbery among the Indians; (d) utilized all sources of food production; (e) left the Indians in total ignorance. The teachers' exam books listed *a, c,* and *e* as the "true" answers.[16]

Many Mexican leftists attached great importance to convincing the public, especially lower-class people and potentially liberal elements in the middle sectors, that traditional Spain and its socio-cultural legacy in Mexico stood for evil things: clericalism, obscurantism, oppressive political reaction, and aristocratic exploitation of the masses. They saw the Spanish colonial tradition, Mexico's Spanish colony, and the Hispanophile Catholic church as obstructing their plans to create a "proletarian" society. Thus labor leader Vicente Lombardo Toledano denounced the Spanish record in Mexico again and again, his attacks keeping the controversial issue a predictable feature of newspaper commentary. Lombardo himself wrote regular columns in *El Universal,* a paper that he rather ungraciously labeled as "Fascist" when addressing union audiences. Pro-Spanish *Excelsior* enjoyed answering Lombardo, and its columnists often exposed flaws in his logic or errors in his facts.[17]

If the Revolution had generally heightened such anti-traditional, anti-Spanish feelings, it also had made widespread sympathy for Spain's new Republic possible in Mexico. Various Revolutionary sectors identified with their peninsular counterparts. All supporters of the ruling National Revolutionary Party (PNR), moreover, could feel solidarity with the progressive Spain that had given them so many of their values. Mexican Revolutionaries saw the "other" Spain embodied in the Republic. PNR liberals in the 1930s admired and identified with Spanish liberalism; Mexican radicals and totalitarians saw hope for a proletarian victory over bourgeois capitalism in Spanish extremism. After the civil war started, Revolutionaries could work together to help the Republic battle its "Fascist" enemies, domestic and foreign. Mexico's industrial workers and even some peasants, organized and directed mainly by Marxist leaders, took to heart Republican Spain's struggle. This in itself was a rather extraordinary development, for in a country where prejudice and ill-will toward resident Spaniards prevailed, anti-Spanish sentiment ran strongest among working-class people. On local Spanish businessmen poor Mexicans frequently vented the hostility produced by their many frustrations and deprivations.

Mexico and the Spanish Republic Prior to the Civil War

Mexico suffered from a weak international position in the 1930s as a consequence of its "revolutionary" reputation. It had reason to fear the major powers as enemies of the country's economic nationalism, relations with the United States being especially strained. Among its Latin American neighbors, virtually all of whom had highly traditional governments, Mexico had few friends. These aristocratic regimes, supported by conservative newspapers, reacted angrily to the PNR's leftist rhetoric and to its attacks on Catholicism. Alejandro Gómez Maganda, a PNR politician with some diplomatic experience in the hemisphere, blamed lack of knowledge about Mexico and an unfriendly capitalistic press for hostile Latin American attitudes toward his country.[18]

The Secretariat of Foreign Relations acknowledged the problem early in 1933 and called for public relations campaigns to deal with it. Foreign Secretary J. M. Puig Casauranc asked all Mexican ambassadors and consuls to give regular speeches about their country. These lectures "should tend to destroy prejudices by establishing the truth about Mexico, since our social and political convulsions of the past twenty-two years have led to erroneous judgments abroad concerning all our affairs." As a result, it had become "urgently necessary to carry out methodically and constantly a systematic campaign in favor of our country." In 1933 Mexico did not even have diplomatic relations with Venezuela and Peru. Its relations with Guatemala had deteriorated due to (among other things) the murder of some Guatemalans in Campeche state in 1930. Mexico had a "bad reputation" in Costa Rica, which Secretary Puig believed was due to "propaganda" spread by intellectuals sympathetic to José Vasconcelos and, consequently, still angry about the Mexican presidential election of 1929.[19] Spain constituted the PNR's only diplomatic bright spot, just as Mexico was one of the few foreign friends of the Republic. Spanish Republicans had long admired the Mexican Revolution, and Ambassador Julio Alvarez del Vayo established a warm personal friendship with General Calles and various members of his regime.

Many Mexicans greeted the new Spanish Republic enthusiastically because its liberal-left government (1931–33) appeared committed to social programs similar to those of the Revolution, a point usually emphasized by those who have written about attitudes toward the *madre patria* in 1931.[20] This is a valid interpretation for those Mexicans who supported the PNR or who agreed with the political principles embodied in the Constitution of 1917, but it overlooks a large group who welcomed the Republic for very different reasons: conservative, Catholic opponents of the Revolutionary government. They tended to be more impressed by the seemingly democratic character that Spanish politics had assumed (excellent ideological ammunition to fire at Calles) or by the new opportunity for a genuine, effective Hispanism that would "unite" Spain with its former colonies, revive Spanish culture in Latin America, and thus provide new defenses against the encroachments of American imperialism.

Some Mexicans looked favorably on the Republic simply because it appeared to represent so many noble ideals and to offer prospects for more humanitarian government in Spain. Looking back from the vantage point of 1936, with the civil war in progress, Vasconcelos observed that from the mid-1920s to 1931 "throughout the world, all enlightened opinion sympathized with those who desired a Republic. . . . We were all ardent republicans in those placid days of conspiracies in Madrid cafés." According to Vasconcelos, optimistic Mexicans at that time expected a Spanish Republic to bring about land reform in Andalusia, to end graft and theft of public monies, and to institute civilian rule by intelligent men. In brief, they had anticipated a Republic that would be a model for Latin American countries to copy.[21]

Alfonso Reyes, a liberal writer whose acceptance of the Revolution had been rewarded with a diplomatic appointment in Spain in the 1920s, was one of countless Mexicans *pleased* by expectation of Mexican-style reforms in the peninsula. "As a believer in a regenerated Mexico," one of his biographers notes, "he could easily understand and be understood by the Spanish reformers." He had lived in Spain for over a decade, knew intimately many Spanish leaders, numbered himself among the authors of the Republican revolution, and claimed to be its principal prophet in America.[22] "Pedro Gringoire" (pseudonym for Gonzalo Báez Camargo, a Methodist minister and liberal journalist) also endorsed the "great transformation" of Spain begun by the Republicans. Gringoire found their projected agrarian reform and their intent to change church-state relations by reducing ecclesiastical influence especially praiseworthy.[23]

One of the major reasons that many conservative, Catholic Mexicans welcomed the Republic in 1931 was their hope that it would provide sufficient stimulation for a revival of "democracy" in Mexico. They saw Spain's example as possibly leading to a resurgence of opposition to PNR "tyranny," and they also thought that Calles could be shamed into imitating the principles and procedures of Republican Spain, should Spaniards succeed in making their new political freedom work. Diego Arenas Guzmán's right-wing newspaper *El Hombre Libre* initially took this line. For some time the paper had been proclaiming in its headlines the PNR's "putrefaction" as its cartoonists mordantly satirized Calles and other Revolutionary politicians.[24] In mid-April a front-page article on the Republic was topped by the headline: "Here's Hoping That Spain Does Not Suffer the Sad Fate of Our Republics of Bosses and Puppets!" Next to the story a cartoon depicted King Alfonso XIII handing his crown to "the Spanish people" as to his right a heavily armed man ("PNR") clubbed a Mexican voter. A short text emphasized the difference in political behavior between "old monarchies consecrated by tradition and a glorious history" and under identical circumstances "improvised mobocracies of our republics which have remained on the margin of civilization."[25]

Mexican opponents of the PNR also tended to be encouraged by what Spanish Republicans were doing and saying about Hispanism and relations with the Latin American countries. By the summer of 1931 the Republic had taken steps to reinforce Spain's political and cultural influence overseas. A new constitution promulgated that year mandated the "cultural expansion of Spain," especially in Latin America, and the Republicans had committed themselves to full peninsular citizenship for all Spanish Americans. PNR politicians also professed to see the creation of a new "union of the Iberian peoples" as a healthy development, but they remained vague about its purposes, and their sentiments on the subject did not approach the passionate intensity of such ardent Hispanophiles as Vasconcelos.[26]

Despite misgivings and disappointments about some prominent Republican leaders because they openly praised Calles, Vasconcelos rejoiced over Spanish political developments. From Madrid in 1931 he urged Spanish Americans to join with Spain in forming a Hispanic-American Federation. All Spanish-speaking peoples, he said, had an obligation to "reintegrate the race" and thus to move Latin America away from Pan-Americanism, a harmful misalliance between imperialistic Yankees and unpatriotic military dictators. The Republicans should lead in preserving Latin America's threatened Hispanic culture, for Spain now enjoyed more liberty than its former colonies: "For this reason we place our hope in the new Spain. Madrid can become the center of an Empire more important than that of Philip II, the moral Empire of nations that have lost their way."[27]

Rodolfo Reyes (Alfonso's brother) was an ultraconservative Hispanist who also lauded the new Republican government for its promises to bring Spain and Latin America closer together. Lecturing at Madrid's Ateneo in November 1931, Reyes observed that "genuine interhispanic life" could replace the past's "poetic Hispanic-Americanism" now that the monarchy had disappeared. There were several good omens for future relations between Spain and America: the Republic's role in helping Mexico enter the League of Nations, the high quality of many Republican diplomats assigned to Latin American countries, and the Cortes's offer of peninsular citizenship to all Spanish Americans. A fresh, aggressive Spanish foreign policy in America, long urgently needed, would bolster the "Hispanic American Nation" in its fight against Pan-Americanism and U.S. imperialism. Formerly, many Spanish Americans had turned to the United States for cultural leadership because they perceived monarchical Spain to be static and museumlike. Regarding American culture as more vital and dynamic than that of Spain, they became "dehispanicizers" and thus agents of Yankee imperialism. With the Republic's birth, however, Spain had an opportunity to reestablish its cultural dominance in the region and so prevent destruction of its legacy.[28]

Those Mexican conservatives who welcomed the Republic in 1931 had hoped that Spanish politicians would *lead* Mexico into an orderly, more tolerant era, not *follow* its examples of social radicalism, religious persecution, and "anarchy." As a group of wealthy political scapegoats who felt oppressed, they yearned for freedom, respect for their "rights," and an end to demagogic government by an official party composed of what they regarded as social upstarts. They were horrified by the PNR program, which threatened to destroy some of their most cherished institutions and values: the church and Catholicism, traditional family life, upper class privileges, and Hispanic culture. But events in Spain and the conduct of Spanish diplomats in Mexico soon indicated that from the Republic their traditionalism and their plight in Callista Mexico would receive no support.

Although most Mexican observers expressed pleasure when Spain's new Republic appeared, some dissenters predicted disaster. In retrospect these men seem to have possessed prophetic vision. Nemesio García Naranjo, a cabinet member under Huerta and one of Mexico's most widely published conservatives, argued that the 1931 election results, although clearly indicating repudiation of King Alfonso XIII, did not represent popular desire for the kind of Republic that had been established. Spaniards had accepted the Republic due to "patriotic frenzy and hope of redemption," but they would soon realize that mere political turnovers did not alter the nature of things: "Poor people do not become rich simply because they change from Crown to Republic; misery is not eradicated by covering it with a democratic mantle; and all this will soon become apparent to the Spaniards as they lose their most cherished illusions." There were already ominous signs. The government had made two serious mistakes: failure to deal forcefully with Catalan separatism and weakness concerning attacks on the Catholic clergy. More and more Spaniards would turn against the Republican administration "on seeing Spain divided by regionalism and inflamed with religious conflict."[29]

Querido Moheno, another old Huertista veteran of many political battles, also offered a pessimistic appraisal of the Spanish situation. In June 1931 he maintained that since the new regime had not been institutionalized, no Republic really existed. President Alcalá-Zamora was "an overseas Madero" whose "suicidal optimism" boded ill for Spain's political future. Moheno wondered how Alcalá-Zamora could continue to speak of the Spanish people's "romantic enthusiasm" for the Republic "after the burning of over one hundred churches, convents, and public monuments." There had indeed been enthusiasm in the Republic's first days, "but it was not exactly romantic." The only romanticism Moheno saw in Spain was in the political outlook of its president, whose obsolete ideas belonged to the nineteenth century. The immediate dangers to Spain—totalitarian impulses from left and right, the threat of dictatorships patterned after either Mussolini or Stalin—would have to be confronted by something more realistic than the Republic's present spirit of faith and confidence.[30]

Mexico and the Spanish War: An Overview

Among the Latin American countries Mexico played a unique and rather lonely role in Spain's civil war. When the conflict started, President Lázaro Cárdenas, without hesitation, committed his country to support of the Spanish Loyalists. After consistently supplying generous military, economic, and diplomatic aid to the Republic during the war, Mexico rescued thousands of Republican refugees by helping them emigrate to the Americas, where they could reconstruct their shattered lives. Mexico itself took in about thirty thousand refugees between 1937 and 1945.[31] Other Spanish American republics either remained neutral or openly sided with General Franco. For many of them, Cárdenas's support of the "Red" Spanish Republic provided additional evidence that the PNR regime could not be trusted. Combined with its economic nationalism, Mexico's Spanish policy also increased the exasperation of Western powers, especially England and the United States. As the country's political isolation deepened, Loyalist Spain remained virtually its only friend.

Ideological sympathy for the Republic unquestionably was a major factor behind Cárdenas's diplomacy, but the president and such key advisers as diplomat Isidro Fabela had additional motives for supporting the Republic so resolutely. The Mexican president loved Spain, felt a strong sense of justice wronged, and abhorrently feared fascism. Both he and Fabela, moreover, realized that Spain gave Mexico a chance to strengthen its own sagging international position. They wanted to persuade the Western powers that the Spanish war was another instance of outside aggression against weak countries that endangered world peace (fascism on the march); then the powers might commit themselves to saving the Republic and at the same time agree to oppose in principle *any* "imperialistic" intervention by one country in another's affairs. The United States had already made nonintervention promises to the Latin American nations. Such a development would benefit Mexico, whose nationalistic economic policies rendered it still susceptible to foreign attacks. Despite Washington's assurances, the Mexicans continued to fear U.S. intervention. Unfortunately for Mexican foreign policy, the major powers never interpreted the Spanish conflict as Cárdenas did. Europe's most outspoken advocate of resistance to Fascist aggression, Winston Churchill, *favored* Franco's rebellion.[32]

Long before the Spanish civil war, Mexico had been campaigning in the League of Nations for collective resistance to imperialism. Mexican delegate Narciso Bassols urged assistance to Ethiopia, and Cárdenas issued a flurry of decrees in November 1935 to comply fully with the League's sanctions against Italy.[33] As the Spanish war raged, moreover, Mexico consistently brought up Japan's invasion of China, linked it to Spain and resistence to imperialism, and urged the League to help the Chinese as well as the Loyalists.[34]

In contrast to partisan claims of overwhelming popular sympathy for Republican Spain in Mexico, available historical evidence suggests an opposite thesis: only a minority of Mexicans backed the Republic from 1936 to 1939, most people remaining apathetic about the civil war or even siding with the Nationalists.[35] Despite the PNR's claim to speak for the nation, General Franco's traditionalist crusade against the Republic had many Mexican supporters. For years Mexicans had been bitterly divided over their own Revolution. Hispanic conservatism and Catholicism still had a powerful hold on much of the population and was not limited to higher social levels. Mexico contained millions of traditionalist rural people as well: impoverished peons and peasants. For the middle and upper classes, Republican Spain's "horrors" confirmed fears about their own likely fate if the PNR continued along its antireligious and demagogic course. The Spanish civil war gave them numerous arguments to use against Cárdenas's Revolutionary administration. Since 1931 they had been able to see striking parallels between the social and political struggles of Spain and those of their own country. After July 1936 they could draw many anti-Revolutionary lessons from these similarities.

From 1931 to 1939 Spanish events and the manner in which they were perceived became integral aspects of Mexico's political life. The experience came to have lasting importance for Mexicans as political leaders after the civil war refused to recognize Franco's regime, and a large colony of Loyalist exiles found a second home in the country. Both of these circumstances, along with the debacle and worldwide repudiation of fascism during World War II, helped Mexico's role in the Spanish conflict achieve the status of a national myth. History seemed to be vindicating at last a policy that had received little sympathy at the time Cárdenas put it into effect. The United Nations, for example, ostracized Franco for almost a decade after the war. Yet Mexican traditionalists could still point to Spain as a place where "Western civilization" took a stand against "Communist barbarism," finding justification for their views in the West's many confrontations with the Soviet Union and China after 1945 and also in their own government's steadily increasing conservatism. As the decades passed and great changes swept across the world, however, the Spanish civil war became less useful as a propaganda instrument for Mexican rightists. Decolonization in Asia and Africa, civil rights movements, students' and women's revolutions, and the impact of television and massive tourism eroded the cultural and social norms on which so much enthusiasm for Franco had been based. Even the papacy and the Latin American clergy moved to the left. Caught up in all this innovation, and increasingly a cultural as well as an economic satellite of the United States, Mexico ceased to be a place where conservative ideological axes could be ground with any profit on the stone of Franquism. It was just too hard to sell Hispanic traditionalism in the 1960s to a nation composed predominantly, in the cities at least, of young people in love with the Beatles. The Spanish dictator's regime, despite some resemblance to Mexico's authoritarian, elitist government, was simply too retrograde culturally, too clerical, and too repressive politically to be anything more than an embarrassing anachronism in the contemporary world. By the 1970s, shopworn right-wing talk about anti-Bolshevist lessons to be drawn from the peninsular conflict of the 1930s had long ceased to have popular appeal or validity.

In dealing with most foreign countries, Cárdenas usually protected his right international flank by downplaying Mexico's political and ideological sympathies with the Republican government. Mexican diplomatic notes on the civil war implied that the PNR had formed no political alliance with the Popular Front regime, and they denied that Mexicans were Communists helping other Communists. Even in routine "thank you" messages sent to people who had congratulated Mexico for helping the Loyalists, Foreign Relations included a statement that "Mexico has acted in the Spanish conflict only in accordance with law and justice."[36] Some Mexican diplomats, however, indiscreetly linked their country's support of the Republic to common leftist sentiments. In August 1936, during a discussion among members of the diplomatic corps in Madrid, Embassy First Secretary Francisco Navarro opposed a proposal of Chilean Ambassador Aurelio Núñez Morgado that all foreign envoys leave the Spanish capital because its government could not guarantee their safety. Navarro said that the Mexicans would remain despite the obvious dangers, for they "had suffered a struggle similar to the one that has developed in Spain . . . [and] out of this struggle . . . arose our left-wing government, which in heart and spirit is with the Madrid regime."[37]

Mexico Helps Arm the Republic

Early in August 1936, Cárdenas responded to a Republican plea for arms. Without waiting to negotiate a sale price with the Spaniards, he had the Mexican army move twenty thousand 7mm Mauser rifles and twenty million cartridges to Veracruz, from where they went to Spain on the Republican ship *Magallanes.* Not until October did Republican Ambassador Félix Gordón Ordás sign a Mexican government contract covering the arms sale. The Spaniards agreed to pay Mexico 3.5 million pesos ($962,000) for this initial shipment. Since the Republic anticipated more arms purchases, it sent to Gordón through banks in Paris and New York six million dollars to cover them. At the Republic's request, Cárdenas also authorized Minister Adalberto Tejeda in Paris to buy for the Spaniards arms and aircraft sufficient to equip two regiments. Later the Mexican president permitted Tejeda to acquire unlimited supplies of European arms for Republican Spain. Cárdenas also tried in August to obtain arms for Spain in England, but the British government refused to authorize any such sales. Although Mexico's diplomatic representative in England promised that the material his country wanted (thousands of rifles and machine guns, millions of bullets) was destined solely for its own army, the British refused "to risk the possibility that these arms would be reshipped to Spain."[38]

Cárdenas knew that his action would create an international uproar, so he at first tried to keep secret the Mexican arms sale to Republican Spain. Newspapers all over the world, however, reported the story even before the shipment reached Veracruz. Mexico thus began its long commitment to the Spanish Republicans in a burst of highly unfavorable publicity. From his vantage point at the legation in Lisbon, Minister Daniel Cosío Villegas observed that in Europe and Latin America hostile countries were scoring propaganda victories at Mexico's expense. A newspaper cartoon sent from Portugal by Cosío showed a hydrophobic-looking Spanish "Red" murdering several noncombatants with a gun marked "from Mexico." In Chile, where radio stations joined newspapers in calling for a break in diplomatic relations with the Cárdenas regime, the Mexican ambassador considered the situation serious enough to ask President Arturo Alessandri to announce that his government intended to maintain friendly relations with Mexico. After about three weeks of silence on the matter, Cárdenas confirmed what the press had reported by detailing his action to congress during an annual report to the nation at the beginning of September.[39]

Cárdenas initially intended to supplement Mexican arms sales to the Republic by purchasing airplanes, airplane engines, and other war materials for it in the United States. Ostensibly, Mexico would be acquiring the military hardware for itself. Late in 1936 Mexico bought ten planes in the United States after assuring the State Department that they were destined for the Mexican air force. A Mexican corporation purchased six other planes from American Airlines, presumably for use in the mining industry. But in January 1937 all sixteen planes were in Veracruz awaiting shipment to Spain on the Loyalist ship *Motomar.* On discovering this, the American press, led by Hearst's papers, played up the story. American warplanes, the Washington *Herald* objected, were being sent to help "the Spanish Communist forces." President Roosevelt was determined to avoid domestic political trouble on the issue and asked Cárdenas not to forward planes or any other American-made arms to Spain. The Mexican leader canceled the plane shipment, then announced that Mexico's policy henceforth would be not to send foreign-made weaponry to Spain unless it had permission to do so from the government of the country concerned.[40]

From September 1936 to September 1937, Mexico sold to the Republic armaments worth about eight million pesos ($2.2 million). Most of these weapons, which included artillery pieces, anti-aircraft guns, mortars, and gas masks, as well as more rifles and ammunition, left Mexico on the Republican ships *Motomar, Ibai,* and *Mar Cantábrico;* the last was captured by the Nationalist navy in 1937. The Mexicans also loaded food, medical supplies, fuel, and military clothing that the Republic had bought on these ships, and occasionally Mexican volunteers sailed off to Spain on them.[41]

Mexican diplomatic officials in Paris purchased (outside of France) substantial quantities of European-made arms for the Republic throughout the civil war. Foreign Relations warned Minister Tejeda in Paris to avoid antagonizing the French government, so Tejeda either operated in secrecy or informed the French that he was buying the weapons for Mexico's army. In August 1936 the Mexicans in Paris contracted to buy fifty thousand bombs and two hundred thousand hand grenades from a company in Brussels. The sales agreement allowed Mexico to cede contract rights to a third party, and this it did, naming as third party Antonio Fernández Balaños, an agent of Republican Spain. In October Tejeda reported additional purchases of military equipment for the Republic from companies in Switzerland and Poland, observing to Foreign Relations that payment had been made "in a way that will not compromise our government." Tejeda continued to seek sources of weaponry for Spain as long as he remained in Paris. When he left at the end of 1937 to become ambassador to the Republic, his successor carried on with the project.[42]

On the Diplomatic Front

Diplomatically, too, Mexico stood by Loyalist Spain. When the League of Nations took up the Spanish question in late September 1936 and responded with a "Nonintervention Committee" rather than assistance to Azaña's regime, Mexican delegate Narciso Bassols objected at his first opportunity. Speaking to the League's Assembly on October 2, 1936, he called nonintervention a tragic step backward in international relations. Mexico would continue to aid the Republic; its policy rested on "solid juridical bases" and stemmed from a sympathetic understanding of the Republican government's dilemma, for Mexicans themselves suffered frequently from "the scourge of antisocial military uprisings."[43]

Early in 1937 Isidro Fabela replaced Bassols at the League. Fabela was a distinguished old liberal from the Revolution's early days and an experienced diplomat. His name invariably comes up in connection with Cárdenas's decision to champion the Loyalist cause, for he and Bassols are regarded as important influences on the president at that critical moment.[44] Prior to Fabela's departure for Geneva, Cárdenas personally gave him instructions. Mexico must defend not only Republican Spain but "any country that suffers foreign aggression from whatever power." It would insist that Spain, having been attacked by Germany and Italy, could properly request and rightfully expect protection from the League's member states under provisions of Article Ten of the organization's charter. Azaña's government being legitimate, Mexico would recognize no other Spanish regime. Fabela must remain intransigent on these points and also on the question of Ethiopia, which Mexico would continue to regard as being illegally occupied by a foreign power.[45]

Cárdenas sent additional instructions in February to his new representative at Geneva. He wanted Fabela to make clear that Mexico considered the League's nonintervention policy to be a form of indirect aid to Franquista rebels and to the foreign powers helping them. Fabela should state emphatically that Mexico's assistance to the Republic, including arms shipments, was the "logical result" of a *correct* interpretation of nonintervention, namely that aggression was to be discouraged by resistance. He must also emphasize Mexico's "scrupulous observance of the principles of international morality" on which the League justified its existence; and he must explain that Mexico transshipped arms to Spain only when the government of the country from whence they came gave its approval.[46] On his arrival Fabela made these and other points orally and in writing, and he repeated Mexico's position on Spain at every opportunity.

Mexican Diplomacy and the Republican Terror

Mexico's ambassador at Madrid in July 1936 was General Manuel Pérez Treviño, a follower of Carranza and Obregón in the Revolution. With Calles he had been one of the PNR's founders. Pérez had held cabinet posts in several administrations and had unsuccessfully tried for the official party's presidential nomination in 1933. In his mid-forties, the ambassador had a spreading paunch, fleshy jowls, a rapidly receding hairline, nervous eyes, and very little political luck. He and some other Callistas considered to be major rivals of Cárdenas (Tejeda, for example) had been assigned to diplomatic posts in Europe, primarily to get them out of the country. Pérez went to Spain in 1935, the year of Cárdenas's break with Calles.[47]

Pérez's first crucial decision when the civil war started involved requests for political asylum by over eight hundred people, most of them conservative Spaniards. When the ambassador chose to harbor them in the embassy and other buildings protected by Mexican diplomatic immunity, leftists at home called him a "Fascist." Pérez's action also displeased President Cárdenas, for it created several complex problems, not the least of which was Spanish Republican anger with its ally for shielding people marked for execution. The United Press correctly reported in October that Cárdenas would replace Pérez with Ramón P. de Negri, Mexico's ambassador to Chile. The UP story indicated that the president's major grievance against his diplomat was the granting of asylum to Emiliano Iglesias, former Spanish ambassador to Mexico during Lerroux's conservative administration of 1933–36 and a man especially hated by the Loyalists. Despite circulation of this wire story, Spanish leftists never learned that Iglesias was at the Mexican embassy.[48]

Cárdenas had an even better reason for removing Pérez from Spain, however. He knew that his envoy saw the Spanish war in terms that contradicted Mexico's official interpretation of the conflict as being between a constitutional, democratic government and seditious militarists in league with international fascism. In October the ambassador had told Foreign Relations:

> The formation of popular militias occurred so quickly and on such a large scale that their Committees immediately assumed almost all government functions. This created a situation that, far from involving the struggle of the legitimate government against the rebellious army, should be seen as an extremely violent clash between two uprisings—one militarist and of completely conservative tendencies and the other popular, Red, of the masses, undoubtedly aimed at the revolutionary transformation of Spain.[49]

Ambassador Pérez and other Mexican officials in Spain had been profoundly shocked by the magnitude of indiscriminate Republican terror. Pérez explained this to Foreign Relations after learning that the president was angry with him. He informed Secretary Eduardo Hay:

> Despite my recognized revolutionary and left-wing sympathies . . . I have given asylum to many people obviously in immediate danger of death. I want to make clear that these persons . . . are not, for the most part, political refugees in the strict sense; their anxieties did not result from specific accusations or prosecutions on the part of the constituted authorities; rather they feared becoming victims of the numerous *chekas* operating anarchically in Madrid and other locations.[50]

Loyalist terror in the summer of 1936 shocked another Mexican diplomat, Consul General José Rubén Romero in Barcelona. Writing to Under-Secretary Ramón Beteta at Foreign Relations, Romero described conditions that filled him with much anxiety.

> The militiamen, armed and deployed throughout the city, give rise to constant unrest, since many of them act irresponsibly, and outrages, public assassinations, vengeances, and persecutions are repeated much too frequently. We witness here in 1936 scenes reminiscent of the French Revolution, the only difference being that Madame Guillotine has been replaced by the modern Mauser. Every day people accused of being fascists, industrialists, landlords, etc. are taken from their homes and shot. One urgently hopes for the emergence of a popular caudillo with the necessary energy and intelligence to dominate the situation and stop the lawless movement that is consuming so many lives and gravely endangering the military campaign at the fronts.[51]

Romero added that the Catalans presented another serious problem for the Republican war effort. They seemed determined to separate their province from Spain "in order to establish a soviet-type state, with abolition of private property and bureaucratic regulation of all of the individual's activities."[52]

As had been the case with arms sales to the Republic, the refugee and terror issues became diplomatic nightmares for Mexico. (Comparable atrocities by General Franco's forces aroused little protest or censure in the international community.) Other countries asked the Mexicans to intercede with the Loyalist government to obtain an easing of Madrid's tense situation, to get safe conduct out of Spain for thousands of refugees in numerous embassies, and to prevent their own nationals or Spaniards related to their nationals from being killed by militiamen. Some countries also pressured Mexico to join them in demanding that Republicans strictly observe their right to grant political asylum. When Mexico refused to cooperate fully with the hard line taken by Argentina and Chile, who wanted all Latin American countries to break relations with the Republic if there were any violations of asylum, several governments and much of the world press accused Mexico of preparing to yield to demands by Popular Front officials that many of the refugees be turned over to them for punishment.[53]

Given the frightful situation in Madrid and elsewhere in Spain, Mexico's justifications for its refusal to join other governments in demanding that the Popular Front end the terror were lame enough to cause many people to wonder whether or not Cárdenas really cared about this issue. As thousands of Spaniards were slaughtered, embassies and diplomatic missions invaded, and foreign nationals shot down in cold blood, Mexicans officially voiced unwillingness to "exert excessive pressure on a legitimate government with which friendly relations are maintained." Mexican politicians also complained that the pressure being applied by such countries as Argentina and Chile threatened "moral injury" to Azaña's administration. Such statements enabled unfriendly critics to accuse the Mexicans of being willing to hand over the political refugees in their embassy if they thought they could get away with it.[54]

Rámon P. de Negri replaced Pérez early in 1937. Opportunism and good political connections had provided the new Mexican envoy with high government posts in the 1920s: chargé d'affaires in Washington; Secretary of Agriculture under Obregón; ambassador to Germany and Secretary of Industry, Commerce, and Labor under Calles. By the 1930s he had settled comfortably into the foreign service. Cárdenas made him ambassador to Chile, then assigned him to Spain at the end of 1936. At the time of this appointment De Negri was a flabby, bespectacled, gray-haired man of middle age. Deceptively innocuous in appearance, he resembled more an insurance salesman than a diplomat. He had an attractive Argentine wife (her second marriage) and a decidedly unattractive stepson, Carlos, a chronic drunk given to violent rampages. An enigma (to say the least), De Negri proved to be such a total diplomatic failure in both Chile and Spain that some people suspected him of having been recruited as an agent either by the Germans or the Russians or by *both* of these powers. Others thought that his many failings stemmed from the evil influence of Carlos, who dominated his stepfather.[55]

De Negri got off to a typically disastrous start in Spain. It took him sixty-seven days (*not* counting allotted travel time) to arrive at his new post. En route he stopped in Paris and began to defame the character of former ambassador Pérez. He also embarrassed Cárdenas by suggesting to the press when he finally did reach Spain that he would turn over political refugees at the Mexican embassy in Madrid to the vengeful Loyalists. On his arrival in Valencia, Republican capital for much of the war, De Negri immediately began to quarrel with his staff, virtually all of whom he had selected himself. When he asked Foreign Relations to allow him to fire Second Secretary Efraín Brito Rosado, Foreign Secretary Eduardo Hay refused permission, reminding the ambassador that he himself had chosen Brito and that to fire him so soon "would give the impression that we choose our personnel carelessly." De Negri then scandalized Republicans by failing to observe any diplomatic protocol when presenting his credentials to the Azaña government. He arrived at the ceremony attired in nondescript street clothes and accompanied by two "aides," both of whom wore Mexican cowboy hats and carried large pistols on their hips.[56]

De Negri badly wanted to turn the refugees over to Loyalist "justice." Even before he reached Spain he sent inflammatory reports to Cárdenas about their alleged behavior in an effort to persuade the president to let him clear them out of the embassy. From Paris he had Minister Tejeda forward to Cárdenas a message accusing the refugees of numerous outrages: conspiring against the Republic, celebrating religious acts, expressing disdain for the Mexican government. He promised the president that when he arrived in Spain, "I will energetically move to put an end to the embarrassing and abusive refugee situation." Cárdenas responded with a cable ordering De Negri to refrain from expelling the refugees and to treat them with all the "consideration" that their position as guests of the Mexican government merited.[57] If at this time De Negri *was* secretly a German agent only feigning leftist sympathies, his ability to have the refugees massacred would certainly have pleased the Germans, as the deaths would have been a devastating propaganda setback for both Mexico and the Republic. Having failed to move Cárdenas, De Negri was left with the unwanted job of negotiating safe conduct out of Spain for the refugees. When he eventually achieved this in the spring of 1937, he also had to escort them from Madrid to Valencia, from where they could sail for France. On March 13, after some dangerous moments at the pier when crowds of workers and militiamen insisted on executing several of the departing rightists, De Negri managed to get all but four of them aboard a ship bound for Marseilles. Four refugees had to stay in the country under Mexican diplomatic protection because the Loyalists accused them of possessing military secrets.[58]

De Negri remained in Spain a mere six months, from late January to late July 1937, yet his stay in the peninsula must have seemed an eternity to the Republican government and to responsible Mexican officials at Foreign Relations. Terrified by Nationalist air raids against Valencia, the ambassador domiciled himself in a village far removed from the city. Even during working hours his appearances at the embassy were rare. Business did not get transacted; communications from Mexico City went unanswered. Reviewing his performance in July, Foreign Relations told Cárdenas that De Negri had not sent back one useful report on the Spanish situation. In addition he had ignored instructions to protect *all* Mexicans in Spain, regardless of their politics, and Secretary Hay thought that he did not even know how many of his countrymen remained in the peninsula. Hay further charged De Negri with mishandling negotiations over several hundred Republican war orphans sent to Mexico as refugees.[59]

The ambassadorial interlude between De Negri, recalled by Cárdenas in July 1937, and Adalberto Tejeda, who arrived in Spain from France at year's end, was ably filled by General Leobardo Ruiz, Mexican Consul General in Barcelona. An astute, no-nonsense soldier-politician in his forties, Ruiz worked well with the Republicans, did not meddle in Spanish politics or cause scandal, and kept a suspicious eye on Communist and Russian activities. When Tejeda took over the embassy, Ruiz returned to his consular office in Barcelona.[60] Colonel Tejeda was big, bald, and fifty-four. He looked both mean and cunning. If ever a man had "boss" stamped all over his face, that man was Tejeda. A terror to Catholics in Veracruz, where he had been governor, Tejeda nonetheless could be warm and compassionate. At the Mexican embassy in Barcelona (the Republican government having moved there from Valencia), Tejeda maintained an orphanage-school for two hundred children, and he adopted one of these waifs and raised her in Mexico as his own daughter. By the time of his appointment, Tejeda had already accomplished his major services to the Spanish Republic in Paris, where as Mexico's minister to France he had labored tirelessly in providing Mexican cover for arms shipments to Spain. Although his diplomatic work in Spain was largely ceremonial (visiting factories, hospitals, peasant communes, and schools), Spaniards developed strong affection for him. Despite his friendship with the Communists, he apparently avoided any involvement in the Republic's internal politics. Consequently, he came out of Spain with his reputation intact, although some Spaniards found him rather crude and stupid. Tejeda, along with Isidro Fabela and Narciso Bassols, played an important role in rescuing thousands of Republican refugees in France by keeping the issue before Cárdenas in 1939. Spanish exiles in Mexico never forgot this. Years after the war had ended they still came to Tejeda's house in Coyoacán to thank him personally for helping them escape from certain death at the hands of Franco or as a result of French indifference.[61]

The Problems of Mexican Diplomacy in Spanish America

Cárdenas tried to find support for the Spanish Republic in Latin America, but political dominance by conservatives in Spain's former empire doomed his efforts to failure. As has been noted, with few exceptions regimes throughout the hemisphere viewed Revolutionary Mexico with as much animosity as they did Popular Front Spain. Right-wing politicians, the press, middle- and upper-class people, and the Catholic church tended to lump Mexico together with the USSR and the Republic as major components of a world Communist conspiracy. In addition, the pro-Republican activities of Mexican diplomats in Latin America drew some of them deep into local left-wing circles, and these associations only confirmed existing suspicions about Mexico's revolutionary intentions in the Americas. In 1937 most Latin American members of the League of Nations voted to expel the Spanish Republic from the League Council, an action that Mexican newspaper columnist Salvador Novo ironically noted "clearly shows us how much sympathy we enjoy among our dear sister republics to the south."[62]

Led by Chile, several South American countries were trying in 1936 to organize "an American front against Communism," a movement that included Mexico as one of its targets. At the same time, Mexico was under heavy fire in Paraguay, where a "National Committee of Paraguayan Rightists" repeatedly accused the Mexican legation in Asunción of distributing Communist propaganda and of supplying funds to local Marxists. The Argentine political situation as reported by Ambassador Alfonso Reyes afforded Mexicans small hope of gaining their foreign policy objectives. Reyes claimed that "a thousand Fascist influences and pressures within and without the government" were working against the Spanish Republic. Mexican diplomats in Peru also found themselves in a totally unpromising situation. Local leftists had been suppressed by a conservative military dictatorship, the press universally lauded Franco, and some newspapers were serving as outlets for Italian attacks on both the Spanish Republic and Mexico as "Communist states."[63]

Mexico's diplomatic position in Central America was perhaps even worse than in the southern continent, for military rulers of the small states in this area, as well as sharing Franco's social and political outlook, viewed their "Communist" northern neighbor with visible apprehension. Both Guatemala and Nicaragua early in the war recognized the Nationalist government and courted its favor. Guatemalan dictator Jorge Ubico sent an ambassador to the rebel regime in 1937 who assured Franquistas that his country stood as "a bulwark against Bolshevism" in Spanish America and that "Guatemala was following with sympathy and interest the Nationalist uprising's development." When a Franco spokesman later responded to this by praising Guatemala as Spanish America's first line of defense against "Bolshevist Mexico," major Guatemalan newspapers gave his remarks special emphasis.[64]

Official attitudes toward Mexico in Costa Rica, Honduras, and El Salvador were just as unfriendly.

Cuba and Colombia offered some hope of success for Mexican civil war diplomacy in Spanish America, yet even they disappointed Cárdenas. Cuban strongman Fulgencio Batista adopted a friendly attitude toward Mexico and seemingly toward Republican Spain, in part because he was cultivating a progressive image at home. When he made a state visit to Mexico in 1938, the ruling party welcomed him as a hero, and a joint session of the Mexican congress cheered wildly when he promised that "Cuba will never recognize Franco." Yet concrete Cuban support for the Republic never materialized. Batista, moreover, *did* recognize Franco (rather soon after the war ended), and the Cuban government responded less than enthusiastically to Mexico's postwar pleas for acceptance of large numbers of Loyalist refugees.[65] In Colombia, Mexico could always count on expressions of solidarity with the Republic by liberal politicians, labor organizations, and even major newspapers, but Colombians never fulfilled their many promises to join Mexico "eventually" in helping its Spanish friends. To some extent the behavior of Colombian liberals when approached by Mexicans on the Spanish issue resembled that of French premier Léon Blum, who told the Republic's ambassador to France that he could not help a regime he loved. Blum urged the ambassador to "tell the Spanish workers that you have seen me weep for them."[66]

Mexicans in Spain

Much misinformation has been published about the Mexican volunteers who went to Spain. In *Mexico and the Spanish Republicans,* Lois Smith asserted that 150 Mexicans fought in Spain, that they "formed part of the International Brigades," and that "several" of them were killed, all inaccurate statements. Spanish Republican politician Juan-Simeón Vidarte got closer to the truth when he wrote that approximately 300 Mexicans went to Spain, but he also incorrectly assigned them to membership in the International Brigades. *El Universal* made a similar error in 1938 by printing a UP story from Barcelona that mentioned "the battalion of Mexicans" being concentrated in that city for repatriation. Actually, these men were the surviving 59 out of roughly 330 Mexicans who had enlisted.[67] Far from being members of the same battalion, most of them had never even seen each other in Spain, so widely scattered were the army units to which they had been assigned. Several other Mexican volunteers escaped death but did not come home with this group. They were prisoners of war, repatriated after Franco's victory.[68] Finally, Republican Ambassador Gordón wrote in his memoirs that neither the Spanish embassy nor any Spanish consulates ever solicited or accepted Mexican enlistments. The embassy, however, both recruited Mexicans and paid their way to Spain.[69]

Two major factors prevented the Mexican government from actively encouraging or helping combatants go to Spain: Mexico's weak international position and the unpopularity of Cárdenas's pro-Loyalist policy with so many Mexicans. The PNR gave very little financial assistance to volunteers. Usually such men were recruited by Spanish Republicans at the embassy or by the left-wing Mexican Workers Confederation (CTM), which also supplied funds to cover travel expenses. The fares of Communists who joined up were paid by the party. Some men sailed to Spain from Veracruz on the Republican freighters *Magallanes, Motomar,* and *Mar Cantábrico.* On August 21, 1937, three Mexicans and several Spaniards were on the *Motomar* when it left Veracruz loaded with arms and food for Spain. Other recruits traveled by train to New York, where they boarded luxury liners bound for Europe. A few Mexicans appear to have sailed off to the Spanish war on the *Queen Mary.*[70]

Probably most Mexican soldiers in Spain had been recuited by the Mexican Communist party (PCM). Communist writer Miguel A. Velasco said that "many" PCM militants went to Spain to help the Republic in various ways, including enlistment in its armed forces, but he provided no specific numbers or names. Velasco and other sources, however, have precisely described one ill-starred group of four Young Communists who sailed for Spain on the *Mar Cantábrico* in 1937. Nationalists took them prisoner and shot them after capturing the ship off Spain's coast. PCM member Rosendo Gómez Lorenzo apparently recruited most of the Communists who went to Spain.[71]

The youngest Mexicans to enlist were four teenage ex-cadets from Mexico's prestigious Colegio Militar. In the summer of 1937, they and five other cadets "deserted" from the Colegio to take ship for Spain. They had been recruited by Captain Ricardo Balderas Carrillo of the regular army and several anonymous persons (from the Spanish embassy, *Excelsior* charged). All were caught and returned under military arrest; authorities at the Colegio then discharged them dishonorably from the Mexican army. Captain Balderas went to prison for his part in the affair. Five of the youths dropped their plans to fight for the Republic, but the remaining four went on to Spain. Commissioned as lieutenants in the Popular Army, they served in different units: Roberto Vega González (20th Corps); Roberto Mercado Tinoco (23rd Corps);

José Conti Varcé (9th Corps); and Humberto Villela Vélez (unit unknown). Conti died in combat. Vega was captured by the Nationalists and remained a prisoner of war for several years after the Franquista triumph but eventually made it back to Mexico.[72]

Mexican civilians also played an active role in the peninsula during the Spanish conflict. The most prominent noncombatants belonged to the League of Revolutionary Writers and Artists (LEAR). They specialized in propaganda assistance to the Republicans. These activities were secretly financed by the Mexican Treasury, which in 1937 subsidized LEAR's delegation to an international writers' conference in Spain. (The Mexican government also paid the expenses of Cuba's largely Communist delegation to this meeting.) Some LEAR notables who went to Spain were: José Revueltas, Octavio Paz, Carlos Pellicer, Blanca Trejo, and Susana Gamboa. Miss Trejo later charged that Susana Gamboa worked as a Soviet agent under the direction of Narciso Bassols. LEAR was headed by José Mancisidor, a fat, middle-aged teacher who belonged to the PCM. His sectarian "servility" before Russian and Spanish Communists alienated some of the organization's less doctrinaire fellow-travelers, who could not reconcile Stalinist cruelties and intrigues with their conception of Spain's battle for freedom and democracy.[73]

The Home Front: Conservatives Justify Their Support of Franco

When the Spanish civil war was in progress, Mexicans acknowledged that the conflict divided them. Even PNR zealots admitted that Cárdenas's support for the Republic enjoyed only limited approval. Alejandro Gómez Maganda, left-wing federal deputy from Guerrero and Mexican consul general in Barcelona during part of the war, described the "Revolution in power" as backing the Popular Front; but "traitorously" siding with Franco were many other Mexicans, among them capitalists and businessmen, "creole Fascists," conservative survivors from the Porfirio Díaz era, and "workers with bourgeois ideas."[74] Gómez might have added several other obvious Franquista elements in the Mexican population: Roman Catholics and their clergy, those students opposed to the PNR's "socialistic" programs, many government employees, political moderates, and middle-sector people in general.

Despite sympathy for Franco's "religious" crusade, Mexico's Roman Catholic hierarchy spent little time writing or preaching about the peninsular conflict. They had serious problems of their own, such as getting exiled bishops back into the country and preventing Catholics from being murdered by mobs or by the police. Their principal antagonists, moreover, remained President Cárdenas and the PNR, not communism or Spain's Popular Front. Noisy advocacy of the Nationalist cause certainly would have been counterproductive and might have been interpreted by Cárdenas as breaking the truce negotiated by ecclesiastics and the PNR in 1929. At that time, the church had pledged to shun politics in return for the right to exist. During the civil war, Pius XI and the Vatican made far more official references to Spain than did Mexico's bishops, and that was evidently the way the pope wanted it. Less than two weeks after issuing a papal encyclical on communism in 1937, the Vatican published another one, *On the Religious Situation in Mexico,* in which the pope specifically instructed clergy and laity in Mexico to avoid any political activism that might produce renewed government persecution.[75]

The Mexican church supported Franco, but not aggressively. In 1936 the hierarchy's executive committee instructed bishops to tell all priests to join their parishioners in offering up "fervent and persistent prayers for the peace and true liberty of the Spanish nation, from which we have received our civilization and our faith, and which is now undergoing one of the most sorrowful crises of its history." Mexican bishops also sent to Spain's clergy in 1937 a message of sympathy that made clear their desire for a Nationalist victory.[76] Beyond this modest moral and spiritual support, however, Mexico's church chose not to go. This left the polemical burden of advocating Spain's military rebellion to individual Catholics and conservatives. Their activities showed none of the Church's calculated reserve.

Rubén Salazar Mallén, a young law professor and journalist, enthusiastically stumped for Franco and for "Spanish fascism" throughout the war. One of his first articles on Spain appeared at the end of July 1936 and made him a hated figure in pro-Republican circles. Salazar wrote that even if the Nationalist revolt failed it would have served as a noble protest against communism. Spain's Western culture had made the army uprising inevitable, for culture and communism were antithetical terms, the latter only thriving in the East, "where men are used to slavery and patiently endure [its] slow suffocation." Spain's rebels were telling the world that their country still had a Western culture. The civil war did not represent a conflict between monarchism and republicanism, since Franco's movement had "Fascist roots" and promised to supercede those political forms. It would synthesize fascism and democracy to produce a pure political order superior to anything that had preceded it. "Spain," he concluded, "preserves its historical prestige by means of the present rebellion."[77]

Catholic militant Fernando Robles interpreted the Nationalist uprising in Spain as a move toward corporatism and authentic Hispanidad that should be imitated in Latin America. Robles still openly sympathized with Mexican Cristeros, whose cause he had championed in the 1920s. In 1937 he paid homage to the Franquistas and to the memory of Ramiro de Maeztu, a Spanish Catholic author who had long argued that corporatism and Hispanism were essential bases for Spanish and Spanish American societies. After a period of material and spiritual poverty, during which Spaniards had lost faith in themselves, forgotten their historic destiny to defend Western civilization, and embraced the false doctrine of materialism, they had rediscovered their native spiritualism. In response to the Republican attack on Christianity, Spain had become the principal battlefield between incompatible philosophies of life. As heirs to the Christian ideals of their Spanish ancestors, Latin Americans had a vital interest in the conflict.[78]

The conservative journal *Lectura* had a clearly pro-totalitarian bias, and Spain occupied a central position in its ideological promotions. Edited by Catholic nationalist Jesús Guisa y Azevedo, *Lectura* mixed together clericalism and fascism. In addition to printing articles by Mexican rightists, it featured considerable foreign material: excerpts from the propaganda classic *Blood Drenched Altars;* translations of speeches and articles by General Franco and Portuguese dictator Antonio Oliveira Salazar; and the writings of Frenchmen associated with "Action Française," a political movement with fascistic inclinations.[79] For Guisa y Azevedo, a Catholic totalitarian state that would unite the Mexican people by eliminating "democracy and class warfare" could best defend Mexico against the United States, which was trying to destroy the country's Hispano-Catholic culture as a prelude to actual takeover.[80] Such a state would also be a bulwark against communism, an infectious disease that had originated in the Soviet Union and was being spread all over the world by "the children of Israel." Revolutionary Mexico had voluntarily allowed entry to the disease for reasons that were not clear —perhaps due to a superstitious belief that this would cause it to "treat us with a certain leniency," or possibly from mere "suicidal desperation" among political leaders, or possibly from their hope that "something new and better will arise from our ruin, as is the case now in [Republican] Spain."[81]

By 1936 José Vasconcelos had altered profoundly his earlier opinions about the Republic and its leaders, many of whom he had known for years. These changes are readily seen in his major statement on the Spanish civil war, *Que es el comunismo.* Vasconcelos had once praised Ramón del Valle-Inclán for endorsing the Mexican Revolution in the

1920s; this had improved Spain's image in the country. Now he denounced the late novelist as a "bad Spaniard" for his comments on Mexico. Valle-Inclán's references to the Spanish colony as exploitative *gachupines* had been damaging to national interests, since resident Spaniards had always helped Mexicans defend their country against "foreign absorption." In commerce, for example, Spanish businessmen formed a barrier against Jewish, Syrian, and Lebanese merchants, "the real enemies of Mexico."[82] Revising almost everything that he had written about Spain in 1931–32, Vasconcelos accused the Loyalists of being from the start in league with the world's "evil" forces: Calles, Léon Blum, Jewish newspapers, international bankers, and the United States of America. Rather illogically, he also accused them of being Communists; their misrule in Spain demonstrated the need for middle-class people in Mexico and elsewhere to protect themselves against Marxism's tendency to destroy them.

Vasconcelos inaccurately claimed to have warned his Republican friends in 1931–32 against starting a religious conflict, saying that he had been appalled by their anticlericalism. Their most grievous offense, however, was to allow Russian agents to infiltrate the Spanish army during the months of the Popular Front regime. Franco's rebellion thus represented a struggle against communism and for civilized life. Only the future would tell if the rebels were Fascists, monarchists, or republicans, but they were definitely "nationalist patriots." Franco wanted to make Spain a world power once again; after the leftists had been defeated, it *would* become such a power. Mexicans and other Spanish Americans could then shed their inferiority complex, for they would be children of a Great Spain. Under Popular Front rule the peninsula could be no more than "a poor imitation of Callista Mexico."[83]

After September 1, 1939, Mexican conservatives had an increasingly difficult public relations problem. History inexorably linked the Spanish Nationalists to totalitarian regimes in Germany and Italy that had become objects of hatred throughout the West. General Franco overtly consorted with his civil war allies, and his dictatorial state ostentatiously displayed the heavily symbolic trappings of fascism. The situation grew darker for Mexican Franquistas in 1942: President Manuel Avila Camacho declared war on the Axis powers. Yet pro-Franco Mexicans braved the unfavorable climate of opinion and continued to use Spain as a political issue in attacking the Revolution. Many of them were Catholic ideologues who had long since repudiated totalitarianism as contrary to Christian doctrine. Satisfied—in their own minds, at least—that Spain remained free from fascism or Axis domination, they insisted on the indigenous, traditional character of the Nationalist movement. Franco represented Catholic Hispanidad, not fascism, and Hispanidad had a natural compatibility with Mexican culture. To be true to their own nature, and to defend the country patriotically against American inroads (a greater threat than German foreign policy), Mexicans had to be Hispanic; and to be genuinely Hispanic, they had to be Catholic.[84]

Conservative writer Alfonso Junco rather perfunctorily rejected totalitarianism (nonexistent in Spain, he insisted) while at the same time eulogizing José Antonio Primo de Rivera. Falangism was an inspiring, "truly democratic" solution to the Hispanic world's modern crisis. An accountant originally from Monterrey, Junco had won a prominent place among right-wing polemicists in Mexico City with his tireless pro-Catholic journalism. In 1940 Junco published *El difícil paraíso,* a series of essays on Spain that he had written the year before. He characterized the Spanish war as having originated in a "desperate insurrection of a people resolved to live, and to live with honor." Franco's supporters had revolted against the "social chaos of arson and assassination" produced by a "criminal Bolshevist invasion" of Spain. This Russian influence had so "infected" the Republic that "it became an urgent need to save Hispanic essence from Muscovite gangrene." Not just a military rising, the rebellion had much civilian support: Carlists, "the admirable youth of the Falange," many women, and members of Spanish Renovation. When they captured an area, the Nationalists immediately established "social euphoria" by restoring order and reviving "joyful work." Even the Loyalist military had finally wearied of communism, and they ended the civil war by doing what the insurgents had done at the start: use force to suppress a "Bolshevist conspiracy."[85]

Junco denied charges that Franco's government was totalitarian. The general headed a Catholic regime that had "instituted a bold program of social justice," had rejected "idolatry of the state," and had repudiated "those aspects of Fascism and Nazism that were unacceptable." In formulating his policies Franco had followed the Spanish hierarchy's antifascist leadership. Under Franco, Christian humanism prevailed in Spain, a country whose political resemblance to Italy was only superficial. Although the Spanish leader fostered "such excellent things as patriotism and corporate organization," he refused to deify the state, suppress liberty, or establish "violence as a norm." Spanish America had much to gain from close association with Nationalist Spain. Spanish tutelage could help in "exaltation of the values of our truest essence," which Hispanic Americans could use profitably in opposing "a fraudulent and incoherent Pan-Americanism that is nothing more than the sarcastic brotherhood of sheep with the wolf!" With its war over, "resurgent Spain" experienced the "difficult paradise" that José Antonio Primo de Rivera and the Falange had desired.[86]

The Home Front: Support for the Republic

Dissemination of pro-Loyalist publicity became a PNR concern in all parts of the country at the start of the civil war, and various government agencies regularly promoted and financed ideological programs about Spain. In September 1937, for example, Republican Ambassador Gordón gave several speeches in Morelia under the auspices of Michoacán's state government and state university. Two months later he appeared at a Mexico City rally sponsored by the Public Education Secretariat, where he and a series of left-wing speakers paid tribute to the Spanish American volunteers killed in Spain. The Mexican government's Official Propaganda Department broadcast this rhetoric to the nation.[87] Cárdenas also did what he could to offset private communications media bias in favor of Franco. Programs on the government's "Radio Nacional" featured pro-Republican commentary by Mexicans and "ideological" speeches by Ambassador Gordón. Communications Secretary Francisco J. Múgica prohibited privately-owned networks and radio stations from broadcasting Franquista propaganda or even news of Nationalist victories. The PNR's newspaper, *El Nacional,* printed much material favorable to the Republic, and during the last half of 1936 alone it ran eight articles on the civil war by Gordón. Other PNR publications made contributions, too. *Revolución,* a monthly journal put out by leftists in the Chamber of Deputies, contained articles written by peninsular Loyalists praising Spanish workers and "the masses" for their "resistance to fascism."[88] Supplementing Secretary Múgica's ban on pro-Franco radio broadcasts, the PNR prohibited movie theaters or private organizations from showing films that backed the Nationalists. Cárdenas's censorship of movies and radio programs, when he made no similar moves against the pro-Franco press, suggests that unfriendly newspaper comment in predominantly illiterate Mexico did not overly worry him.[89]

Whether out of genuine conviction, political ambition, or simple prudence, most Mexican army officers gave Cárdenas their cooperation in regard to his Spanish policy. Indeed, some of the Republic's most enthusiastic and helpful adherents came from the military. Many of these officers had risen to prominence by commanding troops in the Revolution; some had been famous radicals in earlier decades. Among those providing especially valuable assistance to the Republic were generals Manuel Avila Camacho (Secretary of National Defense); Francisco J. Múgica (successively Secretary of National Economy and Secretary of Communications); Leobardo Ruiz (chargé d'affaires and consul in Spain); and Colonel Adalberto Tejeda (diplomat in France and later in Republican Spain). Despite their friendship toward the Republic, however, Mexican professional soldiers tended to be disturbed by its revolutionary politics. Colonel Reynaldo A. Híjar, military attaché at the embassy in Barcelona in 1938, recorded his criticisms in a report sent to the Foreign Relations and National Defense secretariats. He complained that "establishing control of the armed forces has been extremely difficult for the authorities" and that even after a "titanic struggle" there still remained excessive political meddling with the Popular army by left-wing parties and labor groups. "The military authorities are gradually trying to free the army from partisan influence so that it will become truly the army of the people," he noted.[90]

For many officers the Spanish conflict provided a clear lesson for Mexico: organized labor must never become a rival armed force, nor should its political influence be permitted to grow too strong. Broad military support for Cárdenas's Spanish policy thus coincided with deep foreboding in the minds of many officers about "leftist" influences on Cárdenas. They worried about Mexico's becoming "another Spain," they voiced their fears publicly, and they made concerted efforts to forestall any such development.[91]

The Mexican Congress reflected presidential patronage within the PNR rather than popular will; consequently, it gave Cárdenas no trouble in regard to Spain. His foreign policy moves, such as the arms sales, received rubber-stamp approval, and the most active congressional group, the left-wing Revolutionary Bloc, periodically staged emotional tributes to Republican Spain in the Chamber of Deputies. The Congress also sent messages to U.S. lawmakers, urging them to rescind their embargo on arms to Spain. Such differences over Spanish policy as existed between the president and PNR legislators generally involved congressional appeals for more extreme measures by Cárdenas to aid the Spaniards. CTM leader Lombardo had friends in the national legislature, and they frequently helped along his demagogic schemes by demanding repressive action against pro-Franco resident Spaniards and Mexican conservatives, invariably depicted as "Fascist conspirators against the Revolution." The president refused to be intimidated by these maneuvers, so Mexican rightists remained free to support the Nationalists in most ways. Any fund-raising activities on behalf of Franco that came to light, however, were suppressed.[92]

Organized peasants and rural laborers under PNR of leftist control also showed sympathy for the Republic. Some of them marched to pro-Loyalist rallies, others gave money to be sent to "Spanish militia-men." In the fall of 1937 villagers from Ytztacapa and Tetlapa, Hidalgo, collected a modest sum that they sent to Spain through the Regional Confederation of Workers and Peasants (FROC). Accompanying the money was a letter offering a "fraternal salute" to the Republic's "noble combatants."[93] Yet few Mexican peasants in the 1930s could have had anything beyond a dim conception of Spain, and most of them had probably never even heard of the Spanish Republic. The rural majority lacked PNR or leftist direction and had been largely by-passed by agrarian reforms. Not surprisingly, these people remained susceptible to traditionalist appeals from the clergy or Catholic laymen, and the number of them that ever felt any solidarity with their Spanish "brothers" had to be relatively small.

Without question Lombardo's CTM proved to be Mexico's most effective pro-Loyalist pressure group and source of funds. Gigantic labor rallies took place all over the country to publicize the Loyalist cause; money was raised for transmittal to Spain; workers in the armaments industry volunteered free labor so that weapons and munitions could be sent to the Republicans as cheaply and as rapidly as possible; and a large volume of propaganda circulated through the labor press, books and pamphlets, radio programs, films, and special benefit programs.[94] CTM appeals to its affiliated unions for assistance to the Republic usually evoked generous responses. Union members contributed one day's pay to be sent to Spain by the Republican embassy in Mexico City. In August-September 1936, electrical and streetcar workers in the capital began their donations, as did school teachers throughout the country.[95] Money, food, clothing, and other supplies continued to be collected for the Republic by CTM unions until the war ended. A letter sent to Ambassador Gordón in January 1937 by two officers of a small union in Monterrey illustrates rank-and-file cooperation. In compliance with a CTM request each worker had given a day's wages to help finance the Republic's war effort. The letter informed Gordón that a check for 309.47 pesos had been sent to him through the Banco de México. Poorly typed and marked by unconventional syntax and spelling, the letter indicated that the money was for

> the comrade worker militiamen of Spain . . . who are sacrificing so heroically their lives in defense of the liberty and sovereignty of their country and for the government over which Don Manuel Azaña so honorably presides, under attack by the hordes of Hitler and Mussolini who wish to muzzle the liberties of the proletariat, drowning them in blood, but they will not accomplish this, those Dictators.[96]

Like the CTM, Mexico's Communist party became a persistent advocate of the Loyalists and raised money for shipments of food, clothing, and medicine to Spain. From its ranks, moreover, came many of the Mexican volunteers who fought for the Republic. Communists operated through the party itself and less openly through front organizations that they created. PCM members were especially active in Spain, where the Popular Front government gave them more political latitude than they enjoyed at home. In Mexico as in Spain, much party activity was channeled through the League of Revolutionary Writers and Artists. A LEAR "educational" program at Bellas Artes Theater in February 1938 consisted of lectures by individuals recently returned from Spain. All of the principal speakers had Marxist backgrounds or PCM affiliation. LEAR's José Mancisidor also helped run the Friends of Spain Society, a source of pro-Loyalist publicity that closely followed the Communist line on the civil war. Communists also controlled the Spain-related projects of the Mexican Popular Front, a coalition of labor groups and political parties. In addition to having one official representative on the organization's governing board, the PCM could count on the CTM's vote here as well: Party member Miguel A. Velasco served on behalf of the labor confederation.[97]

Despite the scope of its actions relevant to Spain's civil war, PCM sincerity on the matter seems open to doubt. One wonders how much interest the party would have taken in the plight of Spanish Loyalists had not the Soviet Union decided to support them. There can be no question that the PCM line coincided exactly with that of the Russians on major international issues or about the party's complete subservience to Soviet dictates on even internal Mexican matters. In 1939, after almost three years of protesting "foreign aggression against the Spanish people," the PCM called the Finns "instruments of imperialism" and lauded the Soviet invasion of their country. Following the Spanish Republican defeat, moreover, José Mancisidor cheerfully made himself president of the newly-created Friends of the USSR Society.[98] (Mancisidor and the Communists did work hard on behalf of the Loyalists who fled to France after the Franquista victory; but many of these refugees, of course, were also Communists.)

Mexican Politics and the Republican Refugees

During the civil war's last weeks, Ambassador Tejeda and the Mexican embassy moved along with the Republican government from town to town in northeastern Spain and then followed its members into France, finally stopping at Perpignan. Cárdenas called Tejeda home to report on March 1, 1939. In April Ambassador Gordón closed the Spanish embassy in Mexico City; he left the building and its archives in charge of the Cuban ambassador. Republican consuls closed their offices, too. In those foreign countries where the Republic still had diplomatic representation, Spanish officials entrusted buildings, archives, and funds to their Mexican friends for safekeeping. Cárdenas refused to recognize Franco's regime, but he did permit some indirect trade with the peninsula to continue after the war, shipments being routed through such third countries as Cuba and Portugal. Yet he would not yield to Mexican commercial interests who called for resumption of full-scale trade with Spain. Although permitting this small amount of private contact, Cárdenas nonetheless refrained from communicating in any way with "the Franquista authorities." This made it impossible for Mexico to intercede directly on behalf of those Mexican civilians and volunteer soldiers held prisoner in Spain. It also forced Cárdenas to decline invitations from other Latin American countries to join with them in collective appeals to Franco to release all the Latin Americans taken prisoner by Nationalists during the war.[99] Mexico's lonely civil war alliance with the Republicans thus ended on an exceedingly dismal note. Still ahead for the Mexicans lay the melancholy task of trying to rescue as many Spaniards as possible from the miseries and uncertainties of internment camps in France.

Months before the Popular Front government in late 1937 asked Cárdenas if Mexico would accept thousands of Republican immigrants, Daniel Cosío Villegas (from Portugal) and Alfonso Reyes (from Argentina) had already proposed to the Mexican president that he bring "the dispersed Spanish intellectuals" to Mexico and help them find useful employment. Cosío made his initial plans on a small scale, suggesting that Cárdenas invite to Mexico about thirty prominent Spaniards. While waiting for official approval of the project, Reyes did what he could to aid personally some of his old friends hurt by the war and certain to be among those invited: José Ortega y Gasset, Juan Ramón Jiménez and his wife, and Ramón Gómez de la Serna. Reyes also raised money for the widow of his late friend Ramón del Valle-Inclán. Important support for the idea came immediately from other Mexican intellectuals and politicians. From these roots grew a plan that culminated in July 1938 with a presidential decree creating the Casa de España, an institute of research, higher learning, and literary production in which exiled intellectuals would be employed. Conceived initially as a temporary facility, the Casa began operations that same year. Cosío and Reyes served on its board of directors. Included in the first group of Spanish staff members to arrive were José Gaos, Adolfo Salazar, Juan de la Encina, and Jesús Bal y Gay. When a Spanish club in Mexico City, also called the Casa de España, protested use of its name, Cosío and the board redesignated their creation El Colegio de México. Under that name the institution has developed into the country's finest graduate school for humanities and social sciences. Picturesquely located near volcanic mountains south of Mexico City, it stands as a living memorial not only to the humanism and love of Spanish culture of Reyes and Cosío, but also to the one historical moment since its independence in 1821 when Mexico, by supporting the Republic, drew genuinely close to Spain.[100]

The origin of massive Republican emigration to Mexico can be traced to the secret mission of Juan-Simeón Vidarte, a Spanish Socialist politician. According to Vidarte, when he asked Cárdenas in 1937 how he would respond to such an appeal, the president without hesitation replied that Mexico would welcome an indefinite number of exiles. Cárdenas further assured his guest that the immigrants would discover a "second fatherland" when they arrived.[101] Late in 1938, with the war's end in sight, Cárdenas indicated that Mexico would take in about fifty thousand of the Republicans already interned (under appalling conditions) in French camps.[102] Yet he made no immediate move to implement this offer or to fulfill his pledge to Vidarte. Knowing that his decision would be resented and opposed by many Mexicans, including some of his supporters, the president had no desire to bring on that crisis any sooner than necessary. In addition, Mexico had just accumulated enormous debts by nationalizing foreign oil companies; the expensive Republican immigration project would be another burden on the federal treasury.

Several Mexicans in Europe, however, sensed impending catastrophe for the growing number of Loyalist exiles in France. Three of them successfully appealed to Cárdenas to begin a rescue operation at once: Isidro Fabela, Adalberto Tejeda, and Narciso Bassols. Fabela toured the dreadful camps in France and wrote directly to Cárdenas. Bassols came back to Mexico from his diplomatic post in France in spring 1939 to confront the president in person. Tejeda wrote to Cárdenas by way of Foreign Relations from Perpignan, where he and the Mexican embassy had come to rest along with the itinerant, virtually defunct Popular Front government. Fearing that France would send the refugees back to prison or certain death in Spain, Tejeda urged that Cárdenas "initiate international action" on behalf of all of them and that he bring to Mexico as rapidly as possible a selection of the "talented people" among them: intellectuals, writers, teachers, and other professionals.[103] Moved by these entreaties, in April 1939 the president authorized Minister Bassols in France to announce that Mexico "would accept an unlimited number of refugees if the Republican authorities would arrange to finance their transportation and settlement in Mexico." A subsequent presidential decree enabled Loyalist Spaniards to acquire Mexican citizenship quickly and simply.[104]

The first few shiploads of refugees reached Veracruz in the summer of 1939; subsequent departures from France continued throughout the years of World War II. By 1945 about thirty thousand Spanish exiles had entered Mexico.[105] As the evacuation of Republicans from France proceeded, the Mexicans constantly had to pressure French authorities to prevent them from extraditing people back to Franco's Spain. The problem became especially critical in 1940 after the fall of France and the establishment of the Vichy government. Although some Loyalists were sent back to their deaths in Spain, Mexico generally succeeded in protecting their wards from Franquista vengeance.[106] In this matter, representations from Mexican diplomats in France were supplemented by an international publicity campaign on behalf of the refugees that had its base in Mexico. Carried out by the Federation of Organisms of Aid to Spanish Republicans (FOARE), these concerted efforts probably had more effect on the spineless French regime (by shaming it before an increasingly anti-Fascist world) than did official protests by the Mexican government. FOARE enjoyed the backing and nominal membership of almost every government, CTM, and left-wing organization and affiliate in the country. Two of the four women composing its "Honorary Presidency" were the wives of President Cárdenas and of the 1940 presidential candidate Manuel Avila Camacho. Yet José Mancisidor, the Communist who had manipulated LEAR to make it serve Stalinist interests in Spain during the civil war, ran FOARE's daily operations as its president. Working with leftists and other Republican sympathizers throughout the Americas, FOARE kept the welfare, protection, and hoped-for evacuation of the refugees in France a major issue throughout World War II.[107]

Mexican efforts to facilitate Republican emigration from France, begun officially in the spring of 1939, thus continued well into the 1940s and involved Mexico in negotiations with the Vichy regime after the Germans occupied the country during World War II. In addition to enabling Spaniards to come to Mexico, Cárdenas also sought homes elsewhere in the Americas for those still stranded in France, and he authorized substantial payments from the Mexican treasury to care for the needy exiles who probably never would leave that country. Mexico's foreign service personnel in France continued to assist the Loyalists in many ways.

After unsuccessfully making private appeals in early 1939 to several Latin American countries for help in relocating the Loyalist refugees, Cárdenas publicly asked all of them in June 1940 to accept Spanish exiles and thus relieve them from the threat of being turned over to the Germans or sent back to Spain. He hoped that each country would admit at least some Republicans as immigrants. Only Ecuador and Cuba, however, responded favorably to the Mexican president's request. Ecuador promised to accept five thousand families, but the Cuban regime attached very restrictive conditions to its affirmative answer. Cuba would only take in Spaniards "willing to dedicate themselves to agricultural labor" or who "could create new industries by means of capital investment." Petty merchants would not be admitted under any circumstances. Other Latin American countries either made excuses, declined without comment, or offered only "moral support" for Mexico's project. All in all, it was a sorry, even shameful, performance. Uruguay claimed that "domestic politics" prevented any humanitarian move on its part. El Salvador pointed to a "coffee crisis" as the reason it could not help. Bolivia claimed to be "too poor" to take in any Spaniards. Peru reminded Cárdenas of its 1940 law that prohibited *any* immigrants from entering the country. Panama wanted to take in several thousand Republican immigrants (allegedly to "whiten" its predominantly Black or mixed population), but the country's Foreign Secretary informed Mexico that U.S. President Roosevelt had specifically proscribed this because "Spanish radicals would threaten the Canal's security."[108]

The Legendary Republic

During the post–civil war decades, Mexicans continued to be interested in peninsular phenomena, but perhaps no more so than in things American. Spanish entertainers and bullfighters came to Mexico in the 1960s, generated much excitement, and received cheers or jeers depending on the tastes and prejudices of Mexican audiences. But the diplomatic rift between their two countries kept Spaniards and Mexicans rather distant from and generally ignorant about each other.[109] By the late 1960s this remoteness contrasted sharply with the intimate knowledge that most urban and even many rural Mexicans had about life in the United States and with the massive volume of American tourist traffic to its southern neighbor. Such a situation facilitated Mexico's ever-increasing cultural gravitation toward the United States, which by 1977 had so swamped Spain in mass media representation that one had to search hard for samples of Spanish television fare among the multitude of U.S. sports programs alone. (In addition to Saturday afternoon baseball and college football, Sunday NFL football, and Monday night football, covered by several channels, one Mexico City TV station specialized in showing all games played by the Dallas Cowboys.)

Yet the legendary Republic retained its symbolic importance in Mexico despite all the changes. The roots of this phenomenon go back to the civil war itself and to the early 1940s, a propitious time for self-serving versions of the Spanish story as democracy battled fascism during World War II. Several postmortems on Spain in the spring of 1939 by young writers associated with the journal *Taller* presented a thesis that would be repeated for decades in artistic and literary circles. PCM member José Revueltas claimed that history had picked the Spaniards to serve as oracles of an imminent worldwide conflict between freedom-loving people and the evil forces of fascism. In their struggle the Loyalists had constituted the "voice of man," uttering a message of monumental importance. The Western democracies had been too stupid or criminally negligent to listen, yet the battle would continue; and the world would witness "a transformation without precedent" after the fight had been won.[110]

Isidro Fabela, who had played a major role in elaborating Mexico's official line on Spain, emphatically restated this view in subsequent decades. As a widely respected figure, his pronouncements carried considerable weight and always had the stamp of genuinely Revolutionary dicta. Fabela in the 1940s and 1950s characterized the Republicans as representing "authentic" Spain. Azaña's Popular Front regime in 1936 had been "democratic," and it had been supported by "the real Spanish people." The Loyalists had fought for "liberty" and for "legality." Their defeat had left the nation "trampled under foot by foreign hosts." Azaña himself had been a great patriot, a romantic yet noble idealist; he represented "the modern, comprehensive Spaniard who fought for ... a Spain internally free and independent abroad."[111]

This denial of the Spanishness and even the humanity of General Franco and his supporters became a major feature of the legendary Republic in Mexico. Some Mexican accounts of the conflict give the impression that automated machinery rather than people carried out the Nationalist uprising. Republicans had dubbed their opponents "the Anti-Spain." Pro-Loyalist Mexicans adopted this term and were still using it pejoratively against Franco's dictatorship in the 1970s. Concen-

tration on the idealistic principles of Azaña and other Spanish liberals
when writing or speaking about the Republic has been another common
ploy is sustaining the myth. Such a tactic leaves unmentioned irresponsible left-wing violence and extremism during the Republican years,
and it avoids the whole question of the extent to which, if at all, Spanish
liberals ever actually governed the country or exercised control over the
radicals who were nominally on their side.

   During the 1950s and 1960s depiction of Mexico's civil war role
as the mutual struggle of two democratic governments for justice and
liberty became an entrenched national belief. The idea also took root in
American academic and political circles, where liberals in the 1940s and
1950s persisted in characterizing the Spanish Republican and Mexican
governments as "democratic" regimes.[112] In 1954 Roberto Vega González, who had been a young Mexican volunteer in Spain, published his
story and reflected on the war. Like so many of his countrymen, Vega
recalled a pristine Republic unsullied by political vice. The Popular
Front innocents had been cruelly victimized by heartless generals and
Falangists in league with Mussolini and Hitler "to slaughter the Spanish
people" and annihilate their democratic principles. Loyalists had waged
an unsuccessful battle against the "enemies of democracy."[113] Two
notable Mexican writers also gave impetus to the myth in the 1950s:
Andrés Iduarte and Octavio Paz restated certain of its premises. Com-
menting on Mexico's perennial "identity" problem, they linked their
country and its culture to "the other Spain," that is, to the liberal side
of peninsular life that they saw manifested in the Republic. Iduarte,
who was in Spain when the war started, praised the "Spanish spirit"
that fought in 1936 "against the same feudal, clerical, and military
privileges that were fought against in 1810 by the founders of the
Spanish American republics."[114] Paz had an identical perception. Mexicans were "part of the universal tradition of Spain, the only one that
Spanish Americans can accept and carry on." But that tradition linked
Mexico to the liberating ideals represented by the Republic, not to the
repressive negations of General Franco. In his famous *Labyrinth of Solitude* (1959) he wrote: "There are two Spains: the Spain that is closed to
the outside world, and the open, heterodox Spain that breaks out of its
prison to breathe the free air of the spirit. Ours is the latter."[115]

   In the 1960s the gap between fact and fiction in regard to the
Spanish Republic grew wider. For his 1962 thesis in international relations at the National University, Omar Martínez Legorreta wrote *Actuación de México en la Liga de las Naciones* (Mexico's Record in the League
of Nations). Martínez portrayed the Republic as a political Cinderella
abused from the start by wicked relatives: professional soldiers, monar-

chists, Falangists. Martínez made no mention of anticlericalism or of Spain's radical left, and in fact gave the impression of a Republic without faults or weaknesses. To explain the outbreak of civil war, therefore, Martínez had to invoke a plot whose only apparent motivation was the conspirators' evil nature. Mexico's Spanish policy had been totally altruistic. Cárdenas had helped the Republic in 1936 because of his devotion to the principles of the League of Nations and international law. No ulterior motives were involved. "In its Spanish policy, Mexico was not defending any private economic or political interests; the interest it defended was the pure cause of Legality."[116]

Although one might be tempted to dismiss Martínez as willfully obtuse and hence not representative of the Mexican mind, it is clear that for most members of his generation myth had indeed become reality. Young José Emilio Pacheco, for example, would appear to have little in common with Martínez but age. He admitted to a strong liking for the writings of Salvador Novo, an eminent Mexican literary figure who had been sarcastically hostile to Cárdenas and often cruelly satirical about Republican Spain. Yet Pacheco's foreword to a 1964 collection of Novo's old newspaper columns presented a version of the Spanish war that would have puzzled Novo: "The [Spanish] generals aided by Hitler and Mussolini rose up in arms against the defenseless ... Republic while the whole world indifferently contemplated the tragic struggle of a people against its army." President Cárdenas, however, by helping the loyalists and through his overall foreign policy "maintained Mexican dignity."[117]

By the 1960s it was clear that Mexicans in general had come to see the Spanish experience in terms of national greatness. The country had acted selflessly to champion a just cause. Committed to liberty at home and abroad, the Mexican nation had helped Spaniards fight for their freedom while other countries, from stupidity or cowardice, did nothing. The Revolutionary party had given Mexico one of its finest historical moments. There would never be recognition of the odious Franco regime, for justice demanded continued relations with the legal Spanish government-in-exile (maintained by the Mexicans rather threadbarely in the dilapidated old embassy building on Londres Street). Eventually many moderates and conservatives began to echo official thought, an increasingly easier thing to do as the Revolutionary party itself moved to the right and as Franquism became more obviously anachronistic in the contemporary world. The myth not only survived the test of time, it grew ever stronger as years passed.

Franco died in November 1975. After an initial period of uncertainty and struggle for power, King Juan Carlos and Prime Minister

Adolfo Suárez moved to dismantle oppressive institutions created by the dictator. Spain moved warily toward political freedom, and by early 1977 Spaniards were experimenting with representative government. Mexican politicians reacted by rejoicing at Spain's "return to democracy." At long last justice had triumphed, and Mexican diplomacy had been vindicated. As the Spanish process developed in 1975–76, the Revolutionary party added another flight of fancy to the old civil war myth. Official commentary on Spanish events included a depiction of democratic Mexico leading a fascistic, imperialistic world toward discovery of an international order in which human rights and dignity would be respected and weak nations would no longer fall prey to the strong. President Luis Echeverría (1970–76) made this idea one of his favorite oratorical themes. All of these notions characterized the words and deeds of Mexican leaders from 1975 to 1977 as they first attacked moribund Franco and then proceeded toward reunion with Spain after the Caudillo's death.[118]

Early in 1977, after Spain had moved shakily but inexorably toward representative government under the aegis of a king, Mexico resumed diplomatic relations with the *madre patria*. President José López Portillo then visited Spain in October, the first such trip by a Mexican chief of state. In official circles the Mexican president received many courtesies during his stay in Spain. King Juan Carlos bestowed on him the Order of Isabella the Catholic, the highest honor accorded to foreigners. Seville's municipal government named him an "adopted son," and the people of Caparroso, Navarre, home town of one of the president's ancestors, welcomed him as "honorary alcalde." The Spanish Cortes invited him to speak.[119] Leaders of Spain's left-wing opposition, many of them recently returned from decades of exile, warmly greeted López Portillo and praised "Mexican democracy," but most Spanish leftists saved their greatest tributes for Lázaro Cárdenas. Even Communist octogenarian Dolores Ibarruri, who had turned furiously on Mexico over the Trotsky asylum issue, praised the late president. López Portillo publicly returned these compliments. Following a speech to the Spanish Cortes, for example, he vigorously applauded Ibarruri and blew her kisses with his fingers in what he evidently intended to be another manifestation of Mexico's long-standing devotion to peninsular "democracy" as well as an indication of his esteem for the old woman. That a conservative Mexican president would risk offending his equally conservative hosts by such a demagogic gesture cannot be related exclusively to his need to placate left-wing opinion at home. His behavior in the Cortes also reinforces one's impression that the civil war myth continues to play a major role in sustaining the Revolutionary party's self-image as a popularly approved, hence legitimate, political regime.[120]

Much of the rhetoric of the Mexico-Spain rapprochement struck a strongly Hispanist note. Writers and political leaders called attention to the "common destinies" of Mexico and Spain and placed special emphasis on Hispanidad as a basis for lasting union between the peninsula, Mexico, and all Spanish-speaking countries. Yet López Portillo, shortly before going to Spain, observed that "economic imperialism" still constituted an insuperable obstacle to unity among the American republics.[121] The Spanish king himself used the occasion of "Day of Hispanidad" ceremonies, over which he and the Mexican leader jointly presided on October 12, to lament the "poverty, ignorance, and emigration" that was eroding the sense of identity of so many Spanish-speaking people.[122]

In Mexican government circles the degree of Hispanism manifested in 1977 was unprecedented. Predictably, in a country where Spaniards and the Spanish record have always been controversial subjects, journalistic reaction to this phenomenon ranged from approbation to derision, and some critics even questioned official optimism about Mexico's new relationship with Spain. Hispanist Iñigo Laviada found it encouraging that so many administration members, "who until recently denied their Iberian blood," now admitted not only that they had Spanish parents but also that they were full-fledged Hispanophiles. Planeloads of these bureaucrats had accompanied the president on his journey, and Laviada thought that the "returns" to Mexico were worth all the public money it took to pay their expenses. Were he there with them, "I would be convinced that Spain, Hispanism, and the reconciliation merit these expenses . . . and that López Portillo and the . . . Mexicans accompanying him have taken an important step toward the rediscovery of our identity."[123] Fellow journalist Antolín Martínez, however, laughed at the way each bureaucrat suddenly sought to appear more Spanish than any of his colleagues. Their Hispanism, he predicted, would expire with López Portillo's term of office, for each Mexican president seemed to spark a particular fad that died as abruptly as it had been born. Martínez recalled that the same individuals who had been "frantic Socialists" under Cárdenas spent the six years of Avila Camacho's presidency as "fervid believers" [i.e., Catholics]. Observing that in Madrid López Portillo had proudly pointed out those members of his cabinet who had Spanish parents, Martínez suggested that other cabinet officials were now "ready to swear that their father is also a *gachupín*, even at the risk of being eliminated as possible presidential candidates."[124] Pedro Gringoire, veteran of half a century of political journalism, also had reservations about the euphoria accompanying Mexico's reunion with the *madre patria*. He wondered how anyone could take completely seriously the government's present "honeymoon" with monarchical Spain when it had plunged into so many contradictory love affairs in the recent past—with Castro's Cuba, Allende's Chile, Mao's China, and even "the Arab band led by Yaser Arafat."[125]

López Portillo's visit to Spain naturally prompted much press comment on the Spanish civil war and its significance for the nation. By this time, however, the noble heroism of the democratic Republicans and the propriety and courage of Mexican policy had the status of truisms among most journalists. Even conservative *Excelsior* took positions indistinguishable from those of *El Nacional.* In the former paper both an anonymous editorial writer and columnist Jorge Calvimontes recalled the "necessity" of Mexico's long alienation from Spain due to "the triumph of Franquism." Calvimontes added that all Mexican governments had spurned Franco after 1939 because they refused to legitimize with diplomatic recognition his "spoliation of democracy." It had been "morally essential" for Mexicans to await the demise of Franco's "unjust regime of repression" before re-establishing relations with Spain. Mexico's present role in the peninsula was to provide external approval and hence moral stimulation for the "new democracy and liberty of the nation of García Lorca and [Antonio] Machado."[126]

The Revolutionary party's 1977 decision to go along with Spain (for the record at least) and back a revival of Hispanism in Mexico that could be used for defensive purposes against American "imperialism" and cultural influence seemed destined to fail. Mexicans did *not* appear to be finding their "lost identity" by embracing their Spanish roots. Just the opposite, in fact, was happening: day by day the country and its people came under increasing U.S. influence. In the peninsula, moreover, Spaniards (despite what they told Mexicans and other Latin Americans) showed much more interest in union with their European neighbors than with their former colonies in the Western Hemisphere.[127] Still, the Mexicans would always have their special relationship with Republican Spain in the 1930s. It had contributed importantly to their self-esteem and to a rediscovery of "the other Spain" that many of them had forgotten. Through their civil war role Mexicans obtained another national myth to justify their Revolution and their government, and they could relish their country's "admirable" diplomatic stand at a time when ignoble cowardice and appeasement were the prevailing norms. Especially in regard to their rescue of the Loyalist refugees stranded in France, Mexicans can forever rejoice at what they did when the rest of the world remained indifferent to human suffering. Although Mexico's defense of the often-exasperating Spanish Republic in reality cast little glory on the country, it has come to have great importance today. Legendary versions of that story, now accepted as dogma by an overwhelming majority of the people, contribute to a growing national pride for which Mexicans have long and painfully searched.

Acknowledgments

The author expresses profound gratitude for assistance received in preparing this chapter to: Fredrick B. Pike, Mark Falcoff, Robert E. Quirk, Ana Staples, and Albert L. Michaels. Financial help from the State University of New York Research Foundation and the State University College at Buffalo made the study possible. Additional aid came from Sarah Emery and other staff members at Buffalo State's Butler Library and from Carol Julian of its History Department. José Héctor Ibarra and María Lourdes de Urbina at the Archives of the Mexican Secretariat of Foreign Relations assisted the author in various ways. Thanks are also extended to Francesca Linares de Vidarte, Juan Vidarte, María Luisa Tejeda Chardí, and Donald and Coralia Hetzner, and to helpful staff members at the following libraries in Mexico City: Biblioteca Nacional, Hemeroteca Nacional, Biblioteca Daniel Cosío Villegas, and Benjamin Franklin Library.

Notes

1. Richard A. Sinkin, "Modernization and Reform in Mexico, 1855–1876," Ph.D. dissertation, University of Michigan (1972); T. G. Powell, *El liberalismo y el campesinado en el centro de México (1850 a 1876)* (Mexico City, 1974); Friedrich Katz, "Labor Conditions on Haciendas in Porfirian Mexico: Some Trends and Tendencies," *Hispanic American Historical Review* (hereafter *HAHR*) 54, no. 1 (1974): 1–47; Jan Bazant, *Cinco haciendas mexicanas* (Mexico City, 1976).

2. Rodney D. Anderson, *Outcasts in Their Own Land: Mexican Industrial Workers, 1906–1911* (Dekalb, 1976); John M. Hart, *Los anarquistas mexicanos, 1860–1900* (Mexico City, 1974).

3. Fernando Rosenzweig et al., *Historia moderna de México. El Porfiriato: La vida económica,* 2 vols. (Mexico City, 1965); Charles C. Cumberland, *Mexican Revolution. Genesis Under Madero* (Austin, 1952); Stanley R. Ross, *Francisco I. Madero, Apostle of Mexican Democracy* (New York, 1955).

4. Robert E. Quirk, *The Mexican Revolution and the Catholic Church, 1910–1929* (Bloomington, 1973).

5. Charles C. Cumberland, *Mexican Revolution: The Constitutionalist Years* (Austin, 1972); Michael C. Meyer, *Huerta, a Political Portrait* (Lincoln, 1972); John Womack, Jr., *Zapata and the Mexican Revolution* (New York, 1969); Martín Luis Guzmán, *El águila y la serpiente* (Mexico City, 1928).

6. Robert E. Quirk, *An Affair of Honor. Woodrow Wilson and the Occupation of Veracruz* (New York, 1962) and *The Mexican Revolution, 1914–1915. The Convention of Aguascalientes* (Bloomington, 1960); Howard F. Cline, *The United States and Mexico,* rev. ed. (Cambridge, Mass., 1963); Kenneth J. Grieb, *The United States and Huerta* (Lincoln, 1969).

7. John W. F. Dulles, *Yesterday in Mexico. A Chronicle of the Revolution, 1919–1936* (Austin, 1961).

8. Fredrick B. Pike, *Spanish America, 1900–1970. Tradition and Social Innovation* (New York, 1973), pp. 46–55.

9. José Elguero, *España en los destinos de México* (Mexico City, 1929), pp. 9–11; Jesús Guisa y Azevedo, "No hay crítica donde hay decadencia," *Lectura* 1, no. 3 (1937): 193–96; Fernando Robles, "La religión y la hispanidad," *Lectura* 1, no. 4 (1937): 345–49.

10. *La Antorcha,* 1, no. 3 (1931): 3–9. The author thanks Mark Falcoff for making microfilm copies of *La Antorcha* available to him.

11. Barbara B. Aponte, *Alfonso Reyes and Spain* (Austin, 1972), p. 193.

12. Alfonso Reyes, *Momentos de España. Memorias políticas, 1920–1923* (Mexico City, 1947), pp. 11, 35–36, 60.

13. José Vasconcelos and Miguel Alessio Robles, *México y España,* 2nd ed. (Mexico City, 1929). The first edition appeared in 1919.

14. Mark Falcoff, manuscript biography of José Vasconcelos, pp. 112–21. The author thanks Professor Falcoff for permission to use this material.

15. Mary K. Vaughn, *History Textbooks in Mexico in the 1920s* (Buffalo, 1974), p. 37 and passim.

16. *Excelsior,* November 14, 1935, p. 5 (unless otherwise specified, all newspapers cited were published in Mexico City); Emiliano Iglesias to Eduardo Hay, Mexico City, December 3, 1935, Archivo Histórico de la Secretaría de Relaciones Exteriores (hereafter AHSRE), III/243(46–72), III–315–13.

17. *Excelsior,* October 12, 1934, p. 5.

18. Alejandro Gómez Maganda, *España sangra* (Barcelona, n. d.), p. 44.

19. *Boletín Oficial de la Secretaría de Relaciones Exteriores* (hereafter *BOSRE*) 60, nos. 1–2 (1933): 73; 61, nos. 8–9 (1933): 7.

20. See, for example, Félix F. Palavicini, *México: Historia de su evolución constructiva,* 4 vols. (Mexico City, 1945), IV, 256–57.

21. José Vasconcelos, *Que es el comunismo* (Mexico City, 1936), pp. 9–23.

22. Aponte, *Reyes and Spain,* p. 188.

23. *Excelsior,* April 20, 1931, pp. 5–6: interview, Francesca Linares de Vidarte, Buffalo, N.Y., April 24, 1978. Hereafter Linares de Vidarte interview.

24. *El Hombre Libre,* May 14, 1931, p. 1.

25. Ibid., April 18, 1931, p. 1.

26. Mexico, Embajada en España, *Relaciones internacionales iberoamericanas. Discursos pronunciados con motivo de la presentación de credenciales del primer embajador de los Estados Unidos Mexicanos ante el gobierno de la República Española* (Madrid, 1931), pp. 21–22. For a detailed study of Hispanism in the twentieth

century, see Fredrick B. Pike, *Hispanismo, 1898–1936: Spanish Conservatives and Liberals and Their Relations with Latin America* (Notre Dame, 1971).

27. Vasconcelos, *Que es el comunismo*, pp. 18–23; *El Hombre Libre*, June 11, 1931, pp. 1, 4. See also *La Antorcha*, 1, no. 1 (1931): 16.

28. Rodolfo Reyes, *Cuatro discursos* (Madrid, 1933), pp. 6–22.

29. *El Hombre Libre*, May 5, 1931, pp. 1–2.

30. Ibid., June 13, 1931, pp. 1–3.

31. Patricia Fagen, *Exiles and Citizens: Spanish Republicans in Mexico* (Austin, 1973), pp. 38–39.

32. Joseph P. Lash, *Eleanor and Franklin*, Signet edition (New York, 1973), p. 856.

33. *Memoria de la Secretaría de Relaciones Exteriores. Períodos 1934–35 y 1935–36*, 2 vols. (Mexico City, 1939), II, 89–117.

34. See, for example, Isidro Fabela's remarks to the League, September 20, 1937, quoted in Omar Martínez Legorreta, *Actuación de México en la Liga de las Naciones: El caso de España* (Mexico City, 1962), p. 203.

35. Víctor Alba, *The Mexicans. The Making of a Nation* (New York, 1967), pp. 182–83; interview, Spanish Republican who wishes to remain anonymous; Lois E. Smith, *Mexico and the Spanish Republicans* (Berkeley, 1955), pp. 171–72, 177.

36. Ignacio García Téllez to Ernesto Hidalgo, Mexico City, November 5, 1937, AHSRE, III/510(46)"37"/1, III–767–11.

37. "Acta de la sesión celebrada por el cuerpo diplomático en la embajada de Chile, el día 13 de Agosto de 1936," AHSRE, III/510(46)"37"/1, III–764–1, part 1.

38. Lázaro Cárdenas, *Apuntes, 1913–1940* (Mexico City, 1972), p. 354; copy of contract signed by Efraín Buenrostro and Félix Gordón Ordás, Mexico City, October 9, 1936, Gordón Ordás to Eduardo Hay, Mexico City, November 28, 1936, J. Rendón y Ponce to Anthony Eden, London, August 20, 1936 and H. J. Seymour to J. Rendón y Ponce, August 28, 1936, AHSRE, III/146(46)/1, III–1325–5.

39. New York *Times*, August 21, 1936, no page number, clipping in file; Ramón P. de Negri to Secretary of Foreign Relations, Santiago, Chile, September 2, 1936, Luis Quintanilla to Secretary of Foreign Relations, Washington, August 24, 1936, and Daniel Cosío Villegas to Secretary of Foreign Relations, Lisbon, November 8, 1936, AHSRE, III/146(46)/1, III–1325–5.

40. "Venta de armas y municiones a España, 1936," AHSRE, III/146(46)/1, III–1325–5; Washington *Herald*, January 3, 1937, and New York *Times*, January 3 and 4, 1937, no page numbers, clippings in ibid.: F. Jay Taylor, *The United States and the Spanish Civil War* (New York, 1956), pp. 67–68.

41. Smith, *Mexico and the Spanish Republicans*, pp. 190–95: Félix Gordón Ordás to Eduardo Hay, Mexico City, March 15, 1937, AHSRE, III/510(46)"37"/1, III–764–1, part 3; Ramón P. de Negri to Secretary of Foreign Relations, Valencia, February 8, 1937, and Hay to De Negri, Mexico City, February 16, 1937, AHSRE, III/510(46)"37"/1, III–764–1, part 2: Pascual Gutiérrez Roldán to Eduardo Hay, Mexico City, March 4, 1937, AHSRE, III/146(46)/1, III–1325–5; Leobardo Ruiz to Secretary of Foreign Relations, Valencia, November 9, 1937, and Luis Bobadilla to Eudardo Hay, Mexico City, November 16, 1937, AHSRE, III/510(46)"36"/1, III–766–1, part 6; *Renacimiento* (Tegucigalpa), November 30, 1937, p. 13.

42. Adalberto Tejeda to Secretary of Foreign Relations, Paris, July 28, 1936, Hay to Tejeda, Mexico City, July 29, 1936, and Tejeda to Hay, Paris, October 10, 1936, AHSRE, III/510(46)"37"/1, III–764–1, part 2; Tejeda to Hay, Paris, December 27, 1937; Jaime Torres Bodet to Eduardo Hay, Brussels, February 3, 1938, AHSRE, III/146(46)/1, III–1325–5.

43. Martínez Legorreta, *Actuación de México,* pp. 104–105, 199–202.

44. Salvador Novo, *La vida en México en el período presidencial de Lázaro Cárdenas* (Mexico City, 1964), p. 37; Luis Echeverría Alvarez, *Posición de México ante el franquismo* (Mexico City, 1975), pp. 3–4; Linares de Vidarte interview.

45. Isidro Fabela, "La política internacional del presidente Cárdenas," *Problemas Agrícolas e Industriales de México,* 7, no. 4 (1955): 3–10.

46. Ibid.

47. Dulles, *Yesterday in Mexico,* pp. 392–93, 409–10, 430–32, 469, 494–95, 519, 524, 541–43, 574–77. Interview, María Luisa Tejeda Chardí, Coyoacán, D. F., September 10, 1977 (hereafter Tejeda Chardí interview).

48. *La Prensa* (New York), October 21, 1936, pp. 1, 6.

49. Manuel Pérez Treviño, "La situación española," October 10, 1936, AHSRE, III/510(46)"37"/1, III–764–1, part 1.

50. Ibid.

51. J. Rubén Romero to Ramón Beteta, Barcelona, August 30, 1936, ibid.

52. Ibid.

53. Alfonso Reyes to Secretary of Foreign Relations, Buenos Aires, October 18, 21, 23, and 24, 1936, AHSRE, III/516(46–0)/2, III–1246–6.

54. Alfonso Reyes, "Memorandum," Buenos Aires, October 22, 1936, AHSRE, III/510(46)"36"/1, III–766–3.

55. Francisco A. Ursúa to Secretary of Foreign Relations, Santiago, Chile, November 13, 1936, AHSRE, III/146(46)/1, III–1325–5; interviews with Mexican and Spanish Republican sources who wish to remain anonymous.

56. "Memorandum confidencial para el C. Presidente de la República," unsigned, undated, Ramón P. de Negri to Secretary of Foreign Relations, Valencia, January 25, 1937, and Eduardo Hay to De Negri, Mexico City, February 11, 1937, AHSRE, III/510(46)"37"/1, III–764–1, part 2; Tejeda Chardí interview.

57. Adalberto Tejeda to Lázaro Cárdenas, Paris, January 8, 1937, and Cárdenas to De Negri, Mexico City, January 10, 1937, AHSRE, III/510(46)"37"/1, III–764–1, part 2.

58. Ramón P. de Negri to Secretary of Foreign Relations, Valencia, April 2, 1937, AHSRE, III/516(46–0)/2, III–1246–6; *Memoria de la Secretaría de Relaciones Exteriores: 1936–1937* (Mexico City, 1938), pp. 35–36.

59. "Memorandum confidencial", Eduardo Hay to Ramón P. de Negri, Mexico City, February 15, 1937, Juan B. Arriaga, "Informe sobre la actuación del señor embajador en ésta," and "Continuación del informe confidencial al Sr. Secretario de Relaciones Exteriores" (undated), Hay to De Negri, Mexico City, July 21, 1937, and Hay to Leobardo Ruiz, Mexico City, July 21, 1937, AHSRE, III/510(46)"37"/1, III–764–1, part 2; Ruiz to Hay, Valencia, September 20 and November 10, 1937, AHSRE, III/510(46)"36"/1, part 6; interview with Spanish Republican source who wishes to remain anonymous.

60. *El Mercantil Valenciano* (Valencia), October 13, 1937, no page number, clipping in file, and Leobardo Ruiz to Secretary of Foreign Relations, Ma-

drid, November 21, 1937, AHSRE, III/510(46)"36"/1, III-766-1, part 6; Ruiz to Secretary of Foreign Relations, Valencia, October 1 and November 19, 1937, AHSRE, III/510(46)"37"/1, III-770-3.

61. Dulles, *Yesterday in Mexico*, pp. 579, 585-86, 641-42; Tejeda Chardí interview; interview with Spanish Republican source who wishes to remain anonymous.

62. Novo, *La vida en México*, p. 144.

63. Alfonso Reyes to Secretary of Foreign Relations, Buenos Aires, October 10 and November 4, 1936, February 11 and July 3, 1937, AHSRE, III/510(46)"36"/1, III-766-3; Salvador Pardo Bolland to Secretary of Foreign Relations, Asunción, August 20, 1937, AHSRE, III/510(46)"37"/1, III-769-3, part 1; Moisés Sáenz to Secretary of Foreign Relations, Lima, August 11 and December 8, 1936, and Bernardo Reyes to Secretary of Foreign Relations, Lima, April 15 and May 31, 1937, AHSRE, III/510(46)"36"/1, III-768-8.

64. Adolfo Cienfuegos y Camús to Secretary of Foreign Relations, Guatemala City, June 9, 1937, and Enrique Solórzano to Secretary of Foreign Relations, Guatemala City, July 31, 1937, AHSRE, III/510(46)/"37"/1, III-767-14.

65. "Sesión solemne, Cámara de Diputados, Febrero 17, 1939," *Revolución* 2, no. 2 (1939): 47; Fernando Lagarde y Vigil to Secretary of Foreign Relations, Havana, May 27, 1939, AHSRE, III/510(46)"37"/1, III-767-6; Romero to Secretary of Foreign Relations, Havana, June 22, 1940, AHSRE, III/533.1(46)/1205, III-2394-15.

66. J. D. Ramírez Garrido to Secretary of Foreign Relations, Bogotá, June 11, July 21, and September 7, 1937, AHSRE, III/510(46)"36"/1, III-767-4.

67. Smith, *Mexico and the Spanish Republicans*, pp. 196-97; Juan-Simeón Vidarte, *Todos fuimos culpables* (Mexico City, 1973), pp. 546, 807; *El Universal*, November 24, 1938, p. 2.

68. David A. Siqueiros, *Me llamaban el coronelazo* (Mexico City, 1977), p. 348; Roberto Vega González, *Cadetes mexicanos en la guerra de España* (Mexico City, 1954), pp. 201-217.

69. Félix Gordón Ordás, *Mi política fuera de España*, 2 vols. (Mexico City, 1965-67), I, 350; Leobardo Ruiz to Secretary of Foreign Relations, Valencia, November 2, 1937, AHSRE, III/510(46)"37"/1, III-770-3.

70. *Excelsior*, August 22, 1937, p. 1; Vega González, *Cadetes mexicanos*, pp. 39-40.

71. Miguel A. Velasco, "El partido comunista durante el período de Cárdenas," in Gilberto Bosques et al., *Cárdenas* (Mexico City, 1975), pp. 37, 47 n. 33; *Excelsior*, August 21, 1937, pp. 1, 8; Donald L. Herman, *Comintern in Mexico* (New York, 1974), p. 127.

72. Vega González, *Cadetes mexicanos*, pp. 14-30, 62, 66, 75; *Excelsior*, August 3, 1937, pp. 1, 10, and August 4, 1937, p. 5.

73. Blanca L. Trejo, *Lo que vi en España* (Mexico City, 1940), p. 49 and passim.

74. Gómez Maganda, *España sangra*, pp. 24-25.

75. *Revista Eclesiástica de la Diócesis de Zamora*, 1936 and 1937, passim; on Pius XI's instructions to the Mexicans, see Elwood R. Gotshall, "Catholicism and Catholic Action in Mexico, 1929-1941: A Church's Response to a Revolutionary Society and the Politics of the Modern Age" (Ph.D. dissertation, University of Pittsburgh, 1970), p. 143. (*Revista Eclesiástica* hereafter cited as *REDZ*.)

76. *REDZ* 4, no. 9 (1936), p. 221; Smith, *Mexico and the Spanish Republicans,* p. 174.
77. Rubén Salazar Mallén, "La rebelión en España," *El Universal,* July 30, 1936, pp. 3, 8.
78. Fernando Robles, "La hispanidad y nosotros los hispanoamericanos," *Lectura* 2, no. 4 (1937): 358–64.
79. *Lectura,* 1937, passim.
80. Albert L. Michaels, "Mexican Politics and Nationalism from Calles to Cárdenas" (Ph.D. dissertation, University of Pennsylvania, 1966), pp. 288–91.
81. *Lectura,* 1, no. 1 (1937): 95–96.
82. Vasconcelos, *Que es el comunismo,* pp. 10–11.
83. Ibid., pp. 32–33, 39–43, 49–54, 95–98.
84. Efraín González Luna, "Pasión y destino de España," *Ábside* 4, no. 1 (1940): 3–16.
85. Alfonso Junco, *El difícil paraíso* (Mexico City, 1940), pp. 7–18.
86. Ibid., pp. 19–62, 79–93, 109–13, 126–27, 239–61.
87. Gordón Ordás, *Mi política,* I, 481–82.
88. Ibid., pp. 378, 482, 487; Albert L. Michaels, *The Mexican Election of 1940* (Buffalo, 1971), p. 9; *El Nacional,* June 13, 1937, p. 1; *Revolución* 2, no. 1 (1939): 59–61, and 2, no. 4 (1939): 18–23.
89. *Excelsior,* August 3, 1937, p. 1; Gordón Ordás, *Mi política,* I, 351.
90. Reynaldo A. Híjar, "Informe sobre el Ejército Popular Republicano," November 1938, AHSRE, III/510(46)"37"/1, III–763–9, part 2.
91. Edwin Lieuwen, *Mexican Militarism: The Political Rise and Fall of the Revolutionary Army* (Albuquerque, 1968), pp. 115–29.
92. Novo, *La vida en México,* pp. 229–35; Gordón Ordás, *Mi política,* I, 351–52; Smith, *Mexico and the Spanish Republicans,* p. 188; *Revolución* 2, no. 3 (1939), pp. 6–7; *Excelsior,* August 3, 1937, pp. 1–2, and August 21, 1937, pp. 1, 8.
93. *El Diario de Puebla* (Puebla), October 29, 1937, p. 3.
94. Gordón Ordás, *Mi política,* I, 477–79; Vega González, *Cadetes mexicanos,* pp. 37–39.
95. *El Diario Español,* August 27, 1936, p. 2, August 29, 1936, p. 2, and September 5, 1936, p. 2.
96. José Ma. G. Garza and Luis Mata to Félix Gordón Ordáz (*sic*), Monterrey, January 6, 1937, AHSRE, III/510(46)"37"/1, III–770–5.
97. *El Universal,* July 31, 1936, p. 1, February 14, 1938, p. 8, February 17, 1938, p. 2, and February 18, 1938, p. 10; Herman, *Comintern in Mexico,* p. 115.
98. Bosques et al., *Cárdenas,* pp. 37, 44 n. 34; Armando de María y Campos, *Por un mundo libre* (Mexico City, 1943), pp. 16, 53–56, 338–95.
99. Smith, *Mexico and the Spanish Republicans,* pp. 198–206; Vega González, *Cadetes mexicanos,* pp. 62–66, 187–92; Jorge Zawadzky (of Colombian legation) to Eduardo Hay, Mexico City, March 19, 1940 and Hay to Zawadzky, Mexico City, March 21, 1940, AHSRE, III/524.9/94, III–2398–10.
100. Aponte, *Reyes and Spain,* pp. 188–92; Daniel Cosío Villegas, *Memorias* (Mexico City, 1976), pp. 168–79.
101. Vidarte, *Todos fuimos culpables,* pp. 788–89.
102. Palavicini, *México,* IV, 272; Fagen, *Exiles and Citizens,* pp. 32–33.

103. Fagen, *Exiles and Citizens*, pp. 32–33, 40–41; Amaro del Rosal, *El oro del Banco de España y la historia del "Vita"* (Mexico City, 1976), pp. 9–10; Adalberto Tejeda to Secretary of Foreign Relations, Perpignan, February 18, 1939 (message relayed by Narciso Bassols to Secretary of Foreign Relations, Paris, February 18, 1939), AHSRE, III/510(46)"37"/1, III–767–13; Tejeda Chardí interview.

104. Fagen, *Exiles and Citizens*, pp. 31–33, 59.

105. Ibid., pp. 34–39; Smith, *Mexico and the Spanish Republicans*, pp. 231–37; Pablo de Azcárate, "Service pour L'Evacuation des Refugies Espagnols (S.E.R.E.). Memoire sur son origine, constitution et activities," February 1940, AHSRE, III/553.1(46)/1205, III–2394–15. For one version of the controversy between Negrín and Prieto over the Republican treasury funds, see Del Rosal, *Oro del Banco de España*.

106. Smith, *Mexico and the Spanish Republicans*, pp. 209–11; Bernardo Reyes to Secretary of Foreign Relations, Paris, March 15, 1940, AHSRE, III/553.1(46)/1205, III–2394–15.

107. Federación de Organismos para la Ayuda a los Republicanos Españoles, hereafter FOARE, *Memoria de las actividades de ayuda a los Republicanos Españoles. Estados Unidos, Cuba, México* (Mexico City, 1943); FOARE, *Boletín,* numbers 10–11 (mimeographed, undated), AHSRE, III/524.9/94, III–2398–10; Octavio Campos Salas to Secretary of Foreign Relations, Mexico City, June 23, 1940, and Executive Committee of FOARE, "Al pueblo de México. Imped que el pueblo francés entregue millares de españoles a sus verdugos," undated flyer (but February or March 1940), AHSRE, III/553.1(46)/1205, III–2394–15.

108. Pablo Campos Ortiz to Secretary of Foreign Relations, Santiago, Chile, April 3, 1939, AHSRE, III/510(46)"36"/1, III–767–7; two unsigned, undated "Memoranda" (but post-June 1940), Romero to Secretary of Foreign Relations, Havana, June 22, 1940, and Alfonso Rosenzweig Díaz to Secretary of Foreign Relations, Panamá, June 21, 1940, AHSRE, III/553.1(46)/1205, III–2394–15.

109. See, for example, the comments of Carlos A. Medina, *Las Últimas Noticias,* October 14, 1977, pp. 1, 10, and the remarks made by Spanish newspaperman Miguel Higueras, quoted in *El Nacional,* October 8, 1977, p. 1; see also *Excelsior,* October 8, 1977, pp. 1, 9.

110. José Revueltas, "Profecía de España," *Taller* 2 (April 1939): 28–30.

111. Isidro Fabela, *Azaña y la política de México hacia la República Española* (Mexico City, 1943), and "La política internacional," *Problemas agrícolas e industriales de México* 7, no. 4 (1955): 3–10.

112. See, for example, William C. Townsend, *Lázaro Cárdenas, Mexican Democrat* (Ann Arbor, 1952); Josephus Daniels, *Shirt-Sleeve Diplomat* (Chapel Hill, 1947); and Claude G. Bowers, *My Mission to Spain. Watching the Rehearsal for World War II* (New York, 1954).

113. Vega González, *Cadetes mexicanos,* pp. 12–14, 28, 39.

114. Andrés Iduarte, *Pláticas hispanoamericanas* (Mexico City, 1951), pp. 9–18.

115. Octavio Paz, *The Labyrinth of Solitude: Life and Thought in Mexico,* trans. Lysander Kemp, 2nd ed. (New York, 1959), p. 154.

116. Martínez Legorreta, *Actuación de México,* pp. 1–10, 159, 177.

117. José Emilio Pacheco, "Nota preliminar," in Novo, *La vida en México,* p. 11.

118. Echeverría, *Posición de México ante el franquismo,* passim; José López Portillo, *Regresar a España con dignidad* (Mexico City, 1976).

119. "En Contacto Directo," news program, Channel 5 (Mexico City), October 8, 1977; "México en España," news program, Channel 13 (Mexico City), October 13, 1977.

120. *El Nacional,* October 8, 1977, p. 1, and October 10, 1977, pp. 1, 4; *Excelsior,* October 8, 1977, pp. 1, 9, October 13, 1977, pp. 1, 8, and October 15, 1977, p. 1.

121. *El Universal,* October 2, 1977, pp. 1, 7.

122. *Excelsior,* October 13, 1977, pp. 1, 11.

123. Iñigo Laviada, "Reencuentro de la Identidad," ibid., October 15, 1977, p. 6.

124. *Las Últimas Noticias,* October 14, 1977, p. 4.

125. *Excelsior,* October 15, 1977, pp. 7–8.

126. Ibid., October 8, 1977, pp. 6–7.

127. On the tenuous nature of Hispanism in Mexico and elsewhere in Latin America in the years since 1977, see Howard J. Wiarda, "Does Europe Still Stop at the Pyranees? Or Does Latin America Begin There? Iberia, Latin America, and the Second Enlargement of the European Community," Optional Papers Series No. 2, The Center of Hemispheric Studies of the American Enterprise Institute for Public Policy Research (Washington, D. C., 1982), mimeo.

Cuba

Alistair Hennessy

The Spanish civil war was the great revolutionary failure of the first half of this century; the Cuban revolution has been the revolutionary triumph of the latter half. At first sight, there may seem little to link the two phenomena. Nevertheless, that two countries whose histories have been more closely intertwined than any others in the Hispanic world should have provided the touchstone for revolutionary enthusiasm on a world-wide scale is surely remarkable and thought-provoking.

For too long, Spanish and Latin American specialists in the English-speaking world have cultivated their own separate gardens. An exploration of links between Spanish and Cuban history, using the Spanish civil war as a focus, provides one opportunity to break down the hedges of academic particularism.[1] This essay is an attempt to do so, and, by suggesting comparisons and contrasts, it hopes to open up four areas for further investigation.

First, historians of twentieth-century Cuba, Cubans and foreigners alike, have tended to concentrate on the island's external relations with the United States and to explain how this relationship has worked to the island's disadvantage. In so doing, they have ignored the important economic and social role played by the country's Spanish community since independence and the distortions this in turn created in Cuban society.

Second, Spain and Cuba both experienced acute political and economic tensions in the early 1930s, and both suffered revolutionary failures. In Spain, the overthrow of the monarchy in 1931 brought a period of experimentation that had revolutionary potential. In Cuba, the deposition of General Gerardo Machado in 1933, after eight years of dictatorship, had similar results. But whereas in Spain this revolutionary process extended over a period of five years and ended in civil war, in Cuba it was telescoped into under five months. Cuba's Revolution of 1933, although initiating a wide-ranging series of reforms, aborted and did not usher in the democratic regime desired by its participants. Instead, it fell victim to betrayal by one of its authors, Sergeant (later Colonel) Fulgencio Batista, who became the strongman behind all Cuban governments for nearly a dozen years to come. Subsequent government repression destroyed illusions and drove idealists into exile, many of whom found in the plight of the Spanish Republic a cause with which to identify. The effect of this experience on those who later returned to Cuba, and their influence on Cuban politics in the 1940s and after, has yet to be studied.

Third, the violent suppression of opponents in 1934–35, as well as Batista's record as dictator in the 1950s, have tended to obscure the significance of his first period of rule (1934–44), which, although destroying the 1933 Revolution's democratic intents, nevertheless consolidated most of its social achievements in a populist-style multi-class coalition, the unique feature of which was the involvement of Cuba's Communist party. It was the Spanish civil war, acting as a catalyst, that helped to end the party's isolation and powerlessness by facilitating an understanding with Batista.[2] This is turn laid the foundations for a subsequent period of power and influence for the Cuban Communists. If the survival of Castro's revolution is due in large measure to the role played by the Communist party—with its discipline, organization, and links to Moscow—then the process by which it became a political force requires elucidation. The decade when this occurred—between 1934 and 1944—is, understandably perhaps, the least-studied period of Cuban history. These are the silent, unheroic years. The volte-face in Communist thinking, through which Batista was transformed from fascist enemy to beacon of democratic rectitude, can be explained by the demands of Comintern strategy, as well as by the imperatives of Cuban domestic politics, but the Communists' unequivocal support for the Spanish Republicans helped to legitimate the new policy, by making both Batista and the Communists joint partners in supporting a popular cause. Indeed, a greater proportion of the Cuban population seems to have sympathized with the Republic than any other in Spanish America.

Fourth, the civil war's literary impact in Spanish America, and its influence on intellectuals there, has been unjustly neglected. There seems to be little awareness among English-speaking critics, for example, that arguably the greatest literature to be written on the civil war by foreigners was the poetry of Chilean Pablo Neruda and Peruvian César Vallejo. Among Cubans, the poet Nicolás Guillén was profoundly influenced by the civil war: he related the Republican struggle to his own concern with the Black renaissance in Cuba and to the wider anti-imperialist and anti-colonial struggle. This has considerable relevance today, when Cuban intervention in Africa is legitimated through reference to the island's African heritage. The way in which both Cuban and Spanish American responses differed from those of European intellectuals also needs stressing.

This last can be related not only to specific Hispanic literary traditions but also to the different social, political, and economic milieux in which Spanish American writers worked. Whereas many European Communist intellectuals and their sympathizers found the civil war disillusioning and subsequently left the party or refused to cooperate with it, a number of Latin Americans—notably Neruda, Vallejo, Guillén, Marinello, and Roumain—reacted by moving toward it. The explanation for this is not so much that they were "tontos útiles" (useful fools) but that Latin America lacked a viable bourgeois liberal or social-democratic tradition and culture. The Communists' anti-imperialist stance had an obvious appeal for intellectuals who, after the Great Depression, attributed the ills of Latin America to the ties of economic dependence on the United States. Furthermore, the organization and discipline of the Communists—which, in other contexts, intellectuals might count a drawback—could often be seen in the context of factional politics as a source of appeal.

In the final section of this essay, some comparisons and contrasts between Spanish and Cuban historical experiences are suggested. Their purpose is to open up inquiry in a field that has been neglected but, since the demise of Franco in 1975 and the subsequent unfreezing of politics in Spain, might have some relevance for the future.

The Spanish Community in Cuba

Historically, the Spanish civil war had a greater effect on society in Cuba than in any other Spanish-speaking country. It could hardly fail to do otherwise. The presence of a large Spanish community—some 16 percent of the population—many of whom were constantly traveling between the two countries, had created a dense network of familial relationships that transcended political frontiers.[3]

Cuban attitudes toward Spain were complex, arising out of the dilemmas of national identity. Proximity to the United States, and the growth of American influence, led Cubans to assert their Hispanic heritage in order not to be engulfed by a more powerful alien culture. This, more than anything else, conditioned the development of a Cuban nationalism that was directed against the more immediate threat from the north and that inclined Cubans to echo José Martí's distinction between "good" and "bad" Spaniards and between "official" Spain and the "people". Regenerationist Spanish intellectuals themselves preferred this distinction, which in turn underpins the "White Legend" of Spanish history, subsequently elaborated by Cuban friends of the Republic during the civil war.

The length and bitterness of the anti-colonial struggle in Cuba between 1868 and 1898 meant that when the island finally achieved independence, it possessed a more highly developed sense of nationalism than any of the other Spanish American countries at the same stage of their histories three-quarters of a century before. Whereas, in the earlier instances, the state preceded a developed sense of nationhood, in Cuba the reverse was the case. The war of independence had generated a sense of national identity that should have given Cuba advantages not obtaining elsewhere. But Cuban nationalism had serious weaknesses. The "nation in arms" existed only in myth, and a genuine national consensus failed to appear. The defeat of the Spaniards had been achieved in the countryside by means of guerrilla warfare in which the towns had played little part. The historiography of the war reveals how Cubans have sought to interpret the defeat of Spain as a Cuban victory: in this version the Americans intervened only after the Cubans, by their own efforts, had broken the back of Spanish resistance.[4] Interpretations, especially and increasingly on the left, emphasize the role played by Blacks and mulattoes who, as the backbone of the rural guerrilla forces, were whole-heartedly *independentistas,* whereas the urban creoles could lay claim to that label only with some qualification, for most of them usually desired some form of autonomous relationship with Spain or, alternatively, once faced with the *fait accompli* of U.S. intervention, had no difficulty in accepting the limitations imposed on Cuban sovereignty by the Platt Amendment, which was intended to protect them from social revolution and disorder. The "nation," therefore, was fragmented: white creoles, many of whom had family ties or commercial links to Spaniards, kept aloof from the colored population. Other divisions existed: between those who accepted U.S. protection and those who did not; between plantation owners and their workers; and, finally, between Cubans and Spaniards. Had there been a greater sense of unanimnity among Cubans, Spaniards might well have found post-1898 Cuba a less congenial place in which to live.

Until more historical work has been done on the island's Spanish community, it is difficult to say just how integrated into Cuban society it had become. One of the most surprising features of the new republic was the privileged position, guaranteed by the peace treaty, that the Spaniards continued to enjoy. Spanish immigration into Cuba had begun to accelerate after the formal abolition of slavery in 1879, and in the twelve years before the independence war broke out in 1895 some 224,000 Spaniards entered the island, of whom 82,000 remained. So, far from declining after independence, immigration increased, and the percentage of Spaniards among the island's population climbed from 8.2 percent in 1899 to 11.1 in 1907, 14 in 1919, and 15.8 in 1931.[5] Cuba, along with Argentina and Uruguay, is predominantly an immigrant country, but it is uniquely a country of *Spanish* immigrants. Comparable figures for other foreigners in each of the above years were 2.8, 2, 4.5, and 5.7 percent. From independence until 1919, 66 percent of the 660,958 immigrants were Spaniards, who also made up 97 percent of all immigrants from Europe. Unlike Argentina and Uruguay, therefore, Cuba's immigrant stock has not been diluted by non-Hispanic Europeans. There is nothing comparable to the Italian influx, without a consideration of which, Argentine social history makes little sense. In common with Argentina, though, Cubans did not strictly enforce immigration restrictions. Children born of Spanish parents in Cuba remained Spanish unless they opted for Cuban citizenship on coming of age, and Spaniards had little incentive to become Cuban citizens until the mid-1930s. By 1919 only 14 percent of them had done so.

Considerable turnover, with a high proportion of *retornos,* also characterized the Spanish immigrants to the island. In the period 1924–28, 123,798 Spaniards entered Cuba, but 117,254 left. This transatlantic mobility can be observed in the life of the Galician father of Enrique Lister, the Republican general, who crossed over to Cuba eight times as a migrant worker. Some of this mobility can be explained by the seasonal migration of laborers, similar to the *golondrinas* of Argentina's wheat harvests, and it meant that many of the Spanish community thought of themselves as *peninsulares.* They identified with metropolitan rather than creole values, an anomaly eventually attenuated by increasingly cheap labor in the sugar harvests provided by Jamaicans and Haitians.

Spanish immigrants, whether seasonal or permanent, tended to be poor. Galicians were the largest group, making up 47.68 percent of all Spanish immigrants between 1911 and 1958. As in Argentina, the generic term for Spaniard was *gallego.* Only Canary Islanders show a higher percentage of emigrants from the total regional population than Galicians, but the pattern of *isleño* migration differed in some respects from that of peninsular Spaniards, for many tended to settle in rural areas.

The Galicians were the first Spaniards in Cuba to organize a social club on a regional basis.[6] In 1879 they founded the Centro Gallego, to be followed in 1886 by the Centro Asturiano, the latter becoming the largest of all the clubs, with 34,000 members in the 1930s, although in its heyday it had over 60,000. Other regions were similarly represented: Catalans, Basques, Castilians, and Andalusians also established their own *centros*. Most clubs spread branches throughout the island, the Centro Asturiano having over a hundred. Even within regional groups, further compartmentalization occurred. The Centro Asturiano had forty-two autonomous associations based on *comarcas* (villages or smaller regions within Asturias); the Centro Gallego had fifty-seven similar organizations. They fulfilled a function similar to that of the *cofradías* of penisular Spain, serving to perpetuate links between immigrants from particular villages and to maintain contacts with the parent village.

The lavishness of *centro* premises, with their chandeliered ballrooms, restaurants, and recreation rooms, never failed to impress foreign visitors as evidence of the success, thrift, and hard work of these immigrants from northern Spain. *Centros* also illustrated how Spaniards helped each other, for they also functioned as cooperative, mutual aid societies. Spanish immigrants could therefore move in a virtually closed world. Regional affiliations and addiction to the *patria chica*, combined with familial ties and *compadrazgo* links, served to cushion immigrants, to protect them from what otherwise could have been a harsh competitive world, and to decrease the likelihood of swift assimilation. It is difficult to say just how encysted this Spanish community was. One would have to know much more about the incidence of intermarriage and the effect of this on Spanish attitudes. A popular proverb had it that Cuban women "sweetened" the Spanish character, mellowing the hardworking Spaniards' scorn for what they considered to be the creoles' easy-going, feckless ways.

The most striking feature of the Spanish community was its domination of the island's commercial life, especially the retail trade. Spaniards controlled many export-import houses, dominating both the considerable import trade from the peninsula and the export trade, mostly tobacco, back across the Atlantic.[7] Family concerns, these Spanish businesses employed compatriots without capital by taking in apprentices, who would lead a protected life under the patriarchical care of the family head. Few immigrants arrived with capital resources, and many were illiterate (hence the importance of the *centros'* night schools). Like the *montañeses* in eighteenth-century Mexico, they tended to be frugal, parsimonious, austere, and hard-working. They invested their money in their protectors' businesses, or sent it back to Spain as remittances, or invested in urban real estate or in insurance schemes run by the *centros*. Spaniards also had an important place in banking. The Banco Español, founded in the colonial period, maintained fifty-five branches, and the Banco Nacional, founded with U.S. capital, was bought out by a Galician in 1911.

This pattern perpetuated and strengthened certain Spanish values and prejudices among all immigrants except those who broke out of the protective carapace. For the vast majority of Spanish residents, health needs were met by the hospitals of the cooperative societies and spiritual needs by Spanish priests; credit was arranged by Spanish discount houses; their children were educated in private schools, and perhaps their sexual needs were met by Spanish prostitutes. Those who married Cuban women—and the predominance of male over female immigrants suggests prima facie that many did so, although precise figures are lacking—assimilated more quickly to Cuban mores. Children of such marriages sometimes identified all the more fiercely with Cuban nationalist aspirations, as in the case of José Martí, son of a Valencian soldier and a Canary Island mother, or Fidel Castro, first-generation son of a self-made Galician sugar planter who had fought against the Cubans in the war of independence.

By no means all immigrants accepted paternalistic restrictions and controls. As Spanish businesses increased in size, tensions between owners and employees increased, and peninsular workers began to organize unions and form their own cooperative societies, such as the Asociación de Dependientes del Comercio de la Habana. "There are here labor unions so controlled by Spanish workers that only a few Cubans, and no Negroes, work in them," complained Carlos Baliño.[8] As in other Latin American countries, Spanish anarchists and other radicals had been among the first to organize labor movements. The Cuban government deported many of these men back to Spain. José Miguel Pérez, for example, first secretary-general of the newly-formed Communist party, was forcibly returned to the Mother Country in 1925. Franquista rebels subsequently shot Pérez early in the civil war, when he was a Communist official in the Canary Islands. Indicative of the prominence of immigrants as labor organizers was the legislation passed in 1933 that restricted positions as union officers to Cuban citizens.

Spaniards outnumbered Cubans as commercial salesmen, innkeepers (women included), factory clerks, charcoal burners, priests, and nuns. Agricultural workers and traders were the two largest immigrant occupational groups. Although many immigrants stayed in Havana or other Cuban cities, many Canary Islanders went to the countryside, where they came to form a large percentage of the *guajiros,* that is, white peasants. Some Spaniards invested in sugar plantations. In the mid-1930s, thirty-six mills producing 17 per cent of Cuba's sugar crop had Spanish owners, but this proportion declined in later years.[9]

Some professional associations had strict regulations confining membership to Cuban nationals. Hence Spaniards were excluded from those groups that tended to be most vociferous in their expressions of nationalist sentiment. Since the 1870s, Havana University had been the focus of Cuban nationalism, partly because it was the one institution dominated by creoles. In contrast, Spaniards dominated the Cuban Catholic church. The 1919 census showed 426 out of 667 priests and 128 out of 213 nuns to be Spaniards. This Spanish-dominated church, however, did little to help Franco's cause during the civil war, for the institution never struck deep roots in Cuban soil; its reputation had been tarnished by its pro-colonial posture during Cuba's independence struggle. In contrast, Masons, with their anticlerical ideas, played an important role in the rebellion.

There were other reasons as well that explained the weakness of the Cuban church in comparison with its opposite numbers in other Spanish American countries.[10] In contrast to Mexico, for example, Cuba's church had little influence in rural areas and little visible presence in the countryside. The building of churches in Mexico, which served as a means of spiritual domination as well as a way of incorporating a profoundly religious indigenous population into the new society by utilizing their skills, had no parallel in Cuba, where the early disappearance of native peoples left few to proselitize. The Cuban church, therefore, remained an urban institution, and one of the reasons for the general social neglect of rural areas can be partly attributed to this fact. Religious charity in rural areas was minimal, and the religious fiesta did not provide that particular feeling of cohesion that characterizes rural life in most other Spanish American countries. Nor did cults of local saints contribute to the strengthening of regional loyalties and provide a cultural basis for resistance to centralizing revolutionary policies, as they did in Mexico. Alternative religious traditions further weakened Catholic influence. Protestant sects, often linked to parent bodies in the United States, took root during the intervention period (1899–1901; 1906–9). Africanist cults survived slavery and flourished in independent Cuba, supported in turn by Machado, Batista, and Castro. Currents of

Masonic thought and rationalism, moreover, which derived from the liberation movement, mingled with the quasi-religious cult of José Martí, a secular "Apostle," regarded with ambivalence and distrust by orthodox Catholics.[11] Separation of church and state in the Constitution of 1901 further undermined church influence by depriving it of state funding. In the crucial area of religion, therefore, Cuba was unusual among Spanish American countries. Hence a religious issue with high emotional potential—such as that aroused by the Spanish civil war—did not have the resonance in Cuba that it possessed elsewhere in the region. Indeed, the more the Spanish-dominated church tried to use religion to rally support for Franco, the more distrustful Cubans became. Friends of the Republic consistently found sympathetic audiences for their anti-Catholic viewpoint, and Catholic Basques obviously were unconvinced by Francoist propaganda that the war was a religious crusade.

By 1936, the Spanish community in Cuba had lost its privileged position and faced a rising tide of nationalist sentiment. Cubans even rioted against Spaniards in 1933 and 1934. The visible, often ostentatious wealth, symbolized in the ornate premises of the *centros,* aroused envy, and the Spaniards' control of much of the retail trade, and their function as local moneylenders, built up anti-peninsular sentiment at a time of economic depression and political tension.

This anti-Spanish feeling, as well as the disturbed political scene, whose principal motif was urban terrorism, had started a reverse flow back to Spain as early as 1931 and 1932, when the number of Spaniards returning to the peninsula from Cuba began to exceed the numbers entering. One of the most attractive features of the Spanish *centros* had been their hospital insurance schemes for people of the moderate means.[12] But these schemes became a major source of friction with the Cuban medical profession. Cuban doctors who provided services in the well-equipped Spanish hospitals at reduced fees, for reasons of prestige and professional advancement, decided during the depression that many of their patients could afford to pay the ordinary rates. When the Spanish clubs refused to confine the insurance benefits to their poorer members, doctors called strikes throughout the island. Resentment against Spaniards, therefore, was shared by the Cuban professional class as well as by workers and the lower middle class. Push factors of declining opportunities in Cuba, rather than pull factors of better opportunities in Spain, explain this backflow, for Spain was plagued by unemployment throughout this period.

A turning-point in the history of the Spanish community, however, was Cuba's nationalization law of 1933, the most important nationalist legislation decreed by the revolutionary government of Ramón Grau San Martín. The law required at least 50 per cent of all employees in any enterprise to be Cuban,[13] and it resulted in a marked decline in the percentage of Spaniards in Cuba's population. The peninsular presence dropped from 15.7 percent in 1931 to 2.5 percent in 1943, and finally to 1.3 percent in 1953; and whereas Cuban citizens made up 78.5 percent of the population in 1931, they amounted to 95.7 percent in 1943. Whether this decline stemmed primarily from Spaniards leaving for the United States, for other Latin American countries, or for their native land is unclear. As extremely few returned to the peninsula during the civil war years, the most likely explanation would seem to be that they took out Cuban citizenship. In any case, after the promulgation of Cuba's 1940 Constitution, all children born on the island of Spanish parents were automatically Cuban citizens.

Inevitably, this legislation made inroads on Spanish exclusivity; Cubans increasingly joined Spanish clubs (although Blacks and Chinese were still excluded). Spanish firms could no longer be monopolized by Spaniards, and some employers had to discharge their own relatives to make way for Cubans. Citizenship gave little relief to Spaniards, since only naturalized Cubans with special technical qualifications were exempted from the nationalization law. Moreover, Cuban frustrations, caused by pent-up anti-imperialist feelings could now be vented against Spaniards, who were more accessible (and vulnerable) than Americans. Mobs ransacked many of their shops, sometimes in riots organized by unions, on other occasions spontaneously. Demonstrations demanded that 80 percent of all jobs be reserved for Cubans. The outbreak of the civil war therefore found the Spanish community on the defensive, and anxious about how Cubans would react both to it and to them.

To the Cuban left, and especially to the influential student and labor organizations, the Spanish Republic had provided inspiration for their own struggle against first Machado and then Batista. Cuban intellectuals, moreover, had come under the influence of Spain's own post-1898 cultural renaissance. Thus two of the most vocal, coherent groups in Cuba were predisposed to support the Republicans from the war's earliest days. But restrictions on free expression in 1936–37 meant that this remained difficult to manifest until the government itself took a pro-Republican stand in 1938.

Those Spaniards who backed the Nationalists could not look to any specific social group in Cuba for support. Félix Gordón Ordás, Spanish ambassador to both Cuba and Mexico, estimated that 80 percent of Cubans favored the Republicans, and "unlike in Mexico, the majority of Spaniards" did so as well.[14] Affluent Spaniards in Cuba, he commented, had indeed forgotten their humble origins and thus supported Franco. But most members of the Spanish community there remained loyal to the Republic. By way of contrast, those in Mexico, who had suffered from Revolutionary legislation and who regarded President Lázaro Cárdenas as a crypto-Communist were natural allies for the well-organized pro-Nationalist Spanish business community in Mexico City. Elsewhere in the region, countries such as Ecuador and Colombia possessed a powerful church that could produce support for the Spanish Insurgents with little prodding. In the majority of Latin American countries where the landowning oligarchy remained in control, the Spanish Nationalists, with their defense of property rights, found a natural reservoir of sympathy. Cuba, however, lacked a landowning oligarchy in the accepted sense. The creole plantocracy had been decimated during the war of independence and the sugar crisis of the 1880s, when many had sold out to American investors. Defense of property rights, therefore, could not provide an effective rallying cry in Cuba at the very time when nationalist sentiment there sought to reduce economic control exercised by foreign, predominantly American, corporations. The sugar-cane growers (*colonos*), rapidly emerging as one of the island's most powerful pressure groups, were themselves passionately concerned about securing their property rights at the expense of foreign sugar-mill owners.[15] Hence, Spanish rebels styling themselves "Nationalists" did not deceive Cuban nationalists; the two inhabited different ideological universes, and what inspiration Cuban nationalists derived from Spain came from Republican ideals and traditions.

Before considering the course of Cuban politics up to 1933–34, we must briefly examine the major consequences of the Spaniards' historic domination of Cuban society. Colonial administration and politics had been a Spanish monopoly on the island. In the nineteenth century, this monopoly (also extant in Puerto Rico) provided openings for those Spaniards whose prospects at home were restricted due to the country's lack of commercial and industrial development. The removal of Spaniards from the Cuban administration after independence made bureaucratic employment a coveted profession. Officeholders not only enjoyed the exercise of power itself but also fell heir to the material rewards of the island's lucrative spoils system. Opportunities that in the colonial period had been confined to a small creole elite were now open to a wider clientele.

In immediate postcolonial situations, politics and bureaucracy carry high prestige. It is a mimetic response to what the colonizers have done. In the Cuban case, an element of necessity also stimulated the drive for public employment. Had the Spaniards been expelled, they would have left openings in commerce as well as administration. As it developed, however, Spaniards—now excluded from politics and the bureaucracy—tightened their control of business. Cubans, lacking commercial expertise and contacts, and denied the all-important credit controlled by Spanish discount houses, had no choice but to turn to the bureaucracy. Even the technical needs of the growing sugar industry were largely met by foreigners.

In spite of the influences of pragmatic American educational practice, limited employment possibilities for the middle classes distorted Cuba's school system. This problem is most clearly reflected in higher education. Law and medicine were strengthened as elite academic disciplines.[16] Law was an obvious preparation for politics and for manipulating the graft system, as well as for the lucrative representation of U.S. business interests on the island. Not surprisingly, the per capita proportion of lawyers in Cuba reached 1:900, the highest in Latin America.

Subjects relating to the production of the country's wealth, such as sugar chemistry and agronomy, had few students. Thus, Cuba's sugar industry remained backward, and lack of technical expertise delayed diversification of the economy. The university overproduced unemployed and unemployable graduates, whose ambition was either to learn how to manipulate the graft system or to overthrow it altogether. Cuban history provides an exaggerated example of the common Latin American phenomenon of students arrogating to themselves the role of revolutionary vanguard—a role they played in the struggle that reached a climax in the Revolution of 1933.

The 1933 Revolution

No other country in Spanish America in the 1930s experienced a revolutionary movement of such proportions as the Cuban Revolution of 1933.[17] It was a turning-point in twentieth-century Cuban history, bringing to an end the first period of the republic and ushering in the years to be dominated by those who had overthrown Machado—the "Generation of 1930," who were to be the pace-makers of Cuban politics until the 1950s.

The Great Depression hit Cuba no harder than many other Latin American countries. But the coincidence of economic crisis, the tyranny of Gerardo Machado, the lack of a workable political system, and increasing domination of the economy by the United States combined to give Cuban revolutionary nationalism a febrility and persistence that has few parallels elsewhere.

Independence had only intensified Cuba's economic dependence on sugar exports. The quickening of U.S. investment and a readier market nearby underlined the benefits to be derived from comparative advantage. But these assets were offset by the fact that the United States bought 90 percent of the sugar crop with wide variations in quantity and price from year to year. As early as the 1880s, José Martí had warned with remarkable prescience of the dangers of economic penetration by the United States and of the illusion that political independence could be a reality unless accompanied by some degree of economic autonomy. Not until the mid-1920s, however, after the collapse of the sugar boom and a drastic drop in world market prices exposed the vulnerability of the existing economic structure, did Cuban intellectuals recognize the full relevance of his ideas. Nationalist writers then began to question the whole basis of the sugar economy. Neglect of other agricultural activities, the brake on industrialization, the undercutting of wages by massive importations of cheap Haitian and Jamaican labor, the corruption of public life, and the generalized absence of challenge in many areas of Cuban society were all attributed to the domination of sugar. Of all such consequences, Cubans felt the most pernicious to be the boom-slump psychology and a fatalistic gambling mentality that instilled a feeling of helplessness in the face of external economic forces.

The sugar mentality bred economic opportunism, shiftlessness, and a capriciousness that dogged Cuban politics. As Fernando Ortiz, the country's greatest anthropologist and scholar of Afro-Cubanism, wrote, sugar was "an oppressive, weakening force." It had "created two extremes. . . . the proletariat and the rich. There is no middle class in Havana, only masters and slaves."[18] Obviously, Cuba had never sloughed off its colonial legacy. Outside of the Spanish community no strong bourgeois tradition offset the *rentier* mentality of the *capas medias,* the Cuban middle classes. Some economic security might be found in real-estate investment in Havana or Miami, but government employment provided no assurances for the future, because each victorious politician rewarded his own supporters by giving them official posts at the expense of incumbents held over from the previous administration. Some writers have applied the scornful term "lumpenbourgeoisie" to describe these groups. They certainly lacked the homogeneity of an economically secured and psychologically confident bourgeois class, and their political activity consisted chiefly of feverish aimlessness.[19]

Until 1933, politics had been dominated by veterans of Cuba's independence struggle, generals who regarded political power as their legitimate patrimony and who grew rich from the spoils system. Both the Liberal and the Conservative parties were factions and personalist cliques. "Revolutions," such as those of 1905 or 1917, involved changes in government personnel rather than social change or political reform.[20] Successive regimes banned attempts to organize parties based on region, race, or class. For example, the Morúa Law of 1912 forbade Blacks from forming their own party, and in 1925 President Machado outlawed the formation of new parties shortly after assuming office. Machado, a war veteran whose experience as quartermaster was a useful apprenticeship for graft politics, soon reneged on his nationalist promises, and after he extended his term of office in 1928 his regime degenerated into a harsh dictatorship.

In a spoils system, *continuismo* rallies those denied opportunity to be enriched by the fruits of office. But Cuban opposition to Machado had deeper roots than self-interest. The nationalist revival, for example, had a moral commitment to the ideals expressed in the the writings and life of José Martí, and dated from the early 1920s. Nationalist writers and students led the crusade against the dictator. Writers formed the Grupo Minorista, regarding themselves as spokesmen of the people, in the "Protest of the Thirteen". This intellectual renaissance had a direct relationship to an exploration of social and economic problems, such as the position of Blacks in Cuban society and an analysis of the sugar industry. It also opened up Cuban intellectual life to European and other Latin American influences through the pages of the magazine *Avance* (1927–30).[21] More important, because of its institutional base, was the creation of the Federación de Estudiantes Universitarios (FEU) in 1923. Henceforth, students occupied the center stage of political life. They played a crucial role in the overthrow of Machado and of the Céspedes government that briefly replaced him, in elevating Grau San Martín to the presidency in 1933, in the political gangsterism of the 1940s, and in the resistance to Batista in the 1950s. Demand for and achievement of university autonomy in Cuba demonstrated the lasting influence of the University Reform movement, which had fanned out from Argentina after 1918. Although directed in the first instance toward academic renewal, the University Reform movement had radical social and political overtones. One manifestation was the new "popular university" to provide night school education for workers. In such schools, students first established contact with the proletariat.

Early links between Communists and students made the Cuban case somewhat unusual.[22] Julio Antonio Mella—handsome, athletic, and a vibrant orator—had been a university student when he helped to found the Cuban Communist party. Mella and poet Rubén Martínez Villena, a signatory of the Protest of the Thirteen, joined other intellectuals in the party from the very beginning. Cuban students and intellectuals seem to have been influenced by Marxism even more than is normally the case in Latin America; as a result, there has always been a penumbral area around the party, made up of intellectuals sympathetic to but not members of it.

The student movement lost some of its direction when Machado exiled Mella in 1925. But with the foundation of the Directorio Estudiantil in 1927 and its radical wing, the Ala Izquierda, in 1930, students again became a focus of opposition to the dicator. Another was the ABC, a terrorist organization created by intellectuals and professional men in 1931, after all attempts at legitimate opposition had been sealed off. A third focus was the growing labor movement. The Confederación Nacional de Obreros Cubanos (CNOC), in spite of internal divisions between anarchists and Communists, gathered sufficient strength by 1933 to organize a general strike.

This strike, in conjuction with the ABC's terrorist campaign, opposition from the Directorio and the Ala, decline in U.S. support for Machado, and internal divisions within the army, led to the dictator's fall in August 1933 and ushered in five months of confusion and revolutionary promise. After several ineffectual weeks in office, Carlos Manuel de Céspedes, backed by the conservatives, the ABC, and the American ambassador, was replaced by Dr. Ramón Grau San Martín, a physician-professor brought to power through student agitation and a military coup led by Sergeant Fulgencio Batista. Grau lasted slightly less than five months, and was himself replaced by Batista, now a colonel, in January 1934. Within eight days the new government received the diplomatic recognition from President Franklin D. Roosevelt withheld from Grau. For the next ten years, Batista dominated Cuba. He exercised power first through a series of puppet presidents and then, after 1940, as constitutionally-elected president in his own right.

From January 1934, conditions in Cuba were not propitious for overt political activity. Grau went into exile, and later founded the Partido Revolucionario Cubano (PRC—often referred to as the "Auténticos"), symbolically linked through its title with Martí's party of the same name. Antonio Guiteras, Grau's able young radical minister of labor, remained behind to organize the paramilitary "Joven Cuba," evidently believing that Batista could be ousted by armed action.[23] If Guiteras still retained his socialistic beliefs it is questionable if his followers shared them. Communists distrusted the *guiteristas* for their addiction to violence, sensing in it the same fascistic propensities they had condemned earlier in the ABC.

Divisions among Batista's opponents led to the failure of the last and greatest of the general strikes in March 1935, organized by the PRC, the students, Joven Cuba, and the unions. In the repression following the strike's failure, Guiteras was killed while trying to escape into exile. His followers subsequently joined the PRC or scattered until the outbreak of the Spanish civil war gave them an alternative field for heroism.

In spite of mass participation in politics in 1933, a completely new phenomenon in Cuba, the collapse of Grau's government underlined its lack of a firm power base. The various revolutionary groups represented little more than their own frustrations and vague dreams of a free society. This did not prevent Grau from decreeing a remarkable amount of social legislation, but he lacked the means to defend his government against resolute opposition. The sectarianism of the Cuban Communists, who regarded Grau as a "social fascist" and consistently opposed him, might have been justifiable had they an alternative policy themselves, but they had not. Of the various revolutionary groups, the ABC had been deeply divided—a fact that the nature of their clandestine organization before Machado's fall made inevitable—and had been prepared to come to terms with moderate forces. The students had enthusiasm, idealism, and energy, but they lacked direction and experience. Although the Ala Izquierda saw the need for contacts with the labor unions, the humdrum nature of this sort of political work did not interest most students. In this, Antonio Guiteras was an exception. He had recognized the need for the government to base itself on the organized working class, but his approaches to the Communists were rejected. Grau had to work without U.S. recognition and under the threat of U.S. intervention (with warships offshore), all of which contributed to a growing sense of helplessness.

Legacies of the 1933–35 period exercised a lasting influence on subsequent Cuban history. In the short term, they forced government critics into exile or into cynical, passive acceptance of Batista's pragmatic populism. What idealism remained was channeled into support for the Spanish Republic. Thus the surprisingly enthusiastic Cuban response to Spain's civil war may partially be explained by the absence of other feasible causes nearer home. In the longer term, this vacuum led to a reorganization and reorientation of opposition forces. Cuban Communists recognized the failure of their previous ultra-left line and replaced it by offers of Popular-Front-style cooperation with other opposition groups. Grau, however, repudiated these approaches. He preferred to cooperate with such other political parties as the Apristas (local branch of Peruvian Víctor Raúl Haya de la Torre's Alianza Popular Revolucionaria Americana) and Joven Cuba in the enlarged and reorganized PRC.[24] New policies and better organization, however, did not eliminate the fundamental weakness of the opposition. Cuba's tradition of action politics died down under Batista's cossetting in the late 1930s, but burst out again in the 1940s, but then as a degenerate form of gangsterism with little or no trace of the pre-1933 idealism.

Too much stress, though, should not be laid on the negative aspects of 1933. A remarkable amount of legislation had been passed during Grau's short-lived government. The Platt Amendment had been abrogated and the basis laid for Cuba's economic recovery, but perhaps the most significant and arguably the most popular achievement of Grau's government, and the high point of his nationalism, was the 50 percent law, which, as has been suggested, was directed primarily against the Spanish community, which was a more visible and present threat to the majority of Cubans than the United States, the particular obsession of middle-class intellectuals. From the Spaniards' point of view, the 50 percent law posed the decision of whether or not to become Cubans. The outbreak of the Spanish civil war hastened the process whereby they began to identify with the nation in which they no longer enjoyed privileged status.

The Communists and Batista

As for the Communists, Cuba's 1933 Revolution underlined their isolation from the masses and from the revolutionary nationalists. Their failure to exert any influence on events stemmed from adherence to the Comintern's ultra-left Third Period line (1927–34). Communists had to argue that Cuba's revolution would be made by the organized working class and that all other classes and parties, however revolutionary in word, were "social Fascists", reformists at heart whose purpose was to preserve bourgeois rule.[25] Cooperation with these forces, they said, would only obscure the aims and weaken the resolve of true revolutionaries. Thus Communists refused to join the general strike against Machado, and opposed Grau throughout his brief term of office. They based this policy on the view, not without foundation, that middle-class nationalists had such close ties with U.S. interests that they could not possibly lead a national-bourgeois revolution.

Particularly revealing was Communist opposition to nationalistic legislation designed to restrict immigrant labor from Haiti and Jamaica and to the 50 percent decree. They condemned both as examples of "demagogic" nationalism. In the former case, they believed that curbs on migrant labor would reduce the number of potentially revolutionary workers. In reality, however, deep cultural differences between Cuban laborers on one hand and Haitian and Jamaican workers on the other, as well as the transitory nature of migrant employment, were major reasons for rural labor's lack of organization and unity. Similarly, Communists opposed the 50 percent decree, theoretically in the interests of proletarian solidarity, but they did not fully appreciate how many Spanish workers in Cuba possessed the petit-bourgeois mentality they so vehemently despised.

This self-isolating attitude left two legacies that influenced subsequent Cuban politics. Worker distrust had to be overcome by intensive proselitization (and it says much for the Communists' dedication that they were able subsequently to win back a great deal of lost ground in this area); more significantly, it led to undying hatred of the party by Grau and other nationalists, who rejected all subsequent Communist appeals for a Popular Front against Batista.

One immediate consequence of Communist weakness and divisions on the left had been the crushing of the general strike in March 1935. The change in Comintern strategy came too late for Cuba's Communists to readjust to changed circumstances, and they refused to join the committee of proletarian defense, on which were represented the PRC, Joven Cuba, Trotskyists, the Apristas, and the ABC, which originally launched the strike.[26] The widespread response to the strike call was due to the efforts of students and unionists acting independently of the Communists.

After the strike's failure, Batista began to normalize the situation, and his position in early 1936, on the eve of Spain's civil war, seemed strong. He had divided, intimidated, or scattered his opponents. Grau languished in exile; Guiteras was dead; the Communists remained isolated. An economic upturn that came as a result of the U.S. Reciprocity Act of 1934, which benefited the sugar industry, gave the colonel a modest measure of popularity. Employment prospects improved as Cubanization opened up jobs previously held by Spaniards and as restrictions reduced Haitian and Jamaican competition. Abrogation of the Platt Amendment (1934) removed a long-standing nationalist grievance; women were enfranchised. Batista claimed to be continuing the 1933 Revolution and applying Martí's precepts. His *septembrismo* involved a wide-ranging social and economic program by which the military performed social and economic functions, such as was to occur later in the "Nasserist" movements of the 1960s in some other Latin American countries.[27]

Presidential elections in May 1936 were intended to signal a return to normality, although only the pre-1933 parties participated.[28] At this time, Batista had no presidential ambitions himself, and intended to rule through civilian figureheads. The first of these, Miguel Gómez, proved too independent for Batista. Gómez wanted a general political amnesty, the reopening of the university, and a constituent assembly. In addition he rewarded his own supporters with jobs at the expense of Batista's appointees, many of whom were fired. Military men even began to worry that their privileges and pay would be cut back. The prospect of a civilian backlash underlined the need for Batista to widen the base of his support. This was to be achieved later by a comprehensive social program embodied in an ambitious Three Year Plan. A network of councils, partly staffed by soldiers, was set up to administer social services and support private and public welfare agencies. The linch pin of this social policy was the rural school project, together with an agricultural education program designed to rehabilitate the hitherto neglected rural population. Expansion of the military into education, traditionally a field for middle-class employment, underlined the far-reaching ambitions of the new military establishment, and provoked a civil-military crisis that rose to a climax in December 1936 when Gómez vetoed legislation proposed by Batista to finance construction of rural schools by a tax of nine cents on each bag of sugar. Intimidated by military-sponsored demonstrations, lacking an independent power base, and with Washington strictly neutral, refusing to intervene ("morally or otherwise"), Gómez had no choice but to resign after he was impeached by the Senate.

To the Communists, Gómez's impeachment seemed to be another step toward a Fascist-military dictatorship, and they drew parallels between it and the military rising in Spain. In April 1937 they argued that members of the congressional "democratic bloc" who voted not to accept Gómez's resignation should be cultivated as allies in the struggle against Batista. The Communists had moved to this position only gradually. At the Second Congress of the party in 1934, they had maintained that "of all the groups and parties in Cuba, the most dangerous for the revolution are the parties of the 'Left,' particularly the Cuban Revolutionary party of Grau."[29] In October, 1935, a Cuban delegate at the Seventh Comintern Congress admitted that the "neutral position taken by the party with regard to the struggle between the Grau government and the reactionary ABC party . . . objectively facilitated the coming to power of the present reactionary government."[30] Following the Popular Front victory in Spain in February 1936, the party admitted publicly for the first time that its attitude toward Grau had been mistaken and that now "a government of national unity must be created that would represent the interests of the working class, the peasantry, and the petit bourgeoisie and that would defend national producers."[31]

The party expected to ally with Grau and Joven Cuba, but these two organizations had already signed a pact in exile early in 1936.[32] Grau had been adamant in excluding the Communists. Joven Cuba did not wish to exclude any anti-Batista group, yet it continued to favor an armed uprising and, with this in view, established a revolutionary committee. The Communists, for their part, considered an armed rising inadvisable and premature without careful preparation, and therefore drew up a comprehensive program designed to draw together all anti-imperialist forces. Whatever hopes the Communists may have had of rallying mass opinion on the basis of an all-embracing program vanished, however, as Batista's social legislation began to cut the ground from under their feet. In July 1937 he announced an ambitious Three Year Plan promising extensive social and economic reforms, including closer state control of the sugar and tobacco industries, insurance and health schemes for workers, and a new taxation system. However demagogic this might have appeared to some, immediate tangible benefits resulted from his Law of Sugar Coordination (September 1937), the high point of Batista's nationalism.[33] This law comprehended virtually all social and economic aspects of the sugar industry, regulating relations between employers and labor, between mills and planters, and between the agricultural and industrial sides of the sugar industry. By giving the *colonos* security of tenure, it transformed the landowning pattern and, together with a law at the end of the year distributing state lands, widened Batista's support. When, therefore, Batista proposed to legalize the Partido Unión Revolucionaria, a front party under the Marxist intellectual Juan Marinello, Cuban Communists agreed, and thus ended their political isolation.

Batista's motives for his policy change are obscure. From 1936 on, he apparently wished to become president in free elections but felt that his chances of doing so were thin. He had alienated older politicians by ousting Gómez; he was distrusted and despised as an upstart by large landowners, and even those of them who had welcomed his coup as a guarantee of order, and who saw him as a defender of property rights, were alarmed by his social and economic reforms. Most seriously, the revolutionary nationalists, the intellectuals and professional groups, the "doctores", continued to be his implacable foes. When, therefore, the Communists made approaches, they found a receptive audience, for Batista saw an opportunity to widen the base of his support in an area where he feared Grau would find a following.[34]

Full legalization of the Communist party came by stages. Batista authorized a general political amnesty in late 1938, and on May 1, 1938, he permitted the Communists to start publishing *Noticias de Hoy* (later *Hoy*), a daily newspaper that served as party organ into the 1960s.

Finally, in September 1938, the party won complete legalization and merged with the PUR to form the Partido Unión Revolucionaria Comunista (PURC), after a closed meeting between Blas Roca and Joaquín Ordoquí and Batista. It would seem that for this—that is, in return for legalization of the party, a free hand to organize a new union structure, and the promise of a constituent assembly—the Communists agreed to support Batista's presidency. Cuban Communists explained their new-found admiration for the regime by arguing that Batista had been forced into democratic paths by popular pressures under their influence. Now no longer dubbed the "Cuban Franco" and "a focal point of reaction," Batista became "the defender of democracy," in the words of the party's Tenth Plenum. Party leader Blas Roca put it even more disarmingly: "When Batista found the road to democracy, the party helped him."[35]

Although Communist support for Batista "caused indescribable confusion, and contributed to the intensification of the crisis in which the revolutionary movement found itself," the benefits to the party were enormous: respectability and acceptance, an expanded membership from 5,000 in 1937 to 23,000 in 1939 to 122,000 in 1944, an influential daily paper and later a radio station, domination of Cuba's labor movement, and influence in drawing up the Constitution of 1940, the most advanced of its day in Latin America. Finally, two party members, Juan Marinello and Carlos Rafael Rodríguez, joined Batista's cabinet in 1942, becoming the first Communist ministers in any Latin American government.[36] Although the party suffered setbacks later when they lost presidential protection on Grau's return to power in 1944, they still retained an influential position in Cuban politics, with trained and experienced cadres who were to be invaluable after Castro had come to power. The basis for this was laid in the years between 1937 and 1944.

If the Communists had gained, so had Batista, whose power grew as his social reforms began to rally support. Communist influence helped him to the presidency in 1940 and was apparent in the Constitution of that year. Communist domination of the newly-formed Confederación de Trabajadores Cubanos (CTC) ensured that Grau's Auténticos would not be able to mobilize the unions against Batista.

When Batista's term as president ended in 1944, Blas Roca wrote to remind him how the party had been "the most energetic promoter of your inspiring platform of democracy, social justice, and defense of national prosperity," and reaffirmed that Batista had "our affection and our respect and esteem for your principles as a democratic and progressive leader."[37]

Without a favorable international conjuncture, such a rapprochement would have been impossible. Change in Comintern strategy by itself would have been insufficient. Originally, the Communists' switch to a Popular Front strategy was directed against Batista and his American backers. The change from this to an understanding with Batista came as a consequence of Grau's refusal to compromise with either them or the former sergeant. Understanding between Batista and the Communists was therefore a marriage of convenience. Another indication of the changing international signs of the times was the sudden tempering of Cuban Communist attacks on the United States. American party chief Earl Browder, appointed by the Comintern to oversee the new Popular Front strategy in Latin America, promised financial help when Blas Roca visited him in the fall of 1938. When Batista returned from official visits to Washington and to Mexico in 1938–39, the Communists welcomed him back home effusively.

President Roosevelt's cautious Spanish policy, expressed in the neutrality legislation and in compliance with non-intervention (which did not prevent American trucks and oil from reaching the Nationalists), was not criticized by the Cuban party. Washington's refusal to intervene "even morally" to support Gómez at the end of 1936 indicated that Batista's radicalism was not regarded as a serious threat. Roosevelt saw no reason to jeopardize the Good Neighbor Policy in order to bail out Gómez and his ex-*machadista* supporters, and if the Sugar Coordination Act might be seen as a potential threat to American interests, reciprocity was some compensation for American exporters. With the oil controversy looming in Mexico, Washington did not wish to have Cuban complications on its hands as well. Since a tamed Communist party cooperated with an ostensibly democratic Batista in maintaining internal peace in Cuba, Washington could afford to ignore Batista's rhetorical expression of solidarity with Mexico in its struggle with the United States over the nationalization of oil.[38]

By the time the Spanish civil war ended, Batista had become respectable: he had justified American trust, and he was eulogized by Lázaro Cárdenas, his fellow corporatist president of Mexico.[39] He had dispelled all suspicion of pro-Fascist proclivities by overt support of the Spanish Republicans. In Mexico, however, support for the Republic was an indication of pro-Cárdenas sympathies, whereas in Cuba the civil war was not a touchstone for domestic political alignments. Batista's conversion to the Republican cause may have been as opportunistic as the Communists' recognition that Batista was a democrat. But mutual cooperation in a cause with which the majority of Cubans sympathized did much to legitimate the otherwise unlikely union of two incompatible bedfellows.

Official Attitudes toward the Spanish War

Although prima facie a military-dominated government might have been expected to sympathize with the Nationalists in Spain, certain factors restrained Batista from the very beginning. After 1933, when sergeants became colonels through a peculiar barracks revolt of their own, the Cuban army could no longer be regarded as a conservative force, and so, of course, did not immediately identify with a reactionary military rebellion. Furthermore, questing for a legitimate basis for his own power, Batista could ill afford to sanction revolt against a legally-constituted government in Spain. In addition, Republican propaganda constantly stressed the military help given to the Nationalists by Italy and Germany while downplaying similar Soviet aid to the Loyalists. This put the Cuban strongman under additional pressure. A struggle between a legitimate government and foreign intervention roused strong emotional echoes among Cuban nationalists, a group with which Batista anxiously sought identification. Batista's desire for popularity and his ambition to become a constitutional president made him responsive to public opinion once he had overcome the initial challenge to his position.

When the civil war broke out, Cuba's official attitude was neutral, but with a tilt that seemed to favor the Spanish rebels. Outspoken commitment to the Republican cause would have exposed Batista to attacks from a small but influential business community that sympathized with the Nationalists. Batista thus obstructed recruitment of volunteers for Spain as well as fund-raising for the Republic. The same repressive apparatus that limited union and student activity after 1935 likewise stifled expressions of sympathy for the beleaguered Loyalists. Relations between Cuba and the Republic became so strained that in January 1937 the Spanish ambassador was withdrawn, and Republican interests were looked after by the consul-general until a change occurred in Cuban policy in mid-1938, when Félix Gordón Ordás, ambassador in Mexico, was appointed also to Havana.[40]

The breach arose from the action of the Cuban government in November 1936 when it impounded the *Manuel Arnús,* a Republican ship sailing from Alicante to Veracruz to load Mexican arms.[41] The ship had been militarized, but when it put into Havana all the officers, with the exception of the captain, refused to obey orders, and deserted after causing damage to the vessel that temporarily disabled it. Pressured by pro-Nationalist Spaniards, the Cuban authorities blocked every attempt on the part of the Spanish Embassy to arrange for its departure. Police harrassed embassy officials when they tried to interview the captain, refused to grant papers for relief officers to be sent from Bermuda, threatened to embargo the ship for non-payment of debts, and refused a Mexican offer for their naval officers to take the ship on to Veracruz. The Mexican chargé in Havana attributed Cuban intransigence to a sense of inferiority about their sovereignty,[42] but it seems more likely that it expressed the caution of a government that was not yet sufficiently established to take a positive stance at a time when the civil-military conflict between Gómez as titular president and Batista was coming to a climax. As the Spanish ambassador reported in November 1936, his efforts to release the ship had come to naught because he had failed to overcome the "rightist conspiracy supported by the Secretary of Defense against which the very weak civil power has no influence."

Meanwhile, in Mexico City, Ambassador Górdon, frustrated by the lack of communication with Havana and the Ministry of State in Valencia, attempted to resolve the dispute by sending a member of his staff to Havana in the company of Cuban Minister of Education Juan Remos, whom he had met when the latter was on an official visit to Mexico City.[43] Remos, soon to become foreign minister, was staunchly pro-Republican, and Gordón acted without authorization from Spain in order to take advantage of the minister's sympathies.

By mid-March 1938, final arrangements had been made through the good offices of the Mexican chargé in Havana, who was not only —in Gordón's opinion—one of the "most enthusiastic friends of the Republic" but also a friend of Batista. Remos, now foreign minister, expedited matters, and on March 27 the *Manuel Arnús* sailed from Havana under the command of Mexican naval officers. But, in the end, all there was left to show for the affair was a bill for $74,285 and a useless hulk, for the ship was in such bad repair on its arrival in Veracruz that it could not sail back to Spain and could not be adequately repaired without going on to Galveston. At least Gordón could console himself that his initiative had succeeded; as he ruefully commented, "As an industrial enterprise [it was] a disaster, but as a revindication in law, magnificent." In this, as in so many other things, Republicans in exile after the war could find consolation that in justice, at least, they were the victors.

The *Manuel Arnús* "odyssey," as Gordón described it, well illustrates the problem of Cuban-Spanish relations in this period by showing the anti-Republican animus of Batista's regime in 1936–37. The Cuban boss hesitated to alienate influential pro-Nationalist Spaniards until his power had been consolidated. It also underscores the difficulties of Republican diplomacy, its frustrating search for arms and the means of conveying them, and the lack of contact between the Ministry of State and ambassadors abroad. Gordón constantly complained that his official telegrams received no answer.

The resolution of the *Arnús* affair indicated that Cuban policy had changed, and prepared the way for the resumption of ambassadorial representation and for an improvement in Cuban-Spanish relations. In July 1938, Gordón Ordás arrived in Havana to temporarily take up his duties as ambassador. Describing himself as "a Republican pure and simple, neither Socialist nor Communist," he typified in many respects the Republican intelligentsia, with his professional training, his legalistic and rhetorical qualities, his keen sense of personal honor, and his consciousness of historical mission. He was, however, unusual in the range of his practical experience and his scientific background.[44] He was a technocrat who by the time of his arrival in Havana in mid-1938 had to deploy all the skills of a literary orator to plead a lost cause. Born in 1885, he considered himself a member of the "Generation of 1905," those men associated with the Junta para Ampliación de Estudios, a body created to improve the quality of Spanish science by endowing scholarships for study at home and abroad. He began his career as a veterinary surgeon, taught, edited scientific journals, served as an inspector of hygiene, and in 1931 became director-general of mines. Elected a deputy to all three Republican Cortes, he was a founder-member and vice-president of the Unión Republicana. As minister of industry and commerce in 1933 he negotiated a commercial treaty with France. This varied experience, as well as previous visits to South America and Mexico, was sound preparation for his appointment as ambassador to Mexico and Cuba, although some of the Spanish community in Havana resented having their interests represented by a political appointee rather than by a professional diplomat. Nevertheless, his rhetorical skills, his forcefulness, his unshakeable Republican conviction, and his wide culture did much to improve the image of the Republic in both Cuba and Mexico. He was, as the Havana daily *El País* described him, "*simpático,* hearty, amiable, communicative."[45] He was certainly "amigo de las palabras," liking nothing so much as the opportunity to address a public meeting. On his earlier visit to South America he had given forty-two speeches in under three months, and those he gave in Cuba rarely lasted less than an hour.

On his way to take up his Mexican appointment, Gordón had called in at Havana for fifteen days to represent Spain at the inauguration of Miguel Gómez in May, 1936. Depressed by the "complete disorientation" of the Spanish community in Cuba as regards Azaña's Popular Front government, Gordón seized every opportunity to correct what he considered to be the misinformation and false image of events in Spain conveyed by such papers as the influential *Diario de la Marina,* "one of the most pernicious organs of reactionary publicity in Spanish America."[46] He addressed four regional *centros* and then spoke to several Spanish political clubs. Spaniards on the island were in a political limbo, unable to vote either in Spain or Cuba, so these political clubs, reflecting peninsular alignments, constituted a surrogate form of political expression. Although in his enthusiasm he overstepped the bounds of diplomatic prudence and became involved in a polemic with the Cuban press, he impressed his audiences sufficiently to elicit an official request from the Casino Español that he should stay on in Havana permanently. The most positive achievement of this first short visit, however, was the revival of the defunct Instituto Hispano-Cubano under the presidency of Fernando Ortiz. This became the most important center of nonsectarian, pro-Republican activity run by Cubans.

When Ambassador Gordón returned in July 1938, therefore, he was already well known to a number of leading Spaniards and influential Cubans, including Foreign Minister Juan Remos. It was immediately apparent that the official mood had changed. He was surprised, as was the Havana press, at the size and warmth of the public ovation when he presented his credentials.[47] Similarly, the official speech of welcome by President Col. Federico Laredo Bru, who, in describing himself as a "veteran of the wars of independence," indicated that all rancor was forgotten. This address, the Spanish ambassador reported home, "was more than stiff, customary protocol." Gordón had in fact arrived as the understanding between Batista and the Communists had begun to unfreeze official attitudes toward the Spanish Republic. Such a situation enabled Republican sympathizers to work more openly, and allowed Communists to benefit from their domination of front organizations as well as to use *Hoy* as a vehicle for pro-Republican propaganda. The party's Tenth Plenum in June was the first evidence of their new pro-Batista line, and in early August Blas Roca and Joaquín Ordoquí had the secret interview referred to above, which led to the full legalization of the party in September.

Batista was thus open to suggestion when Gordón had a number of meetings with him in August in order to brief him on the Spanish situation.[48] He found Batista attentive and apparently disposed to be impartial: "If it would be unjust to say that he inclined to favor the Francoist cause, neither could it be truly said that he sympathized with the Republican government." In his view, Batista was more sinned against than sinning. In a letter reassuring Angel Ossorio y Gallardo, the Spanish ambassador in Buenos Aires, that his friendship with Batista was not misplaced, he argued that the colonel was more a stenographer than a military man, a liberal and a democrat who had been forced to become a dictator by the inexperience of the left when they deserted him after September 1933, leaving him open to advances from the right.[49]

On August 11, 1938, Gordón could report that the recent ministerial reshuffle favored the Republican cause, as there were now four ministers on the left, three center-left, one right-wing liberal, two Fascist-inclined, and one uncertain. At the same time, Foreign Minister Juan Remos and the new Cuban ambassador to Spain were both ardently pro-Republican. For his part, Batista first publicly expressed his support for the Republic in a speech on September 5 commemorating the Sergeants' Coup of 1933.[50]

Although this official sympathy made the work of Republican aid societies easier—an immediate financial repercussion was exemption from the 5 percent export tax on sugar and tobacco sent to Spain—it was too late to be of much use. By fall 1938 Republican armies were on the defensive, exhausted after the last desperate fling on the Ebro in August, and in November the International Brigades were withdrawn. The Russians' concern about Munich and the German threat, as well as the Japanese in the Far East, had reduced their interest in and aid to the Republic. The importance of the new policy, therefore, lay mainly in one of its domestic political consequences: it helped to forge the understanding between Batista and the Communist party, which at last began to be integrated into Cuba's political system.

Popular Pro-Republican Sentiment in Cuba

Although exiles might identify with the idealistic aims of the Republicans, for the majority of Spaniards in Cuba the outbreak of war posed more practical questions, such as the rupture of transatlantic sailings from northern Spanish ports as ships were commandeered for war service. Whereas 3,882 Spaniards returned to Spain in 1936, the number dropped to 8 in 1937. Shut off from possible return, and penalized by the nationalization legislation, the Spanish community had to face up to the prospect of integrating into Cuban life. Since the enactment of this legislation, Spaniards had been on the defensive, and although there were deep divisions among them, reflected in conflicts in the *centros,* there was a reluctance to expose these differences to public scrutiny.

Resident Spaniards expressed diverse views on the civil war in their own newspapers, but the Havana press, except for the oldest and most respected capital daily, the *Diario de la Marina,* and several other papers, was pro-Republican. Founded in 1938, the *Diario* had always represented conservative Spanish business interests. Financed by a Spanish advertising clientele, and ably edited by the formidable José ("Pepín") Rivero, an admirer of Franco, the *Diario* regularly attacked Ambassador Gordón, accusing him of accepting commissions on the purchase of arms and drawing him into a polemic with a Jesuit that earned him a rebuke from Spanish Minister of State Julio Álvarez del Vayo and a warning not to be provoked into public controversy.[51] *El Debate, Alerta,* and *El País* also took pro-Nationalist editorial positions, but the bombing of the latter's offices in September 1936, causing more than thirty casualties, was a grim warning whither the dangers of uncritical support for the Nationalist cause could lead. The Falange had a following of its own, and published a monthly, *Arriba,* throughout the war, and on the news of Franco's victory it could turn out twelve thousand supporters to listen to Rivero.[52]

Most other dailies, such as *El Pueblo,* the leftist paper with the widest circulation, *El Mundo, Prensa, Heraldo de Cuba,* and *Crisol,* were pro-Republican. A publishing house, Editorial Facetas, brought out a monthly review on Spanish issues, and also published a series of books on aspects of the war. The Spanish government distributed its own bulletin, *El Servicio Español de Información. Bohemia,* the leading weekly, which had a radical tradition, was also pro-Republican. From May 1938, the most outspoken pro-Republican daily was *Hoy.* But as early as June 1936, the Communists already had a mouthpiece in their monthly *Mediodía,* which within a week of the outbreak of the war had published a manifesto of solidarity with the Republic. Copies of *El Mono Azul,* the organ of the Alianza de Intelectuales Antifascistas, published in Madrid during the siege, were circulated among Cuban intellectuals.[53]

The *centros* were too divided to express unqualified views except for the Basque and Catalan centers, where support for the Republic was based on the latter's recognition of their claims for autonomy. The Casino Español supported the rebels, but this was a special case. Founded as early as 1869, when it had become the headquarters of the notorious *voluntarios* (bully-boys who beat up known advocates of Cuban independence), it had declined to being an exclusive social club for the wealthier Spaniards. In the two largest *centros,* the Asturiano and the Gallego, opinions were bitterly divided. In the Centro Gallego, the Hermandad Gallega under the leadership of Álvarez Gallego, a regular contributor to *Hoy,* challenged the executive committee by establishing a pro-Republican radio station, "Hora Loitia."[54]

Wider in appeal were front organizations, integrating both Spaniards and Cubans, that sprang up all over the island. The Frente Democrático Español took the lead in orchestrating demonstrations, organizing meetings, sponsoring declarations, and briefing the Spanish ambassador on his arrival. It drew together many disparate groups that had been set up on sectional lines—the Centro Republicano, the Ateneo Socialista, the Izquierda Republicana, the Círculo Republicano Español, the Unión Democrática de Hijos de Galicia, to name only a few. In addition, there was the Alianza Latinoamericana, patronized by those Latin Americans in Cuba who wished to express their solidarity with the Republic, as well as the main Cuban cultural association, the Casa Hispano-Cubana de Cultura, "for strengthening the democratic struggle in general, and for supporting in particular the glorious cause of Spanish legitimacy," presided over by Fernando Ortiz. The Casa had branches throughout the country, with over ten thousand fees-paying members, and published its own journal, *Nosotros*.[55]

The Cuban movement for solidarity with the Republic did not get under way properly until early 1937, by which time it had become clear that the war would be a long one and that the Republicans would not receive the aid they might legitimately expect from the Western democracies. Pro-Republican Cubans set up committees to raise money, clothes, tobacco, and food. After the death in Spain of her husband, volunteer Pablo Torriente, his widow Teresa Casuso returned to Cuba and founded the Asociación de Auxilio al Niño Español, for which she claimed a membership of 300,000. It maintained a childrens' shelter at Sitges throughout the war.[56] In 1938, the Comité Nacional de Ayuda a España coordinated aid efforts and pressured the Cuban government quite effectively. Thanks to its efforts, sugar and tobacco exports to the Republican zone left Cuba exempt from duty. In addition to private gifts channeled through the Comité, the Cuban government itself sent consignments of cigarettes, tobacco, sugar, and tinned milk. Pressed by Ambassador Gordón, Batista even used his personal influence to persuade the conservative Asociación de Hacendados, whose president was allegedly a "Fascist sympathizer," to cooperate in releasing sugar for this purpose.[57]

Whenever he could, Gordón addressed public meetings in both Havana and the provinces. On one level, his speeches simply refuted anti-Republican propaganda by arguing the justice of the Loyalist cause, the legitimacy of the Republic, the violation of international law by the intervention of the Axis powers, and the denial of the Republic's basic right to buy arms in self-defense from whomever it wished. On another level, however, they elaborated what might be called a "White

Legend," that is, a version of Spanish history that stressed, among other things, Spain's civilizing mission in the New World. This new interpretation ran counter to the Black Legend of Portestant propaganda, but in the present context, and even more relevantly, it challenged the Nationalists' version of the past (Hispanidad). Gordón scarcely needed prompting by Álvarez del Vayo to use the speechifying on October 12, the *Día de la Raza,* for propaganda purposes. Addressing an audience estimated at fifteen thousand, crowded into the cathedral square, he and Chacón y Calvo, a colonial historian, gave academic speeches assessing Spain's civilizing mission in positive terms.[58]

According to the White Legend, Spain's greatness stemmed from variety, not uniformity, and was rooted in a federal, decentralizing tradition as expressed in revolts against Hapsburg and Bourbon centralization and in resistance to Napoleon. Nineteenth-century political disturbances and Spain's imperial domination of Cuba could then be attributed to the attempt to force regions and colonies into the artificial mould of a foreign-inspired liberal state. In this view, Spain was a union of regions, and the right-wing accusation that the Republic fomented separatism was a canard. By granting autonomy to regions, the Republic was replacing an artificial uniformity with a natural unity. This interpretation of Spanish history finds its most cogent expression in the writings of "that lay saint" Francisco Pi y Margall, the most influential ideologue of nineteenth-century republicanism, and the one Spaniard of that period whose memory was revered in Cuba because of his courageous and uncompromising hostility to the Hispano-Cuban war of 1868–78 and his support for Cuban rights in the 1890s.[59]

In the White Legend, *señoritismo* (rule by a foppish upper class), bureaucratism, militarism, and a militant and intolerant church were products of alien centralist ideas introduced into Spain by the Austrian Hapsburgs and the French Bourbons. Similarly, fascism was a foreign importation, alien to the basic democratic ideals that operated as defining components of Spanish society and that had found their supreme literary expression in Lope de Vega's play *Fuenteovejuna,* in which the hero is the collective *pueblo.*[60]

The real Spain—that of the *pueblo*—had been hidden from view in Spanish America, where the conquest had been mistakenly seen as a Spanish undertaking, rather than one inspired by Austrian and French example. Las Casas, not Charles V or Philip II, was the true representative of Spain's civilizing mission. From this it followed, apparently, that the Republic of 1931 was an attempt to return to the true Spain of the *pueblo* and to revert to the traditions of freedom and tolerance that predated the modern, centralizing, authoritarian state. From the Spain

of the *pueblo,* Spanish America had nothing to fear. The White Legend
is as much fantasy as its black counterpart, but it served its purpose in
reconciling Spanish Americans to a Mother Country they had hitherto
tended to reject and despise.

Cubans in the War

Repression after the 1935 strike scattered the revolutionary opposition,
driving it underground or forcing it into exile. Guiteras himself was
shot, together with Venezuelan expatriate General Carlos Aponte, as
they were about to go into exile. Other members of Joven Cuba were
more fortunate. Many reached the United States. For these men, Spain
offered an alternative to aimless plotting or, as for the best-remembered
of them, Pablo de la Torriente Brau, an escape from "carrying trays and
washing dishes" and occasional journalism. It was while covering a
solidarity meeting in New York's Union Square for the Cuban review
Bohemia that he suddenly recognized his mission. "I have had a marvel-
ous idea," he wrote in a letter. "I am going to Spain, to the Spanish
revolution . . . where the hopes of the oppressed of the whole world are
throbbing. The idea exploded in my brain." His friend Raúl Roa tried
to dissuade him, but "the fever of the Spanish revolution had taken
possession of him, absorbing all his capacity for service, his inexhaust-
ible energy, and his heroic sense of life." Torriente told Roa that it was
useless to try to dissuade him—"I go to Spain precisely in order to give
to the Cuban revolution all my experience. I believe that if, for any
reason, the journey does not come off, I would retire to a corner to die
alone, to die of grief and fury."[61]
  In September he left as war correspondent for the American Communist paper *The Masses* and for the Mexican *El Machete.* Three months
later he was dead, killed on the Madrid front at Majadahonda. After
hearing an impassioned plea from La Pasionaria and Margarita Nelken
for all able-bodied men to go to the front, he felt he had no choice but
to join up. He became a commissar in the brigade commanded by
Valentín González ("El Campesino"), who described him as the "greatest, most intelligent, most honorable, and purest person at my side."[62]
He had been a student militant in the anti-Machado struggle, experienced a period in prison, and was then active as a radical journalist from
1933 until forced into exile after the strike of 1935. He was an exceptional person by any standard, extroverted, passionate, and idealistic,
making an immediate impression on all those who came into contact
with him. He was "like a figure out of a legend," a fellow-prisoner

recalled, a "Cuban John Reed."[63] He was the only Cuban serving at the front to leave a first-hand account of his impressions, and in the idealism and commitment of his writings he unites in revolutionary ideology the anti-Machado struggle, the Spanish civil war, and the Cuban Revolution in an ancestry of heroic self-denial.

The figures for Cuban participants in the Spanish war are very uncertain. A hundred young Cubans reportedly left for Spain in the early months, but in addition to these volunteers there were also Spaniards living in Cuba, or whose parents were living there—such as Enrique Lister, the Republican general who had been initiated into politics on a Havana construction site. In addition, there were Cubans volunteering from exile, and some who joined from Spain, where they were resident at the time the war broke out. As early as October 1936 there were already more Cuban volunteers than from any other Latin American country.[64]

Published estimates of volunteers refer to the Republican side; we do not know how many fought for the Nationalists. According to Castells, 136 Cubans served in the International Brigades, most of them in the 24th Spanish Battalion of the Abraham Lincoln Brigade, a unit in which Mexicans, Puerto Ricans, and other Latin Americans also reportedly served. With as many as 60 members of Joven Cuba, a *centuria* was named after Antonio Guiteras. Its commander, Rodolfo de Armas, in his early twenties, was killed within a few months of his arrival. In common with the Americans, many of the Cubans seem to have been students —youth was certainly their characteristic, and even those who had been initiated into the gun battles of Havana streets had not yet been hardened, as had many European volunteers, by years of exile or by the discipline of political militancy. A Russian source gives the number of Cubans who fought for the Republic as 850, 90 percent of whom allegedly served in units other than the International Brigades. Predictably, this source describes the volunteers as "workers."[65] If this estimate is correct, then Cuba contributed one of the highest per capita proportions of volunteers of any country, although the hundred or so killed was comparatively low for foreigners, whose casualties were notoriously high.

There may have been a tendency for Cubans to transfer to units where their compatriots were in positions of command. Such was the case of machine-gun captain Basileo Cueria, a Black baseball player who had lived in New York since 1926 and who had served with the Lincoln Brigade for five months until Policarpo Candón, whom he had known in New York, arranged for his transfer.[66] No reference is made elsewhere to Cuban Blacks, which, in view of Guillén's stress on the importance of the war for Blacks, suggests that Cueria may have been unique. Although the Communist party was making a point of proselitizing among Blacks in Cuba, they were conspicuous by their absence from the predominantly middle-class and student revolutionary groups from which so many volunteers were drawn. Without more detailed research, it is impossible to be more precise about the social origins of Cuban volunteers. A number of officers are listed, presumably men purged from Batista's army as unreliable. It is equally difficult to ascertain party affiliations. Some half-dozen Cubans, in the Russian estimate, were designated political commissars, indicating party membership; of these, two have Jewish names, which could reflect the high proportion of Jews in the party's initial membership.

In 1936, as indicated earlier, activities related to giving military help to Spain were not allowed in Cuba, and so had to be carried on underground. The Communist party established a committee to organize the dispatch of volunteers, which included those from other groups like Joven Cuba, the Ala Izquierda, the PRC, and even members of the old parties. For the anti-Batista opposition, sending volunteers to Spain was a way to train and harden veterans for the struggle against the regime at home. In practice, however, it turned out rather differently. Those who had left at a time when Batista was still in his dictatorial phase returned to find him now accepted by the Communists as a democratic leader. This itself may have been a cause of disorientation, but Cuban politics in the 1940s provided no outlet for idealism. Politics may have been more democratic but was now dominated by gangsters, which put a premium on skills of violence even inside the university, where political gangsterism ("bonchismo") was inextricably fused with student politics. Civil war veterans provided the leadership for many of these terrorist groups,[67] including the Acción Revolucionaria Guiterista (ARG) and the revamped Joven Cuba, led by lawyer-journalist Dr. Eufemio Fernández, who had fought in Spain. The Movimiento Socialista Revolucionaria (MSR), a smaller group, was led by Rolando Masferrer, who had fought in the civil war as a Communist and had been wounded at the battle of the Ebro. On his return to Cuba, still only twenty-nine, he combined a brilliant student career with violent politics, founding the fiercely anti-Communist MSR in 1944. Escaping to Florida in his yacht with a considerable fortune on Batista's overthrow, he was blown to bits by a car bomb while in exile.

The Unión Insurreccional Revolucionaria (UIR), with which Fidel Castro had some tenuous links as a student activist, was led by Emilio Tro, who had served in the American army between the civil war and his return to Cuba; he was appointed Grau's chief of police in Marianao, where he was shot down in a gunfight in 1947. Jorge Agostini, who had served in the Republican navy, became head of Cuba's secret police during the presidency of Carlos Prío Socorrás (1948–52) and was assassinated in 1956. Spanish exiles were also involved in gunfights in the 1940s, as well as in anti-Batista conspiracies in the 1950s. Carlos Gutiérrez Menoyo, born in Spain, where his elder brother had been killed, came to Cuba to join his family after service in the French army, only to be killed himself, together with another Spanish exile, leading a commando group in the famous attack on the presidential palace in March 1957. His younger brother Eloy became a Fidelista guerrilla but was later to be imprisoned for attempting to assassinate Castro. Yet another exile, Daniel Martín Labandero, an ex-Republican officer, was implicated in a conspiracy against Batista and was killed in a bid to escape from prison. Many escaped death in Spain only to die violently in the bloody factional fights of Cuban gangster politics or in the revolutionary cause of the anti-Batista struggle.

The Cuban government, unlike that of Mexico, did not welcome an influx of refugees.[68] In answer to a request from Álvarez del Vayo to accept ex-volunteers from any country, the Cubans refused to take any except those who had previously been residents in Cuba, which at least left it open for Spaniards who had lived there to return. There was no desire, though, to strengthen the merchant element, which the 1934 nationalization law had been designed to reduce, and only those prepared to invest their capital (as if refugees had any!) in industry or to become agriculturalists would be admitted. Professionals and teachers were welcome, but restrictions on foreigners teaching in the public educational system meant that Cuban intellectual life did not benefit from an influx of Spaniards as did so many other Spanish American countries.[69] In any case, the violent atmosphere of Havana University in the 1940s was scarcely propitious for serious academic work.

Many university professors and literary figures, such as the poet Juan Ramón Jiménez, the philosopher Ferrater Mora, and the poet-typographer Manuel Altolaguirre, who had published Guillén's *España* in Valencia in 1937, only stayed for a short time. Some minor literary figures who found employment in journalism did put down roots, as did some musicians, actors, architects, and doctors. But many other middle-class professional men passed on to the United States, Venezuela, or Mexico. José Gaos, vice-rector of Madrid University, who had spent some time in Cuba during the war trying to arrange visits by Spanish academics, left for Mexico, where he was instrumental in establishing the Colegio de México and in strengthening the *orteguista* emphasis of Mexican thought. Thus Cuban cultural life did not benefit from a large-scale immigration of intellectuals as did that of Mexico, where, in addition, exclusion from the closed political system directed the energies of many Spaniards into cultural, entrepreneurial, and media activities. In Cuba, by contrast, an open political system was to draw many into turbulent political activity.

Only one major Republican politician came to Cuba—Alvaro de Albornoz, a leader of the Radicals, and friendly with Gordón Ordás. But he too soon went on to Mexico, as did Gordón himself, who turned down the offer of a post in the local administration after relinquishing the embassy when Cuba recognized the Franco regime in March 1939.

Under Mexican pressure, Cuba agreed to help find homes for refugees in France and also agreed that Havana could be used as an "intermediate station" for refugees on the way to other countries. To many refugees, Cuba was not more than a transit camp.

Most professional soldiers also passed on to other Spanish American countries, but one, Alberto Bayo, was to provide an interesting and important link between the civil war and Castro's revolution.[70] Bayo had been born in Cuba, and eventually returned to die there in 1967. In his youth he had gone to Spain and became an officer in the air force. During the civil war he led a successful invasion of Ibiza and an unsuccessful attack on Majorca. He then tried with indifferent success to mount guerrilla campaigns behind the Nationalist lines on the Madrid front. He was one of the few Republicans to take guerrilla warfare seriously. After the war he was active in exile organizations in Mexico. In addition to being director of the School of Military Aviation, he was also in demand as an instructor in guerrilla warfare, training young Spaniards for a return to Spain, Nicaraguans to overthrow Somoza, and Cubans to overthrow Batista. Carlos Prío financed him from Florida, and it was from Bayo—not the classical guerrilla theorists—that Castro and his followers learned the rudiments of guerrilla warfare, as well as listening to him retell the heroic exploits of the civil war.

The history of the Spanish Caribbean and Central America in the late forties and early fifties is one of turbulence and undercover activity, as Communists and non-Communists alike cooperated and clashed over strategy and tactics. The long-standing regimes of Somoza in Nicaragua and Trujillo in the Dominican Republic, and the Pérez Jiménez regime in Venezuela after 1948, became targets for the Caribbean Legion organized by the democratic left. Most of these activities were directed from, and operated out of, Central America, especially Costa Rica, where José Figueres had come to power in 1948, and from Guatemala, where a revolution had brought Juan José Arévalo to power in 1944. Spanish Republican exiles contributed military skills and experience to the Legion's exploits. Bayo had taken leave of absence from his Mexican post to organize the revolutionaries' air power for a strike against Nicaragua in 1948, and other units also had Spanish officers. In a projected attack on the Dominican Republic in 1949, Bayo was so worried by the number of his countrymen involved that it was decided to leave them behind, to avoid the charge that the expedition was dominated by "Red" Spaniards.[71] Cuba was the main base for attacks against the neighboring Dominican Republic, many exiles from which were active in Cuba. Civil war veterans, including Masferrer and Eufemio Fernández, were prominent in the Cayo Confites expedition of 1947, in which Fidel Castro also participated.

In spite of the repressive nature of the Trujillo regime, some nine hundred Spanish refugees were admitted to the Dominican Republic, of whom as many as a hundred and seventy may have been Communists.[72] In marked contrast to that in Cuba, the Communist party in the Dominican Republic owed its origins to the Spanish civil war.

Although returnees and exiles figure in many Cuban and Caribbean conspiracies of the 1940s and 1950s, it would be wrong to give the impression that they constituted a disproportionate element, or that they were in some way responsible for the politics of violence. Their involvement does, however, suggest a difficulty in keeping on the sidelines when this sort of politics put a premium on the experience they would have acquired in the civil war (or the Second World War). Nor is it surprising that, in this atmosphere of corruption, ideals were dimmed. Many illusions about the Communists had been dispelled during the war, although some, like Bayo, not a Communist himself, admired them for their fixity of purpose. Others sensed that in the fluidity of Cuban politics the Communists, as the only organized party, had a future— or, as Francisco Pares put it, "the fidelismo of Fidel is not enough to ensure the survival of fidelismo."[73]

It is hypothetical how far other expertise or experience from the civil war was to be useful or influential in the course of the revolution. Ramón Nicolau, a commissar in Spain, was to be an important contact man between the Directorio Estudiantil and the 26th of July movement at the Cabaña fortress in 1959. Manuel del Peso, another commissar, was one of the few Communists to be active in the guerrilla campaign against Batista in the 1950s; he later became military attaché in Moscow. Joaquín Ordoquí, who had persuaded Nicolás Guillén to join the Communist party when in Spain, was to be one of the foremost Communist (PSP) members in the 1960s, but finally fell from grace because of his implication in the Marcos Rodríguez affair. As with Aníbal Escalante, who had been the first editor of *Hoy* in 1938, was prominent in pro-

Republican gatherings in Cuba, and fell foul of Castro in 1962, his sectarianism was to be his undoing.

The Literary Effects

It may appear odd that more Spanish Americans did not fight in a war that prima facie would seem to involve them more intimately than their non-Spanish European contemporaries, most of whom had little interest in or knowledge of Spain before the triumph of the Popular Front in February 1936. The difficulties and cost of travel and the organizational and financial weaknesses of Latin American Communist parties, as well as the closer proximity of the Fascist threat in Europe, provide part of the explanation. Quantity, however, is not all, and another aspect of the question, pro-Republican sympathy among Latin American writers, left its impress on Spanish American culture far out of proportion to the number of those involved.

In July 1937 the Republic hosted the Second International Congress for the Defense of Culture, with meetings in Madrid, Valencia, and Barcelona.[74] Some sixteen writers from Spanish America seem to have been present, and their names read like a roll call of the masters of modern Hispanic literatures. The Cuban delegation of five was the largest from any Latin American country, consisting of Nicolás Guillén, Alejo Carpentier, Juan Marinello, Félix Pita Rodríquez, and Leonardo Fernández Sánchez.[75] The only one of these who was not a Communist, or did not become one as the result of the civil war, was Carpentier—"one of the most neutral men I have ever known," as Neruda described him.[76]

At that time Carpentier was a minor literary figure. He had been associated with the *Revista de Avance* in Cuba in the mid-1920s but, after a brief spell in prison, went into self-imposed exile in 1928; for the next eleven years he lived in Paris on the margin of the literary world, so inconspicuously that Neruda refers to him as a French writer. He had only written one novel—*Ecué-Yamba-O*—published in Madrid in 1933, reflecting his early interest in the Afro-Cuban movement. His career as a novelist lay in the future, after his return to Cuba in 1939. The civil war does not seem to have influenced him to the same extent as other Spanish American writers. He wrote only a handful of articles for the Havana magazine *Carteles,* and there are no references to the war in any of his novels until *La consagración de la primavera,* published in 1979. Nevertheless, Carpentier was profoundly influenced, as were so many other Spanish Americans, by José Ortega y Gasset and his *Revista de*

Occidente, which since its foundation in 1923 had been the major disseminator of trends in European (especially German) culture. The cultural relativism of Ortega's "perspectivism," together with Spengler's *Decline of the West* (translated into Spanish in 1923), legitimated the assertive new cultural nationalism of the mid-1920s, in which writers began to throw off European and especially French influences.[77]

The remarkable cultural renaissance in Spain reflected in the generations of 1898, 1927, and 1936 predisposed Spanish American writers to take their counterparts in the peninsula seriously for the first time and to discover significance in their own Spanish—as well as Indian and African—heritage.[78] At the same time, in the early 1930s, when every Latin American country except Mexico experienced a military coup, the Spanish Republic was a beacon of hope and optimism; in effect it was a political counterpart to the cultural renaissance, and a regime with which literary intellectuals could identify. Carpentier's obsession with his origins, rising from his mixed Russian-French ancestry, predisposed him to explore the African roots of Cuba's culture, and for this reason, perhaps, Spain did not have the same resonance for him as it did for other Spanish Americans.

For Nicolás Guillén, Afro-Cubanism was not a literary stance—not simply the "alluring other"—that enabled alienated writers to escape from the thralldom of European example, but an intimate process of self-discovery. His mulatto origins and the murder of his father by soldiers in the Liberal Revolution of 1917 roused his political interest and heightened his awareness of the problem of Cuba's unassimilated Black population, which was becoming a major cause of concern for Cuban intellectuals in the mid-1920s. His poetry was rooted in the African rhythms of the speech and music of the burgeoning Havana slums, swollen by Blacks from the countryside through the importation of cheap Haitian and Jamaican labor. Comparatively untouched by French influences, he was steeped in classical Spanish poetry, like Miguel Hernández, "cantor de las trincheras," the great peasant-poet he was to know and admire in Spain. He was also influenced by the contemporary revival of the *romance,* the traditional Spanish ballad, interest in which had been roused among Spanish poets by the researches of the medievalist Ramón Menéndez Pidal, and which had been popularized before the civil war by Federico García Lorca.

The most remarkable feature of the literature produced during the civil war was the resurrection of the *romance* and its use by leading poets to bridge the gap between popular and elite culture.[79] Guillén recounts a discussion he had in Valencia with Hernández, Langston Hughes, the Black American poet, Mexican Octavio Paz, and Argentine Raúl Gon zález Tuñón. The subject was the relevance of the *romance* form in revolutionary literature. Only González Tuñón thought the *romance* was worn out. The others believed that its popular roots made it an ideal form for revolutionary poetry.[80] This view was vindicated by the three hundred *romances* collected by Emilio Prados for the Madrid congress.

With regard to the revival of the *romance,* the centrality of Andalusian poet and dramatist Federico García Lorca to Spanish American writers cannot be exaggerated. No Spanish poet had ever made a comparable impact in the New World. Not only did his poetry and personality make a profound impression, but the brutal manner of his death at the hands of Insurgent minions in the early days of the war made it difficult for writers not to be Republican supporters. Cuba was the first Spanish American country Lorca ever visited, and the effect was all the greater because he came in March 1930 straight from his brief but devastating sojourn in New York, which had depressed him with its economic and racial tensions. The relief at returning to a Hispanic country is reflected in the one poem he wrote in Cuba. Guillén was profoundly influenced by Lorca, as he was to be by Rafael Alberti, who in 1935 also visited Havana.[81] When, therefore, Guillén arrived in Spain in 1937, unexpectedly invited by Neruda to attend the congress, he was going to one of the sources of his inspiration.[82] Curiously, though, Guillén published no poetry based on his experiences in the civil war. His one volume inspired by the war, *España, cuatro angustias y una esperanza* was written in Mexico on the eve of his departure for Spain, although published in Valencia in 1937. However, he did write a number of prose pieces, interviews, sketches, and speeches for the Havana Marxist journal *Mediodía.*

In Madrid, Guillén was impressed by the Alianza de Intelectuales Españoles, the cultural center run by Alberti in a commandeered palace.[83] Here, against a background of exploding shells, bombs, and sirens, lectures were given, conferences organized, and evening classes conducted throughout the siege of the city. The Alianza also published *El Mono Azul,* which, in addition to acting as a newspaper, also published poems. Poets like Miguel Hernández, a political commissar in the 59th Regiment, read their poetry in the trenches. For intellectuals, marginalized and despised in their own countries, often in impotent opposition and struggling against censorship, as in the case of the Cubans, the Spanish experience was a revelation. In Guillén's case, the attraction of the Communist party, which he joined in Valencia in 1937, was partly due to its recognition of the social and political functions of the writer, as well as to his admiration for Alberti, who had been a party member since 1931.

Guillén identified himself with Spain as a writer, for whom defending culture was a "sacred duty"; as a mulatto, because fascism with its racialism was the greatest barrier to the universalization of the human spirit; and as a Cuban, because he identified the cause of the struggle at home against the "Fascist" dictator Batista with the cause of the anti-fascist struggle in Spain. "I come from a small country" he wrote, "under a military and Fascist dictatorship that destroys free expression and kills the slightest attempt to restore democracy.... Spain and Cuba . . . have identical enemies, identical destinies, identical solutions."[84]

He was to take up the first theme, on his return to Cuba, in a talk that expresses clearly what Spain meant for Spanish American writers.[85] Earlier in the century, he argued, Paris had been the Mecca where literary reputations were won and lost. Paris symbolized the highest aspirations of the dominant bourgeoisie. Although they might not be aware of it, writers worked for the class they despised, and with few exceptions the man of letters was "an animal domesticated by the man of wealth." The First World War did not fundamentally alter the writers' outlook except in Russia. Not until the Spanish civil war did a fundamental change occur. The war moved not only simple men but also complex, sophisticated intellectuals, cautious in spirit, accustomed to avoiding politics, which might sully the purity of their thought. Guillén looked back to the Madrid congress as a reunion of writers facing their tasks with simplicity, uninterested in posturing and attitudinizing.

Readers of Stephen Spender's account of the congress—that "spoiled childrens' party"—will scarcely recognize it in Guillén's account, but much eluded Spender, as it did the other "war tourists" whom Spender himself castigated. European writers did not react in any way comparable to the Spanish Americans, whose responses were conditioned by a sense of solidarity based on the common bond of language and by the feeling that in "working for the triumph of Spain they were working for the triumph of Spanish America," in the words of the manifesto signed by the Spanish Americans at the congress.[86] Exile, rootlessness, and a sense of cultural orphanhood had been the experience of many of them. Pre-Republican Spain had been the *madrasta,* as Bolívar's said, the step-mother who provided no spiritual sustenance. Writers did not look to Madrid for inspiration; the scorn they had for Spain's backwardness was reciprocated by the Spaniards' contempt for what was considered to be the nouveau-riche pretentiousness, political instability, and racial inferiority of Spanish Americans. For their part, it was difficult for Spanish Americans to see beyond the official Spain to the "pueblo." Contact with Spaniards was ordinarily confined to immigrants who, if economically successful, were resented and, if economic failures, were despised. The civil war provided an opportunity to make contact with the non-official Spain, and from that experience was to grow the "White Legend" of the Spanish past.

The civil war also inevitably hastened an on-going rapprochement between Spanish and Spanish American writers. Peninsular authors had first become aware of a distinctive Spanish American literature through the poetry of Rubén Darío, who initiated *modernismo,* the Spanish equivalent of the symbolist movement in France. Links between Spanish and Spanish American writers were immeasurably strengthened in the late 1920s by such Mexican intellectuals as Alfonso Reyes and José Vasconcelos, both of whom maintained intimate relations with the literati of the Mother Country. The influence of Ramón del Valle Inclán on his Spanish American counterparts was significant, if not as important as that exerted later by García Lorca. Finally, Pablo Neruda's appointment to the Chilean embassy in Madrid in 1936 made him a central figure in Spanish literary circles and an important influence on Spanish poets.

Madrid, which previously symbolized a centralized imperial system and unjust oppression, became, during the siege, "Madrid the heroic, astonishment of the world and honor to the human race." Guillén repudiated Paris in an article in which he contrasted the frivolous reception of air-raid practices in the French capital with the grim reality of Madrid under fire.[87] Madrid was not only the center of the world but also the forge of a new consciousness and a new humanity:

> The heroic resistance of the Spanish people was the culmination of its great spiritual life. . . . To the wars of territorial conquest and imperial aggrandizement has succeeded the war for the affirmation of man's permanent values, the war for the defense of culture and love.

Guillén saw in Spain's war more than a mere civil conflict. To him it ultimately represented "the gestation of the man of the future, his slow and sure birth in a field of blood like the bed of a woman who has just given birth."

In this sort of writing can be sensed the apocalyptic and messianic streak that runs through much Spanish and Spanish American thought, from the Franciscans through its secularized form in Bolívar, on through Martí and Vasconcelos, and up to Castro, and which was to find during the war its supreme poetic expression in the work of César Vallejo, who was to describe Spain's mission more prosaically in his speech to the congress: "In the Spanish people, America regards its own extraordinary destiny within human history, a destiny whose continuity consists in the fact that it has been given to Spain to be the creator of continents: today she is saving the entire world from nothingness." [88]

Guillén also identified with Spain as a Negro. "I come as the representative of one of the inferior races of the Fascists," he remarked, but he did not preach an exclusive Black racism. His mixed ancestry and roots in classicial Spanish literature went too deep for him to repudiate his Spanish heritage, and in his search for universal values he was concerned to link the cause of Cuban Negroes with that of the Republic: "In Cuba the Negro lives the tragedy of Republican Spain . . . but the Cuban Negro is also *Spanish,* because together with the infamous marks of slavery he received and assimilated the elements of Spanish culture."[89]

Guillén spent much of his time in Spain with Langston Hughes, the Black American Communist writer who was chronicling the contribution of American Blacks to the Republican cause.[90] Hughes had visited Havana in 1927, and had translated Guillén's poetry, and thus he served as an important link in the Black literary renaissance that had begun to stir in the United States and the Caribbean in the late 1920s. Guillén saw himself as the spokesman of this renaissance, and in so doing foreshadows the Castro Revolution's emphasis on Cuba's African heritage as part of its opening toward African revolutionary movements.

Juan Marinello, the official spokesman for the Cuban delegation, also produced a number of articles. A member of the Grupo Minorista of the 1920s, he was also Cuba's foremost Marxist literary critic and one of the most sensitive interpreters of the writings of José Martí. Marinello emphasized the distinction that Martí had consistently evoked between "good" and "bad" Spaniards, between "official" Spain and the "people." Recalling an incident in Oriente when he had witnessed a crowd of Cubans shouting "Long live Spain!" Marinello contrasted it with the hatred inspired by Cuba's long struggle for independence:

> The cry "Death to Spain" of 1868 and 1895 is the same cry that we shout today . . . the desire, that is, to see dead and buried the Spain of Weyler and Queipo, of Balmaceda and Franco, the death of the Spain that killed Maceo and Pablo de la Torriente, death to the stupid and rapacious military, to gun-toting priests, to idle *señoritos,* and to parasitic nobles.[91]

Martí's distinction between "good" and "bad" Spaniards—echoed here by Marinello—and the moral content of his philosophy have exercised a potent influence on Cuban radical thought. At the same time, his concept of redemption through suffering led—in this particular context

—to an emotional identification of Cuban with Spaniard, as well as to a desire for reconciliation. Just how far this was reflected in Cuba itself in the relationship between Spaniards and Cubans is difficult to say, but in the peninsula during the war it seems to have been a reality.

Comparisons and Contrasts

At the moment that the civil war ended and dictatorship was being established in Spain, Cuba was about to enter a period of economic prosperity and constitutional rule, exemplified in the Constitution of 1940, with Batista becoming president in the freest elections in Cuban history. And yet appearances were deceptive. Batista was the guardian of the new order, guaranteed by the Communist party. In 1944 he was replaced in free elections by Grau San Martín. The long-postponed hour of the men of 1933 had finally come, but with results very different from what had been expected. Grau's period of office became a by-word for corruption, and in order to buy off the opposition he resorted to bribery and violence. The university was neutralized by gangsterism, and Grau could only widen the basis of his support among the Communist-dominated unions by illicit means. The four-years' presidency of Carlos Prío Socorrás (1948–52) were no improvement. Grau's party, the Auténticos, split, with a reformist, moralizing wing, the "Ortodoxos," under Eddy Chibás, claiming to be the rightful heirs of its idealistic 1930 tradition. When Batista returned to power in 1952, this time through another coup and with no pretensions to democracy, the opposition hardened. The conspiratorial tradition reasserted itself, finally triumphing in the successful deposition of Batista at the end of 1958 and ushering in the most profound social and political revolution the Hispanic world had yet seen. While Cuba experienced a total transformation, Spain too was undergoing changes—but by very different means. After three decades of technocratic, managerial corporatism, peninsular society was almost unrecognizable from that of the 1930s.

The political incompatibility of the two regimes did not prevent economic cooperation, and one of the more bizarre features of Cuban-Spanish relations under Franco was the Spanish contribution to Cuba's economic survival.[92] Madrid was linked to Havana by the only air connection existing between the island and Western Europe, and some fifteen thousand Cuban exiles left for Spain. But after the death of Franco, relations have not been as close as might have been anticipated. Santiago Carillo's "Euro-Communism" is too critical of Moscow at a time when Cuba is drawing closer to the Russians. And Cuba does not provide a model for what is now Spain's most serious problem—the assertion of regional aspirations.

But although direct influences are limited, it may still be worth drawing parallels between the experiences of two countries that have been the touchstones for revolutionary enthusiasm. Why did Cuba succeed where Spain failed?

Both countries have had ambivalent attitudes toward their northern neighbors, and each country's history has been conditioned by the interests of foreign powers. In Europe, the Great Powers could never leave Spain to work out its own political solutions, whether in the War of the Spanish Succession (1700–13), the Napoleonic War (1808–14), or the civil wars of the nineteenth and twentieth centuries. Strategic need prompted this interest, as it did that of the United States in Cuba.

Rivalry between Britain and the United States guaranteed the continuance of Spanish rule when the rest of the Spanish empire became independent. Under Spanish control, Cuba experienced the sugar revolution, which made it the richest colony for its size possessed by any European power. In the nineteenth century the colony's function was to satisfy the "empleomanía" of the impoverished Spanish middle classes and to provide a protected market for Catalan industry, especially for textiles unable to compete in the Spanish domestic market with cheaper English imports. In Cuba, the tensions rising from contradictions between an expanding capitalist economy and a slave system, and between the plantocracy's economic and social power and its lack of political control, found expression in annexationism, reformism, autonomism, and, finally, independence. With the decline of British strategic and economic interests in the Caribbean, independent Cuba now became economically, strategically, and to some extent even politically dependent on the United States.

As the dynamic of capitalist growth seemed to condemn independent Cuba to an unlimited expansion of sugar monoculture, this dependence became an obsession with Cuban thinkers. The anxiety that had been expressed in the admonitory writings of José Martí in the 1880s and 1890s was to become a leitmotif of Cuban intellectuals. But a sense of powerlessness and resentment was tempered by admiration for the positive aspects of American democracy (as may be seen in Martí, too), as well as by admiration for American efficiency. The attitudes of Cuban nationalists have been determined by this complex love-hate relationship.

In Spain, by contrast, there was no comparable overwhelming sense of economic dependence: foreign economic interests, although extensive in railways, mines, and public utilities, were more diffuse.

Modernization created imbalances reinforcing regional differences, which ultimately developed into full-fledged nationalist movements, the main thrust of which was against the internal enemy—Castilian centralism—rather than a foreign power.

Spanish attitudes toward Europe have been varied, ambivalent, complex, and contradictory. Spanish thinkers have been divided in their admiration of and attraction toward British, French, and German culture. The dichotomy of the "two Spains" that runs through peninsular history since the Enlightenment, and that was given a new twist by the writers of the Generation of 1898, oversimplifies the complexity of the response to the rest of Europe, but on the other hand it does reflect the divisions over the role accorded to the Catholic church and traditional values as the key defining element in Spanish culture. The church was galvanized into action by the threat from the new secular elite produced by the Libre Institución de Enseñanza, but instead of leading to a modernization of attitudes it resulted in an even more exclusive Catholic culture.

In Cuba, intellectuals were spared having to choose between hermetically sealed cultures. With the collapse of the creole plantocracy during the independence wars and the sugar crisis of the 1880s, there was no dominant social group representing comparable traditionalist values, and, with the defeat of Spain and the discrediting of the church, Cuban intellectuals elaborated a secular nationalist mythology on which consensus politics could be based. Without the advantages of the Mexicans, who were able to elaborate an *indigenista* nationalist mythology drawing sustenance from a pre-Hispanic past, Cuban nationalism was at first defined by negatives. It was only in the 1920s, with the rediscovery of Martí and the exploration of the African contribution to the island's culture, that Cuban nationalism acquired a more positive dimension.

Martí is central to any understanding of the new nationalism. He is the symbol and model of civic patriotism, devoting his life in exile to the cause of independence with the self-dedication of a Lenin or a Mazzini, and ultimately embracing death, at the end of a life that reflected the redemption through suffering of Cuba itself. The simplicity of his language and his short essays made him easily accessible to a wide audience. His ideas provided both a practical program and an alternative, but also, through their vagueness, enabled a wide spectrum of opinion to use him to legitimate their ideas. Most important were the moral imperatives of his thought, which transcended economic divisions. At the core of his writings there is a populist model of class harmony that appealed to the nationalist mood of Cubans living in the shadow of external pressures, where class divisions would only have weakened the nation.

Moral intensity and redemptionist fervor have been the distinctive features of the Cuban radical nationalist tradition, with each new generation of students as its missionaries. The extraordinary role that students have played in Cuban politics can be explained by the fact that Havana University had an institutional continuity unparalleled by that of any other Cuban body and that, since the mid-nineteenth century, it has been the forging-house of nationalism. Student attitudes were conditioned by the myth of the incorruptibility of youth, which was integral to the University Reform movement throughout Spanish America but was given greater force in Cuba by a student martyrology stretching back to 1871. Although students have exercised political influence in Spain—in the 1860s, at the end of the Primo de Rivera dictatorship (1931), and during Franco's regime—there was no opening for them to play a comparable role as a political catalyst. Spanish political parties and trade unions generated their own leadership. This is not to deny the importance of youthful political cadres in the 1930s—either the *cedistas,* young Socialists, or Falangists—but a youth movement linked to a party is very different from the Cuban students' arrogation to themselves of the role of revolutionary vanguard.

Closely related to the function that students have played in politics has been the tendency of Cubans to interpret their history in generational terms. Literary and cultural historians have found the generational concept useful in defining and delimiting literary moods, but its value as a tool for political analysis is more questionable. In any society in which there are discontinuities caused by war or revolution, the concept of a "generation" is useful to distinguish groups subjected to different influences. But unless it is rooted in structural analysis, the concept can easily become banal. Where there are sharp discontinuities, generational analysis often exaggerates conflict between groups, but for every student rebelling against what he might have felt to be his father's betrayal of the ideals of Martí, there was probably one or another *niño bitongo,* spoiled children prepared to live off their patrimony.

The popularity of the use of generational categories in Spain as well as Cuba reflects the idealist and elitist perspective popularized by Ortega y Gasset.[93] Ortega's lifework was in one sense devoted to drawing attention to Spain's need for enlightened elites. Despising politicians, and attributing to them the nation's ills, he sought Spain's salvation in an elite of thinkers of high moral purpose—the equivalent of the "moral censors" contemplated by Bolívar in his Angostura Constitution (1819).

Unlike such theorists of the elite as Mosca, Pareto, or Michels, who repudiated liberal parliamentarism, or Gramsci, who widened the definition of the intellectual by stressing his crucial role in the construction of a genuine socialist society, Ortega's political attitudes were ambivalent. But his inflated view of the role of intellectuals, disseminated among a wide audience through his journalism in *El Sol,* his books, and the *Revista de Occidente,* bolstered the traditional image of the *pensador* in Hispanic culture as someone removed from, and above, the ordinary run of life, and to whom deference is due.

Conclusion

The Republic of 1931 was the political counterpart of Spain's post-1898 cultural renaissance—a republic of humanist intellectuals unable to meet the demands of a modernizing revolution that required agronomists rather than parliamentary orators. It is also paradoxical that, at the moment Republican Spain embarked on a program of transformation, intellectuals should rediscover an unchanging Spain, with writers turning for inspiration to the *campesino* and his relationship with the earth.[94] The imagery of poets was derived from rural rather than urban themes. The war strengthened this trend, whereby Republican fortitude was rooted in the values of a rural culture. In the process, rural simplicity was set against urban sophistication, rural innocence against urban subtleties, rural loyalties against urban betrayal. The nontechnological world of rural Spain was comprehensible to humanist intellectuals faced by a crisis in which holistic schemes of thought of the middle ground were dying and in which scientific and technological developments seemed to make humanist intellectuals irrelevant.[95]

Faced with the need to provide a new legitimating ideology, Republican intellectuals could only turn to an unsuccessful and discredited nineteenth-century tradition and to the myth of *the pueblo* enshrined in the verities of rural life.[96] As a simpler society, Cuba had a limited choice of options, but most Cubans shared a set of common assumptions embodied in Martí and the radical nationalist tradition. Departures from this were ascribed not so much to ideological differences as to moral lapses. The strength of this native tradition lessened the influence of foreign ideologies, whether anarchism, socialism, *aprismo,* or communism. Any revolutionary ideology, for example, that did not assign a key role to intellectuals and students would have had little chance of acceptance by the "doctores," whose influence in a weak and heterogeneous middle class has always been out of proportion to their numbers. Disillusionment with orthodox communism, with its emphasis on the proletariat as a revolutionary vanguard at a time when it seemed to have become corrupted by consumerism or coopted into tied labor movements as in Mexico (and to some degree in Cuba itself), was perhaps one reason why the Cuban revolution received such a sympathetic response from intellectuals, especially students both in and outside Cuba. Their new role was to rouse the consciousness of a downtrodden and neglected peasantry, who were now regarded as a more promising revolutionary potential in developing societies than the organized working class.

The Cuban Revolution sanctified the role of intellectuals without forcing them to become apparatchiks, although Castro expected them to fulfill a different function once the Revolution had entered an institutionalizing phase.[97] In developed societies, intellectuals can fulfill the role of Mannheim's "unattached intellectual"—universities pay them for doing so —but in developing nations this function can become a luxury, self-defeating and self-immolating. In a scientifically- and technologically-based society, Castro expected a sacrifice of individualism, an acceptance of the primacy of communal effort, and the replacement of a humanistic by a technical intelligentsia. The reorientation of educational priorities so as to generate cadres of technicians and so reduce dependence on outside assistance was given top priority. But such a reorientation was only possible because, in the period needed to restructure the educational system, the Eastern bloc countries could provide the necessary technicians and economic assistance. No such possibility was open to the Spanish Republic. Economic depression, political instability, and the absence of specialized agencies to provide expertise condemned it to pursue modernization without modernizers.

At the other end of the political spectrum were the military, but they play a very different role in the two countries. In Spain, the military were an integral part of Liberal politics, with the *pronunciamiento* fulfilling the function of a general will theory. Only after defeat in the Cuban war of independence did the military, now on the defensive, become defender of the status quo and protector of national unity against threats from the left and regionalism. The Cuban army in the twentieth century, incorporated into the graft system, was not obsessed by military "honor," but under Batista in the 1930s soldiers fulfilled a civic role in the Instituto Cívico Militar. Increasingly urban-oriented, it could not cope with the rural guerrillas of the 1950s. In Spain, the Nationalist army might also have been unable to meet a challenge from guerrillas but, puzzlingly, it did not have to do so. The war was fought on traditional lines—albeit with novelties like dive-bombing and whippet tank warfare—and although Hemingway's *For Whom the Bell Tolls* (the book that together with the film has probably done most to mold the image of the civil war in the American consciousness) catches an echo of a guerrilla incident, guerrilla warfare was an exception, and Orwell's description of trench warfare, reminiscent of the Western Front, was closer to reality. In Cuba, by contrast, there was no other tradition than that of the guerrilla, and Bayo saw his ideas, which were never taken up seriously in Spain, succeeding in Cuba.

To return to the question we posed at the beginning of this essay, two factors that help to account for Castro's success seem worth emphasizing. The rapid disillusionment of large sectors of the middle classes with a revolution that went beyond the reforms of the 1940 Constitution posed a serious potential threat that Castro met, not by modifying his radicalism, but by allowing the discontented to go into exile. This provided a safety valve, much as the emigration of Spaniards to other European countries was to do for General Franco. Had Castro closed the door to emigration, in all probability internal opposition would have broken out into civil war, with the threat of foreign intervention and a failure comparable to that in Spain.

Further, the emigration of middle-class technicians and administrators compelled Castro to move closer to the Communist party, whose organization and cadres provided the discipline the Revolution needed in the early 1960s. Ironically, Castro's revolution owes its survival partly to their cooperation, much as Batista's counter-revolution did in the late 1930s.

The politics of national unity—the elusive goal of Martí's populist strategy[98]—has exercised a potent fascination in Cuba since 1933. The weakness of class formation, combined with the sense of dependence on the United States, explains the prevalence of populist parties, but, because of the dead end of sugar monoculture, populist coalitions were inherently unstable.

In contrast, although Spanish politics had deeper roots in class allegiances than in Cuba, political alliances in Spain were difficult to maintain; even between different sections of the working class, divided by exclusivist proletarian political traditions, or between sectors of the middle classes, divided by regional loyalties.[99] Of all Spanish politicians and parties, Lerroux and his Radicals were the nearest thing in Spanish politics to the Cuban examples. But Lerrouxism was an aberration in the context of Spanish political life.[100] The stabilizing role that the Communists played in Cuba during the first Batista period, and during the Revolution itself, was absent in Spain because of their weakness until the outbreak of the civil war. The war gave the Communists their chance, due partly to the non-intervention policy of the Western powers and partly to the anarchists' giving priority to the social revolution rather than to the war.

War provided the Communists with their opportunity, as it has in other twentieth-century revolutions, even in Cuba with the surrogate of the Cold War. It has been the Cuban Revolution's good fortune to survive because the balance of international forces favored it, whereas Spain became a battleground because the balance had still to be tested. In the final instance, the contrasted fate of both has been decided not so much by differences in their domestic politics but by decisions of great powers beyond their control.

Acknowledgments

The author gratefully acknowledges a British Academy grant that facilitated the preparation of this essay.

Notes

1. Hugh Thomas, in *The Spanish Civil War* (London, 3rd edition, 1977) and in *Cuba: The Pursuit of Freedom* (London, 1971), has written the fundamental books on both topics. Quarrying in the latter yields many nuggets, and anyone working on modern Cuba is indebted to him for doing so much of the groundwork.

2. Fabio Grobart, Blas Roca, and Carlos Rafael Rodríguez were all Communist activists in the 1920s and early 1930s. So were those who have only recently died, like Juan Marinello and Lázaro Peña, or those who have been disgraced, such as Aníbal Escalante or Joaquín Ordoquí. A useful interview with Blas Roca appears in *Granma* (Havana), August 20, 1978.

3. The paucity of material on Spanish immigration into Cuba and of studies on the Spanish community reflects the backward state of immigration studies in Latin America generally. There is still no general book on the subject. This lacuna was recognized by the Conference of European Historians of Latin America in Cologne in 1975, which took immigration as its theme. For Cuban immigration, there is a short introductory article by D. C. Corbitt, "Immigration in Cuba", *Hispanic American Historical Review* 22, no. 2 (1942): 280–308. For the Spanish community in Cuba see the exploratory article by M. Kenny, "Twentieth-Century Spanish Expatriates in Cuba: A 'Sub Culture'?", *Anthropological Quarterly* 34, no. 2 (1961): 85–93.

4. For a brief analysis of trends in Cuban historiography, see R. F. Smith, "Twentieth Century Cuban Historiography", *Hispanic American Historical Review* 44, no. 1 (1964): 44–73. In 1940 revisionist historians organized the Sociedad Cubana de Estudios Históricos e Internacionales under the inspiration

of Emilio Roig de Leuchsenring. It was left-wing in orientation. One of its symbolic victories was to get the Cuban Congress to rename the Spanish-American War the "Guerra Hispano-Cubanamericana". The emphasis on the Black contribution is reflected in the treatment of Antonio Maceo. See P. W. Fagen, "Antonio Maceo: Heroes, History, and Historiography", *Latin American Research Review* 11, no. 3 (1976): 69–93, and the biography by P. S. Foner, *Antonio Maceo: The Bronze Titan of Cuba's Struggle for Independence* (New York, 1976). For a Spanish audience—as may be seen in the references to speeches during the Spanish civil war—José Martí was the brave hero of reconciliation who, as a "genuine freedom-loving Spaniard," only sought to free Cuba from "official" Spain.

5. For figures see the various censuses of *1899* (Washington), *1907* (Washington), *1919* (Havana), *1931* (Havana, 1938–39), *1943* (Havana, 1945), *1953* (Havana, 1955). The only one providing an adequate occupational breakdown is 1919. Thomas, *Cuba,* passim, extracts much information. See also Cuban Economic Research Project, *A Study on Cuba* (Coral Gables, Florida, 1965), pp. 300–303. For Lister, see *Nuestra Guerra* (Paris, 1966). An insight into one *retorno* may be gained from J. F. Marsal, *Hacer la América: Autobiografía de un inmigrante español en la Argentina* (Buenos Aires, 1969). This edition of an extraordinary autobiography is a model of what is needed in the neglected field of qualitative studies of the immigration process in Latin America. Oral historians need to start moving before *retornos* and immigrants die off.

6. For clubs see Kenny, loc. cit., and *Problems of the New Cuba: Report of the Commission on Cuban Affairs* (Washington, 1935). This is one of the most perceptive and detailed analyses of Cuban society, and fundamental to an understanding of the early 1930s. It influenced radical thinking.

7. For Cuban-Spanish trade see *Problems,* p. 404. This trade was only a small proportion of Cuba's total trade, perhaps some 5 per cent.

8. Quoted in Luis Aguilar, *Cuba, 1933: Prologue to Revolution* (New York, 1972), p. 80. Baliño was a friend of Martí, and also knew Mella. He is thus an important link in the ancestry of the Revolution. He tried to found a socialist party without much success.

9. For mill ownership, see *A Study of Cuba,* p. 238, and *Problems,* pp. 226–30.

10. During the colonial period the Church played a crucial social control function, as is clear from M. Moreno Fraginals, *The Sugar Mill, 1760–1860,* tr. Cedric Belfrage (New York, 1978). The Cuban film, *La última cena* (1977), based on a historical incident, illustrates this well.

11. For the Martí cult see R. G. Gray, *José Martí: Cuban Patriot* (Gainesville, 1962).

12. *Problems,* pp. 119–20; R. Hart Phillips, *Cuba, Island of Paradox* (New York, 1959), pp. 80–81.

13. For repercussions of the 50 percent decree, see *Problems,* pp. 213–14, and M. Kula, *Rewolucja 1933 roku na Kubie* (Warsaw, 1978). I am grateful to a student, M. Debinski, for help in translating this interesting analysis. The decree hit Jamaicans particularly hard, as may be seen from letters sent to the British embassy. Grau and Batista disagreed over the provisions of the decree. Grau insisted on allowing only native-born Cubans to be counted among the 50 percent. Batista wanted the proportion increased to 75 percent, but this to include naturalized Cubans. In spite of the Spanish ambassador's protest, Grau's

view prevailed. E. A. Chester, *A Sergeant Named Batista* (New York, 1954), p. 171.

14. F. Gordón Ordás, *Mi política fuera de España,* 2 vols. (Mexico City, 1965–67), II, 99. This view contrasts with an anonymous article published in Washington, September 11, 1936, pointing out how "the majority of Cubans sympathize with Franco because many had invested money in Spanish properties after the [1933] Revolution and now the leftists have confiscated them." Jaime Torres Bodet [Washington] to Pablo Torres Campos Ortiz, October 15, 1936, Archivo de la Secretaría de Relaciones Exteriories, III/510 (46) "36"/1. III–7676–7, enclosure. I owe this reference to T. G. Powell.

15. For the *colonos* who emerge as one of the most assertive groups in the late 1930s, see *Problems,* pp. 273 et seq., and J. Martínez Alier, *Haciendas, Plantations, and Collective Farms* (London, 1977), chapter 4.

16. For figures of students graduated from Havana University see *Problems,* pp. 154–55. There is an introductory account in English of the student movement by J. Suchlicki, *University Students and Revolution in Cuba, 1920–1926* (Coral Gables, 1969). The lean years of student activity between 1934 and 1940 when the university was closed for two years has been analyzed by N. Pérez Rojas, *El movimiento estudiantil universitario de 1934–40* (Havana, 1975). Pérez finds that science majors declined but that medicine showed the greatest increase.

17. The best account in English is Aguilar, *Cuba, 1933.* For an application of the "Bonapartist" model, see D. L. Raby, "The Cuban Revolution of 1933: An Analysis", University of Glasgow, Occasional Papers, no. 197. See also S. Farber, *Revolution and Reaction in Cuba, 1933–60* (Middletown, Conn., 1976). For an analysis within the framework of economic dependence, see J. R. Benjamin, *The United States and Cuba: Hegemony and Dependent Development, 1880–1934* (Pittsburgh, 1977).

18. Quoted by F. Ortiz, *Cuban Counterpoint: Tobacco and Sugar,* tr. Harriet de Onís (New York, 1940), p. 65.

19. R. Blackburn, "Prologue to the Cuban Revolution", *New Left Review* 21 (1963): 52–91, has a pungent analysis of the middle classes. For a different view, see J. and V. Martínez Alier, *Cuba: Economía y sociedad* (Paris, 1972), pp. 63–73.

20. C. Chapman, *A History of the Cuban Republic* (New York, 1927), is an old-fashioned political history with an American bias. See Louis A. Pérez, "Scholarship and the State: Notes on *A History of the Cuban Republic",* *Hispanic American Historical Review* 54, no. 4 (1974): 682–90. An unpublished paper by Professor Pérez, "La Chambelona: Political Protest, Sugar, and Social Banditry, 1914–1917", probes deeper into the social origins of the 1917 Revolution.

21. For *Avance,* see R. Rexach, *"La Revista de Avance* publicada en La Habana, 1927–30", *Caribbean Studies* 3, no. 3 (1963): 3–16. The most influential book on sugar was R. Guerra y Sánchez, *Azúcar y población en las Antillas* (Havana, 1927).

22. The best insight into the student movement of the early 1930s are the reminiscences of Raúl Roa, *Retorno a la alborada,* 2 vols. (Havana, 1964). For labor, in English see R. J. Alexander, *Communism in Latin America* (New Brunswick, N. J., 1960), and his *Trotskyism in Latin America* (Stanford, 1973).

23. For Guiteras, see J. A. Tabares, *Antonio Guiteras* (Havana, 1975). The program of Joven Cuba is printed also in *Antonio Guiteras: Su pensamiento revolu-*

cionario, selección y estudio introductorio de Olga Cabrera (Havana, 1974), pp. 183–98.

24. The most detailed analysis of the Cuban Apristas, as indeed of the development of Communist thinking, is A. Anderle, *Algunos problemas de la evolución del pensamiento anti-imperialista en Cuba entre las dos guerras mundiales: Comunistas y apristas,* Acta Universitatis Szegediensis de Attila Jozsef Nominatae: Acta Historica, Tomus LII (Szeged, Hungary, 1975).

25. The best overall treatment in English is Alexander, *Communism.*

26. Anderle, *Algunos problemas,* pp. 38–51, for Communist party thinking in 1934–35; Alexander, *Trotskyism,* p. 221. Sandalio Junco, the leading Cuban Trotskyist in the early 1930s, disagreed strongly with the ultra-left line and is reputed to have told Stalin so to his face; he argued that the Cuban middle class was potentially revolutionary. He was assassinated by the Communists in Cuba in 1942.

27. For "septembrismo," see Louis A. Pérez, *Army Politics in Cuba, 1898–1958* (Pittsburgh, 1976), chapter 9.

28. For the 1936 elections, see R. H. Fitzgibbon and H. M. Healey, "The Cuban Elections of 1936", *American Political Science Review* 30, no. 4 (1936): 724–35, and Thomas, *Cuba,* pp. 703–5.

29. *The Communist* 13, no. 11 (1934), quoted in Farber, *Revolution and Reaction,* p. 67.

30. Quoted in Farber, ibid., p. 69.

31. Anderle, *Algunos problemas,* p. 58.

32. Accounts of these negotiations in ibid., pp. 59 et seq.

33. For the Law of Sugar Coordination see *A Study of Cuba,* pp. 339 et seq.

34. The most detailed analysis is Anderle, supra, but see also J. García Montes and A. Alonso Ávila, *Historia del partido comunista de Cuba* (Miami, 1970). The mediator between Batista and the Communists, according to them (p. 196) was the Mexican ambassador Reyes Spindola, whom Gordón described as "one of the most constant and enthusiastic friends of the Spanish Republic." (Gordón Ordás, *Mi política,* I, 734.) He was also a close friend of Batista. He played an important role in the *Arnús* affair (see below).

35. Alexander, *Communism,* p. 278.

36. B. Goldenberg, "The Rise and Fall of the Cuban Communist Party (1925–1959)," *Problems of Communism,* July-August, 1970, p. 72. The quotation is Roa's. Luis Aguilar, *Marxism in Latin America* (New York, 1968), p. 33; Farber, *Revolution and Reaction,* p. 85, quoting Blas Roca's figures. The higher figures refer to electoral registrations, not to party members.

37. Quoted in Aguilar, *Marxism,* p. 138.

38. I. F. Gellman, *Roosevelt and Batista: Good Neighbor Diplomacy in Cuba, 1933–1945* (Albuquerque, 1973), passim.

39. *El Universal* (Mexico City), November 30, 1938, refers to a meeting of the CTM's National Committee at which it was resolved to send an "homenaje al pueblo cubano" out of respect for its fight against fascism. Batista was regarded as a friend of democracy.

40. Gordón, *Mi política,* II, passim. The relevant sections of Gordón's justificatory memoirs—some 200 pages in vol. 1 and 250 pages of vol. 2—are the major printed source for Cuban-Spanish relations from 1936 to 1939, and include telegrams, letters, speeches, and newspaper articles.

41. Originally the *Cristóbal Colón*, with a cargo of coal from Cardiff, was ordered to Veracruz to collect arms, but it went aground in Bermuda, whereupon the *Manuel Arnús* was ordered to replace it. Gordón telegraphed Valencia to say that it was useless sending a ship without three million dollars to pay for the arms. The difficulties of obtaining arms due to the embargo were so great that Gordón even considered, in desperation, going to Bolivia to buy Chaco war surplus stocks!

42. ASRE, III/510 (46) "37"/1, III–767–6. "Actitud de Cuba en la rebelión de España". Once again, I owe this reference to Professor Powell.

43. Gordón, *Mi política*, I, 728 et seq. Gordón believed the whole incident could have been cleared up with a couple of hours' talk with Batista, but the pressure of work prevented him from leaving Mexico.

44. Gordón, *Mi política*, II, 25 et seq. For his earlier career, see his *Mi política en España*, 3 vols. (Mexico City, 1962–63).

45. Gordón, *Mi política*, II, 55.

46. Ibid., pp. 116 et seq.

47. Ibid., p. 87.

48. Ibid., pp. 94–96.

49. Ibid., p. 96 n. This refers to Batista's post as a sergeant-stenographer. Being present at military trials of students gave him contacts that he would otherwise not have had. Batista fancied his oratorical skills much as Gordón did.

50. Ibid., pp. 97–98.

51. Ibid., pp. 45 et seq.

52. *Discurso pronunciado ante 12,000 personas por J. I Rivero en la fiesta de "plato único" celebrada por la Falange Española, 19–II–1939* (Havana, 1939).

53. A. Augier, *Nicolás Guillén: Notas para un estudio biográfico-crítico*, 2 vols. (Havana, 1964), II, 64–65.

54. Gordón, *Mi política*, II, 189.

55. *Nosotros* 1, no. 10 (1938): 26–27, for a breakdown of the distribution of members.

56. T. Casuso, *Castro and Cuba* (New York, 1961), p. 80.

57. Gordón, *Mi política*, II, 119.

58. Ibid., pp. 193, 221–28. Estimates vary about the number attending Gordón's speeches, but fifteen to twenty thousand seems to have been a normal attendance except for his first speech in July 1938, when the pro-Republicans estimated that a hundred thousand came to the Polar Stadium. This was owned by a brewer who lent it free of charge. The *Diario de la Marina* estimate was fifteen thousand! (ibid., pp. 33–41).

59. Ibid., pp. 154–61. For Pi y Margall's career and ideas, see C. A. M. Hennessy, *The Federal Republic in Spain: Pi y Margall and the Federal Republican Movement, 1868–74* (Oxford, 1962). Pi's ideas were elaborated in *Las nacionalidades* (Madrid, 1876). His ideas are experiencing something of a revival in contemporary Spain, as federalism seems a solution to the desire of regions submitted to Franco's centralization for forty years for a degree of autonomy. Pi was not a regionalist and would have no sympathy for exclusive Basque or Catalan claims.

60. Pedro Crespo in the *Alcalde de Zalamea* by Calderón de la Barca was another hero of the White Legend (Gordón, *Mi política*, II, 229 et seq., "Pedro Crespo y la defensa de Madrid"). Unlike "il popolo" or "le peuple," "el pueblo" means both town and "the people." Hence the word had a resonance, rooted

in that localism that has been recognized as a dominant feature of Spanish life, lacking elsewhere. "La nación," with its artificial connotations in contrast to "el pueblo" or, in the Spanish American context, "madre patria," has little emotional pull. The use of "el pueblo" was preempted by the left, whereas the right significantly used "la nación" to the extent of calling themselves *nacionalistas*.

61. Pablo de la Torriente Brau, *En España, peleando con los milicianos: Selección y estudio preliminar de Jorge Max Rojas* (Mexico City, 1972), pp. 52 et seq. See also R. Roa, *Pablo de la Torriente Brau y la revolución española* (Havana, 1937). Casuso, *Castro and Cuba*, pp. 82–83, denies he was ever a Communist, but the poet Miguel Hernández, who served in the same unit, refers to his party card being found on his corpse (*Peleando*, p. 54). To the Communists, anxious to establish a revolutionary ancestry to match that of the nationalist radical tradition, and the anti-Communists, anxious to deny them one, the issue is far from academic.

62. J. Marinello, *Hombres de la España leal* (Havana, 1938), p. 111.

63. K. Valdés, "A Soldier Named Pablo: Interview with Gustavo Fabel, a Prisonmate of Pablo de la Torriente Brau," *Granma* (English edition), January 2, 1977.

64. Phillips, *Cuba*, p. 176; Thomas, *Spanish Civil War*, p. 547 n.; A. Castells, *Las brigadas internacionales de la guerra de España* (Barcelona, 1974), p. 381; J. A. Tabares, "Los voluntarios internacionales cubanos", *Granma*, December 25, 1971.

65. *International Solidarity with the Spanish Republic, 1936–39* (Moscow, 1975), pp. 102–6. In the 1940s an agreement was signed between Spain and Cuba to repatriate 632 Cubans still in Spain. José D. Cabus, *Batista: Su pensamiento y acción, 1933–44* (Havana, 1944), p. 10. This suggests that the numbers may well be as high as Russian estimates.

66. Guillén, "Un pelotero, capitán de ametralladores," *Mediodía*, December 6, 1937.

67. Information on the groups is in Thomas, *Cuba*, passim, and also R. Bonachea and M. San Martín, *The Cuban Insurrection, 1952–59* (New Brunswick, N. J., 1974). R. Sadler of New Mexico State University at Las Cruces has studied the conspiracies of the 1940s and is publishing his findings in book form.

68. Gordón, *Mi política*, II, 251–54, and Romero (Havana) to Eduardo Hay (Mexico City), June 22, 1940, ASRE, III/553 (46)/1025, III–2394–15.

69. V. Llorens, *La emigración republicana de 1939* (Madrid, 1976), pp. 176–79.

70. See A. Bayo, *Mi desembarco en Mallorca* (Mexico City, 1944), and *Mi aporte a la revolución cubana* (Havana, 1960). He also wrote a miniature handbook on guerrilla warfare and a volume of poems, *Fidel te espera en la sierra* (Havana, 1959).

71. C. D. Ameringer, *The Democratic Left in Exile: The Anti-Dictatorial Struggle in the Caribbean, 1945–59* (Coral Gables, 1974), pp. 81, 92.

72. Alexander, *Communism*, pp. 300–302.

73. Thomas, *Cuba*, pp. 1081–82; he comments that the appointments at La Cabaña mark the beginning of Communist influence in the rebel army. The party in the army is now one of the major loci of power. A majority of the members of the Central Committee of the Communist party are military men.

74. For the congress, see the jaundiced account in Stephen Spender's autobiography, *World Within World* (London, 1951), pp. 238–42; Augier, *Nicolás Guillén*, II, 67–76; J. Franco, *César Vallejo: The Dialectics of Poetry and Silence* (Cambridge, 1976), chapter 9.

75. The Spanish Americans included, Raúl González Tuñón, Cayetano Córdova Iturburu, and Pablo Rojas Paz of Argentina; Pablo Neruda, Vicente Huidobro, and Alberto Romero of Chile; Octavio Paz, José Mancisidor, and Carlos Pellicer of Mexico; César Vallejo of Peru; Jacques Roumain of Haiti; and Jorge Icaza of Ecuador. The Spaniards included Rafael Alberti, José Bergamín, León Felipe, Juan Chabas, Vicente Aleixandre, Luis Cernuda, Antonio Machado, and Emilio Prados. From the United States there were Ernest Hemingway, Langston Hughes, and Malcolm Cowley. In addition, there was a wide range of European writers—Andre Malraux, Julian Benda, Heinrich Mann, Ludwig Renn, Ilya Ehrenberg, Alexis Tolstoy, and Michael Kolstov.

76. Pablo Neruda, *Memorias: Yo confieso que he vivido* (Buenos Aires, 1974), p. 171. His account of the congress is trivialized. He seems more interested in poking fun at Huidobro, whom he disliked, than in illuminating the congress he helped to organize.

77. R. González Echevarría, *Alejo Carpentier: The Pilgrim at Home* (Ithaca, N. Y., 1977), chapter 2. The *Carteles* article was "España bajo las bombas", September 12, 1937.

78. For literary generations of 1898, 1927, and 1936, see in English D. Shaw, *The Generation of 1898 in Spain* (London, 1975), H. Ramsden, *The 1898 Movement in Spain* (Manchester, 1974), C. B. Morris, *A Generation of Spanish Poets, 1920–1936* (Cambridge, 1969), and J. Ferran and D. P. Testa, *Spanish Writers of 1936: Crisis and Commitment* (London, 1973)

79. For the *romance* during the war, see the excellent work of J. Lechner, *El compromiso en la poesía española del siglo XX*, 2 vols. (Leiden, 1968), Vol. 2 reprints some. See also the reprint of E. Prados and E. A. Rodríguez Monino, *Romancero general de la guerra de España* (Milan, 1966), which was originally published in Madrid and Valencia in 1937. Parallels might be drawn with the Mexican *corrido*, which stemmed originally from the *romance*, but, although used by Mexican Communists in *El Machete* in the 1920s, it was never taken up by major Mexican writers, perhaps because it lacked the subtlety of the *romance*.

80. *Mediodía*, October 25, 1937; "Un poeta en espardeñas," in *Prosa de prisa*, 2 vols., (Havana, 1975), I, 88–93.

81. M. Auclair, *Enfances et morts de García Lorca* (Paris, 1968), pp. 205–29, 451–55; *El poeta en La Habana* (Havana, 1961); J. Sabourin, "Federico García Lorca en Santiago de Cuba", *Revista de la Universidad de Oriente*, (March 1962).

82. Guillén and Marinello were in Mexico, where they had been invited to a conference by the Liga de Escritores y Artistas Revolucionarios, when the invitation to the congress arrived. The two then traveled to France via Canada with Octavio Paz.

83. *Mediodía*, November 1, 1937; "La Alianza de Intelectuales españoles", in *Prosa de prisa*, I, 102–5.

84. From his speech in Paris on July 16, 1937, in ibid., p. 85.

85. "La hermosa lección del pueblo español", in ibid., pp. 146–52.

86. Augier, *Nicolás Guillén*, II, 77 n.

87. *Mediodía*, June 20, 1937, "Sirenas en Paris", in *Prosa de prisa*, I, 84.

88. Quoted in Franco, *César Vallejo,* p. 223.
89. *Mediodía,* August 17, 1937; speech to the congress in Madrid in *Prosa de prisa,* I, 81.
90. Langston Hughes, *I Wonder As I Wander: An Autobiographical Journey* (New York, 1956), pp. 321 et seq.
91. J. Marinello, *Momento Español* (Havana, 1939), p. 218.
92. Between 1973 and 1976 Cuban exports to Spain jumped from $55M to $321M, while Spanish exports to Cuba rose from $38M to $182M. Spain is Cuba's third largest customer, after Russia and Japan (*Economist Foreign Report,* June 9, 1976, pp. 7–8). Cuba is the largest buyer of Spanish industrial goods abroad, and Spain has built most of Cuba's fishing fleet. It has been estimated that there may be as many as 250,000 Cubans of Spanish parentage who have a theoretical right to Spanish citizenship.
93. N. Valdés, "Análisis generacional: Realidad, premisas, y método", *Areito* (New York) 3, no. 4 (1977): 19–26, has questioned the usefulness of the concept. The most useful discussion by a historian of the generational concept in a broad focus is A. Spitzer, "The Historical Problem of Generations", *American Historical Review* 78, no. 5 (1973): 1353–85, and that of sociologist P. Abrams, "Rites de Passage: The Conflict of Generations in Industrial Society", *Journal of Contemporary History* 5, no. 1 (1970): 175–90. Two writers who have used the concept to interpret aspects of the Cuban Revolution are M. Zeitlin, *Revolutionary Politics and the Cuban Working Class* (Princeton, N. J., 1965), and E. González, *Cuba under Castro: The Limits of Charisma* (Boston, 1974). We need some studies on Spanish students, but see A. Jato, *La rebelión de los estudiantes: Apuntes para una historia del SEU* (Madrid, 1953), and J. M. Maravall, *Dictatorship and Political Dissent: Workers and Students in Franco Spain* (Tavistock, 1978). In the 1930s the Falange had an appeal for students—and indeed, without support from students and the young, it is doubtful if Fascist movements could have had any success. Not for nothing was the marching song of the Italian Fascists *Giovanezza,* and *Horst Wessel* one of the most favored of martyrs to the Nazis. In Spain, José Antonio clearly had a compulsive attraction for students. In Latin America, in contrast to Europe, students have invariably been left of center, and this can be related to the mystique of the University Reform movement.
94. Lechner in *El compromiso,* supra, remarks on the dominance of rural imagery in the *romances* and other poetry of the civil war, as well as the absence of Catalan contributions.
95. The Saint-Simonian antithesis between "producteurs" and "oisifs" and the technocratic implications of this thought are now coming to be seen as the brilliant insight they were in the 1820s. See G. Ionescu, *The Political Thought of Saint-Simon* (Oxford, 1976). It is extraordinary how long it has taken historians to take the concept of technology transfer seriously. Any balanced analysis of the reasons why Russia was able to survive after 1917 and develop "socialism in one country" must pay far more attention to those reserves of technical expertise on which the Bolshevik leadership could draw. They were able to do this because of the considerable scientific sub-culture that existed in pre-revolutionary Russia—the scientists and technologists who welcomed the opportunities the revolution offered for the exercise of their talents. A unique feature of the Cuban revolution has been the post-revolutionary development of such a scientific culture, aided paradoxically by the blockade and the breathing space it afforded to change the educational structure with Eastern Bloc aid. Cuba is

now an exporter of technicians, and the fact that they could not be utilized in Latin America provides one more explanation as to why Cuba has become involved in Africa. More attention should be paid, in analyses of the reasons for the failure of the Second Spanish Republic, to the dearth of technical expertise. Too much energy has gone into hair-splitting analyses of political rivalries. One historian who senses the problem is E. Malefakis in his magesterial work, *Agrarian Reform and Peasant Revolution in Spain: Origins of the Civil War* (New Haven, 1970).

96. For Spanish intellectuals, see M. Tuñón de Lara, *Medio siglo de cultura española (1885–1936)* (Madrid, 1970).

97. For intellectuals in Cuba, see J. A. Weiss, *Casa de las Americas: An Intellectual Review in the Cuban Revolution* (Chapel Hill, 1977).

98. For the best analysis of the continuing populist tradition, see M. Valdés, *Ideological Roots of the Cuban Revolutionary Movement*, University of Glasgow Occasional Papers, no. 15 (1975). For post-1933, Farber, *Revolution and Reaction.*

99. The Asturias rising of 1934 marks a turning-point, and the Popular Front elections are the culmination of working-class solidarity. Nevertheless, the attitudes between Communists and anarchists continued to be highly ambivalent. In Cuba the anarchist viewpoint got no hearing, as, unlike the Communists, they had no international propaganda organization.

100. The best analysis of Lerroux is J. Romero Maura, *La rosa de fuego* (Barcelona, 1975), which treats of 1909. Lerrouxism in the Second Republic has not been adequately treated.

Colombia

David Bushnell

Within a week of the outbreak of the Spanish civil war both houses of the Colombian Congress had unanimously adopted resolutions of solidarity with the Loyalist regime.[1] This accurately foreshadowed the role of Colombia as the Spanish Republic's most persistent supporter, after Mexico, among Latin American governments. It did not at all accurately reflect Colombian opinion on the struggle, which, just as in the rest of Latin America, was deeply and bitterly divided. Again as in the rest of the region, though undoubtedly more than in most countries, the Spanish struggle had a powerful effect because the issues it posed and the circumstances out of which it developed so closely paralleled the situation of the New World nation itself.

The fall of the Spanish monarchy in 1931 came just one year after the end of the so-called Conservative hegemony in Colombia and the return of the Liberal party to control of the government by electoral means after almost fifty years of Conservative domination. In both countries the change had been greeted by its supporters as the dawn of a new era of fresh ideas and vigorous action for solving problems that the previous regimes—backward-looking, corrupt, and ineffective— had been unable or unwilling to cope with. In both cases, the new rulers eventually fell to quarreling among themselves over the proper pace and scope of innovation, among other things, while their adversaries recovered from the shock of defeat and launched a counterattack. Hence, in Colombia as in Spain, the decade of the 1930s witnessed a rise of political and social agitation, including outright violence. To be sure, there were important differences. Spain, for all the backwardness that appealed to certain romantic spirits at home and abroad, had progressed considerably farther on the road to conventional western-style modernization than Colombia, a country whose capital and largest city, with around three hundred thousand people, did not even have a railroad or highway connection with the next largest, Medellín. Colombia had no heavy industry and only a moderate amount of light industry; though there were enclaves devoted to petroleum and bananas, the production of coffee for export and food for domestic consumption were far and away the principal economic activities. The beginnings of serious labor and agrarian unrest, it is true, were definitely present, but Colombia had no significant Marxist or other leftist parties and, at the beginning of the decade, not much more in the way of labor unions.[2] At least in part, this weakness of the working-class organizations was due to the presence of something that Spain signally lacked: an entrenched two-party system whose traditional allegiances blanketed the entire population and had the effect of diverting popular discontent into sterile Liberal-Conservative partisan feuds.

Starting in 1930, the first phase of the Colombian Liberal regime, under the presidency of Enrique Olaya Herrera, was marked by a generally conciliatory political atmosphere at the upper levels (with even a bipartisan coalition in effect) and numerous outbursts of political bloodletting in the back country, as lesser Liberals set out to avenge a half century of real or imaginary grievances and local Conservatives proved sometimes less ready to accept the election results than Conservative clubmen in Bogotá. Preoccupied with this problem of political violence, not to mention the world depression and eventually the Leticia conflict with Peru, Olaya failed in practice to make a serious attack on the nation's underlying social and economic problems. Indeed, he was himself a moderate Liberal in the traditional mold whose policies were tempered by fiscal orthodoxy and by a conscious deference to U.S. economic interests. In 1934, however, Olaya delivered the presidency to a fellow Liberal, Alfonso López Pumarejo, who discarded coalition government for an all-Liberal administration and embarked on a more sweeping program grandly entitled *La revolución en marcha*. It was ambitious, at least by Colombian standards, both in its expressed objective of fully incorporating the masses and middle sectors into Colombian political and economic life and in certain of its concrete innovations, such as vigorous government support of labor unionization and a first agrarian reform law. Yet it was all too reminiscent of nineteenth-century Liberal-Conservative conflict in that it also included some minor attacks on the position of the church, thus serving to give the religious question a new lease on life in Colombian politics.[3]

López's program in and of itself and his concurrent willingness to accept the support of the nation's tiny Communist party—symbolized by the presence of a Communist leader alongside the president at the 1936 May Day celebration[4]—were portrayed in alarmist terms by the Conservative opposition and by one sector of the ruling Liberals. What was happening in Colombia was compared with that dreadful Mexican Revolution, then at its most radical under Lázaro Cárdenas, and somewhat less insistently, at least prior to July 1936, with the evils being perpetrated by Popular Front supporters in Spain. The fact that Colombian Communists and certain left-leaning Liberals who strongly backed López went so far as to indulge in loose talk of Popular Fronts for Colombia[5] provided additional pretexts for sounding the alarm and further ensured that the Spanish civil war, when it came, would have a major effect on Colombia. No Colombian Popular Front was ever formally created, but there was often tactical cooperation between groups of *lopista* Liberals and Communists or other miscellaneous leftists. And the argument that Colombia did not need a Popular Front because the Liberal party administration already served the same purpose, which appeared to be the official answer to those who raised the question,[6] did not exactly quiet the fears that were expressed.

At the same time, one factor that heightened the emotional and political effect of the Spanish civil war in such countries as Argentina and Cuba was conspicuously absent: a resident Spanish colony of significant size. Among the principal Latin American nations, none had proved less attractive to post-colonial currents of immigration than Colombia. An official count of foreigners living in Colombia, released early in 1939—almost at the end of the Spanish struggle—put Venezuelans in first place with a total of 4,546 (mainly clustered near the border), Germans in second place with 3,637, and Spaniards in third with 2,273.[7] The figures admittedly represented a slight underenumeration and did not include those few foreigners who had become naturalized, but they do reveal the minute size of the Spanish colony in a total population of about nine million. The count of Spaniards would not yet have included more than a handful of civil war refugees, whereas the German total was already swollen with Jewish and other refugees from the Nazis. As was the case with other European colonies in Colombia, the Spaniards were influential out of proportion to their numbers. They included a good many priests (e.g., a comfortable majority of the community of Augustinian religious)[8] and such enterprising business people as the Carulla clan, which later on, after undergoing Colombian naturalization during World War II,[9] would put its name on the principal chain of Bogotá supermarkets. Unfortunately, no detailed occupational or other breakdown of resident Spaniards exists, but even taking into account a higher than average level of achievement by individuals they were not important as a group.

Neither were there significant Spanish investments in Colombia nor a high level of trade between the two countries. In the last pre–civil war year, 1935, Colombia imported 1,278,239 pesos of Spanish goods and sold 643,554, mostly coffee, in return. (At the time, the peso was worth 1.75 to the U.S. dollar.) The figures represented 3 percent and 1 1/2 percent, respectively, of the trade with all countries.[10] The fact that Spain normally enjoyed a favorable balance in trade with Colombia had led the Spanish government to give Colombian coffee relatively preferential treatment in applying the trade restrictions that Spain like so many countries adopted in response to the economic problems of the world depression.[11] Nevertheless, the commercial relationship remained quite limited, and it was not wholly satisfactory to Colombia.

Some Colombians did, of course, have a feeling of cultural affinity with Spain. They took pride in their reputation for speaking the purest Spanish in Latin America, although in reality that reputation was based on the speech of upper-class *bogotanos* and other educated inhabitants of the Andean interior; it certainly did not apply to the speech of Barranquilla or Quibdó. Colombian writings and oratory were well sprinkled with allusions to Cervantes and Calderón and to the heroic virtues of the Spanish discoverers and colonizers. Indeed, Colombians of both white and mixed race made no cult of the fallen Chibchas but were content to identify with the *conquistadores:* the main east-west artery in downtown Bogotá was the Avenida Jiménez de Quesada, whereas no street or major landmark bore the name of Tisquesusa, the last Zipa.[12] However, this easy acceptance of the Spanish heritage did not necessarily imply much familiarity with or interest in current Spanish literature and intellectual trends, and furthermore emphasis on the positive aspects of that heritage was always more common among Conservatives than among Liberals. It was the former who carefully nurtured a political alliance with that preeminent example of the Spanish legacy, the Roman Catholic church, whereas the latter had never fully outgrown the systematic anti-Spanish reaction of the nineteenth century. Yet appreciation for the Spanish heritage was not unqualified even in the rhetorical baggage of Conservatives. In a famous disquisition of 1928 on what was wrong with Colombia, the man who would emerge as the foremost leader of the Conservative party after its fall from power —Laureano Gómez—devoted a good share of attention to the shortcomings of his countrymen's Spanish forebears, who had managed to produce "none of those outstanding luminaries who guide the human spirit and point new ways for the conquest of wisdom." He further exclaimed:

> May heaven forbid that in inheriting the hardness of Asturias or Andulu-sian grace, the impulsiveness of Extremadura or Catalan dryness, the tenacity of the Basques or the haughty inertia of the Castilians, we may have received also the blindness, ineptitude, and laziness of their rulers and the cowardly and damaging resignation to tolerate them.[13]

The same Laureano Gómez, when in 1935 he published an analysis of the contemporary world and its problems under the title *El cuad-rilátero,*[14] wrote it in the form of sketches of the four men he considered to be the most significant figures on the international scene: Hitler, Mussolini, and Stalin, all of whom he condemned unmercifully, and Gandhi, whom he held up as an example for emulation. Clearly, the Gandhian virtures of humility and non-violence were not those conventionally associated either with the Spanish *conquistadores* or with the budding Falange of the 1930s. It is thus hardly surprising that Gómez was not among the Colombian discoverers and early admirers of José Antonio Primo de Rivera. He, and in fact the mainstream of Colombian Conservatives, tended to empathize instead—when they looked at Spain at all—with the parties of the parliamentary right. They had shed no tears over the fall of the monarchy, but they were quick to deplore the anticlerical excesses of the Republic, even while carefully distinguishing between those evils and the republican system itself. In greeting the rightist election victory of 1933, the Conservative daily *El País* quite typically observed: "The reaction has not been against the democratic republican method of government: it has been against the atheist and clerophobe gang that had exalted itself on the anguished backs of a credulous people."[15] Such a view was wholly congruent with the standard Conservative position on politics in Colombia, which was to proclaim democratic republicanism as the creed best suited to the nation's political genius, and the Conservative party as the foremost exponent of that creed, while assailing the Liberals for their failure to honor that same creed in practice.

Only on the extreme right of the Conservative party were there some who even before the outbreak of the Spanish war were prepared to dismiss "the democratic republican method" as hopelessly decadent and corrupt and who were openly attracted to authoritarian, corporatist, Fascist, or proto-Fascist alternatives. Such men tended to claim for themselves the labels "Nationalist" and "Rightist," although other Conservatives denied they had any exclusive right to them. They were few in total numbers, and they very definitely did not include any of those Conservative elder statesmen such as Abel Carbonell, Francisco de Paula Pérez, and Esteban Jaramillo, who since the days of the Conservative hegemony had acquired a reputation for close association with Anglo-Saxon business interests.[16] They did include a disproportionate share of the party's younger activists. Their most prominent spokesman was Silvio Villegas, who in due course published the volume *No hay enemigos a la derecha*[17] that was at least in part a reply to *El cuadrilátero*. Another of their leaders was Guillermo León Valencia, who became the first Conservative president of the later National Front but in 1936 was director of *Claridad* in Popayán, which billed itself as "organ of the counterrevolutionary phalanxes" and called for Colombia to be saved by "a he-man in a black shirt" (*un macho de camisa negra*).[18] Nor did this one branch of Colombian conservatism have any doubt that Spain was in need of the same. A writer in the weekly *Derechas* observed that the defeat of the right in the Spanish elections of February 1936 was a "natural consequence" of the unwillingness of José María Gil Robles to make a clean break with the democratic system. The situation demanded instead "an integral, authoritarian, and modern Fascist"—like José Antonio.[19] For that matter, even Gómez, who occasionally wrote for *Derechas* himself, agreed that the great error of Gil Robles had been to be a compromiser;[20] but Gómez did not automatically look on the observance of democratic formalities as a fateful compromising of sound principle.

On the other side of the party division in Colombia, among the Liberals, a comparable distinction can be made between the mainstream of the party and its outer fringes in their attitude toward the Spanish situation. The former, whose position on any issue was most faithfully reflected in the pages of *El Tiempo*, the newspaper of Eduardo Santos, felt a close affinity with Spain's own liberal and republican center. Liberals of the Santos variety distrusted the CEDA of Gil Robles as clerical and reactionary but were equally opposed to Marxism: what inspired their enthusiasm was a figure like Manuel Azaña, who seemed to want for Spain the very things that they stood for in Colombia. Hence they welcomed Azaña's coming to power in February 1936, although they also had misgivings about many of his Popular Front associates. Between the Liberals who took their opinions ready-made from the columns of *El Tiempo* and those others who considered Santos and his newspaper too complaisant toward the radicalism of the López administration at home, the main difference in assessment of developments in Spain was an even more intense fear among the latter of Popular Frontism. These "right-wing" Liberals eventually obtained a separate mouthpiece in *La Razón,* founded in September 1936 by Juan Lozano y Lozano, but they were hardly rightists in the sense of Silvio Villegas or the youthful Valencia: they were merely unreconstructed nineteenth-century liberals, and as such they still found Azaña, if not his leftist collaborators, more acceptable than José Antonio (or José Calvo Sotelo). Then, at the other extreme of the Liberal party, there was a self-proclaimed leftist minority that wholeheartedly supported López, was not terrified of Popular Fronts either at home or abroad, and rejoiced without seeming mental reservation over the "splendid leftist victory" in the February 1936 Spanish elections.[21] The principal representative of this viewpoint in the press of Bogotá, *El Diario Nacional,* nevertheless showed far more interest in the British royal family than in anything that happened in Spain before July 17, 1936. Perhaps only the Colombian Communists could be said to feel a really intense commitment to the Spanish Popular Front regime prior to the rebellion.

Colombian Views of the Spanish Uprising

When the Spanish civil war began, it immediately absorbed—and retained—a large share of the attention of literate, especially urban, Colombians. The extent to which members of the traditional peasantry were even aware of it is impossible to estimate, but any Colombians regularly reached by the mass communications media could hardly ignore what was happening in the *madre patria.* The Spanish civil war did not once disappear from the first page of *El Tiempo* until December 5, 1936, when it was temporarily pushed off by the combination of the Buenos Aires peace conference and the British abdication crisis; from July 18 to the end of the year, it occupied on the average all or part of 4.1 front-page columns each day.[22] In *El Siglo,* the newspaper of Laureano Gómez that was the main national organ of the Conservative opposition, a similar situation prevailed. As it was more concerned than *El Tiempo* with publicizing domestic calamities and official abuses, *El Siglo*'s front page was more often wholly taken up with Colombian affairs, but the daily average for page-one civil war coverage from the beginning of the struggle through December 31 was almost identical: 4.0 columns. Outside Bogotá, Medellín's *El Colombiano* in the first week of August had to apologize to its readers for a deterioration in its appearance, observing that circulation had increased to such an extent because of public interest in the Spanish events that it ran out of supplies of imported ink and had to substitute an inferior domestic product.[23] Public interest was further manifested in street demonstrations in favor of one side or the other[24] and in the cheers and catcalls that greeted newsreel coverage of the Spanish struggle in Colombian theaters.[25] The show of sympathies elicited by newsreels was perhaps the closest equivalent in Colombia to an opinion poll on the subject, however skewed a sample the audiences may have been. And it was won by the Nationalists, according to the admission of the generally pro-Republican *El Tiempo*.[26]

It need hardly be added that the sympathies expressed correlated rather closely with Colombian political affiliation. In the case of Conservatives, in fact, support for the Nationalists was both unanimous and uniformly exuberant. It transcended factional and ideological differences within the party, although it is also true that not all Conservatives read the same things into the Spanish rebellion. Predictably, to the extreme rightist fringe it was one more landmark in a spreading world reaction against bankrupt liberal democracy and in favor of anti-parliamentary authoritarian solutions to the problems of the modern world. As Silvio Villegas was happy to point out, where Gil Robles and other such maneuverers and compromisers had failed, Franco, by openly establishing a military dictatorship and proclaiming a corporatist state, was now succeeding.[27] Most Conservative spokesmen, however, were not prepared to renounce the traditional forms of democratic and constitutional government that in their view had flourished in Colombia precisely during the years of Conservative hegemony. They accordingly saw the Spanish rebellion as a holy crusade to rid the body politic of Marxist corruptions and reaffirm traditional Catholic values, and only secondarily, if at all, as a movement to establish a new order comparable to those in Germany and Italy. *El Colombiano,* which claimed to be the authentic mouthpiece of *antioqueño* Conservatism, described the uprising in Spain as a reaction of "monarchists and conservative republicans."[28] In somewhat similar fashion, one early editorial of *El Siglo* remarked:

> Therefore we today accompany in spirit the Spanish army, seasoned in battle, adorned with so many and such heroic virtues, illumined by religious faith, in the campaign that it opened a few days ago to restore in its fatherland order, justice, respect for law, properly understood freedom, and peace of conscience.[29]

El Siglo apparently did not assume that "properly understood freedom" (*libertad bien entendida*) would mean quite the same thing in Spain as it meant, or ought to mean, in Colombia, for another paragraph of the same editorial contained the statement, "From Spain we are separated only by profound, almost instinctive, republican and democratic sentiments." Yet clearly it did hope and expect that Nationalist Spain would follow a course somewhere between the totalitarianisms of right and left. And if Franco was not fighting for democracy, at least he could not be accused of destroying it, since from the standpoint of Colombian Conservatives that had already been accomplished by the irresponsibility of Spanish liberals and the savagery of the Spanish left.[30]

Though it did not have an overt affiliation with any party, the Colombian church as of the 1930s normally took the same position on any issue as the Conservative party—or vice versa. Certainly the Spanish civil war was no exception. The episcopate observed the *Día de la Raza* in 1936 by issuing a formal declaration of solidarity with Nationalist Spain.[31] Both in Bogotá and in remote small towns, and on the initiative either of the clergy themselves or of lay Catholics, church functions were repeatedly used to call attention to the Spanish struggle and to show support for the Nationalists in particular. The occasion might be a thanksgiving for the alleged fall of Madrid[32] or prayers for the souls of those fallen in "the good cause."[33] Whether the church was speaking as an institution or whether members of the clergy as individuals were joining in the debate, emphasis was normally placed on the Nationalist movement as a crusade against Marxism and irreligion rather than on its significance as a triumphant reaction against parliamentary democracy, but certainly clerical spokesmen were not inclined to mince words. One can only imagine what back-country priests must have said to their flock from the Sunday pulpit. However, the Jesuits who ran the otherwise sedate *Revista Javeriana* included in it a regular section of "Letters from Spain" with first-hand accounts of both Nationalist heroism and Red barbarism,[34] and one special issue, appropriately entitled *España Mártir*, was later distributed in a "second economy edition" of five thousand copies.[35]

Even at the end of the Spanish conflict, Colombia's *franquistas* were still divided among themselves as to the essential characteristics of the Nationalist movement and what now to expect from its victory. In a sample of political and intellectual figures interviewed by *El Siglo,* however, only one Franco supporter expressed actual concern over what would come next, making clear that either a restoration of "the discredited dynasty of the Bourbons" or a Nazi-Fascist dictatorship—both of which he apparently viewed as possible—would be highly unfortunate.[36] At the same time, the Jesuit Félix Restrepo, high priest of Colombian corporatism, both recognized that Spain under the Nationalists would be in some sense Fascist and predicted that such a phase would last only two years, after which the monarchy would be restored; at least to him, none of this was particularly disturbing.[37] One writer in *El Colombiano,* as the war neared its close, confidently expected Franco's Spain to become an example of "Christian democracy," whereas another in the same newspaper (the only constant of whose editorial policy was distaste for Laureano Gómez's centralized Conservative party leadership) did not hesitate to lump the new Spain with the other European Fascist nations in a "Mussolini-Hitler-Franco axis" that was triumphantly saving Europe.[38] And though many Conservatives saw in a victorious Franco regime a potential rallying point for Hispanic America against U.S. political and economic influence and French cultural tutelage, there were still some who saw no contradiction between their love of Franco and a continuing acceptance of Pan-Americanist verities.[39] What all these views obviously had in common was the conviction that Franco, whatever he did next, had at least saved Spain from several different fates worse than death: from atheism, anarchy, and the sway of Moscow.

Among Liberals, meanwhile, the outbreak of the Spanish civil war had produced a tide of sentiment in favor of the Loyalists that at least initially was almost as automatic as support for the Spanish Insurgents among Conservatives. This was reflected in the unanimous congressional resolutions of solidarity with the Spanish Republic that have already been mentioned: since Conservatives had been boycotting the polls on the pretext that the Liberal regime was engaged in systematic electoral manipulation, the Congress had only Liberal members, who would be joined in 1937 by a lone Communist. Naturally the Communists, together with those Liberals who defined themselves as leftist within their own party, were particularly enthusiastic for the cause of the Republic, which they supported without ever appearing to waver. Both groups were usually in the forefront of pro-Loyalist rallies and demonstrations, at which the speakers were likely to include such Liberals as the journalist-politician José Combariza ("José Mar") and the rising social scientist Antonio García, and the Mexican flag and anthem were probably in evidence alongside the Colombian and Spanish.[40] The leftist minority were also inclined to view the Nationalist uprising as the response of a "parasitic minority" to the Republic's valiant effort to correct "semi-feudal" economic conditions.[41] They did not accept for the Spanish government any appreciable share of blame for the conflict, save insofar as it had been guilty of too much patience toward its declared enemies.[42]

The attitude of other Liberals was more complex, and varied observably over time. All unequivocally denounced the military uprising per se, including some senators who voted for their chamber's pro-

Republic declaration in July 1936 with the specification that they meant to show their condemnation of the rebellion rather than approval of the Communist and anarchist tendencies on the Loyalist side.[43] In fact, most Liberals were sincerely and frankly aghast at the excesses that almost immediately broke out in reaction *to* the uprising, particularly after it was learned early in August that a group of fellow Colombians had been killed by Red militiamen, whereas Nationalist excesses were generally unnoticed or denied by Conservative commentators. The Liberal press—on occasion even including the leftists' *El Diario Nacional*[44] —proved willing to print articles by or interviews with Franco sympathizers, something that Conservative organs virtually never did for the Loyalists. Some Liberals, moreover, ultimately came to the point of deciding that it was impossible in good conscience to support either of the warring parties. One exponent of such a position was Enrique Santos, brother of Eduardo and, under the penname of "Calibán" in the latter's newspaper, the most widely read Colombian columnist.[45] A plague on both your houses was likewise the underlying tone of comments on the war in the pages of *La Razón,* which under the direction of Juan Lozano y Lozano was a frankly anti-López and unabashedly pro-capitalist organ of traditional Liberal thinking.[46]

A few Liberals evolved to the point of actually supporting Franco. *El Siglo* on various occasions claimed that Liberals known to it were supporting the Spanish Nationalists,[47] but it remained unusual for Liberals of consequence to do so, at least for the record. The most interesting example was none other than the Colombian minister to Spain at the beginning of the war, Carlos Uribe Echeverri, a moderate and business-oriented Liberal from Antioquia who admittedly underwent some hair-raising experiences during the disorders of the first few weeks in Madrid. His legation stoned and fired upon by Red militiamen, Uribe seems to have almost lost control of himself, sending back highly alarmist reports to Bogotá in which among other things he suggested that the Colombian government ask the United States and Great Britain to grant him personal sanctuary in their Madrid embassies. The U.S. State Department was quick to extend such an offer, but Uribe never made use of it: instead he took a seat on a German airplane to get out of Madrid altogether.[48] Uribe then returned to Colombia, predicting that Franco and his "fuerzas restauradoras" would surely win in Spain and at the same time launching a round of attacks on the López administration at home for the "Communist" inspiration of its reform programs.[49]

The experiences at the start of the war of the Colombian consul in Barcelona, Carlos Ortiz Lozano, were somewhat comparable, and so were his declarations on returning home, at least insofar as he showed an obvious preference for the Nationalists; he did stop short of equating López with the Spanish Reds.[50] It should in fact be emphasized that the statements of Colombians escaping from the scene of conflict, most of them private citizens, played a very important part in creating the atmosphere of revulsion against Loyalist excesses.[51] They had been chiefly in Republican territory, and more often than not their personal and professional associations were with elements of the Spanish population that were basically pro-Nationalist. Hence their testimony was overwhelmingly harmful to the cause of the Loyalists.[52]

Even so, it would seem that the majority of Colombian Liberals never wholly renounced their support of the Spanish Republic. Their ardor might cool as the weeks and months went by, but they still regarded the Nationalists as a greater evil and as responsible in some measure even for Red atrocities, which they provoked by their treacherous uprising.[53] It was widely felt, too, that the Nationalists' growing dependence on German and Italian support guaranteed that the worst elements among them would prevail, whereas there was always hope that more moderate and responsible forces would reassert themselves on the side of the Republic. What is more, in due course there could be seen a definite rekindling of Liberal enthusiasm for the Loyalists, thanks to the very real admiration aroused by the heroic defense of Madrid, the increasing disapproval of Nazi Germany and thus of the German role in Spain, and, finally, the fact that a more orderly and less radical style did gradually assert itself on the Republican side.[54]

The issue of Nazi intervention in the Spanish War was dramatized by the German naval bombardment of Almería on May 31, 1937. The incident evoked a storm of protest from the Liberal press and intellectuals as well as from the Chamber of Representatives, which adopted a strong resolution of condemnation presented by Jorge E. Gaitán. Its passage was by an overwhelming majority but not quite unanimous, as certain of the less militant Liberals protested that it was an infringement on the executive's prerogative to conduct foreign policy. The president of the chamber, Carlos Lozano y Lozano—who was the brother of the founder of *La Razón* and himself a leading figure of the Liberal party's traditional establishment—objected even to its substance. He explained that he did not wish to "wound the patriotic sentiments of a great nation, traditionally friendly to Colombia, whose sons offered us precious and unforgettable services in a painful moment of the country's life." Yet this allusion to the service of German volunteers in Colombian aviation during the Leticia conflict did not prevent him from reiterating almost in the same breath his personal support for the Spanish Republic.[55] And shortly thereafter his brother's newspaper, while noting once more that Azaña had helped prepare the way for all that happened by misleading and stirring up the ignorant masses, confessed that if the "liberal spirit" had to choose "between the two catastrophes, that of creole communism or that of foreign fascism, it must prefer the plague of communism. Everything is forgiveable, everything is understandable in life except treason to the fatherland."[56] The Nationalists' frank acceptance of German and Italian intervention thus became their unforgiveable sin, in the view of an organ whose raison d'être was to combat "creole communism" (very loosely defined) in Colombia.

On the first anniversary of the outbreak of the war in Spain, *El Tiempo* felt free to describe the struggle as nothing less than one between modern civilization and "the systems of exploitation and domination that have been disappearing from the face of the earth since the dark epochs of the black plague."[57] Three days later, at the opening of a new session of Congress on July 20, the Chamber of Representatives reverted to unanimity as it sent a warm greeting to "the Spanish people in arms, which is defending the cause of universal democracy and its territorial independence against foreign invasion."[58] This new warming of Liberal sympathies toward the Republic was to persist for the duration. Even as the end drew near, in January 1939, a columnist in *El Tiempo*—one other than "Calibán", who held to his personal opinion that neither side was worthy of support—summed up the predominant Liberal attitude: "We accept the fact [of the Republic's defeat] but in the name of democracy and liberty we can never resign ourselves to it."[59]

Colombian Relations with Spain at War

The Colombian government itself naturally shared the sympathy of Liberal opinion for the Republicans. The Mexican minister, it is true, expressed impatience to his own government concerning Colombia's failure to give that sympathy more practical expression,[60] presumably meaning something other than the rhetorical and diplomatic support that the Republic did receive from Bogotá. Yet the kind of overt and covert material support provided by Mexico would have been unthinkable in the Colombian case, even if the government had been inclined to offer it, since not only were most military officers pro-Conservative[61] (and ipso facto pro-Franco) beneath their outward veneer of political neutrality but the Colombian regime did not enjoy the same freedom as the Mexican from the constraint of legal technicalities. In any case, a basically pro-Republican attitude was characteristic of both the Alfonso López administration and that of Eduardo Santos, who succeeded to the presidency in August 1938. The conduct and opinions of Minister Uribe Echeverri were thus a source of embarrassment to the Colombian Foreign Ministry, which went about as far as it could to disown him, even calling attention to apparent inconsistencies in the dispatches he had sent home from Madrid.[62]

The disorders in Republican territory during the early weeks of the war that so upset the Colombian minister nevertheless did place a serious strain on relations between the two countries. The fact that the building that housed the Colombian legation belonged to a known rightist may partly explain the stoning and shooting it suffered at the hands of Red militiamen, but fortunately there was no serious damage.[63] Nor was the Colombian one of the legations that quickly filled up with Spaniards fleeing from the tumult outside: except for his landlord and the landlord's son, Uribe Echeverri appears to have given asylum to no Spanish citizens. This was not merely because the legation was rather limited in space but because the minister, in his alarmed state of mind, feared that granting asylum would create grave dangers for the legation and its staff and accordingly cabled Bogotá for a policy decision. The answer he received, from Foreign Minister Jorge Soto del Corral, was that he should not give asylum until further notice, on the grounds that there was no convention on diplomatic asylum between Spain and Colombia and no information readily available concerning Spanish practices in the matter.[64] Uribe did do what he could to protect Colombian citizens, on whose behalf he rented adjoining quarters and placed them under the protection of the Colombian flag.[65] He also worked to assist them in getting out of the country entirely, for which purpose the government at Bogotá cabled special repatriation funds to its representatives in Spain.[66] But not all who made the attempt got out safely.

From Madrid, the normal route to safety was by train to Barcelona, where Consul Ortiz Lozano would take charge of dispatching beleaguered Colombians on the final leg of their journey to the French border. Generally the evacuation was successful, with Ortiz Lozano also looking after Colombians located in Catalonia itself or in other parts of Spain that were accessible to the Catalonian escape route, and he received almost nothing but praise for his efforts. On August 7, however, a group of seven young religious from a nursing community took a train from Madrid with with safe-conducts obtained by the Colombian legation, reached Barcelona, but were murdered by Red militiamen before the consul could make contact with them. So was a Colombian mechanic who had the misfortune to accompany them. There was at least one other Colombian noncombatant killed in Republican territory: a theology student pulled from a train between Ciudad Real and Madrid, despite his official safe-conduct, on July 28, although news of this incident, unlike that of the martyrdom in Barcelona, did not get out for several weeks.[67]

It was, in any case, the murder of the seven religious that aroused the greatest outcry. Apart from the inevitable diplomatic protests,[68] there were protest resolutions adopted by both houses of Congress and angry demands by Conservatives and some Liberals for a break in relations. To be sure, the congressional resolutions lost much of their effect by virtue of the fact that they were adopted in secret session—ostensibly for fear that publicity could endanger the lives of other Colombians on Spanish soil—and were disclosed only somewhat later.[69] The secrecy involved gave rise to much ridicule and indignation, especially on the part of those who felt that the only decorous response to the Barcelona atrocity would have been an immediate diplomatic break.[70] And such a break did loom as a possibility for a brief time in August 1936. The Colombian government even inquired of the British Foreign Office whether it would be prepared to take over representation of Colombian interests in Spain.[71] However, the inquiry seems to have resulted from Uribe Echeverri's fear for his own and his legation's safety more than from the murder of Colombian citizens, for which Colombia was prepared to accept Spanish apologies and give the Spanish government a chance to make amends.

The British, on their part, showed no interest in taking charge of Colombian interests, and in the end it made no difference, since no break occurred. Uribe Echeverri did leave, as already mentioned, but the Colombian legation remained in operation under a chargé. Not surprisingly, Uribe was widely criticized for abandoning his duty station just when most needed, to which he replied that he was due to be replaced anyway and was coming home more or less on schedule; yet in fact no new minister reached Madrid until after the war was over.[72] Consul Ortiz Lozano left too, soon after the Barcelona killings, but he was virtually run out of Spain by Catalan militia units that were not content with tearing the Colombian flag from his car and violating his correspondence but gave him to understand that his very life was in danger. This degree of animosity toward the consul was due not just to the vigor of his protests over the deaths of the Colombian religious but to the fact that, without any special authorization from Bogotá, he had been giving shelter in the consulate to Spanish Nationalists as well as Colombian citizens and in some cases providing the former with Colombian passports to escape the country. The Catalan authorities, who may not have been fully aware of his passport manipulations, expressed regret that they could not assure his safety and advised him to leave, which he did.[73] But by that time the hardest part of the repatriation process was probably over. In all, more than two hundred Colombians were brought home safely. Some others stayed on in Spain by their own choice, but after the first few weeks of war the experiences of Colombians in Spain generally ceased to raise diplomatic problems.[74]

It took somewhat longer to settle the problem of the nine who had died. As might have been expected, the official investigation into the deaths that was promised by the Republican authorities never yielded concrete results, and Colombia more than once expressed annoyance at the slowness of the Spanish government in providing the indemnification it had also agreed to pay to the victims' families. It was even alleged that Colombia revived the threat of a break in relations in order to prod the Spaniards into making payment. But they did pay 250,000 pesos to the families of the nine known Colombian victims, in February 1938, at which point the Colombian government considered the matter closed.[75]

The harboring of Nationalist refugees in the Colombian legation never became a diplomatic problem at all, even though two more, both related to Colombians, were accepted in September 1936. Unlike various other foreign missions, the Colombian kept the Spanish government informed of the names of asylees, and on the Spanish side no questions were raised as to the propriety of Colombian conduct in the matter. Instead, questions were raised at home, where the policy adopted by Soto del Corral was denounced as shameful by Liberals as well as Conservatives, once it became generally known, and in October 1936 the policy was liberalized.[76] By that time, however, most of those who might have taken advantage of Colombian diplomatic hospitality were probably dead, in prison, or in some other legation, and it does not appear that anyone else joined the small band of asylees already present.

Colombia did not play an active role in the repeated attempts by Latin American governments to promote a settlement of the Spanish war. On several occasions, starting in August 1936, when Uruguay proposed mediation by the American nations, the Colombian government expressed support in principle but saw no likelihood that the contending parties would prove amenable, and chose not to devote any serious effort or attention to such overtures. Colombia was even less sympathetic to the Uruguayan proposal of August 1937 that the American nations recognize both sides in Spain as having formal belligerent status. Gabriel Turbay, who had succeeded Soto del Corral as foreign minister, dismissed the idea as flatly opposed to the doctrine of non-intervention in the internal politics of other nations.[77] Colombia further showed support for the Spanish Republic by voting (unsuccessfully) for it to retain its semi-permanent seat on the Council of the League of Nations in September 1937.[78] And it was one of the last Latin American nations to accept the fait accompli of Franco's victory. The Colombian government, by then presided over by Eduardo Santos, withdrew recognition from the Republican regime only in mid-March 1939, when it was already in an advanced state of dissolution, and the very next day President Santos gave a luncheon in honor of the Republican minister to Colombia, Rafael de Ureña, whom he had just de-recognized. Actual recognition of the Nationalists was delayed a bit longer, until April 1. This was just one day after the United States had done the same, and naturally Santos was attacked in the Conservative press as a puppet who had been waiting for State Department approval before recognizing Franco. But there is no reason whatever to suppose he would have liked to do so earlier than he did.[79]

Ureña had not been the Spanish minister at the beginning of the war. The post was originally held by Manuel del Moral y Pérez, who showed his zeal for his government by lodging a formal complaint with the Colombian Foreign Ministry at the end of July 1936 against one particularly offensive depiction of Manuel Azaña in a cartoon in *El Siglo*. He soon withdrew the complaint, on the ground that he had received satisfaction in the form of messages of solidarity from countless Colombians and resident Spaniards.[80] In September 1936, however, Moral himself resigned in protest against the course of developments in Republican Spain, leaving the legation in the hands of a succession of chargés until the arrival in mid-1938 of Ureña[81]—who achieved great success in polishing the image of what by then was a clearly doomed regime.

An able and experienced foreign service officer as well as a political moderate,[82] Ureña exemplified the very kind of centrist republicanism in Spain toward which Eduardo Santos felt an intense emotional commitment. Moreover, August 1938 marked both the inauguration of Santos as president and the fourth centennial of the founding of Bogotá. To celebrate the latter, a series of special events was organized in which the Spanish government participated with a cultural exhibit under the care of two distinguished special emissaries, the historian José María Ots Capdequí and the botanist José Cuatrecasas, and at the opening of the Spanish exhibit Santos himself was among the speakers. The theme of Spain's continuing devotion to culture in the midst of fratricidal strife received repeated emphasis, with Professor Ots proudly citing the cultural vocation of Republican soldiers who were learning to read even in the trenches.[83] Ureña, on his part, struck the same note as he participated fully in the observances, and early in September he received the special tribute of a banquet organized by an array of Liberal luminaries ranging politically from Jorge E. Gaitán to Juan Lozano y Lozano and including such cultural figures as Baldomero Sanín Cano and Germán Arciniegas. The Mexican minister was present, as usual on such occasions, and also the Ecuadorian; so were a group of young rightists, including Laureano's son Alvaro Gómez Hurtado, who tried to disrupt the proceedings with shouted allusions to the Barcelona martyrs.[84]

Nationalists and Republicans on the Colombian Front

While the Spanish legation, remaining in Loyalist hands, sought to rally the Spanish colony in Colombia in support of the Republic, the existing Círculo Español of Bogotá tried initially to maintain a degree of neutrality. In April and May of 1937 it launched a nationwide fund drive for the purpose of founding a home in Spain for war orphans, with the money to be delivered to whatever government emerged in control at war's end. The drive claimed to have the participation of both Nationalist and Republican sympathizers, Colombian as well as Spanish-born, but the presence of such figures as Guillermo Camacho Montoya among the organizers and the fact that *El Siglo* (on which he was an extreme right-wing collaborator) took the lead in publicizing it suggests that pro-Nationalists predominated.[85] They would also appear to have commanded an actual majority among Spanish residents in Colombia, although it may only have been that the Conservative press did a better job of playing up the views and activities of Spanish Nationalists than Liberal newspapers and the Communist *Tierra* (whose circulation was a mere three thousand) did for the Spanish Republicans.[86]

The Republicans and their Colombian adherents at some point established a Comité de Amigos de España as their own fund-raising arm, with affiliated organizations in various Colombian cities and in labor unions. Primarily for cultural and propaganda activities, they founded an Ateneo Republicano Español in Bogotá at the beginning of January 1938.[87] But the founding of the Ateneo attracted less attention even in the pages of *El Tiempo* than the creation, in the same month, of the Círculo Nacionalista Español. The formal inauguration of the new Círculo's headquarters took place on January 29, in the presence of Franco's "special envoy," Ginés de Albareda. The latter was dissuaded from one earlier attempt to visit Bogotá by the threat of hostile demonstrations, of which he had suffered a foretaste at Barranquilla, but this time all went well. Even the British minister, M. Paske-Smith, turned out for the ceremony. More predictably, the archbishop coadjutor of Bogotá, Juan Manuel González, was also present and gave the church's blessing both to the Nationalist cause in general and to the image of the Sacred Heart, which, together with that of Francisco Franco, presided over the locale.[88] The principal speaker was Laureano Gómez, whose remarks at this ceremony became one of the key pieces of evidence cited by those critics who, as will be discussed below, claimed he had abandoned democratic ideals precisely under the influence of European events.

Ginés de Albareda stayed in Colombia for a number of months, engaged in both substantive and symbolic acts on behalf of the Franco regime. He placed the representation of Nationalist interests on a regular footing by appointing Dr. Antonio Valverde Gil, who was also president of the Círculo Nacionalista Español, as provisional delegate of the Falange Tradicionalista de las J.O.N.S. in Colombia. Valverde Gil would in effect have immediate charge of propaganda, economic, and other concerns of Nationalist Spain in Colombia.[89] Ginés de Albareda likewise performed such necessary rituals as placing decorations at the tomb of Jiménez de Quesada and at the bust of the Liberator in the Quinta de Bolívar. *El Siglo*'s reporter noted, however, that the Spaniard could not contain a cry of anguish on observing Bolívar's French-style bed in the Quinta: the "corrosive influence" of French "encyclopedism" had extended even to this![90] Obviously, Franco's envoy had not mastered the art of co-opting the Liberator for whatever contemporary cause one happens to be serving, while blithely ignoring contrary evidence. He nevertheless received the tribute both of a dinner given by the Spanish colony, at which one matador made paella and another recited poetry,[91] and of a Jockey Club banquet offered by the high command of Colombian conservatism. Esteban Jaramillo headed the banquet organizers. Laureano Gómez, Mariano Ospina Pérez, and countless others attended to express their support for him and the Nationalist cause. In his introductory remarks, Jaramillo made clear that he, at least, had not renounced his democratic faith: he expressed the firm hope that Spain would emerge from the present struggle "to enjoy the inestimable gifts of liberty, social justice, and democracy."[92]

One task of Valverde Gil and the Círculo Nacionalista Español was, naturally, to coordinate the work of related organizations in other cities, including a Cartagena branch of the Falange whose officers had been approved by authorities in Spain[93] and a Círculo Nacionalista in Medellín that was soon bickering with Valverde over alleged mishandling of funds collected for the Franco cause. From the publicity given to the latter episode by *El Colombiano,* which was both stalwartly Conservative and ever ready to denounce centralist infringements on the dignity of Antioquia, one can reasonably infer that there was an element of Colombian regionalism involved, whatever the financial details may have been.[94] In any case, the efforts of Valverde and others to raise funds for Franco attracted widespread support, even if the total sums were not overly impressive. The wholehearted collaboration of *El Siglo,* whose national network of agencies served to receive donations, was clearly one positive factor. Perhaps the most intensive single campaign was that launched in January 1938 as a subscription to buy Colombian coffee and cigarettes for Franco's soldiers. Over three hundred pesos were raised the first day, and during the next few weeks further contributions were recorded regularly in the columns of *El Siglo,* coming from remote villages as well as large cities, chiefly in small amounts from individuals of modest means. The Franciscan community of Bogotá was one of the contributors, for some ten pesos.[95]

There is less information concerning the effectiveness of comparable drives of behalf of the Loyalists. *El Siglo* reported in April 1937 that an "enormous shipment" of foodstuffs had been sent to "Red Spain," by supporters in Cali, but it may well have exaggerated because *El Siglo* was interested in highlighting the supposedly illegal methods used.[96] *El Tiempo* did not publish regular lists of donors to the Republic, and neither did *Tierra,* even after it had promised to do so. Instead, the Communist organ sadly complained that Colombian support for the Republic was more rhetorical than practical. Certainly the staff of *Tierra* had reason to know, since it was the most persistent solicitor of donations for the Loyalists, including both donations in kind (cigars and cigarettes, *panela,* coffee) and money to support an Hogar Colombia for war orphans in Spain. At one benefit function for the Hogar Colombia in Santa Marta, a young man performed as a violin solo a piece entitled "Abajo Franco!" If, as reported, an institution by such a name was really created, there is no reason to suppose that it was wholly or even mainly supported by Colombian contributions.[97] Conceivably, some Republican sympathizers may have rationalized their failure to do more by assuming that the Liberal administration would somehow take care of Colombian aid to the Loyalists, but official assistance, too, was mainly verbal. In September 1938, the lower house of Congress did briefly consider drafting formal legislation on noncombatant aid to the Spanish Republic, but the motion was referred to a committee that brought forth the proposal—readily adopted—that the executive branch be authorized to do what was needed.[98] As the war came to a close, the executive under Santos made a genuine effort to bring limited numbers of Republican refugees to Colombia; it did not do much if anything more than that.

Much less did Colombia serve as a significant source of volunteers on either side of the conflict. There were no organized recruiting drives, and only six fully authenticated instances have come to light of Colombians fighting in the Spanish war, four for the Republicans, two for the Nationalists. One of the Republican volunteers was a certain Ramón Paz, in Barcelona when the war began, who enlisted in the government forces, was later sent to the United States on a propaganda mission, ultimately returned to Spain, and was killed in action.[99] Another was Efrén Díaz, who was in Prague when the war broke out but joined an international contingent in Paris, fought for a time in Spain, and by mid-1938 was again in Colombia.[100] Of the Colombian José María Mariño it was reported only that he had been captured by the Nationalists while serving as a Republican messenger and imprisoned for the duration. Finally, there was Mario Sorzano Jiménez, son of the *santandereano* Liberal diplomat and political figure Francisco Sorzano, who was a medical student in Madrid when war began. He immediately volunteered for medical-related work with the Loyalists and even earned a Spanish decoration; he left Spain just before the final collapse.[101] On the Nationalist side there were two Colombians, both professional military men who were already with the Spanish armed forces as of July 1936. One of these, Lt. Luis Serrano Mantilla, had been studying military aviation in Granada and remained to serve in Franco's air force.[102] The other, who was the most prominent of all Colombians to serve, was Major Luis Crespo Guzmán, brother of the influential Conservative director of *Diario del Pacífico* in Cali, Primitivo Crespo, and nephew of the archbishop of Popayán. Crespo was a long-time volunteer in the Spanish Foreign Legion, married to a Spaniard, and identified as much as or more with the *madre patria* as with the land of his birth—he fought for Franco as a matter of course, and died from wounds received in the capture of Irún.[103] It is, needless to say, entirely probable that a few other Colombian nationals fought in the war without attracting attention in the news media at home, but it is still obvious that Colombia ranked near the bottom among Latin American nations as a source of recruits.

The Impact of the Spanish Struggle on Colombian Ideas and Behavior

Even though nothing Colombia did or did not do had an observable effect on the outcome of the war in Spain, it is an article of conventional wisdom that the conflict did have a significant influence on political trends within Colombia. Most obviously, it was a topic of heated argument—as already seen—among Colombians of different ideological leanings, and to that extent it contributed to the polarization and bitterness of political debate that with occasional respites were characteristic of the mid-1930s and following years. To be sure, Liberals and Conservatives and the rival currents within each of the major parties would have been engaged in debate no matter what; without the civil war in Spain they might only have raised their voices a little higher in arguing about other things, with no great difference in the intensity of discussion or in the fundamental attitudes expressed. However, it has also been maintained that the Spanish conflict in and of itself altered the political thinking of some Colombians, or at least accelerated and exaggerated certain changes in their thinking that would otherwise have been less pronounced. More specifically, such Liberals as Germán Arciniegas often suggested that Conservatives were led by their enthusiasm for Franco and their grateful acknowledgment of the help he received from Hitler and Mussolini to adopt anti-democratic, pro-Fascist positions in domestic as well as international affairs.[104]

It is quite true that support of Franco in Spain was often associated with expressions of admiration for right-wing dictatorship generally and with approving comments of Hitler and Mussolini. One regular contributor to *El Siglo* observed, with specific reference to the lessons to be learned from the Spanish experience, that "a country of order can today do no less than have recourse to dictatorship."[105] Another writer in the same newspaper made the point that the responsibility of Communists and Jews for what happened in Spain had proved Hitler fully right concerning the danger they jointly posed for Western civilization.[106] The premature announcements of the fall of Madrid in November 1936 brought forth black shirts in celebration on the streets of Pasto,[107] while singing of the Fascist anthem "Giovinezza" marked one Colombian tribute to the memory of José Antonio.[108] A student group at the Universidad del Cauca, protesting the protests of the bombardment of Almería, was so carried away as to acclaim Hitler the "greatest contemporary cultural force against international hoodlumism."[109] A certain Legión de Extrema Derecha in Bucaramanga, having first stated that "we are *Fascists* because we seek a strong, imperialist, and fecund Fatherland," explained that it was "present-day Spain" that "is showing us the path of duty."[110] And so forth.

Though similar citations could easily be multiplied, it is not entirely clear what they prove. They mostly derive from individuals or groups situated on (or just beyond) the far right fringe of the Conservative party, and it is perhaps doubtful that these people, most of whom were declaring their disillusionment with liberal democracy well before

July 17, 1936, would have sounded much different had the Spanish struggle not occurred. Much less can one assume that because some Fascist-sounding comment on the struggle appeared in *El Siglo* it must reflect the thinking of Laureano Gómez and the official leadership of the Conservative party.[111] As a hardened anti-Semite, Gómez could easily have accepted the comment cited above about Hitler, the Jews, and the Communists, but this would not necessarily make him an admirer of Hitler, who elsewhere in *El Siglo* was damned as a new Luther (*un nuevo Lutero sin desenfrailar*).[112] In fact, Gómez delivered a public lecture in August 1937 on the combined topic of the persecution of Catholics in Hitler's Germany and in Red Spain.[113] Hence the Fuehrer was seen as a German Largo Caballero as well as a latterday Protestant reformer.

In the same way, Gómez and other mainstream Conservatives were perfectly capable of considering certain political systems acceptable for Spain (or for Italy) that they were not prepared to recommend for Colombia—at least not yet. An editorial of *El Siglo* that Gómez might even have written himself argued that governmental forms were in themselves unimportant compared with the overriding need to save Spain from Bolshevism. What mattered was the "Christian notion of government" that guided the Nationalists and that might presumably express itself throught other forms in countries where circumstances differed.[114] The one thing that could be seen most clearly in Laureano Gómez was simply an upsurge of admiration for the *madre patria* or, more precisely, for the historic, Catholic Spain that Franco was defending against Marxist assault. Although in 1928 Gómez had taken a rather critical view of Colombia's Spanish heritage, and although his newspaper at the beginning of the civil war had seen fit to stress the instinctive democratic sentiments that separated Colombia from Spain even while declaring enthusiastic support for the Nationalists, in his January 1938 address at the opening of the Círculo Nacionalista Español he made an eloquent and seemingly unqualified evocation of the glorious Spanish traditions that were eclipsed during the age of liberalism—when "the womb of Spain became infertile"—but were now being resurrected. As arms rose in the hall in the Fascist salute, he concluded with his own unswerving endorsement of the Nationalist cause: "In whose phalanxes we enlist ourselves with indescribable joy. . . . Up Spain, Catholic and imperial!"[115]

To *El Tiempo,* Gómez's speech was proof that he had finally made a "spiritual surrender," abandoning the democratic tradition that he previously defended against critics within his own party.[116] The same conclusion, interestingly enough, was reached by Silvio Villegas, who first observed that Gómez for purely opportunistic reasons had once written "a rather mediocre book, but saturated with democratic bile," against European totalitarianism, and then went on to note with pleasure that in view of "the growing sympathy of the Conservative masses for the rightist movements of Europe Dr. Gómez himself and his people have joined the Spanish Falangists with the delicious fervor of catechumens."[117] Both Villegas and another Conservative of the same school, the columnist of *El Colombiano* José Mejía y Mejía ("J"), made the further point that there was no essential difference between the Spain of Franco and the current regimes of Germany and Italy, so that in embracing Franco the author of *El caudrilátero* was really embracing Hitler and Mussolini. Mejía y Mejía did add that Gómez, the veteran parliamentarian, might not be wholly aware of this last implication of his new profession of faith, but he too welcomed the Conservative leader into the company of those who had outgrown belief in liberal democracy.[118]

The patronizing suggestion by one on Colombia's extreme right wing that Gómez himself did not quite understand the logic of his remarks should perhaps have been a warning not to read too much into his glowing tribute to the new Spain of Francisco Franco. He had inscribed his name in "the phalanxes" of the Generalísimo, but not necessarily *the* Falange. And the fact remains that neither in his January 29 speech nor on any occasion in the following months did Laureano Gomez explicitly forswear traditional democratic objectives, much less call for the adoption in Colombia of the same system that Franco was imposing in Spain. As of June 1938 he was still condemning that "deviation to the right" that "implies the destruction and death of liberty. It is the [form of] dictatorship predominating in some great peoples, which offers material well-being in exchange for servitude."[119] Least of all did he have any but the most back-handed praise for Franco's friends, Hitler and Mussolini. Yet in the last analysis the most important reason to question the assumption that Gómez had abandoned democratic faith under the combined influence of the Spanish civil war and Nazi-Fascism is the sheer opportunism—an overriding concern with tactical political considerations—that Silvio Villegas also alluded to.

Convinced that Colombia was a country with a solid Conservative majority temporarily excluded from power by Liberal chicanery, Gómez saw no reason to turn his back definitively on representative procedures. As still another *El Siglo* editorial expressed the matter, it might well be necessary in the face of Liberal repression for "the Conservative party in opposition" to adopt certain "Fascist modalities" of combat, but always with the expectation of being "essentially democratic" once it returned to power.[120] Neither did Gómez wish to take excessive risks in regaining power, with the result that he was bitterly condemned by Silvio Villegas for having failed to support a somewhat harebrained military conspiracy in 1936.[121] (Villegas contended that conditions in Colombia that year had been as favorable as in Spain but that Gómez was too cowardly to take advantage of them.) Mainly, Gómez was content to assail the Liberals in the name of their own democratic creed while boycotting the polls both to dramatize his lack of faith in Liberal electoral practices and to create a situation in which the Liberals might feel free to fight among themselves.

Gómez began moving again toward full political participation only with the victory of Eduardo Santos in 1938, which suggested that a more acceptable brand of Liberalism was coming to the fore; and the early months of the Santos administration witnessed a veritable love-feast of *convivencia* as Gómez and his newspaper acclaimed the honorable intentions and worthy acts of the new president and declared themselves ready to cooperate in restoring Colombian democracy after the dark years of Alfonso López's misrule.[122] Then, suddenly, on January 8, 1939, Liberal policed fired on a Conservative rally at Gachetá, Cundinamarca, killing ten persons—and almost overnight Gómez and the majority faction of the Conservative party began proclaiming their utter lack of faith in Colombian democracy generally and Santos in particular, at the same time advising Conservatives to use violence as necessary in political self-defense.[123] Thus, as of the close of the Spanish struggle, Gómez "and his people" seemed definitely to be veering away from a commitment to democratic procedures. But the reasons had little to do with European events: Gómez may have really felt deceived by Santos, but, even more important, he felt the need to assume a militant posture so as to keep alive the fervor of his own followers and to answer those critics within the party who were depicting him as little more than a lackey of the Liberal regime. Of course, this posture did not prevent Gómez from finally ending abstentionism in time for the congressional elections of 1939: an overly rigid consistency was not one of his failings.[124]

If further evidence is needed of the primacy of domestic tactical considerations over European influences, one may look at the behavior of the self-styled *derechistas* who so scorned the Gómez of *El cuadrilátero.* Although they had found his clinging to an ostensible belief in democracy opportunistic at best, they did not hesitate to attack him for his policy of abstention from an electoral process that they dismissed as farce even more categorically than he did. Electoral campaigning, they suggested, was nevertheless a good way to keep the Conservative party in fighting trim.[125] When Gómez adopted a conciliatory line toward the Santos administration, they naturally assailed him for going too far. But when Gómez abruptly shifted gears again in response to Gachetá, his critics on the right lost no time in doing the same themselves, now joining hands with such Conservative paladins of democatic orthodoxy and moderation as Esteban Jaramillo as they attacked him for his provocative recommendation of direct action in defense of Conservative rights and for presuming to doubt the assurances given by Eduardo Santos that justice would legally be done.[126]

It is perhaps significant, too, that overt exponents of corporatist thinking in Colombia made only infrequent references to the Spanish Falangist model. There were two main currents of such thinking, of which one was a mere facet of more generalized admiration for Fascist and other right-wing authoritarian regimes that practiced (or claimed to practice) corporatism as a form of social and economic organization. For those who espoused this sort of political option, corporatism was a handy codeword signifying rejection of the various excesses of modern individualism, but there was generally little evidence that they had given serious thought to its theory or practice,[127] and in any case its official adoption by Nationalist Spain served only to reinforce a rhetorical application mainly suggested by Italian and Portuguese usage. The other and more serious current was less politically committed and was firmly grounded in social Catholicism. It was associated above all with the Jesuits: with Father Félix Restrepo as its best known interpreter, with the *Revista Javeriana* as an organ of opinion, and with such recent graduates of the Universidad Javeriana in Bogotá as Jorge Leyva, who expounded corporatist doctrine in the pages of *El Siglo.* [128] Corporatists of this school were uniformly Conservative in Colombian party loyalty and ardent supporters of Franco, but they went out of their way to emphasize that corporatism as a system of social organization based on Christian teaching was compatible with widely different political systems.

In his own principal work on the subject, *Corporativismo*—published in 1939 though incorporating earlier writings—Father Restepo observed that Germany and Italy, by their denial of human liberty, had actually tended to discredit corporatism. Salazar in Portugal apparently had not. Yet Franklin D. Roosevelt had "at one stroke, with entirely democratic methods, by means of his famous codes of loyal competition, filled his country with corporative organizations." Restrepo thus conveniently ignored the Supreme Court decision striking down NRA, the better to claim "the great North American democracy" as a key example of corporatism in action. He also gave passing mention to corporatism in Spain, but less than to the United States or for that matter to the Ecuadorian constitution of 1929.[129] It may well be that he played up the U.S. example to score debating points, but it is nevertheless striking that a man who was perhaps the leading intellectual figure of the Colombian right and a hardened propagandist for the Nationalists should have given almost no evidence of Spanish influence on his own social and political thinking. The same can be said of most discussions of corporatism that passed beyond mere sloganeering in the major Conservative newspapers: a reference to the teachings of José Antonio in such a context stands out simply for its rarity.[130] Restrepo, on his part, was careful also to point out the implicitly corporatist nature of certain key Colombian institutions, notably including the Federación Nacional de Cafeteros.[131] Yet it cannot be said that corporatism of any kind or degree was a major public issue in the Colombia of the 1930s. In fact, Conservatives were prone to unfurl the banners of classic individualism themselves in their struggles against creeping "collectivism,"[132] and the classic liberalism of Eduardo Santos was quite satisfactory to the Gómez wing up to the eve of Gachetá—and to most of Gómez's opponents within the party once he turned to denouncing that Liberal statesman.

One could almost argue that the Spanish conflict had more decisive influence on the thinking of Liberal supporters of the Republic than on that of Conservative Franquistas. Even among Liberals, the excesses of Red militiamen and scenes of anarchy in the early months of the struggle were repeatedly cited as an argument against anything approaching a Popular Front in Colombia and more generally against the "opening to the left" represented by the programs of Alfonso López.[133] Though the *Revolución en marcha* would have lost its momentum in any case, it is not at all unlikely that events in Spain strengthened the *santista* wing of the Liberals in the struggle for control of the party and at least added to their ultimate margin of victory. Santos himself, it should be noted, was one of those who forcefully maintained that the critical weakness of the Spanish Republic had been the lack of a strong center party: those Spaniards who "represented the liberal idea" were therefore swept up in "a veritable mosaic of groups and tendencies linked only by the vague bond of leftism," and this in turn helped prepare the scene for Spain's catastrophe.[134] The failure of the López administration itself to react more vigorously to the death of innocent Colombians in Spain was also effectively used in the anti-government propaganda of both Conservatives and dissident Liberals and may have further contributed, in some small measure, to the weakening of the *lopista* faction. To that extent, however, it merely played into the hands of Santos, who was more effusively (though also selectively) pro-Republican than López.

One other way in which the civil war debate influenced the outlook of Colombian Liberals was by its effect on their attitude toward the Conservatives. As suggested above, there is no very clear evidence that the Spanish conflict was responsible for a sharp rightward or *fascistizante* drift of Conservative opinion; yet there was a conviction on the part of many Liberals that such a shift was occurring. The conclusion drawn by *El Tiempo* from the speech of Laureano Gómez at the Círculo Nacionalista is in this respect fairly typical of Liberal thinking. Naturally, Liberals attributed the supposed upsurge in anti-democratic ideas among Conservatives to the influence of Hitler and Mussolini as well as Franco; but then the Spanish example was not disturbing only for its ideological dimension. Franco, after all, had led a military rebellion against a government that Conservative spokesmen were all too fond of comparing with the Liberal regime in Colombia. If Conservatives really believed what they said to the effect that Alfonso López was leading Colombia into the same predicament in which Spain found itself in July 1936,[135] and if they further believed that the Nationalists were saviors rather than criminals in rising up against the legally constituted authorities, would they not be prepared to save their own country in the same manner? Indeed, some Conservatives were quite ready to predict that if things continued deteriorating at the present rate in Colombia a Spanish-style explosion could be expected. As the Tunja firebrand Fray Francisco Mora Díaz proclaimed after reciting a long litany of *lopista* sins that he readily equated with those of the Popular Front in Spain, "The bomb is more than loaded: the only thing lacking is to apply the spark."[136] And the mere fact that Silvio Villegas would publicly reprimand Gómez for *not* having followed the example of Franco was another indication that such thoughts were at least thinkable. Therefore it is not hard to understand why Liberals often expressed a growing distrust of their traditional adversary. Nor did they hesitate to exploit the allegedly subversive implications of Colombian Franquismo in their own quarrels with the Franquistas. Thus *El Diario Nacional,* as it scolded the Jesuits for their outspoken defense of the Spanish Nationalists, asked whether an organization that in this way preached the doctrine of rebellion should continue to have use of government facilities and other forms of official support for the teaching activities by which it sought to mold—in effect, to corrupt—the minds of Colombian youth.[137]

The Colombian Legacy of the Spanish Conflict

The notion among Liberals that a Franco was somehow lurking behind the Conservative party's democratic façade did not die with the end of the civil war; it continued to provide a standard reference point in political debate during the following decade. In this respect, the post-Gachetá Laureano Gómez repeatedly fueled the Liberals' fears. In September 1940, to cite just one instance, he rose in the Senate to declare that the proposed reelection of Alfonso López at the end of Santos's presidency could only be accomplished in defiance of the majority sentiment of both Liberals and Conservatives; it would therefore be seen as a declaration of war, and Conservatives would not evade their responsibility to fight back. When certain Liberal colleagues appeared to ridicule his threat, Gómez was quick to respond with a provocative reference to the Spanish example: in a comparable situation the Spanish right had risen to meet the challenge, and even though initially it lacked arms, it had managed to find all those it needed. The latter remark was construed by Liberals to mean that Gómez would seek foreign military assistance for his own revolt just as Franco had done, which is not quite literally what Gómez said.[138] However, the episode conformed to a persistent pattern of rash remarks by Conservatives, made rasher in the retelling by Liberals. Similarly, a polemic was touched off in the first part of 1942 by the Communist leader Gilberto Vieira, and taken up by Liberals as well, over purported Falangist documents seized in Cuba that told of requests to the Spanish Nationalists from Colombian Conservatives for aid in preparing an uprising, all seemingly in line with Gómez's Senate remarks.[139] But no Franco-style rebellion occurred. The abortive Pasto coup of Colonel Diógenes Gil, in July 1944, fell pathetically short of developing into one. Thus, instead of imitating Franco, the Conservatives followed the path of Gil Robles, returning to power by exemplary democratic means in the election of 1946.

Yet it was not just continuing fear of the Nationalists' example that served to keep Spain and its recent conflict a live issue in Colombia. The domestic controversies set off at the time by the Spanish struggle continued to be rehashed in political debate, as when the policy of the López administration on diplomatic asylum and the vagaries of Minister Uribe Echeverri's behavior and opinions were made the subject of still another full-dress Senate debate in September 1939, a good half-year after the end of the war and even longer after the events in question. Uribe himself was converted in retrospect almost into a Conservative folk hero, so that his defense of his conduct, presented to the Congress of 1939, elicited a flurry of telegraphic congratulations along the lines of: "From Conservative trenches where I stand watch, rifle in hand, I congratulate a great patriot who knows always to subordinate partisanship to the interest of the Fatherland."[140] And in due course he was being touted as a possible coalition candidate against Alfonso López's reelection bid of 1942.[141]

The formal relations between Colombia and the new Spanish government were also subject to a number of strains and irritations. The tardiness and seeming bad grace of the Santos administration's recognition of the Nationalist victory had produced sour comments from Colombian Conservatives, and the Liberal president's attitude can hardly have been lost on the Nationalists either. The Spanish legation in Bogotá (of which the Colombian Foreign Ministry had taken custody) was finally delivered to Franco's first minister to Colombia, Luis Avilés y Tíscar, in June 1939, but the same Avilés got things off to a bad start with an ill-tempered public protest over a headline in the *lopista* organ *El Liberal*, and when he finally presented his credentials to Santos in August there was a conspicuous lack of accompanying publicity and rhetoric.[142] Meanwhile, the first Colombian minister to Franco's Spain, the *boyacense* Liberal politician Francisco Umaña Bernal, had already taken possession of his post the previous April.[143] At least he did not inherit any problems of diplomatic asylum, for the Colombian legation (unlike some other Latin American missions) had not discharged its Nationalist asylees only to fill up again with terrified Republicans. He did face a rather pale counterpart to the assassination of Colombian citizens by Red militiamen in the form of the Nationalists' detention of a small number of Colombians on grounds that Colombian officials considered strictly political. Colombia naturally entered formal protests over these cases, and sought to rally the support of sister Latin American governments to the same effect.[144]

Though it did not become a formal issue between Colombia and the Franco regime, the welcome that Santos extended to limited numbers of Republican refugees caused greater domestic controversy. The controversy had antecedents that went back well before the end of the war, including a series of sporadic alarms (the earliest no later than November 1936)[145] over the rumored arrival of Communists or other leftist undesirables from the *madre patria*. Another antecedent was the presence in Colombia during the war, under official or semi-official auspices, of select Spanish educators and cultural figures who were looked upon with suspicion at best by Conservative spokesmen. *El Siglo* objected, for example, to a tour by the Spanish actress Margarita Xirgú, who insisted on presenting leftist and immoral plays by the likes of Federico García Lorca and tendentious adaptations of the classics—all with the support of the Colombian Ministry of Education.[146] It was even more indignant on discovering that a Catalan professor imported to direct a girls' secondary school in Medellín had, supposedly, been removing religious statues from the premises and teaching her young charges the clenched-fist salute.[147] And then there was Luis de Zulueta. This politically centrist man of letters and former Republican diplomat was brought, not from the trenches of Madrid, but from Paris, early in 1937, as a technical consultant and expert adviser to the Ministry of Education. In addition he gave public lectures and became a frequent contributor to *El Tiempo,* of whose management he was a special favorite. To judge from the thoroughly conventional tone of his published remarks, Zulueta cannot have told Colombian educators and literati much they did not already know, but he had been acquainted with Eduardo Santos since the time when the latter was doing diplomatic assignments in Europe for Olaya Herrera. At least in public, he avoided controversial statements on current issues. Nevertheless, he was the target of a steady stream of abuse, as a "pseudo-intellectual," from the writers of *El Siglo.* [148]

"Pseudo-intellectual" or not, and thanks above all to his close relationship with Santos, Luis de Zulueta was to become the unofficial head of the Republican exile colony in Colombia when, by staying on in Bogotá after the war ended, he in effect became an exile himself. Another Spaniard of Republican sympathies, who came to Colombia on his own initiative during the war and remained to play an important role afterward, was Fernando Martínez Dorrien, who proceeded to found Editorial Bolívar and the weekly illustrated magazine *Estampa,* whose first number appeared in November 1938. *El Siglo* subjected Martínez Dorrien not to ridicule but to charges of having acquired his venture capital through arms contraband;[149] he used his publishing enterprise, in any event, to promote impeccably pro-Liberal and anti-Franco viewpoints. The last Republican minister, Rafael Ureña, on his part simply settled in Bogotá for good, becoming a legal adviser to one of the international oil companies. However, as the defeat of the Republic approached, there were also concerted efforts—both official and otherwise—to promote the entry into Colombia of at least a small part of the vast and increasing concentration of fugitive Republicans in Europe who were seeking resettlement across the Atlantic.

Feelers from Basque organizations interested in group emigration to Colombia had already begun in the latter half of 1938 and continued into the early part of World War II. They initially received the warm endorsement of President Santos and were relatively uncontroversial: neither did anything come of them.[150] At the same time, the Colombian government continued and intensified the practice of recruiting particular Spanish specialists to serve in Colombia, exactly as had been done earlier with Zulueta.[151] It likewise granted visas to a number of other emigrés, despite a generally restrictive immigration policy recently adopted for the primary purpose of controlling the entry of Jewish refugees from central Europe—an influx small in absolute numbers though large for Colombia, especially in relation to the pre-existing Jewish community. The entry of at most two or three thousand Jews[152] in a country most of whose inhabitants had never laid eyes on a Jew at any time in their lives was a source of concern not only to lunatic-fringe anti-Semites but to moderate and otherwise reasonable Liberals of the *santista* school. And the regulations adopted to make more difficult the entry of European Jews now threatened, as in such other Latin American nations as Argentina, to obstruct the entry of Spanish Republicans. However, given the urgency of the Spanish refugee problem in the early months of 1939 and the perfectly genuine desire of the Santos administration to help, the application of the rules was relaxed by means of "a discreet exception" for the benefit of Spaniards of "good antecedents" and needed skills or capital who applied for visas through the Colombian consulate in Paris.[153]

The reference to "good antecedents" naturally meant, among other things, that no Communists or anarchists need apply. Military officers, it was decided, need not apply either, since in Colombia there was no "immediate and useful application" for their skills. What Santos really wanted was select figures in science and medicine, university teaching, and the liberal professions generally, in which Colombia did not necessarily suffer an undersupply of trained personnel but in which the newcomers would face few problems of adaptation and could be expected to bring some fresh ideas, methods, and techniques in their respective fields that would beneficially stimulate their Colombian colleagues. Certainly, the numbers involved were not great. From Colombian statistics it is impossible to derive the total number of Spanish refugees who entered the country, but it is clear that there was no great increase in the general population of resident Spaniards. Whereas 524 Spaniards of all sorts entered Colombia in 1932 and 575 in 1935, the number fell to 359 by 1938, recovering to 405 in 1939 and 389 in 1940; and in each of these years the arrivals in question do not by any means represent a net gain, as there were also departures.[154]

It can be stated further that in March and April 1939, for example, which were presumably two quite busy months, the Paris consulate processed visa applications for 121 Spanish Republicans (including children). By occupation, the largest category was *oficios domésticos*, i.e., housewives, represented by 25 persons. Next came merchants (12), followed by students (9) and clergy (8). Four were listed as professors, although there undoubtedly were persons of other occupations who had taught in Spain and would teach again in Colombia.[155] There is no unequivocal proof that all those who obtained visas made use of them, and obviously the Paris figures for March-April 1939 do not account for all the Republicans who were granted visas or who turned up in Colombia without them and managed to stay. But it is still safe to infer that this was no mass movement: at its greatest, the Republican exile colony amounted to a few hundred individuals. Not even the plea of Lázaro Cárdenas to other Latin American nations in 1940 to accept a massive influx of Republican refugees lest they be engulfed by the Nazi conquest of Europe could induce Colombia to further liberalize the process of admittance. It does not even appear that Colombia replied to the Mexican note.[156]

The failure to receive a more significant number of Spanish Republicans appears hard to reconcile either with Colombia's past support of the Loyalist cause or with the official cordiality shown toward those who did come. Yet most Colombian support for the Republic had been joined all along with sincere misgivings about many of the Republicans. No less widespread was the conviction that in an economy of limited opportunities such as the Colombian any large spurt of newcomers would be directly prejudicial to the native-born: if government funds were required to assist the resettlement, were there not even more pressing domestic needs?[157] Last but scarcely least, the whole matter was politically sensitive from start to finish. Even the limited numbers of refugees accepted in Colombia were enough to alarm *El Siglo,* in whose opinion only the "scum of society" had reason to fear Franco and thus to flee Spain.[158] From the right wing of the Liberal party itself, "Calibán" gravely observed that of the Spanish emigrés "we cannot accept any but the Basques, and of them only the ones who have clean antecedents."[159] Apparently none but the Communists and certain *lopista* Liberals were prepared to fling the gates wide open.[160]

Even the Communists might have drawn the line if a bona fide Spanish anarchist had turned up, but there is no indication that one did. On the other hand, a few Communists entered, despite the precautions taken, not to mention one general, Leopoldo Menéndez, who had been an aide to Manuel Azaña and who taught for a time at the Colombian Escuela Superior de Guerra. There was also José Prat García, a Socialist who had served as an undersecretary in the government of Juan Negrín. Most of those who came, however, were politically from the liberal center or at least not clearly identified with left-wing partisan activity.

The Republicans certainly did include a significant number of distin-guished professional people. Professor Ots Capdequí and the botanist José Cuatrecasas, both of whom had been in Bogotá for the cautricen-tennial, returned as Republican exiles. They were among the dozen "Spanish professors" for whom President Santos gave a luncheon early in September 1939; so were the former dean of the Facultad de Medicina of Barcelona, Antonio Trías, and the authority on commercial law José de Benito.[161] Santos further welcomed many of the Spanish Republi-cans as regular or intermittent contributors to *El Tiempo,* and a few became full-time employees of the newspaper. The medical doctors tended to enter private practice, as was the case with Trías, who as head of the Catalan subgroup of exiles ranked close to Zulueta in overall influence within the Republican colony. A few others entered commerce and industry, including Paulino Gómez, who had served as Minister of Government under Negrín, José María España, a former high official of the Catalonian Generalitat, and the novelist Clemente Airó, who in Colombia entered the publishing business.[162] The Republican colony was thus able, despite its small size, to exert at least some leavening influence—as desired by Santos—in many different areas of Colombian life.

Quite a few of the Spaniards considered Colombian asylum only a way station to someplace else or eventually returned to Spain without waiting for the death or overthrow of Franco. Pedro Comas Calvet, a financial official of the Generalitat, became an adviser to Santos's minis-ter of finance, Carlos Lleras Restrepo, then moved on to Panama, where he continued his work as financial adviser. Ots Capdequí was among those who returned to the Spain of Franco. And few of those who did stay seem to have become naturalized as Colombian citizens. Yet in general they adjusted easily to life in Colombia. Presumably they soon became inured to the tirades of Laureano Gómez and *El Siglo,* which professed a particular antipathy toward fugitive Spanish Republicans even of the sort that Santos was bringing in: one typical outburst had it that such "Spanish Reds" as José de Benito and Ots Capdequí were "barbarizing the country" with their writings in the *Revista de Indias,* published by the Colombian Ministry of Education.[163] Even the return of the Conservatives to power in 1946 made surprisingly little difference in the status of the emigrés. Those on official service contracts or teach-ing at public universities tended not to have their appointments re-newed, particularly once Laureano Gómez himself assumed the presidency in 1950, but cases of outright harassment were rare. Indeed, it is worth noting that Gómez shared with Santos an interest in import-ing Spanish professional specialists. He never retracted what he said about the Republican refugees, but there is an amusing anecdote of his reaction on learning that a recruiting mission sent to Europe by his own government had been avoiding Spain: "Let them bring Spaniards, even if they are atheists" (*aunque sean ateos*).[164] If this can be believed, perhaps we have here an unexpected by-product of the warming toward the *madre patria* of which Gómez's speech to the Círculo Nacionalista Español in January 1938 had been one notable landmark.

Gómez as president was no less interested in political importations from Spain, but these were not to be reminiscent in any way of *España atea*. When he launched his move to revamp the Colombian constitution—a project that would contribute to his own overthrow on June 13, 1953—he proposed that it be done along semi-corporatist lines, with the church and other corporate groups represented as such in the Senate. He likewise favored limiting the suffrage to heads of families at the municipal level, as in the Spain of Franco.[165] This constitutional reform project was the culmination of that process of disenchantment with conventional liberal democracy on Gómez's part whose beginnings are commonly placed back in the mid-1930s and attributed to the influence of the Spanish civil war, among other external factors. Nor is there any reason to deny that some such influence may have occurred. However, it has already been seen that domestic circumstances probably had more to do with Gómez's political thinking and behavior in the 1930s, and their overriding importance in the following decade seems even clearer. After all, on April 9, 1948, the Liberal populace of Bogotá came near to overthrowing the Conservative government of Mariano Ospina Pérez and would have happily lynched Laureano Gómez if he could have been found;[166] Gómez retreated to Spain for safety and stayed there until it was time for him be be elected in his own right—something that was accomplished in the midst of the spreading epidemic of political horrors known in Colombia simply as *la violencia*. Father Félix Restrepo found in all this deterioration new reason to restructure the Colombian political and economic systems after corporatist models,[167] and it is hardly surprising that Gómez, having just appreciated the peace and tranquillity of the new Spain, was in agreement. Even then, he did not espouse a total rejection of liberal democratic niceties. Moreover, the domestic experience of Colombia was so traumatic in the late 1940s and early 1950s as to lessen the need to look elsewhere for root "causes" of ideological trends.

It is also tempting to view *la violencia* as Colombia's own equivalent of the Spanish civil war. In ferocity it was all too similar, and in scale of casualties (though not of physical destruction) it was at least distantly comparable. The Colombian phenomenon was quite different, however, in that the political class of both traditional parties managed to stay alive in the cities while their peasant followers killed each other in the back country over issues that—apart from life and death and possession of spoils—were thoroughly irrelevant to their own situation. Undoubtedly social and cultural maladjustments that were side effects of modernization served as aggravating factors, but the bloodletting began over conventional partisan conflicts and was not really brought under control until the National Front by its ingenious power-sharing devices removed the causes of such conflicts. A more striking parallel between Spain and Colombia can perhaps be seen in the respective aftermaths, for both the civil war and *la violencia* left behind deep-seated fears of triggering another such disaster, which in turn fostered a high degree of political apathy and immobilism.

In the Colombian case, this national mood helped the country's leaders to put off dealing squarely with issues of the kind that were posed in the Spanish civil war, to say nothing of new issues that have surfaced since that time. Nevertheless, the country continues to function with the same two parties, though with a wholesome decline in traditional partisan *mística*. The same or similar economic interest groups are also in evidence, and though no one talks any more about organizing them as "corporations"—for one thing, Gómez as president gave corporatism in Colombia something of a bad name—they share more than a few corporatist features. What Colombia has most conspicuously failed to develop is a viable leftist movement, for which the post-*violencia* mood, contrary to the expectations of some naive revolutionaries, proved decidedly inhospitable. In its own time, the Spanish civil war had not been exactly favorable, either, to the progress of the Colombian left. Mainly, it had served to spur newspaper sales, to dramatize the issues both real and imaginary that were already being debated in Colombia, and to reinforce, at the least, divisive tendencies already present in the political system. In so doing, it also became a prism by which students of Colombian history and politics can perhaps see and understand more clearly a critical period in the nation's development.

Acknowledgments

The research on which this chapter is based was supported in part by a grant from the Penrose Fund of the American Philosophical Society, for which I wish to express my sincere appreciation.

Notes

1. *El Tiempo* (Bogotá), July 23 and 24, 1936.
2. Miguel Urrutia, *The Development of the Colombian Labor Movement* (New Haven, 1969), pp. 55–69, 81–105.
3. No really adequate general survey of the Olaya and López administrations exists either in Spanish or in English. A passable overview is Vernon L. Fluharty, *Dance of the Millions: Military Rule and the Social Revolution in Colombia, 1930–1956* (Pittsburgh, 1957), pp. 43–59.
4. *Revista Javeriana* (Bogotá), Jump 1936, p. 386.
5. See *El Diario Nacional* (Bogotá), June 27, 1936; Presidencia de la República, *La política oficial: Mensajes, cartas y discursos del presidente López*, IV (Bogotá, 1938), 101, 103; *Treinta años de lucha del Partido Comunista de Colombia* (Bogotá, 1960), pp. 36–41.
6. *El Tiempo*, March 4, 1937. The reference is to an address by Eduardo Santos, whose identification with the López administration was not quite complete, and many of whose personal followers would have preferred an outright condemnation of any thought of a Popular Front for Colombia. In this case, Santos was clearly expressing the official Liberal position.
7. *El Tiempo*, February 2, 1939.
8. J. M. Fernández and Rafael Granados, *Obra civilizadora de la Iglesia en Colombia* (Bogotá, 1936), pp. 197, 281.
9. Ministerio de Relaciones Exteriores, *Memoria* (hereafter cited as *Memoria de Relaciones*) (Bogotá, 1942), pp. 61, 64–65.
10. Contraloría General de la Republica, *Anuario Estadístico Nacional 1935* (Bogotá, 1936), pp. 202, 223.
11. Carlos Uribe Echeverri, *Nuestro problema: Producir* (Madrid, 1936), pp. 414–19.
12. Today Bogotá has the Cine Tisquesusa as one of its first-run movie theaters, but this is a much later development.
13. Laureano Gómez, *Interrogantes sobre el progreso de Colombia* (Bogotá, 1970), pp. 45, 46.
14. Bogotá, 1935.
15. *El País* (Bogotá), April 26, 1933.
16. *Colombia Nacionalista* (Medellín), March 23 and May 18, 1935; Minister to Colombia Spencer S. Dickson to Eden, May 4, 1936, Public Record Office (London), F.O. 371–19777/289.
17. Manizales, 1937.
18. *Claridad* (Popayán), May 21, 1936.
19. Daniel Valois Arce, in *Derechas* (Bogotá), March 13, 1936.
20. *Derechas*, June 26, 1936.
21. Armando Solaho in *El Tiempo*, February 19, 1936.
22. This calculation takes account of any materials—including headlines, photographs, and cartoons—relating to the Spanish civil war that filled any part of any column in the standard eight-column format. The figure given for *El Siglo*, below, is similarly based.
23. August 4, 1936.
24. *El Siglo* (Bogotá), July 26, 1936, referring to what may have been the first of any importance.

25. *El Tiempo,* October 21, 1936; *Derechas,* October 22, 1936; *El Siglo,* October 22 and 23, 1936.

26. *El Tiempo,* October 22, 1936.

27. *La Patria* (Manizales), December 10, 1936, reproduced in *No hay enemigos a la derecha,* p. 249; cf. *El Colombiano* (Medellín), November 9 and 13, 1936.

28. *El Colombiano,* July 23, 1936. Yet another writer on the same newspaper clearly predicted and gladly accepted a Fascist outcome (*El Colombiano,* July 29, 1936).

29. *El Siglo,* August 1, 1936.

30. A point forcefully made by Félix Restrepo in *Revista Javeriana,* August 1937, p. 90.

31. *El Siglo,* December 4, 1936.

32. *El Siglo,* November 11, 1936.

33. *El Siglo,* July 2, 1937.

34. *Revista Javeriana,* November 1936, pp. 362–66 and 389–91, and subsequent issues.

35. *Revista Javeriana,* November 1937, "Suplemento," p. 140. *España Mártir* first appeared in August 1937.

36. *El Siglo,* April 2, 1939.

37. *Estampa* (Bogotá), June 10, 1939.

38. *El Colombiano,* January 28 and 31, 1939.

39. *El Siglo,* January 6 and March 27, 1939, and passim; *La Defensa Social* (Bogotá), passim, for the expression of Conservative Pan-Americanism.

40. See *Tierra* (Bogotá), passim, which generally gave the fullest reporting of these events, as well as references to specific functions noted elsewhere in this chapter.

41. For example, *El Diario Nacional,* August 13, 1937.

42. See, for example, Luis Eduardo Nieto Arteta, "El Fascismo en España," *El Tiempo,* July 4, 1937, on the ruinous vacillations of the Republic.

43. *El Diario Nacional,* July 24, 1936; *Anales del Senado,* July 24, 1936.

44. E.g., interview with the long-time Colombian consul in Seville, José María Pérez Sarmiento, in the issue of August 14, 1936.

45. *El Tiempo,* November 17, 1936. Though Calibán was the most forthright, a similar viewpoint was implicit in numerous other commentaries published in *El Tiempo* during September-November 1936.

46. See especially *La Razón,* September 21, 1936.

47. E.g., *El Siglo,* September 5 and 28, 1936.

48. Minister to Colombia M. Paske-Smith to Foreign Office, August 11, 1936, Public Record Office, F.O. 371–20535/133; *Anales de la Cámara de Representantes,* October 16, 1936, p. 979.

49. The fullest statement of these views occurred in an interview with Uribe Echeverri published by *El Espectador* (Bogotá), November 20, 1936. He immediately claimed to have been misquoted, especially with regard to the López administration, but all remarks attributed to him were in line with other comments he had made since his return home. See *El Tiempo,* November 22, 1936; *El Espectador,* November 23, 1936; *El Colombiano,* November 26, 1936.

50. *El Tiempo,* September 26, 1936. Like Uribe, Ortiz Lozano unconvinc-

ingly denied certain pro-Franco comments (*El Siglo,* October 3, 1936). He happened to be Enrique Santos's son-in-law (*El Diario Nacional,* August 20, 1936).

51. *El Tiempo,* September 4, 6, 10, and 24, 1936.

52. An account of the Colombian colony in Spain at the outset of the war, by the consul in Sevilla, appeared in *El Diario Nacional,* August 20, 1936. A rather large number were clergy.

53. See *El Tiempo,* September 30 and October 22, 1936.

54. For an expression of relief at the emergence of Negrín, see *El Tiempo,* June 1, 1937.

55. *Anales de la Cámara de Representantes,* June 2, 1937, pp. 849–50, and June 3, 1937, p. 855; *El Tiempo,* June 2, 1937.

56. *La Razón,* June 21, 1937.

57. *El Tiempo,* July 17, 1937.

58. *Anales de la Cámara de Representantes,* July 20, 1937, p. 4.

59. *El Tiempo,* January 25, 1939.

60. J. D. Ramírez Garrido to Eduardo Hay, September 7, 1937, Archivo de la Secretaría de Relaciones Exteriores de México (hereafter cited as ASREM), III/510(46) "36"/1.III–767–4. This citation and others from Mexican archives came, naturally, by courtesy of T. G. Powell.

61. Anthony P. Maingot, "Colombia: Civil-Military Relations in a Political Culture of Conflict" (Ph.D. dissertation, University of Florida, 1967), pp. 250–51, 257–59, and passim.

62. *El Tiempo,* October 15, 1936; *Anales de la Cámara de Representantes,* October 16, 1936, p. 979.

63. *El Colombiano,* July 30, 1936; Uribe interview, *El Espectador,* November 20, 1936.

64. *Anales de la Cámara de Representantes,* October 16, 1936, p. 979; Raimundo Rivas, report of September 2, 1937, p. 7, in R. Botero Saldarriaga, "Papeles relativos a sus labores en la Comisión Asesora del Ministerio de Relaciones Exteriores," in archive of the Academia Colombiana de Historia (Bogotá). Uribe Echeverri apparently took in his landlord *after* receiving instructions not to accept refugees.

65. *El Tiempo,* September 10, 1936.

66. *Anales de la Cámara de Representantes,* October 16, 1936, pp. 979, 981.

67. *El Tiempo,* September 26, 1936; *El Espectador,* October 6, 1936; *Memoria de Relaciones,* 1937, p. 167.

68. *Memoria de Relaciones,* 1937, p. 168.

69. *El Tiempo,* September 30, 1936.

70. *El Siglo,* September 5, 10, 23, and 29, 1936; *La Razón,* September 30, 1936.

71. Telegram, Paske-Smith to Eden, Public Record Office, F.O. 371–20531/102; *El Siglo,* August 17 and September 16, 1939; *Anales de la Cámara de Representantes,* October 16, 1936, p. 979.

72. *El Siglo,* September 10 and 24 and October 11, 1936; *La Razón,* September 22, 1936; *El Espectador,* November 20, 1936; *Memoria de Relaciones,* 1937, p. 164. Carlos Lozano y Lozano, who had been appointed to take over the post as minister to Spain, resigned in December 1936 without ever going to Spain.

73. *El Tiempo*, September 6 and 26 and October 15, 1936; *Memoria de Relaciones*, 1937, pp. 169–170.

74. *Memoria de Relaciones*, 1937, pp. 174–75, 177.

75. *Memoria de Relaciones*, 1937, pp. 170–74; 1938, p. 327–36; *El Siglo*, September 10, 1938.

76. Raimundo Rivas, September 2, 1937 report, pp. 9–11; *Memoria de Relaciones*, 1937, pp. vii–viii; *El Siglo*, November 22, 1936, September 16 and 17, 1939.

77. *Memoria de Relaciones*, 1937, pp. 165–66; 1938, pp. 325–27; and 1939, pp. xcv–xcvi.

78. *Memoria de Relaciones*, 1938, p. 479.

79. *El Tiempo*, March 10 and 11, 1939; *El Siglo*, March 8 and 30 and April 1 and 2, 1939; *Memoria de Relaciones*, 1939, pp. xcvii–xcviii, 6.

80. *El Siglo*, July 30 and August 13, 1936.

81. *El Tiempo*, September 25, 1936; *Memoria de Relaciones*, 1937, p. 164, and 1938, p. 324.

82. Division of European Affairs, Department of State, memorandum, January 22, 1938, U.S. National Archives (hereafter USNA) 701.5221/13.

83. *El Tiempo*, July 27, August 10 and 14, 1938; *La Razón*, August 10, 1938.

84. *La Razón*, August 25, 1938; *El Tiempo*, September 10, 1938; *El Siglo*, September 18, 1938.

85. *El Siglo*, April 27, May 3, 4, 13, 21, and 31, 1937.

86. See especially *El Siglo*, passim, for news of both Nationalist and Republican Spaniards, naturally belittling the latter. There was also in Barranquilla the separate organ *La Falange*, supposedly sponsored jointly by Fascist Spanish and Italian residents (*El Diario Nacional*, August 15 and 19, 1937). The source for *Tierra*'s circulation is Félix Restrepo, "El comunismo en Colombia," *Revista Javeriana*, February 1938, p. 6.

87. *El Tiempo*, January 9, 1938; *Tierra*, January 14 and November 26, 1938.

88. *El Siglo*, January 30, 1938; report by Spanish chargé d'affaires Juan Climent Molla, February 22, 1938, Archivo General de la Adminstración (Alcalá de Henares), Política General, Caja 3,115, as cited in a study of the López administration by Alvaro Tirado Mejía, which has not yet been published but of which he generously supplied a copy. On Ginés de Albareda's aborted previous trip to Bogotá, see both Molla report and *El Siglo*, September 22, 1937.

89. *El Siglo*, January 23 and February 3, 1938.

90. *El Siglo*, February 3, 1938.

91. *El Siglo*, February 9, 1938.

92. *El Siglo*, February 25, 1938; *Revista Javeriana*, April 1938, "Suplemento," p. 66.

93. *El Siglo*, January 17, 1938.

94. *El Siglo*, February 21, 1938; *El Colombiano*, February 27, 1938.

95. *El Siglo*, January 31 and February 2 and 10, 1938.

96. *El Siglo*, April 17, 1937.

97. *Tierra*, June 10 and 24, August 6, September 17, November 4, and December 2, 1938.

98. *El Tiempo,* September 9, 1938; *Tierra,* October 14, 1938.

99. *Tierra,* January 20, 1939.

100. *Tierra,* July 17, 1938.

101. *Tierra,* June 18, 1937; *Estampa,* May 20, 1939. One problem in the identification of Loyalist volunteers was the lack of a complete collection of *Tierra* even in the Biblioteca Nacional at Bogotá; this may have caused one or two to be missed whose exploits were in fact publicized.

102. *Estampa,* May 20, 1939.

103. *El Siglo,* November 10, 1936, January 15 and 18, 1937; *Revista Javeriana,* February 1937, p. 70.

104. With reference specifically to Laureano Gómez, see Germán Arciniegas, *The State of Latin America* (New York, 1952), pp. 163–64, Diego Montaña Cuéllar, *Colombia país formal y país real* (Buenos Aires, 1963), p. 154, and Fluharty, *Dance of the Millions,* pp. 61–62.

105. *El Siglo,* February 2, 1938.

106. *El Siglo,* September 22, 1936.

107. *El Colombiano,* November 10, 1936.

108. *El Siglo,* June 25, 1937.

109. *El Siglo,* June 13, 1937.

110. *Derechas,* November 5, 1936 (used in place of bold-face type of the original).

111. For a specific disclaimer of editorial agreement with an article in praise of fascism, see *El Siglo,* August 3, 1936.

112. *El Siglo,* June 16, 1938.

113. *El Siglo,* August 21, 1937.

114. *El Siglo,* January 31, 1938.

115. *El Siglo,* January 30, 1938; *El Tiempo,* January 30, 1938.

116. *El Tiempo,* January 30, 1938.

117. *El Colombiano,* February 15, 1938.

118. *El Colombiano,* February 1, 1938; see also issue of February 2, 1938.

119. *El Siglo,* June 16, 1938.

120. *El Siglo,* January 4, 1937.

121. *La Patria,* February 8, 1939.

122. *El Siglo,* November 10, 1938; *Revista Javeriana,* February 1939, "Suplemento," p. 1; and caustic comment in *El Colombiano,* January 5, 1939.

123. U.S. Chargé Winthrop S. Greene to Secretary of State, January 13, 1939, USNA 821.00/1267; *Revista Javeriana,* March 1939, "Suplemento," pp. 45–58.

124. The most conspicuous exception to Gómez's spirit of *convivencia* in the latter part of 1938 had been his opposition to Conservatives' accepting the places offered them by Santos on the Gran Consejo Electoral—even as he moved toward electoral participation. His party opponents, naturally, accepted those seats, even though they had criticized Gómez for being too effusively friendly toward Santos (*Revista Javeriana,* November 1938, "Suplemento," p. 446 [i.e. 246]).

125. Villegas, *No hay enemigos a la derecha,* pp. 219–20; see also Augusto Ramírez Moreno, *La crisis del Partido Conservador en Colombia* (Bogotá, 1937), pp. 44–49.

126. *El Tiempo,* February 7, 1939; *La Patria,* February 8 and 9, 1939.

127. For a typical sloganeering use, see *La Patria,* March 18, 1939, or *Derechas,* passim.

128. *El Siglo*, July 26 and August 15, 1936. See also the reference to Víctor Emilio Jara, *Ideas sobre el estado corporativo* (Bogotá, 1936), a Javeriana thesis in jurisprudence, in *Revista Javeriana,* November 1936, p. 385; José María Uría, "La organización social sobre la base de las corporaciones," *Revista Javeriana,* August 1936, pp.88–93, continuing intermittently in subsequent issues and "En torno a las ideas corporativas," June 1937, pp. 356–63. (Uría was a professor at the Javeriana.)

129. Félix Restrepo, *Corporativismo* (Bogotá, 1939), pp. 32–36 and passim. And the Conservative Party, in formally adopting corporatism as part of its social-economic-cultural platform, in almost the same breath added another denunciation of "the antidemocratic systems that have been appearing in the old continent" (*El Siglo,* February 9, 1939).

130. Guillermo Camacho Montoya in *El Siglo,* February 8, 1939. Laudatory references to the *Fuero del trabajo* and Spanish vertical syndicalism did sometimes appear (e.g., *El Colombiano,* November 25, 1938, and *El Siglo,* January 20, 1939). But the same Camacho Montoya on another occasion could write an article on corporatism without mentioning Spain at all (*El Siglo,* February 2, 1939).

131. Restrepo. *Corporativismo,* p. 39.

132. *El Colombiano,* July 23, 1936, and *La Defensa* (Medellín), January 5, 1937.

133. *La Razón,* September 23, 1936, and "Calibán" in *El Tiempo,* October 18, 1936. The importance of this factor was also stressed by the British minister Paske-Smith, in his dispatch to Eden, October 1, 1936, Public Record Office, F.O. 371-19776/92.

134. *El Tiempo,* March 4, 1937.

135. For example, *El Colombiano,* July 26, August 5, 14, 18, 1936.

136. *El Siglo,* August 1, 1936.

137. *El Diario Nacional,* August 22, 1937.

138. *El Tiempo,* September 26 and 27, 1940.

139. Allan Chase, *Falange, the Axis Secret Army in the Americas* (New York, 1943), p. 203; Montaña Cuéllar, *Colombia país formal y país real,* pp. 166, 167.

140. *Anales del Senado,* September 8, 1939, pp. 412–15; *El Liberal* (Bogotá), September 16, 1939; *El Siglo,* September 16, 1939. In the original Spanish: *Desde trincheras conservadoras donde fusil al brazo vigilo, felicito al gran Patriota que siempre sabe posponer partidismo interés patria.*

141. And when Uribe finally declined the candidacy, an important reason was apparently the unfavorable reaction among Liberals to his service in and opinions concerning Spain (*El Tiempo,* January 30, 1942).

142. *El Liberal,* June 16 and 17, 1939; *Memoria de Relaciones,* 1940, p. 291; Ambassador Spruille Braden to Secretary of State, June 23 and August 25, 1939, USNA 701.5221/14, 16.

143. *Memoria de Relaciones,* 1941, p. 189.

144. *Memoria de Relaciones,* 1940, p. 291; Jorge Zawadsky, Colombian Legation, Mexico City, to Eduardo Hay, March 19, 1940, ASREM III/524.9/ 94.III-2398-10.

145. *El Tiempo,* November 21, 1936.

146. *El Siglo,* November 11 and 20, December 3 and 13, 1936.

147. *El Siglo,* June 1 and 18, 1937.

148. *El Tiempo,* March 5 and 10, 1937; *Revista Javeriana,* April 1937, p. 234; *El Siglo,* April 13 and 15, 1937, and January 31, 1938; Vincente Llorens, *La emigración republicana de 1939* (Madrid, 1976), p. 172; interview with Tomás Ducay, Bogotá, September 22, 1977.

The following treatment of the Republican colony is derived, except where otherwise specified, from the discussion by Llorens, pp. 172–76; the interviews with Ducay, with Roberto García Peña, Bogotá, September 26, 1977, and with Miguel Trías, Bogotá, September 27, 1977; and Miguel Trías, personal communication, December 29, 1978. Professor Ducay came to Colombia directly from Spain in the early 1950s but established close contacts with Republicans who had arrived earlier. Trías had arrived as an exile at the close of the civil war, though as a minor accompanying his father, Antonio Trías. García Peña is not, of course, a Spaniard himself but was for many years a close collaborator of Eduardo Santos on the staff of *El Tiempo.*

149. *El Siglo,* January 15 and March 1, 1939.

150. *El Tiempo,* November 23 and 29, 1938, March 18–20, 1939; *El Siglo,* March 18 and 20, 1939; *Memoria de Relaciones,* 1941, p. 203.

151. *El Liberal,* January 17, 1938.

152. The number of foreigners identified as Jewish was given early in 1939 as 3,474 (*El Tiempo,* February 2, 1939). It is impossible to say how many were recent arrivals.

153. *Memoria de Relaciones,* 1939, pp. 158–65, 181–82, and 1940, p. viii.

154. Contraloría General de la República, *Anuario General de Estadística 1935* (Bogotá, 1936), p. 112; *Anuario General de Estadística Colombia 1940* (Bogotá, 1941), p. 16.

155. *Memoria de Relaciones,* 1939, pp. 182–83.

156. See the essay by T. G. Powell, above.

157. *Memoria de Relaciones,* 1940, pp. vii–viii; *El Tiempo,* March 8, 1939.

158. *El Siglo,* April 17, 1939; see also *El Siglo,* February 23 and 26, and March 23, 1939.

159. *El Tiempo,* February 23, 1939; see also *El Tiempo,* January 29 and March 8, 1939.

160. *Tierra,* passim; *El Liberal,* March 7, 1939; *El Siglo,* March 16, 1939.

161. *Estampa,* September 16, 1939.

162. *Revista Interamericana de Bibliografía* 26:3 (July–September 1976): 347.

163. *El Siglo,* September 15, 1939.

164. Ducay interview. Ducay, who was one of those recruited, had been no Franco supporter but was necessarily apolitical in Spain; as source for the anecdote, he gave the man who was Spanish minister to Colombia at the time, José María Alfaro.

165. Fluharty, *Dance of the Millions,* pp. 129–33; Laureano Gómez, *Los efectos de la reforma de 1953* (Bogotá, 1953).

166. It was Gómez himself who observed that the 9th of April "divides in two the political history of Colombia" (cited in Hugo Velasco A., *Ecce homo, biografía de una tempestad* [Bogotá, 1950], 246).

167. Félix Restrepo, *Colombia en la encrucijada* (Bogotá, 1951). This work, which contains Restrepo's detailed blueprint for a corporatist restructuring of Colombia, did not make explicit reference to *la violencia*, then at its peak; but it was clearly in the author's mind, as final proof of the bankruptcy of previous institutions.

Peru

Thomas M. Davies, Jr.

Similarities and Contrasts: The Peruvian and Spanish Backgrounds

Both Peru and Spain experienced intensified civil strife and political violence in the early 1930s. In both nations the onset of the Great Depression exacerbated long-standing social, economic, and political conflicts, and the challenges of modernization threatened the legitimacy of traditional values and the viability of the old social order. For Spain, this crisis culminated in a brutal civil war that captured the attention of the international community of nations. In Peru, the crisis of the 1930s evolved into a series of illegal regime changes, interim dictatorships, and sporadic civil strife, punctuated by barracks revolts, civilian-military uprisings, political assassinations, and torture of political prisoners. And although the level and intensity of civil strife in Peru never reached the magnitude of that in Spain, Peruvian perceptions of the Spanish civil war and the issues at stake in the Iberian peninsula significantly affected Peruvian political development until the outbreak of World War II. Moreover, the legacy of the political struggles of the 1930s, particularly with respect to civil-military relations, continued to influence Peruvian politicians in the 1970s and early 1980s.

In the 1930s, Peru shared many similarities with Spain. Both were relatively backward nations in which political elites were seeking a peaceful road to modernity (or a peaceful way of slowing or preventing the onset of modernity). Both shared the severe problems of an archaic land tenure system accompanied by dramatic disparities in income distribution. But both also had emergent modern economic sectors in industry and commercial agriculture and had witnessed the rise of increasingly militant bourgeois and proletarian groups who often viewed traditional patterns as obstacles to their present and future aspirations.

Despite these similarities, significant differences in Peruvian and Spanish realities conditioned the response of each nation to the crises of the 1930s. Spanish regionalism, both geographical and cultural, could not compare to the regionalism characteristic of Peru, with the attendant physical barriers to national integration and the overwhelming salience of the "Indian question." Spain's economic fragility did not approach Peru's vulnerability to movements in the international marketplace, nor did the Spanish economy depend so critically on the decisions of foreign investors and foreign entrepreneurs.

Contrariwise, Peruvian internal politics were not so directly conditioned by the looming specter of war in Europe and the confrontation between the great ideologies of the time: liberal democracy, Marxism, and fascism. In this sense Peruvian development was, in international terms, a footnote to the series of events that culminated with World War II. Nevertheless, Peruvians sought to understand the confrontation between modern and traditional forces and values in their country and to place domestic events within the context of the emerging drama of the Western world.

Through the years and with few exceptions, white and mestizo Peruvians have looked down on the Indians and pointed to their degraded state as proof of innate inferiority. So long as such biases prevailed, Peru could scarcely have been expected to advance toward the degree of national integration that most authorities accept as a crucial ingredient of modernization. Nor could it have been expected to undertake one of the concomitant features of modernization, land reform.

If there was one constant in Peruvian elite politics from 1824 to 1968 it was a fundamental agreement on the political, economic, and social dangers of even a moderate land reform program. The semifeudal Indian labor systems so prevalent throughout the sierra served both to maintain Indians under tight control and to prevent them from developing new needs, thereby reducing the danger of revolt.[1] Not surprisingly, then, in the 1930s the Peruvian land tenure system and the position of the Indian peasant in society contrasted unfavorably even with the situation of the rural poor in Spain, which in turn compared unfavorably with that of most of Western Europe. Thus, as in so many other areas, most Peruvians (particularly rightists but some leftists as well) simply could not identify with Spanish Republican calls for land reform.

The Tradition of Militarism in Peru and Spain

If the Indian question distinguished Peruvian politics from its counterpart in Spain, the frustration of military elites with the inability of civilian politicians to unite their respective nations, to provide for the basic needs of the peoples, and to create a modern economy was remarkably similar. Especially since the eighteenth century in Spain and since independence in Peru, most military leaders have blamed the backward conditions of their respective nations on the ineptitude and corruption of civilian politicians. Later the ideologies of republicanism, liberalism, and democracy prompted contempt from the majority of professional military in both nations. Indeed, as Brian Loveman and I have noted elsewhere, the military's traditional distrust and disdain for civilians led to overt hostility toward all things connected with civilian politics and politicians.[2]

What emerges from a study of the historical background of civil-military relations in Spain and Peru is a sense of nearly parallel development leading to a common doom—civil war and protracted military rule. By 1930, military establishments in both nations were firmly committed to the precepts of antipolitics, which by its very nature is anticivilian and antiliberal and which rejects political pluralism. Loveman and I describe military antipolitics this way:

> It assumes repression of opposition, silencing or censoring of the media, and subordinating the labor movement to the objectives of the regime. It does not willingly tolerate strikes by workers nor the pretensions to aristocratic privilege by traditional elites. It seeks order and progress; the latter assumed contingent upon the former. It places high priority on economic growth and is usually little concerned with income distribution except insofar as worker or white-collar discontent leads to protest and disorder. It can pragmatically emphasize either concessions or repression in obtaining its objectives.
>
> Military antipolitics adds several elements to those general characteristics: military leadership, a more insistent demand for order and respect for hierarchy, a less tolerant attitude toward opposition, and an outright rejection of "politics," which is perceived as being the source of underdevelopment, corruption, and evil.[3]

Peruvian Attitudes Toward Spain: The Background

Given the similarities in civil-military relations, one might assume that by 1936 Peruvians would have understood the various forces and factions at work in Spain. The ironic fact is that Peruvians did not really comprehend the Spanish conflict any better than did the citizens of England or the United States who tended to view it as a simple struggle between liberal democracy and Fascist dictatorship.

Much of this misunderstanding was due to Peruvian proclivities for hanging labels on political factions inside Peru and then projecting those labels outward and applying them in other nations—for our purposes, to the various factions in Spain. But political labels such as Communist and Fascist, liberal and conservative, Catholic and anti-Christ really do not help to explain or clarify events in either country —on the contrary, they distort reality and fuel the fires of emotion. Peruvian failure to understand the Spanish civil war was due also to general ignorance about Spanish development or, at best, a fragmentary knowledge predicated on political preference—really another way of saying "label."

Throughout most of the nineteenth century Peru had little contact with Spain, a situation that served only to reinforce the many negative images formed during the struggle for independence. Internal political, economic, and social conditions all but precluded Peruvian attention, either governmental or popular, to foreign affairs in general and, in particular, to the complexities of domestic politics in individual nations, including most definitely Spain. Complicating this was the fact that Peru did not even maintain diplomatic relations with Spain throughout nearly the first fifty years of independence.

A limited number of Spanish immigrants did find their way into Peru, but they would have had no real effect on relations between their *madre patria* and their new homeland had it not been for one minor incident that exploded into war in 1866. The incident arose out of a disagreement over contractual terms between several Basque settlers and a north coast plantation, producing a clash in which two Basques were killed.

The Spanish-Peruvian war was not of great significance in the overall history of either nation, but it proved highly influential in reinforcing the negative attitudes most Peruvians held toward Spain. Indeed, these are permanently embodied in Peru's second most important national holiday (after Independence Day), May 2 (1866), the day Peruvians valiantly beat back a Spanish naval attack on Callao.[4]

The 1898 defeat of Spain at the hands of the United States had less effect on Peru than elsewhere in Spanish America. Nevertheless, some Peruvian intellectuals found their attention drawn to Spain. The great Peruvian writer, iconoclast, and, later, militant anarchist Manuel González Prada wrote a biting essay attacking Spanish attitudes toward Spanish Americans. In particular, he condemned Spanish racist prejudices vis-à-vis miscegenation in the one-time colonies. Six years later, in 1905, he produced the essay "Cosas de España," in which he expressed alarm that Peruvians were becoming increasingly sympathetic to the values of conservative, traditional Spain. By now a convert to anarchism, González Prada offered Peruvians a view of Spain colored and distorted by the sort of political prejudices that he was never inclined to understate.[5] Concluding his tract with a bitter attack on the young Alfonso XIII, he called for an anarchist takeover of Spain to end the corruption of crown and church: "Having come of age, the 'wolf cub' today occupies the throne, which is still stained by purulent secretions and anti-syphilitic unguents. Ugly, with that ugliness that implies moral and physical degeneration, Alfonso XIII promises to be a second edition of Carlos II, the Bewitched" [the physically ravaged and mentally retarded ruler of Spain, 1665–1700].[6]

Pro-Spanish or Hispanist attitudes were also represented in Peru in the early part of this century, especially among Catholics and conservatives. The best statements of this viewpoint are found in the writings of the celebrated intellectual Víctor Andrés Belaúnde and in the magazine that he founded in 1919 and edited for decades, *Mercurio Peruano.* Early in his career Belaúnde called for increased trade and commerce between Spain and her former colonies, declaring that it would lead to the triumph "of the supreme values of the spirit and of the ethical sense of life over the utilitarian philosophy of the Anglo-Saxons." He went on to say that, regardless of the ocean between them, "there exists the one great spiritual *patria:* our mother Spain."[7]

In 1920, on the occasion of the *Fiesta de la Raza* (which celebrates Columbus's discovery of the New World in his capacity as an agent of Spain's "Catholic Monarchs"), Manuel G. Abastos published a highly significant essay comparing Peru and Spain. His principal thesis was that there existed a fundamental similarity in the physical, moral, political, and social traits of "my people and those of the mother country."[8] He argued that both had long suffered from the divisive effects of racial heterogeneity and the isolation caused by a highly incohesive geography. He pointed to the Spanish heritage of "aversion to sustained and persevering labor" and to the disrespect for laws and government prevalent in both cultures. Comparing the decline of Spain under Carlos V (1519–56) to Peru's misuse of guano and nitrate revenues in the mid-nineteenth century, he found in both sets of circumstances a predictable result of traditional Hispanic emphasis on grandiose but unrealizable projects rather than on the laborious and pragmatic accumulation of capital.

Abastos did see hope for both nations if they would return to the traditions, virtues, and hard work of the conquistadors. Out of the ashes of their adversity, Peru and Spain would rise like the phoenix and achieve a greatness never before dreamed of: "The child will do like the mother, like the strong and wise she-lion; he will work with the hammer and the pen, he will exhaust his mind and stimulate his senses in the service of great and beautiful things."[9]

Contact between Spain and Peru increased steadily throughout the 1920s, particularly in the areas of commerce and immigration. Both economies experienced sharp upturns during this decade, and Spain in particular began to expand her commercial trade with Latin America. There was also a marked increase in the number of Spaniards who emigrated to Latin America, and although the vast majority went to Argentina, Cuba, Brazil, and Uruguay, Peru recorded a net gain in Spanish immigrants from 1920 to 1930. For example, between 1924 and 1928 almost a thousand more Spaniards arrived than left.[10]

The factor that contributed most to increased Peruvian contact with and popular awareness of Spain and the Hispanic past, however, was the year-long celebration of the centennial of the 1824 Battle of Ayacucho, the last major engagement in the independence wars. Gone were the rancor and bitterness of those by-gone years, and in their stead was an outpouring of love and praise of the mother by her child. This was reflected in the publication of numerous books and articles on Spain and Peru's primordial ties to her.[11]

The 1920s in Peru, as elsewhere, witnessed the true flowering of the popular press, political journals, and magazines, and a significant growth of "foreign correspondents" and the international wire services needed to flash their stories to people back home. Although important for all Peruvians regardless of political persuasion, the new electronic journalism had particular import for leftists and for the working classes they so yearned to influence. Declining costs of newsgathering and printing made possible smaller circulations, which in turn meant more jobs for young leftist intellectuals. Any list of journalists working in Peru in the period 1918–36 would read like a who's who of the Peruvian left: José Carlos Mariátegui, Eudocio Ravines, Ricardo Martínez de la Torre, César Falcón, Alberto Hidalgo, Armando Bazán, Luis Valcárcel, and many others, including Víctor Raúl Haya de la Torre.

Without doubt, the most influential of these leftist journalists was the political thinker and activist José Carlos Mariátegui. Detailed analysis of his life and work falls outside the scope of this study,[12] but it must be noted that he contributed immeasurably to leftist perceptions of Spain and Spanish society in the 1920s. Forced by President Augusto B. Leguía (1919–30) to choose between imprisonment or exile, Mariátegui accepted a government "scholarship" to study in Europe and spent the period 1919–23 in Italy, with side trips to most of the other European nations, including Spain. Returning to Peru in early 1923, he spent the remaining seven years of his short life writing prodigiously on politics in both Europe and Peru. Moreover, he founded *Amauta,* one of the most influential magazines in twentieth-century Latin America, and *Labor,* a newspaper that had a very limited life (ten numbers, November 1928 to September 1929) but was of no little importance in Peru.

While in Italy, Mariátegui was influenced by Italian Socialists and Communists, including Benedetto Croce, Piero Gobetti, Antonio Gramsci, Antonio Labriola, and Adriano Tilgher, as well as by the works of the Frenchman Georges Sorel. He therefore viewed the Spain of dictator Miguel Primo de Rivera from the perspective of the European left, and in so doing helped to foster in Peru certain myths about the Spain of the late 1920s. Writing in *Variedades* in 1928, Mariátegui offered an analysis of the Spanish Directory and the dictatorship of Primo de Rivera. He concluded that, rather than being revolutionary in any form, the Directory represented a *putsch* of the extreme right that very likely would lead to the establishment of a Fascist government à la Mussolini.[13] Extreme right-wingers in the Directory, he believed, had alienated intellectuals by their reactionary political ideologies and their brutal suppression of freedom of the press, freedom of thought, and freedom in the universities.[14]

Obviously, Mariátegui viewed the situation in shades of black and white. That Spain was neatly divided between an extremely reactionary and repressive group on the right and the forces of progress, reform, and revolution on the left is simply a myth, yet a myth that was to gain increasing acceptance in Peru.

The "Oncenio" Shapes Peruvian Attitudes toward Spain

By 1930, Peruvians of all political shades held largely stereotypical views of Spanish historical development as well as of the meaning of contemporary events in that country. These polarized views were reinforced, indeed hardened, by the tumultuous changes and events that rocked Peru in the 1920s and particularly in the 1930s.

The inauguration of Augusto B. Leguía in 1919 constituted a major turning-point in Peruvian history. Throughout his eleven-year rule (the *oncenio*), Leguía sought to restructure Peruvian society, modernize the economy, and reorder the nation's priorities to favor the urban-industrial sector. Despite this shift in emphasis, Leguía was not a revolutionary. On the contrary, he sought to implement certain reforms and structural modifications in order to preserve basically intact the essential features of the old socio-economic hierarchy. And massive labor unrest (which culminated in the successful general strikes of 1919 in favor of the eight-hour day), together with increasingly vocal middle-sector demands, had convinced him, as well as some civilian and military elites, that a crisis was at hand.

Unquestionably, the groups that benefited most during the *oncenio* were those of middle-sector status. There was a quantum leap in bureaucratic expansion between 1919 and 1930, an expansion that provided large numbers of new white-collar jobs as well as new social services. For example, over eight hundred new primary schools were built between 1921 and 1929, increasing the primary student population from 176,680 to 318,735.[15] Health facilities were also expanded, including the construction of a modern children's hospital in Lima. Most important of all for middle-sector groups was the founding in 1922 of the government-sponsored Society of Employees of Commerce, which counted among its members white-collar workers in commerce, the professions, and the public sector. The 1924 Employees' Statute offered members of the society job protection against arbitrary dismissal as well as retirement and life insurance benefits. Pike correctly characterizes this as "Peru taking a most important step to establish the dependence of white-collar workers on an all-powerful government."[16]

As in Spain, however, traditional socio-economic and political elites did not willingly surrender to the forces of modernization and "progress." Instead, they mustered whatever allies they could find and went forth to "save" Peru and her citizens from the ravages of unregimented laissez-faire capitalism on the one hand and Socialist bureaucratization on the other.[17] The result was unrest, violence, and finally a situation tantamount to civil war.

Disparate, even antithetical, interests could be held in some semblance of equilibrium only so long as the economy continued to expand and flourish. In turn, the health of the Peruvian economy depended on the health of Wall Street. The stock-market crash of October-November 1929 marked the beginning of the end for Leguía and his great experiment, the Patria Nueva. He managed to hang on for almost a year, but in August of 1930 was finally overthrown by Col. Luis M. Sánchez Cerro, a fascinating mestizo officer who enters into the following section of this essay.

The dictator's fall left Peru in a nearly hopeless state of economic, political, and social chaos. The new economic and political groups favored by Leguía and on which he had based his regime never united into a cohesive political party. Instead, they remained divided and often mutually antagonistic. The myriad of splinter parties that formed after the 1930 coup d'etat further complicated the already confused political picture. With two exceptions—APRA and the Unión Revolucionaria (both discussed below)—they were small, powerless, and devoid of those charismatic leaders necessary to attract great masses of people.

The Appearance of the Mass Political Party in Peru

The most important legacy of the *oncenio* may very well have been the creation of a huge body of people who had been displaced or alienated during the course of the 1920s. It has become almost a cliché to note that the process of modernization is often as destructive as it is constructive. Therefore, one might expect the victims of modernization to attempt to forestall its onslaught or to mitigate its consequences. Such attempts occurred in both Spain and Peru. Whether they were "rightists," like the Carlists in Spain or the Catholic corporatists in Peru, or so-called leftists, like some traditional Socialists in Spain and many followers of APRA in Peru, powerful forces resisted the variegated effects of modernization or sought to channel the benefits in their own direction.

To accomplish their goal, however, the latter, the "leftist" groups, needed a new type of political vehicle, one that was large enough to accommodate the masses. Thus there emerged in Peru the mass-based political party, which was vertical in organization and cut across class lines through its populist appeals.[18]

Two new political parties—the Alianza Popular Revolucionaria Americana (APRA) of Víctor Raúl Haya de la Torre and the Unión Revolucionaria of Luis M. Sánchez Cerro—sought to absorb and represent the interests of the urban masses. Both were populist types of parties, intent on the mobilization and manipulation of the masses by elites, yet they had very different political orientations, particularly with reference to future directions in the economic, political, and social arenas. These differences not only shaped the course of domestic policies in the 1930s but helped to determine Peruvian attitudes toward Spain and her civil war.

Founded in Mexico City in 1924 by Haya de la Torre and like-minded young intellectuals who had been exiled by the Leguía regime, APRA has been pictured by its admirers as a grass-roots lower- and middle-class reform movement designed to end foreign and oligarchical domination of the economy, to raise the standards of living of all Peruvians, to incorporate the Indian mass into national life, and to democratize the socio-political structure of the country. In contrast, opponents of the party and its leader point to their propensity for violence and usually characterize their program as being designed to obliterate all that was good in Peruvian society and replace it with a godless form of communistic dictatorship that would reduce everyone to the level of pack animals. Furthermore, dire warnings of bloody racial and class warfare if the Apristas triumphed were couched in such a way as to frighten whites and mestizos regardless of their stations in life.[19]

Both views are highly simplistic and tend to distort the APRA movement and its role in Peruvian society. Though admittedly extremist in many of his earlier statements and writings, particularly in his more radical student days (1918–23), Haya de la Torre never really called for nor favored a leveling social revolution.

In the Plan for Immediate Action, published in 1931 as the official party platform and still the basic statement of Aprista principles, the real aim of Aprismo emerges clearly. The Plan was hardly directed toward the illiterate and culturally isolated Indians of the sierra, who had neither political influence nor the right to vote. Nor was it directed toward the poorest elements in the urban sector. On the contrary, careful scrutiny of the document's salient economic points demonstrates that the focus was on the better-off elements (usually unionized) of the laboring class of urban centers and the large coastal haciendas, on white collar workers in rural and urban centers, on small landowners, and on the middle class in general.[20]

Besides middle-sector support, the party also secured important financial aid from such key northern businessmen as Rafael Larco Herrera, whose medium-sized sugar plantation, Chiclín, was in danger of being engulfed by the huge Gildemeister holdings at Casa Grande. Rafael's brother, Víctor Larco Herrera, had lost his hacienda, Roma, to the Gildemeisters in 1924.[21] Thus, the Apristas enjoyed some northern upper-class support that both influenced the tenor of their party platform and served as an indication of their real ideology.

Another middle- and upper-class element in Aprista ranks that militated against leftist extremism in general and radical unionism and *indigenismo* in particular was a contingent of the followers of former President Augusto B. Leguía. Since neither Leguía nor his supporters had ever been sincerely committed either to supporting the urban labor movement or to alleviating the condition of the Indian, their views coincided nicely with those of the northern coastal and urban supporters of APRA.

There is no doubt that former Leguiístas provided the Apristas with political expertise, campaign funds, and a substantial number of votes. Even more important, Leguiísta support of APRA was one key indication of where APRA stood on the major questions facing Peru in the 1930s. Clearly APRA fully intended to support the newly emergent middle-sector groups against the old oligarchy. That position would lead to conflict and civil war.

The fact remains, however, that Haya did adopt a populist, even radical stance in public in order to attract lower-class support. His principal labor backing came from the sugar plantation workers on the north coast, from certain miner groups in the central Andes, and from the most organized elements of the Lima proletariat. Most of these lower-class workers were young, energetic, brave, and audacious, yet politically immature. They wanted immediate political action and instantaneous success, and thus they constituted a potentially serious threat to Haya's leadership. Herein lay the great dilemma for Haya and the rest of APRA's middle-class functionaries: how to win and hold this radical, lower-class support without frightening or alienating their middle- and upper-class allies, who could hardly have been expected to support either Haya's radical pronouncements of the 1920s or labor's radical demands of the 1930s.[22] All the while, Haya remained basically fearful of unleashing the masses only to lose control over them. This fear would go far toward explaining Haya's later seeking out high-ranking military officers to lead revolutions for him instead of relying on popular uprisings.

Luis Sánchez Cerro's party, the Unión Revolucionaria, was likewise populist, but it sought and received support from groups strikingly different from those backing Haya.[23] Bold and fearless in the style of the old-time military caudillo, Sánchez Cerro was a relatively dark-skinned *cholo* (mestizo) of short stature like most of Peru's lower classes. And he eschewed the flowery rhetoric of the political forum employed by Haya, opting instead for direct communication with the people in their own language, a language he spoke as no other twentieth-century president before him—or after him, for that matter. His closeness to the people is nowhere better seen than in his campaign style: "Daily his campaign headquarters was filled with working class individuals seeking an audience, and he usually obliged them, telling his aides, 'don't turn the people away, because they have come to me to shake my hand. Let them all embrace me. I want to embrace them too.' "[24]

In truth, Sánchez Cerro may have viewed the lower "orders" with disdain, but his military experience had taught him that a patriotic soldier was responsible to the poor in a paternalistic way. In the sierra and the small towns that were isolated from Lima, the local military commander was a true father figure, and thus Sánchez Cerro had long experience in dealing with the poor and in treating them in kindly and deferential manner so as the better to dominate them. Haya could claim no such experience and thus drew little support from the poorer element of the proletariat.

But merely understanding the masses, speaking their language and receiving their support, could hardly guarantee victory in the electrion. To win, Sánchez Cerro needed somehow to counter the Apristas' middle- and upper-class support—not an easy task. Suspect because of his dark skin, rough manners, crude language, and lower-class family background, Sánchez Cerro was initially shunned by Lima's upper classes. But their attitudes changed as they came to understand they would have to choose between two evils, Sánchez Cerro and Haya de la Torre.

Their choice was determined by Sánchez Cerro's basic conservatism and commitment to a corporatist type of state. Despite his appeals to the lower classes, it soon became obvious that he was not a wild-eyed revolutionary bent on destroying upper-class wealth and power. His official "Program of Government" was not only vague, it was moderate to a fault. Finally, the oligarchy was convinced by Sánchez Cerro's campaign of fear. Picturing himself as the candidate of order, he accused the Apristas of being Communists, Leguiístas in disguise, and in general a group of violence-prone, irresponsible agitators who would destroy Peru. Completing his indictment, the resourceful candidate pointed to several of Haya's anti-military statements and charged that if placed in power the Apristas would seek to dismantle the nation's armed forces.

By mid-1931 it was clear that Sánchez Cerro, for better or worse, had become the unofficial Civilista candidate, and support from this quarter tipped the balance in the October election. Although irregularities and fraud affected both candidates, Haya did in fact lose the election, garnering 106,007 votes to 152,062 for Sánchez Cerro. But the issue did not end at the polls, for the 1931 election touched off an era of civil strife that raged off and on throughout the 1930s and spilled over into the 1940s and 1950s.

Peru's Descent into Civil Violence

Not long after the election, Haya was jailed for revolutionary activities. Thereupon his more radical supporters, led by the legendary Manuel Barreto Cisco, "El Búfalo," gained the upper hand in party councils and launched a dawn attack on July 2, 1932, against the army's Donovan garrison in Trujillo. After fierce fighting the Apristas overpowered the army units loyal to Sánchez Cerro and took control of the city. Sánchez Cerro responded by dispatching army and navy units as well as bombers, and by the night of July 8 it was clear the rebels had lost. The top Aprista command, led by Haya's brother Agustín, fled, but many Apristas fought on. When Sánchez Cerro's troops finally won complete control on July 10th, they found the bodies of more than sixty of their comrades massacred in their cells.

The army responded by rounding up all males suspected of having taken part in the rebellion (they looked for powder burns on the fingers or bruises on the right shoulder), took them to the Chimú Empire ruins of Chan-Chan, and executed them. Estimates of the number shot vary widely from a few hundred to the six thousand now claimed by APRA, with the real figure probably around fifteen hundred. Whatever the number, the twin massacres of the soldiers and the Apristas precluded any agreement between the two sides, and the civil war continued to escalate, as in the uprising in Huarás on July 14, after which five more Apristas were executed.

Many historians have pointed to the Trujillo uprising as the incident that made the army and APRA irreconcilable foes for all time, a view supported by the fact that both have commemorated the anniversary each year since. But the truth of army-APRA relations is not so simple, because Trujillo frightened Haya as much as it did the military. It was a horrible example of what could happen if the radicalized masses got out of control. Thus Haya began his lifelong search for a general who would take power and then call for elections that Haya felt he could win. The coup would therefore be orderly and "safe," with no danger of the masses' taking power.[25]

On April 30, Sánchez Cerro was killed, gunned down as he left the race track by the young Aprista fanatic Abelardo Mendoza Leyva. There is evidence to suggest that the assassination was the result of an agreement between Haya and the army general Oscar R. Benavides. The matter is complex and highly polemical, though, and need not detain us now. Following the assassination, the Council of Ministers immediately declared a state of siege and called the Constituent Congress into special session to elect a new president. The election, effected under pressure from military leaders, was no contest—Benavides received eighty-one of the eighty-eight votes cast that day and immediately assumed the presidency.[26]

There was a genuine outpouring of grief and outrage all over the nation as newspaper after newspaper condemned the murder and called for an immediate investigation.[27] The danger, of course, was that embittered and grief-stricken relatives and followers of the martyred president might attempt to kill Haya de la Torre (who was still in prison) as well as other top Aprista leaders. Since such action would have dangerously escalated the conflict, Benavides moved resolutely to protect Haya.

By the end of 1933, however, the level of internal discord had risen and the country was more than ever polarized into warring camps incorrectly labeled extreme right and extreme left.[28] At this juncture the Apristas provoked a minor uprising among non-commissioned officers —the so-called Sergeants' Conspiracy. Although there is no doubt that Haya and other top leaders knew about and supported Aprista infiltration of non-commissioned ranks, it is most unlikely that Haya ordered the early January revolt. Undoubtedly his pragmatic instincts would have led him to respect the sentiments expressed in 1935 by long-time Aprista conspirator Col. César Enrique Pardo: "I do not even consider an uprising based on enlisted men because of professional ethics and because it would represent suicide for the party."[29]

Haya immediately secured an interview with President Benavides (no doubt to deny his party's complicity), and the Aprista media launched a campaign blaming Civilistas for the disturbance.[30] Despite their conciliatory attitude toward Benavides, however, Apristas escalated their attacks on other government figures. Moreover, some party leaders apparently accepted the arguments of Col. Pardo that there should be an Aprista uprising, led by and composed of civilian APRA members, without the intervention of military officers.[31] In any event, Haya was forced into hiding (he stayed much of the 1934–44 period in the house of or under the protection of Benavides's brother-in-law, Augusto Benavides Canseco), and other Apristas were persecuted and driven underground or into exile. Certain moderate elements desperately tried to stop the mushrooming violence, but more often than not they too were silenced by the government.

As the year 1934 wore on, both the plotting and the repression became more serious. Haya returned, unsuccessfully, to his quest for the "right" military officer or officers who might be persuaded to take power for him. This proved to be of no avail, and following the collapse of several uprisings[32] the army closed ranks more than ever behind Benavides, whereupon the APRA was forced even further underground. Haya remained in hiding in Lima, but the rest of the Aprista leadership took refuge in such centers as La Paz, Santiago de Chile, or Buenos Aires. The number of revolutionary incidents declined perceptibly, and Peru settled into a short period of relative peace, although political jockeying among above-ground parties remained at a fever pitch.[33]

The end of 1935 found Apristas engaged in yet another plot, and this one was, in many ways, the most fascinating in their long history. Heretofore unknown, the conspiracy envisioned a full-scale invasion of Peru from Bolivia and was masterminded by Col. César Enrique Pardo, Julio Cárdenas ("El Negus"), and Víctor Colina in La Paz, together with the exiled Aprista colony in Santiago headed by Luís Alberto Sánchez.[34] In order to raise the funds necessary for the invasion, Apristas issued one million dollars worth of bonds. Most of those sold were purchased outside of Peru by the movement's sympathizers and by enemies of, or those dissatisfied with, the Benavides administration. President Lázaro Cárdenas of Mexico is among those reported to have purchased these bonds—to the value of six thousand dollars.[35]

When the bond issue failed to produce the needed funds, Apristas turned to the Bolivian military government of David Toro. In a letter to Toro dated August 17, 1936, Aprista leaders requested 2,000 rifles, 150 machine guns, and 200 pistols with a total of 1.6 million rounds of ammunition and 20,0000 rifles and hand-launched grenades. They further requested $15,000 in cash, all of which was to be paid for with $19,500 worth of Aprista bonds. In return for this aid, the Apristas promised that once in power they would "give positive support, moral and material, to the Revolutionary Socialist Government of Bolivia for its stability and the realization of its socio-political program."[36] There is also strong evidence to suggest that APRA secretly offered the Bolivians a corridor of Peruvian territory for an outlet to the Pacific Ocean.[37]

President Toro agreed to provide the arms, munitions, and money requested, but the whole operation was halted for a time by Haya's sudden decision to participate in the 1936 election. Rejecting advice to the contrary from most of the exiled Aprista leaders, who wanted to pursue the Bolivian invasion, Haya announced that he would run for president on a ticket with Col. César Enrique Pardo as candidate for First Vice-President (to win army support) and Juan Guerrero Química as Second Vice-President (to win lower- and working-class support). Haya's entrance added another confusing element to the already confused and dangerously polarized political picture.

Fearing an Aprista victory, Benavides ordered the National Election Commision to reject the party's application for inclusion on the ballot. The commission duly complied. Balked on this front, Haya, instead of returning as he later would to the planned invasion from Bolivia, went in search of another candidate who would take power for the Apristas. His choice fell on Congressional Deputy Luis Antonio Eguiguren. Although most of the nation's press treated Eguiguren's candidacy as a farce, he had the guaranteed support of the Apristas and picked up a substantial number of votes from moderates who could support none of the other candidates.

The elections were held on October 11, and it soon became apparent that Eguiguren was winning. On October 23, the count was suspended, the elections declared null and void, and a new, entirely military cabinet installed. On November 13, the Constituent Congress passed a law that extended Benavides's term until December 8, 1939, and gave him legislative as well as executive power; then the Congress voted itself out of existence. Thus terminated an electoral campaign that had been brutally divisive because rightists referred to a showdown between the forces of good and evil, of Christ and anti-Christ, of Western Christian tradition and the evils of Russian (sometimes Jewish) communism, while leftists countered with dire warnings of massive social unrest if the black reactionaries triumphed. Peruvian minister plenipotentiary in France, Francisco García Calderón, expressed the sentiments of many of his countrymen when he hailed Benavides's decisive action with these words: "This period of bonanza in which we live, thanks to your measured and just policies and your attributes as a statesman, will not now be interrupted."[38]

Perhaps the actions taken by Benavides and the Congress were in fact the only means of avoiding a new outbreak of violence. Certainly the prospects of an APRA victory were abhorrent to many elements. Benavides, like Franco in Spain, felt that as a military man who had sworn loyalty and pledged his life to the *patria* he must do everything possible to prevent renewed civil strife, with its inevitable aftermath of economic disruption and its possible consequences of delivering the country to starry-eyed utopianists likely to end, wittingly or not, by delivering their country to the international Marxist conspiracy.

Official Peru Responds to the Spanish Civil War

It is within the context of domestic developments that Benavides interpreted the significance of the Spanish civil war that erupted some three months before Peru's aborted presidential election. Benavides undoubtedly sympathized with Franco and felt that Peru was facing similar problems. Indeed, Gabriel Jackson's description of Franco's July 1936 pronouncement could, with the change of only a few words, have been written about Benavides:

> He [Franco] stated that anarchy and revolutionary strikes were destroying the nation; that the Constitution was for all practical purposes suspended;

that neither liberty nor equality before the law could survive in such circumstances; that regionalism was destroying national unity; and that the enemies of public order had systematically slandered the armed forces. The Army could no longer idly watch these shameful developments. It was rising in order to bring justice, equality, and peace to all Spaniards.[39]

Both Franco and Benavides were career military officers who had dedicated their lives to national security. Along the way they had acquired a distrust of and disdain for civilian leaders. To civilian politicians, in fact, they attributed the venal and corruptive influences that weakened their countries. Likewise, neither leader trusted intellectuals, and Benavides in particular excluded them from his government, convinced that they were born threats to stability.[40] Throughout his term, the Peruvian president refused publicly to embrace any ideology save that of patriotism. And the Spanish caudillo, although considered by some to be the epitome of militaristic fascism, was basically non-ideological, relying on his keenly pragmatic instincts.

For Benavides, what mattered was to end the civil war raging in his own country, for he was firmly committed to modernization and industrialization. These goals required a stable business climate, which could only be achieved through the imposition of internal order. So, Benavides imposed tight controls on the press and all but prohibited potentially divisive political activity—deporting both rightists and leftists indiscriminately. Beyond this, he moved to professionalize the military and improve the crowd- and riot-control capabilities of the police. In line with the latter objective, he contracted an eight-man Italian police mission to reorganize and upgrade the various branches of the police establishment.[41]

Internal stability remained, however, merely a means to Benavides's long-range objective of economic development. In pursuit of this goal he hoped to attract foreign sources of investment and simultaneously to reduce Peru's traditional dependence on U.S. capital—a dependence that he suspected undermined internal stability by retarding and distorting patterns of development. Furthermore, Benavides feared the cultural penetration that came in the wake of U.S. economic investment. Preferring a corporatist approach to the socio-economic system, he feared that individualistic, liberal capitalism inevitably undermined political authority.

Economic factors, therefore, joined with internal security considerations and with political values in leading Benavides to look to Europe and Asia for markets and investment possibilities. For a number of reasons too complex to explore within the confines of this paper, German and Japanese influence on Benavides were minimal, but that of the

Italians was extremely important. Not only was Benavides himself a fervent admirer of Mussolini, but he had also had long-standing ties with Italy going back to 1917, when he served as Peruvian minister to Rome. Moreover, the Italian colony in Lima was large (some seven thousand) and extremely influential economically.[42] The Banco Italiano was one of the most powerful financial institutions in the nation, wielding an influence far beyond its total holdings. The bank was heavily involved in industrial development and expansion (which dovetailed neatly with Benavides's own priorities) and also served as a leading lender to the Peruvian government.[43]

Moreover, Peruvian public opinion was strongly pro-Italian, and Peruvians of Italian descent were extremely active in promoting Italian interests and strengthening relations between the two countries. Mussolini was held in great esteem, and this popular identification with Italy helped to reinforce Benavides's sentiments. It must be noted, however, that respect and admiration for Italy and Mussolini did not signify that most Peruvians were Fascists. On the contrary, though they admired the great strides taken by Italy, the majority of Peru's political leadership remained dubious about totalitarianism.[44]

Benavides's staunch commitment to internal order, planned economic growth, and a corporate type of state, plus his admiration for Mussolini's accomplishments in pulling Italy out of chaos, all helped form his attitudes toward the Spanish civil war. By late 1936 it was obvious to him that supporters of the Republic were wild-eyed, violence-prone, anti-religious zealots bent on destroying Western, Christian civilization in Spain. Franco, on the other hand, was the defender of the church and the *patria*. Benavides made no secret of his support for him.

From the outset, Peru was one of the most pro-Nationalist governments in the hemisphere. As early as August 1936 the Peruvian government had quietly sounded out the governments of Argentina and Chile regarding a possible joint recognition of the Burgos government or at least of its belligerancy status.[45] This bias was made even more explicit a few months later. Luis Avilés y Tíscar, who was the Spanish minister plenipotentiary in Lima, defected from the Republic and announced he was now the "minister" of the Burgos government. The Peruvian government allowed him to continue to occupy the Spanish legation, thereby according tacit recognition to the insurgent cause.[46]

Peruvian diplomats in Spain were no less opposed to the Republican government. The Peruvian minister plenipotentiary was Juan de Osma y Pardo, scion of two of Peru's most illustrious families. The counselor of the legation was Raúl Porras Barrenechea, an outstanding

Hispanist scholar whose strong anti-Republican views were well-known before, during, and after the war. Since Porras was in Paris in 1936, the Peruvian Foreign Office sent Jorge Bailey Lembcke to Madrid as acting counselor. Arriving in Madrid in July 1936, Bailey Lembcke left a vivid, emotional portrait of the chaos in that city between July and September. He characterized the Azaña government as a mere shadow with the real authority in the hands of the left. To his mind, all leftists were "reds" and Communists, usually governed by Russian officials. "Madrid," he reported, "like the rest of Spain occupied by the reds, was struck by a wave of looting, pillaging, acts of vengeance, and assassinations that were carried out with incredible cruelty and fury. Leftists of all shades, men and women, seemed to be seized by a thirst for blood and killing before which there was no pity or guarantee for anyone or anything."[47]

Under the direction of Osma y Pardo and Bailey Lembcke the Peruvian legation soon became a haven for upper-class, often titled, Spaniards who rightly feared for their lives in Republican Madrid, which was ruled at night increasingly by leftist death squads. When it became obvious that neither the consulate nor the legation was capable of handling the huge number of Peruvians and Spaniards who requested asylum and protection, Bailey Lembcke housed them in the building he had earlier rented for his personal living quarters.[48] The number of refugees soon passed two hundred, and their situation was made even more difficult by the fact that Spain had never accepted the Latin American concept of the right of asylum.

The Peruvian diplomats encountered little difficulty in evacuating Peruvian citizens residing in Madrid. Even Felipe Sassone, a monarchist who had written for *ABC,* was allowed to leave without incident. The same was true of some of the unimportant Spaniards who were simply helped along in their efforts to get to France. According to Bailey Lembcke, the evacuation of Peruvians was all but complete by the end of August, leaving some twenty-two Spaniards including two dukes and five duchesses, one count and three countesses, and two marquises and one marchioness. Since their family names, positions, and even faces were so well known to leftists, they were finally evacuated in September with great difficulty only after issuance to them of falsified Peruvian passports.[49]

Despite protestations of neutrality, the Peruvian legation was actively though clandestinely supporting the insurgent cause. Both the consulate and the legation continued to grant asylum to Spaniards, many of whom were branded as criminals by the Republican government. Moreover, "the Peruvian and Cuban legations were known centers of espionage, but untouchable because of their diplomatic immunity."[50]

In the late fall of 1936, the Foreign Office learned that the number of refugees in the Peruvian consulate in Madrid (headed by an honorary consul who was a Franquista) was over 400 men, women, and children, including some 50 Peruvians and 360 Spaniards. After preliminary diplomatic haggling over the disposition of these refugees, a group of militiamen, under orders from the director general of security in Madrid, attacked the Peruvian consulate on May 6, 1937, and arrested the 410 refugees as well as the honorary consul, Antonio Ibáñez Gutiérrez. The following day the press in Madrid published an official police report charging that the police had found in the Peruvian consulate a powerful radio receiver and transmitter with which "the conspirators communicated with the rebels, receiving instructions from them and giving them in return secret military information that was found among other documents together with the codes used in the criminal correspondence. These spies had been hidden by the Honorary Consul of Peru in a notable abuse of the Peruvian flag."[51]

Both Osma y Pardo and the Foreign Office protested vehemently, demanding the immediate release of the consul and the return of the refugees, together with guarantees of safe conduct. The Madrid government stalled until May 20, when it finally released the consul, who not only denied all charges of espionage but also claimed he had been forced to sign false statements while in jail. The 50 Peruvian refugees and 342 of the Spanish prisoners were also released at this time, leaving 18 Spaniards in the custody of the Republicans. That group was charged with espionage and high treason and taken to the Model Prison in Valencia.[52]

Since the Republican government refused to satisfy the various Peruvian demands, Peru recalled Osma y Pardo. Nevertheless, the Peruvian government continued to work for the freedom of the 18 Spaniards and for the return of Osma y Pardo's personal belongings, which had been confiscated at an early stage of the dispute. Ultimately, on March 17, 1938, Peru formally broke off diplomatic relations with Spain following the rejection by the Republican government of a Peruvian proposal that the prisoners be handed over to the Chilean Embassy.[53]

The day after printing the offical Foreign Office communique announcing the break in relations, El Comercio (Peru's leading daily, which was owned by the ultra-rightist Miró Quesada family) ran a long editorial praising the break. After recounting the various incidents that led to the rupture, the editorialists concluded that Peru, as a dignified nation, had no choice. Employing the emotion-charged language typical of the period, they described the Nationalists' imminent victory as entailing "the preservation, even exaltation, of the ideal, authentic, and traditional Spanish values that we received as a precious inheritance and that are indispensable to our individual and collective lives."[54] Concluding, *El Comercio* writers urged prompt diplomatic recognition of the Franco government. Within two months they had their wish. In May 1938, Peru granted de facto recognition to the Nationalist regime, followed by de jure recognition the following February.[55]

Throughout the conflict the Benavides administration played down incidents between Peru and Spain, and government officials avoided partisan statements. The Spanish civil war, after all, loomed as a bitter ideological struggle between the same types of implacable foes that had plunged Peru into bloody strife such a short time earlier. Constant attention to the Spanish struggle and the issues it raised could only have exacerbated tensions inside Peru. With the preservation of internal order as his primary consideration, Benavides moved to censor expression of all sentiments that might have fanned domestic discord.

Peruvian Journalists and Intellectuals Assess the Spanish Civil War

Cowed by fear of censorship and outright suppression, many of Peru's smaller, non-ideological newspapers and most magazines avoided mention of the Spanish conflict. The larger dailies in Lima provided extensive coverage of the war from the news services, but they made few editorial comments and kept editorials by Peruvians to a minimum.[56] In fact, of the more than forty periodicals reviewed in researching this essay, fewer than fifteen offered any comment at all, and that figure included those publications founded with the expressed purpose of supporting the Republican position.[57]

The overwhelming majority of the nation's press was decidely pro-Franco, and this was particularly true of Lima's most important dailies: *El Comercio, La Crónica, La Prensa,* and *El Universal.* Of these the most stridently anti-Republic were *La Prensa* and *La Crónica.*

As early as January 1936, *La Prensa* argued that the antics of the left had caused the dissolution of the Cortes, thereby placing in doubt the viability of the government of Niceto Alcalá Zamora and the very existence of the Republic itself.[58] But it was with the Popular Front victory in February 1936 that the paper declared ideological war on the Republic. They blamed the victory on the rightists' failure to comprehend fully the true designs of the Russians and the world-wide Communist conspiracy. This analysis was accompanied by a still more basic commitment that came to characterize their treatment of the Spanish conflict until 1939—there could be no compromise between atheistic communism and Western Christian civilization either in Spain or in Peru. They warned Peruvians that "the voice of alarm that comes from the Spanish electoral process should be heard in every sector of the Peruvian body politic. Everyone should now understand, while there is still time, that it is the responsibility of all to unite in a single front to contain the very real Marxist threat."[59]

More than any other paper, *La Prensa* throughout the war compared events in Spain to actual or potential problems in Peru. Furthermore, the principal enemy was more often than not the centrists, whom the editors felt would simply pave the way for a Bolshevik takeover.[60] Here is one of their typical dire warnings:

> Peru—beloved son of Spain—is also in danger of suffering a period of anarchy. Our political problem is parallel to that of Spain. There exists here the danger of suffering from the eclectic program of Alcalá Zamora and the sad denouement of the philosophy of Anaña. But if some day we have to endure the visit of red Soviet emissaries, we will have an example to follow in the present situation in Spain. . . . Today they are fighting at the gates of Madrid. They could just as well be fighting at the gates of Lima.[61]

Whereas *La Prensa* editorialized against centrist parties, *La Crónica* campaigned against all political parties and favored the establishment of a Fascist state in Spain.[62] Noting that political parties were in crisis all over the globe, its editors exulted that "General Franco" has the patriotic courage to cut the Gordian Knot in one blow—suppress them all."[63]

La Crónica, like *La Prensa,* presented the Spanish conflict as the final struggle between Western Christian civilization and godless, Marxist barbarism.[64] Beyond this, its writers liked to speculate on the political structure of the new Spain. Confidently they asserted that the forthcoming government would be "totalitarian and functional," that all Spaniards would enjoy corporate representation, and that no one would be represented by political parties, as these would be "inexorably abolished."[65] With the remains of democratic politics extinguished once and for all, "the government will be in the hands of an elite group of Catholics, fascists, monarchists, and conservatives who will carry out a program of social justice inspired by the famous encyclical [*Rerum Novarum*] of Pope Leo XIII."[66]

El Comercio, controlled as mentioned by the Miró Quesada family, was not only pro-Franco but extremely pro-Hitler and pro-Mussolini as well.[67] Its editorial writers were every bit as strident and inflammatory in their 1936 comments as those of other rightist papers, but unlike the latter they defied the Benavides government and refused to tone down their attacks following the October 1936 elections.

During the first half of 1938, *El Comercio* ran a series of very important articles by Peruvian journalist (later editor of *La Prensa*) Guillermo Hoyos Osores entitled "Antecedents of the Spanish Civil War." In a classic statement of traditional Hispano-Catholicism, Hoyos Osores blamed the war on intellectuals and the intellectual currents that had been running in Europe since 1650, singling out liberalism for especial culpability. He argued that Spain, and Peru, had to reject those anti-Christian doctrines and return to the greatness embodied in the Counter Reformation.[68] This set the tone for *El Comercio's* coverage of the Spanish scene in the months ahead. With the war finally ended, its editors applauded Franco for having saved Spain from communism and concluded: "Because of Franco, our *madre patria,* the heroic and glorious Spain that discovered the New World ... and colonized the whole American continent, has been restored to brilliant prominence in universal history as a bulwark of our Western Christian civilization."[69]

El Universal was the most moderate of the rightist papers, but it too saw the conflict as one between good and evil, communism and Western tradition. By July and August of 1936 the paper was blaming Spanish chaos solely on the Communists, excoriated for trying in Spain what they had already attempted—with mixed results—in Russia, Hungary, Germany, and Italy. Franco, the editorial writers averred, could hardly sit back and "look impassively at what was happening—how the country was disintegrating politically and morally."[70] Their solution for Spain's dilemma was similar to *La Prensa's*, *La Crónica's*, and *El Comercio's*, but they stated it with less emotion. They argued simply that Italy and Germany had succeeded in implanting order and discipline and that was what Spain needed: "If in a sick world like that of today fascism signifies order, work prosperity, and respect for national traditions and religions ..., communism is associated with chaos and anarchy."[71]

Though definitely not a major Lima daily like those discussed above, *Las Derechas* was nevertheless influential in rightist and some moderate circles. The paper viewed the Spanish civil war in terms similar to those employed by *La Prensa*: a bi-polar struggle with no compromise possible. According to *Las Derechas*, Alcalá Zamora never understood that "the centrist illusion in truth was only a screen behind which extremists feverishly and recklessly prepared their assault on the government."[72] Always underlying its civil war reporting was the fear that the Spanish nightmare might be repeated in Peru. Most of the 1936–37 editorials developed the theme that "we Peruvians should seriously look at ourselves in the mirror and think about what is happening in Spain. Here also they are preparing the insane farce of center politics."[73]

If secular rightists in Peru were concerned about the socio-political ramifications of the Spanish civil war, Peruvian prelates and clergy were terrified of the religious consequences. Speaking through *El Amigo del Clero,* the official publication of the Archdiocese of Lima, Peruvian church leaders early argued that the Republican government had fallen "into the hands of the Socialists, Communists, and Soviet partisans who are venting their fury against defenseless churches and convents and unarmed priests and nuns." Not only were priests instructed to preach against the godless, terroristic communism ensconced in Russia, Mexico, and Spain, but they were provided long lists of atrocities committed by Spanish Communists and Republicans. One particularly gruesome piece held that dozens of little girls had been beheaded and that women (sometimes pregnant) were soaked in gasoline and then set afire.[74]

There is no doubt that the Catholic clergy in Peru saw themselves as the last bulwark in the world-wide struggle against communism, Masonry, Protestantism, and laicism in general. What happened in Spain could happen in Peru unless all good Catholics joined to prevent it. The import of the Spanish conflict was set forth in these terms: "In substance, it is a bloody struggle fought between two diametrically opposed ideologies: the one that defends Christian civilization and the other that imposes barbarism. In this hour, under the noble Spanish sun, the fate of mankind is being decided."[75]

Aiding the church in its "holy crusade" were powerful and influential lay leaders, including politicians, businessmen, and a broad array of conservative intellectuals active in various walks of life. Foremost among them and probably the leading rightist in Peru in the 1930s and 1940s was José de la Riva Agüero y Osma, direct descendant of Peru's first president, renowned historian and literary figure, and arch Hispanist who preferred to be known by his hereditary Spanish title, the Marquis of Aulestia.[76] A militant advocate of rigid, medieval Catholicism and of fascism, particularly as practiced in Italy, Riva Agüero did at least disassociate himself from Nazi racism. At the same time, he proclaimed himself "an unconditional admirer of Hitler and his governmental methods."[77]

In 1936 Riva Agüero organized Acción Patriótica, a coalition of rightest parties united in the common belief that all centrism was evil, for it would lead straight to communism. Riva Agüero called repeatedly for the establishment of a corporate state in Peru and embarked on a personal campaign to publicize and glorify the Mussolini regime, rally support behind the Franco insurrection, and condemn the influence of the United States and England in Peru and Latin America.

In the context of Peru's political scene in the 1930s and 1940s, Riva Agüero was unusual only in the extremism and openness of his rightist credo. A considerable majority of the Peruvian elites were pro-Nationalist, and most of them were also pro-Fascist. A few of the more prominent figures in this company included Carlos Miró Quesada Laos, Víctor Andrés Belaúnde, Raúl Porras Barrenechea, Guillermo Hoyos Osores, Raúl Ferrero Rebagliatti, Pedro Irigoyen, Carlos Pareja Paz Soldán, and Felipe Sassone. Each viewed the struggle in Spain as a war to the death between Western Christian civilization and the barbarous anti-Christ chaos of Marxist Russia. To a man they had fallen into the trap of projecting ideological labels created to explain the civil strife of Peru in the 1930s onto the Spanish situation.

The moderate newspapers in Lima (for example, *La Noche* and *El Callao*) offered a less emotional view of the Spanish civil war, but they too were often misled, even blinded, by label-hanging. In addition, they faced the burden of having to cope with a suspicious and often hostile government. The result was that they were circumspect in 1936 and all but ceased to comment in the 1937–39 period.

The most openly pro-Republic newspaper in Lima was *Excelsior*. Dedicated to fighting all political extremes, the daily very early compared the situation in Spain to that in Peru:

> Against all this reaction, the Spanish people rose up on February 16, as they had risen on April 14, 1931. We should learn from the experience. If the rightists are not open and sensitive to the desires of the Peruvian people, if they are not capable of listening to their needs and desires, if they persist in trying to resolve the transcendental problems of the nation from the salons of the Club Nacional, then there is reason to fear for the future.[78]

By September, *Excelsior* was picturing the conflict as one between Fascist dictatorship and liberal democracy: "We conclude, therefore, that a social war has begun when generals, Fascists, reactionaries, and monarchists revolt against a government elected by the Spanish people."[79] It was that and similar political attitudes that moved the government to close the paper for three months (October 16, 1936, to January 14, 1937).

Once reopened (and then issued only sporadically), the paper was much more circumspect in its commentary. It published only one editorial on Spain in 1937 and none at all in 1938. It finally broke its silence in February 1939 with a very bitter editorial decrying the fall of the Republic, "a Republic of workers as the first article of the Constitution says, but in reality a Republic of intellectuals." That Republic had fought valiantly for three years so that the peasants, the industrial workers, and the disinherited could enjoy greater justice and social equality and greater respect for human rights:

> In these hours the Spanish drama has ended. The workers will again have to grind their faces on the ground and the intellectuals will roam about the earth with their dreams, their ideals, their hopes. Spain is now in the hands of the Army of the Carlists, of the monarchists, of the Navarrese, of the Italian legions, of all those under the command of General Franco. Now that they have won, what are they going to do with Spain?[80]

If the moderates were harassed by the Benavides administration, the political left was effectively silenced and nearly eliminated altogether. There were no leftist newspapers or magazines publishing legally in the period 1936–39, leaving only clandestine publications (such as APRA's *La Tribuna*), leaflets, broadsides, and posters. Due to the very limited space available as well as to the dangers inherent in dissemination, most leftist literature concentrated almost exclusively on internal Peruvian affairs.

Two publications, however, were devoted entirely to the Spanish civil war, but since neither succeeded in publishing more than three or four numbers, their influence was meager at best. The first was *Cadre* (the *Boletín de los Amigos de los Defensores de la República Española*), which issued three numbers between October 1936 and September 1937. Pro-Russian as well as pro-Republic, *Cadre,* like the rightist press, and other leftists publications, adopted the attitude that the Spanish civil war was the final struggle between good and evil, barbarous fascism versus humanitarian democracy. Although it devoted much of its space to attacking world-wide fascism, *Cadre* called on all Peruvians to join the struggle by volunteering time and donating money not only to support the Spanish Republic but also to defeat fascism and the Benavides regime inside Peru.

España Libre, organ of the local committee of "Amigos de la República Española," was even more shortlived and never progressed beyond the mimeograph stage.[81] Like *Cadre, España Libre* sought to counter the pro-Nationalist coverage of the Peruvian press by providing the "real truth" behind the headlines. To that end the publication concentrated on Fascist massacres and crimes against humanity (such as Guernica) and the threat to peace and freedom in Peru and the world represented by the German-Italian offensive in Spain.

The Peruvian Communist party was small and largely ineffectual in the 1930s, as was demonstrated by its weak efforts on behalf of the Spanish Republic. Reflecting the Popular Front line of the period, long-time Peruvian Communist head Jorge del Prado later wrote that the party had developed a "powerful movement of solidarity with the Spanish people," but in reality party efforts were confined to distributing leaflets and broadsides on fascism and its spread to Spain.[82]

The vast majority of Peruvian leftists, as well as most moderates, belonged to the APRA party, and thus one might have expected Aprista publications to be actively pro-Republican. However, in what appeared to be an enormous contradiction, APRA took no position whatsoever and in fact avoided the subject altogether. No Aprista newspaper, magazine, pamphlet, or book of the period mentioned the civil war, and major documentary sources such as the archives of César Enrique Pardo and Julio "El Negus" Cárdenas likewise are devoid of any references to Spain.

In a 1976 interview in Lima, Aprista leader Luis Alberto Sánchez informed me that Haya de la Torre himself had issued a general order forbidding any Aprista from writing or speaking about the Spanish civil war. Sánchez explained that Haya issued the order because he feared that if Apristas focused on the Spanish conflict, attention would be diverted from the more immediate and important problems in America and Peru. Furthermore, open Aprista support of the Republic would have reinforced the rightist charge that APRA was an international and/or Communist party and therefore illegal under the terms of the 1933 Constitution.[83]

Without doubt Sánchez's explanation is well-founded and logical, particularly his second point,[84] but there was another motivation that was dictated by rather unusual internal political conditions. In a recent study, Father Jeffrey L. Klaiber notes that in the 1920s Aprista leaders were openly, even stridently, anti-clerical. By 1931, however, "Aprista leaders displayed their awareness that the popular Catholicism of the lower classes far from being a stumbling block to reform ... could actually be a key resource for galvanizing the people to revolt against and to resist the dictatorial regimes of Sánchez Cerro and his successors."[85] Thus, Haya de la Torre, Luis Alberto Sánchez, and other Aprista leaders sought to counter and neutralize the charge that Apra was anti-clerical and anti-Catholic—charges that had been leveled with some effect by certain high clergy, including Jesuit historian Rubén Vargas Ugarte.[86]

Since much of the rightist propaganda, and that of the Catholic church itself, pictured the Spanish civil war as a death struggle between Catholic and anti-Catholic, Christianity and atheistic communism,

APRA could hardly have afforded to link itself to the Republican or "anti-Christian" side. To do so would have endangered the party's input into and influence over lower-class popular religiosity, which it had so carefully nurtured since 1932.[87]

The neutrality of APRA, the weakness of the Communist party, and unrelenting repression by the Benavides government explain why there was never any open recruitment for the International Brigades as occurred in Europe and the United States and in other Latin American republics, such as Cuba, Argentina, Chile, and Mexico. Information does exist on some thirty Peruvians who fought on the Republican side, but almost all the volunteers were either leftist political exiles, mostly Apristas, who went to Spain from Valparaíso, Arica, and Buenos Aires, or Peruvian students residing in Spain who got caught up in the conflict owing to their membership in the Federación Universitaria Hispano-Americana (FUHA) or in some leftist organization. None of the thirty-odd played a major role in the war.[88]

The most important Peruvians who spoke out for the Republic were several prominent poets and intellectuals who were in Europe when the war broke out. Paris-based journalists Franklin Urteaga and Gonzalo More both worked for the Republicans through a publication entitled *Paix et Démocratie*. César Falcón, who had emigrated to Spain in 1919, first worked on the newspaper *Alta Voz* and later on *Frente Rojo*. He also helped to organize and train troops and saw limited action. Falcón formed part of the Republican delegation to the League of Nations in 1938 and during 1938–39 he edited the newspaper *Voz de España* in Paris and published his novel *Madrid.*[89]

Eudocio Ravines, co-founder of the Peruvian Communist party and high-ranking member of the Latin American bureau of the Comintern, was ordered to Spain from Chile by the Third International. He worked for a short time on the paper *Frente Rojo* and served as a liaison agent between Russian officials such as Stephanov and the Spanish left. According to Ravines, he only worked at journalistic tasks, but according to his various enemies he was a commissar in the International Brigades who played an active role in the Communist effort to eliminate the Poumistas (POUM) and the Trotskyists.[90]

The real giant among these exiled Peruvians, however, was world-renowned poet César Vallejo. Accompanied by poet Julio Gálvez (later executed by Franquistas), Vallejo arrived in Paris in 1923, where he lived and wrote until 1936. He was deeply moved by the Franco uprising and became very active in pro-Republican causes, being one of the founders of the Committees for the Defense of the Spanish Republic. Together with other Latin American intellectuals in Paris (including

Pablo Neruda and David Alfaro Siqueiros), Vallejo worked on the mimeographed publication *Nuestra España*. In December 1936 he spent two weeks in Barcelona and Madrid, and in July 1937 he returned as a delegate to the second Congress of Writers in Defense of Culture. The result of his visits and his commitment to the Spanish Republic is the monumental *España, aparta de mí este cáliz.*[91]

Conclusions: The Lingering Specter of the Spanish Civil War

By 1939 Peruvians of all political persuasions were no closer to understanding the Spanish tragedy than they had been in 1933 or 1936. Blinded as they were by the myths, the political polarization, and the label-hanging of their own internal strife, both rightists and leftists were virtually incapable of perceiving what was under way in Spain. What is more, the vast majority of Peruvians remained indifferent to and grossly uninformed on the struggle.

For Peruvian elites, however, events in Spain provided a horrifying example of what could happen if the forces of popular democracy were unleashed. The landed and commercial oligarchy feared the loss of their power, privilege, and wealth to the anarchistic, godless hordes, symbolized now by Spanish Republicans. For the Peruvian armed forces, the Spanish civil war reinforced traditional disdain of all things connected with civilians and offered one more proof of the corroding influence of partisan politics. To Haya de la Torre and the Aprista leadership, one of the most sobering spectacles of the Spanish struggle was the loss of control by their Iberian counterparts over the rank and file of the new mass parties. Thus the APRA high command determined to redouble efforts aimed at control of underlings.

The specter of the Spanish civil war, together with the very basic issues it raised, have continued to affect, even torment, Peru to the present day. Most of Peru's governing classes had considerable Axis sympathies during World War II (although President Manuel Prado, 1939–45, had the courage and foresight to support the Allies), and their suspicions of pluralistic, liberal democracy did not really abate during the next three decades.

Civilian elites, including even to a certain degree Haya de la Torre himself, were joined by military officers in the fear and distrust of free elections and the trappings of the democratic state. The whole trend of developments during the 1940–68 period points to this conclusion. In the brief resume that follows, military attitudes will be stressed, because it was the officers who gradually became the most potent elite group in shaping national destiny. In part this came about because of mounting consensus among the officers that civilians had grown incapable of preventing social and political leveling.

As the demands of the masses, both rural and urban, increased in the post–World War II era, and APRA persisted in its populist mobilization, the old elite lost its ability to maintain order. Periodically the military stepped into the political arena, seeking to moderate the erosion of control. In the 1962 presidential election Haya de la Torre won the largest number of ballots, but he failed to garner the two-thirds necessary to take power without congressional approval, and the military annulled the whole electoral process. For part of 1962 and 1963 the military arrogated the powers of government to themselves. This time the officers proved far different from those who had terminated civilian rule following the assassination of Sánchez Cerro in the mid-1930s. Part of the difference lay in the fact that the new military rulers were products of the Center for High Military Studies (CAEM). Founded as a military school in 1950, CAEM was patterned after both the Escôla Superior de Guerra in Brazil and the War College in the United States.[92]

Simply stated, CAEM doctrine expanded the concept of national security to encompass all those political, economic, and social conditions that affect the power of a nation. Moreover, the doctrine held that economic development was synonymous with national defense and security. Thus, if they were to fulfill their constitutional *and* institutional charge of guarding the fatherland and maintaining internal order, Peru's generals would have to involve themselves directly in the modernization process, which, in Peru, at least, meant a frontal attack on the traditional land tenure system, recognized as the source of a serious economic bottleneck and burgeoning social discontent.

In the past, the military had often served as political brokers in an attempt to prevent civil strife and social disintegration. To that end, the military intervened frequently, but usually only as a caretaker until the proper combination of civilian politicians could be found. One more application of this technique was all they had in mind when they supported Fernando Belaúnde Terry for president in 1963.

Belaúnde's nearly total failure to achieve meaningful land and industrial reforms, his inability to solve satisfactorily a long-standing dispute with the International Petroleum Company, together with the unacceptable possibility that Haya de la Torre would win the 1969 presidential election, prompted the military to take power again in October 1968. Settling in, this time, for a long stay, the generals quickly embarked on a far-reaching program of economic, social, and political reforms, including a land redistribution program second in scope only to that of the Cuban revolution.[93]

Although they did alter many underlying features of the Peruvian economy and landholding system, the military encountered what appeared to be insuperable problems. Obviously, their restructuring resulted in the enmity of privileged interests. Beyond this, the officers proved unable to meet the aroused hopes of less privileged and marginal sectors. Mired in proliferating problems that forced them increasingly to adopt repressive measures to maintain stability, thereby feeding resentment, they were happy enough to relinquish the burdens of the direct exercise of political power. In 1980 they permitted elections to choose a civilian president. The victor was Fernando Belaúnde Terry. For better or worse, owing to military intervention the country he once more governs is structurally quite different from the one he ceased to rule in 1968 when ousted by the officers.

In spite of change, some things have remained unaltered. Regardless of the rhetoric they employed as they sought to mitigate social problems, the Peruvian military during their twelve years of power sought a type of economic modernization and political stability that would not fundamentally erode the country's pervasive patterns of minority dominance and majority deference. Throughout the 1970s, old themes of anti-Marxism and anti-liberalism had become conspicuous on all fronts, with a concomitant effort to restrain or control popular participation so that government would descend from above rather than ascend from below. Emphasis on hierarchy in an organic society recalled the rhetoric of the 1930s, some of which was analyzed at the beginning of this essay.

Although extensive changes introduced in Peru during the four decades since the civil war in Spain helped draw attention to the pervasiveness throughout the Spanish-speaking world of the clash of traditionalism with modernity, the basic issue has remained the same: how to change everything without really changing anything in the way of basic social values and asymmetrical relationships. Summing up the accomplishments of Franco, a Spaniard remarked: "The ideal . . . has been to assimilate the Western economic models and preserve the specifics of the political and social models that prevailed before the civil war."[94] These words serve as well to capture the end result of Peruvian developments since that country emerged from its own civil war of the 1930s. Thus a common thread connects the causes that gave rise to the civil struggles in Spain and Peru, and links the ultimate results as well.

Acknowledgments

Since the research and writing of this article covered a span of almost three years, I incurred many debts along the way. Jorge Basadre, Gerold Gino Baumann, Félix Denegri Luna, and Luis Alberto Sánchez provided invaluable assistance while I was in Lima, 1976–77. Also, during and after my stay in Peru, Yolanda Ramírez de Llanos served brilliantly as my research assistant, particularly on the voluminous periodical literature. Brian Loveman and Fredrick B. Pike contributed immeasurably to the style and editing of the initial draft. Finally, I owe an incalculable debt of gratitude to my former graduate student and friend Glenn Douglas Stock. Although he was seriously ill, Glenn helped with the final research and served as a knowledgeable and incisive sounding board for my ideas. His seriousness of purpose, dedication to scholarship, and zeal for life should serve as an inspiration for us all. Tragically, Glenn did not live to see the finished product, but it is, in so many ways, a memorial to him.

Notes

1. For an extensive discussion of Indian labor conditions and standards of living in the republican period, see my *Indian Integration in Peru: A Half Century of Experience, 1900–1948* (Lincoln, 1974), particularly chapters 1 and 2.
2. Brian Loveman and Thomas M. Davies, Jr., eds., *The Politics of Antipolitics: The Military in Latin America* (Lincoln, 1978).
3. Ibid., p. 12.
4. There are many accounts of the Spanish-Chilean-Peruvian War; the best succinct one is chapter 10 of James W. Cortada, "Conflict Diplomacy: United States-Spanish Relations, 1855–1868," Ph.D. dissertation, Florida State University, 1973. Also useful is William Columbus Davis, *The Last Conquistadores: The Spanish Intervention in Peru and Chile, 1863–1866* (Athens, Ga., 1950).
5. Manuel González Prada, "Cosas de España," in *Prosa menuda* (Buenos Aires, 1941), p. 237. (This essay was originally published in *Los Parias* 20 [1905]).
6. Ibid., p. 238.
7. Quoted in Fredrick B. Pike, *Hispanismo, 1898–1936: Spanish Conservatives and Liberals and Their Relations with Spanish America* (Notre Dame, 1971), p. 204.
8. Manuel G. Abastos, "El Perú y España," *Mercurio Peruano* 28 (1920): 255.
9. Ibid., p. 269.
10. Calculated from tables found in Mario E. del Río, *La inmigración y su desarrollo en el Perú* (Lima, 1929), pp. 87–91, 110–14, 159–61.
11. Augusto B. Leguía, *Discursos, mensajes y programas del Presidente Leguía* (Lima, 1926), III, 305–6.

12. One must begin with his collected works: *Obras completas de José Carlos Mariátegui*, 10 vols. (Lima, 1959–1970), particularly his classic *Siete ensayos de interpretación de la realidad peruana*, translated into English by Marjory Urquidi as *Seven Interpretive Essays on Peruvian Reality* (Austin, 1971). The Mariátegui family has also made a fine contribution to the scholarly community by publishing beautifully-prepared facsimile editions of *Amauta*, 6 vols. (Lima, 1977), and *Labor* (Lima, 1974). There are literally hundreds of articles and books on Mariátegui, but the best and most complete study is Jesús Chavarría, *José Carlos Mariátegui and the Rise of Modern Peru* (Albuquerque, 1979).

13. José Carlos Mariátegui, "El Directorio español," *Variedades*, December 8, 1923, reprinted in José Carlos Mariátegui, *Figuras y aspectos de la vida mundial* (Lima, 1970), pp. 46–52.

14. *Variedades*, March 1, 1924, reprinted in José Carlos Mariátegui, *Signos y obras* (Lima, 1959), pp. 120–26.

15. For an excellent discussion, see Fredrick B. Pike, *The United States and The Andean Republics: Peru, Bolivia and Ecuador* (Cambridge, Mass., 1977), pp. 181–82.

16. Ibid., p. 182.

17. For a superb discussion of this complex issue, see ibid., particularly chapters 6 through 8.

18. Steve J. Stein, *Populism in Peru: The Emergence of the Masses and the Politics of Social Control* (Madison, 1980), chapter 1.

19. Except where otherwise noted, the material on APRA has been drawn largely from my article "The Indigenismo of the Peruvian Aprista Party: A Reinterpretation," *Hispanic American Historical Review* 51 (1971): 626–45, and chapters 5 and 6 of my *Indian Integration in Peru*. Two highly laudatory and rather uncritical works on Haya de la Torre are Harry Kantor, *The Ideology and Program of the Peruvian Aprista Movement*, 2nd ed. (Washington, D.C., 1966), and Robert Alexander, *Prophets of the Revolution: Profiles of Latin American Leaders* (New York, 1962).

20. For a complete text of the Plan, see Víctor Raúl Haya de la Torre, *Política Aprista*, 2nd ed. (Lima, 1967), pp. 9–30. The economic program is on pp. 14–18.

21. For the allegation that Larco Herrera contributed fifty thousand *soles* to the Aprista election campaign in 1931, see Ambassador Fred Morris Dearing, May 16, 1931, to Secretary of State, Serial Files on Peru, National Archives, 810.43 APRA/83, hereafter cited as D.S. followed by the identification number. Rafael Larco Herrera continued to support Aprista principles, and in 1933, through his Lima newspaper, *La Crónica*, declared himself in accord with various Aprista proposals. See Dearing to Secretary of State, November 16, 1933, D.S. 823.00/1046. For an analysis of the economic change in La Libertad and its effect on the Larco Herrera family, see Peter Klarén, *Modernization, Dislocation, and Aprismo: Origins of the Peruvian Aprista Party* (Austin, 1973), chapters 1 through 3.

22. Víctor Villanueva, *El APRA en busca del Poder* (Lima, 1975), pp. 75–78. Villanueva's principal thesis is that APRA was sharply divided between the bourgeois leadership of Haya and others who wished to achieve power through the liberal, electoral process, and the authentically proletarian mass of campesinos and workers who possessed a predilection for violent revolution.

23. For my analysis of Sánchez Cerro, I have relied heavily on and owe an intellectual debt to Stein, *Populism in Peru: The Emergence of the Masses*, Chapters 2, 4, 5, and 8, and to Villanueva, *El APRA en busca del poder*, particularly chapters 2 and 3. The best and most complete study of the Sánchez Cerro period is vol. 14 of Jorge Basadre's monumental *Historia de la República del Perú*, 6th ed. (Lima, 1970).

24. Stein, *Populism in Peru*, pp. 103–04. p. 188.

25. This is the principal thesis of Villanueva's *El APRA en busca del poder* as well as his *El APRA y el ejército (1940–1950)* (Lima, 1977).

26. Basadre, *Historia de la República*, XIV, 403–9.

27. An entire volume of newspaper clippings on the assassination from all over Peru and the rest of Latin America is in the Sánchez Cerro Archive.

28. For right-wing attacks on the left in general and on the APRA in particular, see *Criterio*, nos. 1–4 (October-November 1933). No. 3 (November 8, 1933) contains a long analysis of the political situation and states matter-of-factly that there are only two parties in Peru, "the Right, which guards the traditions of revolutionary nationalism, and the Left, which is inspired by exotic and unstable forms of socialism. Either we are on one side or the other." *Acción* (November 4, 1933) carries a picture of and a story about Fascists dressed in black shirts meeting at the tomb of their fallen hero, Sánchez Cerro.

29. Private archive of César Enrique Pardo, Lima, Peru, hereafter cited as the Pardo Archive. Cited also in Villanueva, *El APRA en busca del poder*, p. 159.

30. For an account of Haya's January 9th meeting with Benavides, see *La Antorcha* 2, 139 (January 10, 1934). A few days later he met at length with Jorge Prado. See *Acción* (January 17, 1934).

31. Pardo Archive. Reprinted in Villanueva, *El APRA en busca del poder*, pp. 160–61.

32. For fascinating accounts of these events, see Villanueva, *El APRA en busca del poder*, pp. 162–73. For a less satisfactory version see Percy Murillo Garayocochea, *Historia del APRA, 1919–1945* (Lima, 1976), pp. 327–38. The principal Aprista conspirator was Julio Cárdenas García, alias "El Negus." A legend in his own time, Cárdenas was involved in more than twenty major uprisings. He kept a small archive of his activities in the 1930s and 1940s, and much of Villanueva's documentation comes from interviews with Cárdenas. In June 1977, Villanueva and I interviewed Cárdenas and filmed much of the archive. In addition, see a series of articles by Andrés Gallardo Echevarría that appeared in the Peruvian political magazine *Oiga*, July 10 and 17 and August 7, 1970.

33. All the major newspapers, plus the numerous papers created specifically to support one candidacy or another, commented editorially on the changing political structure, almost to the exclusion of foreign affairs. There was almost no mention of the crisis in Spain except to compare it to Peru. For example, in an editorial of December 17, 1935, *El Universal* noted that the prolonged cabinet crisis in Spain, which had been caused by the inability of the parties to cooperate, had finally been settled with the formation of a center-right coalition. Since *El Universal* had been campaigning against the proliferation of parties in Peru, its analysis of the Spanish situation was at once a comment on and a warning to Peruvian politicians. *Excelsior*, though usually conservative in its ideology, took a middle position and blasted both the extreme right and the

extreme left. See especially its editions of August 8, September 19, October 10, November 14, December 19 and 21.

34. The first description of the plot was written by Víctor Villanueva and appeared in *Caretas* 488 (1973). Villanueva then published a more extensive account in *El APRA en busca del poder,* pp. 173–79. Both of these works were based almost exclusively on documents in the César Enrique Pardo Archive, but in 1977 I found several hundred additional documents in the Benavides Archive, and in our book entitled *300 documentos para la historia del APRA: Conspiraciones apristas de 1935 a 1939* (Lima, 1979), Villanueva and I have selected the most important documents on the conspiracy.

35. For a reprint of the description of the bonds, see Villanueva, *El APRA en busca del poder,* p. 176, and Davies and Villanueva, *300 documentos,* p. 37. For two discussions of the bond issue see Louis G. Dreyfus, Jr., to Secretary of State, April 1, 1936, D.C. 810.43 APRA/207, and *Las Derechas* 1, no. 27 (April 6, 1936).

36. Pardo Archive, reprinted in Villanueva, *El APRA en busca del poder,* pp. 174–75, and Davies and Villanueva, *300 documentos,* p. 65. The United States Embassy in Lima was aware of the plot. See Dreyfus to Secretary of State, September 3, 1936, D.S. 823.00/1212.

37. For one public statement of this attitude, see an April 1936 interview in Asunción, Paraguay, in which Manuel Seoane stated that once in power the Apristas would respond favorably to Bolivia's just demands for a Pacific port. See an editorial in *La Prensa,* April 25, 1936, condemning the Aprista proposal.

38. Francisco García Calderón to Oscar R. Benavides, November 21, 1936, Benavides Archive, Legajo 9, Documento 29. For a comparable view written before the action, see Carlos Concha to Oscar R. Benavides, October 29, 1936, Benavides Archive, Legajo 9, Documento 27. Even before the election, many periodicals had pointed to the Benavides presidency as an example of a calm, moderating force between two irreconcilable and undesirable extremes. See for example, *Cascabel* 2, no. 82 (May 2, 1936).

39. *The Spanish Republic and the Civil War, 1931–1939* (Princeton, N.J., 1965), p. 233.

40. Víctor Andrés Belaúnde noted in his memoirs: "Benavides, consciously or unconsciously, wanted to divorce himself completely from intellectual advisers. He quickly got rid of Riva-Agüero, who had consolidated his government in the most difficult moments, and later he also dismissed Carlos Arenas y Loayza" [one of Peru's leading intellectuals and diplomats in the period 1930–50]. *Trayectoria y destino: Memorias completas,* 2 vols. (Lima, 1967), II, 819. It goes without saying that Benavides would have rejected the advice of leftist intellectuals as well.

41. R. M. de Lambert to Secretary of State, June 12, 1937, D. S. 823 105/18. At first the United States embassy in Rome had mistakenly reported that the rank of the mission officers would be very low. See Alexander Kirk to Secretary of State, May 3, 1937, D.S. 823. 105/17.

42. Sherman Miles in Lima to Army Chief of Staff in Washington, May 28, 1940, D.S. 823.00F/20; and James C. Carey, *Peru and the United States, 1900–1962* (Notre Dame, 1964), p. 104.

43. Baltazar Caravedo Molinari, *Burguesía e industria en el Perú, 1933–1945* (Lima, 1976), pp. 66–67. See also Jorge Basadre, *Chile, Perú y Bolivia independientes* (Barcelona, 1948), p. 732.

44. One of the leading members of an upper-class Italian-Peruvian fam-

ily in Lima put it to me this way: "Before Mussolini, the Italians in Peru were ashamed of their origins. Mussolini made us proud again, able to hold our heads up high, but that does *not* mean that we were Nazis—we were not!" One of the earliest favorable accounts of Mussolini and fascism was written in 1923 by Víctor Andrés Belaúnde and published in his highly influential *Mercurio Peruano*. Anticipating themes that later enjoyed considerable vogue, Belaúnde said in part: "It is necessary to admit that fascism arose as a reaction of the Italian national organism, threatened with disintegration at the hands of the communists and the passive complicity of the government. Italy needed order, the reestablishment of respect for authority, discipline, an efficient bureaucracy and all these things have been secured temporarily" (12, no.66 [December 1923], pp. 250–51).

45. Mexican Ambassador to Peru, Moisés Sáenz, to Secretary of Foreign Relations in Mexico City, August 11, 1936, Archivo de la Secretaría de Relaciones Exteriores (Mexico City) (hereafter cited as ASRE), II/510 (46) "36"/1, II–768–8. I am most indebted to Thomas G. Powell for sending me this and the other citations from the Archivo. Unfortunately, the Archive of the Ministerio de Relaciones Exteriores in Lima is closed to researchers as far back as the nineteenth century and is certainly not available for the 1930s. Thus, I have had to rely on Powell's citations, the *Memorias* of the Ministro de Relaciones del Perú, and a couple of memoirs by Peruvian diplomats.

46. Moisés Sáenz, Lima, to Secretary of Foreign Relations in Mexico City, December 8, 1936, ASRE, III/510 (46) "36"/1, III–768–8.

47. Jorge Bailey Lembcke, *Recuerdos de un diplomático peruano 1917–1954* (Lima, 1959), p. 131. The author also recounts a particularly gruesome incident when leftists broke into a room just as a woman was giving birth and killed her husband, driving her permanently insane. In fact, Bailey Lembcke made every effort in his book to picture all leftists as the cruelest and bloodiest barbarians possible.

48. Ibid., pp. 133–45. Again this account is quite emotional and must be used with a great deal of caution. See also Alberto Wagner de Reyna, *Historia diplomática del Perú (1900–1945)*, 2 vols. (Lima, 1964), II, 251–53.

49. Bailey Lembcke, *Recuerdos de un diplomático peruano*, 135, 139–44.

50. Jackson, *The Spanish Republic and the Civil War*, p. 438. Jackson goes on to state that at night shots were fired from the embassy buildings of pro-Franco governments and that many embassy personnel were involved in the black market in Madrid (p. 439).

51. Cablegram from Spanish Minister of State, Julio Álvarez del Vayo, in Madrid to the Peruvian Foreign Office in Lima, May 15, 1937, delivered by the Mexican Minister in Lima, ASRE, III/510 (46) "36"/1, III–768–8. Wagner de Reyna, *Historia diplomática del Perú*, II, 251–52. See also the official Peruvian communiqué on the incident, which was reprinted in *El Comercio*, March 19, 1938: Perú, *Memoria del Ministro de Relaciones Exteriores don Carlos Concha, 20 de noviembre de 1937–20 de abril de 1939* (Lima, 1939), LXX–LXXIV, 262–69. See also Perú, *Memoria del Ministro de Relaciones Exteriores General C.A. de la Fuente, 23 de octubre de 1936 al 29 de octubre de 1937* (Lima, 1939), XXVIII–XXXI, 41–58; and Perú, *Memoria del Ministro de Relaciones Exteriores don Enrique Goytisolo B., 20 de abril al 8 de diciembre de 1939* (Lima, 1940), XIX–XX, 11–16, 38–41.

52. From the official comuniqué in *El Comercio*, March 19, 1938. Perú, *Memoria del Ministro de Relaciones Exteriores, 1937–1939*, pp. 262–69; and Perú,

Memoria del Ministro de Relaciones Exteriores, 1936-1937 pp. 41–58. As U.S. ambassador Claude G. Bowers noted later, the Peruvian minister had the gall to state at one point "that the fifth columnists 'wanted to listen to the official news from the Salamanca situation,' and he had refused permission." See his *My Mission to Spain: Watching the Rehearsal for World War II* (New York, 1954), p. 300.

53. *El Comercio*, March 19, 1938; Perú, *Memoria del Ministro de Relaciones Exteriores, 1937–1939*, pp. 262–69; and Perú, *Memoria del Ministro de Relaciones Exteriores, 1936–1937*, pp. 41–58. See also Wagner de Reyna, *Historia diplomática del Perú*, II, 251–52; and a scathing editorial in *La Prensa*, February 5, 1938. While negotiations were still going on, Peru appeared to adopt a more cautious public stance. For example, in reply to an Uruguayan inquiry of July 15, 1937, about the possibility of all the American nations recognizing the Franco regime at the same time, Peru stated that, although she was in agreement in principle, it was necessary to await a more opportune moment. Moisés Sáenz in Lima to Eduardo Hay in Mexico City, July 15, 1937, ASRE III/510 (46) "36"/1, III–768–8.

54. *El Comercio*, March 20, 1938. See also a stinging editorial in *La Crónica*, May 9, 1937.

55. Wagner de Reyna, *Historia diplomática del Perú*, II, 253.

56. Either I or Glen Stock or my research assistant in Peru, Yolanda Ramírez de Llanos, researched the following newspapers in the Peruvian National Library in Lima. The place of publication of the periodical is in parenthesis. *Acción* (Lima, Organo de la Unión Revolucionaria); *Acción* (Chiclayo); *Altura* (Huancayo); *Alerta* (Cajamarca); *Acción Social del Magisterio* (Lima); *Amigo del Clero* (Lima); *La Antorcha* (Lima); *La Bala Roja* (Chiclayo); *Boletín del Comité Amigo de los Defensores de la República Española* (Lima); *Boletín del Partido Democrático Reformista* (Lima); *Cahuide* (Lima); *El Callao* (Callao); *La Cara y el Sello* (Lima); *El Cascabel* (Lima); *La Colmena* (Arequipa, Organo del Círculo de Obreros Católicos); *El Comercio* (Lima); *La Crónica* (Lima); *Cuaderno Aprista* (Lima); *El Deber* (Arequipa); *Las Derechas* (Lima); *Ecos y Noticias* (Piura); *España Libre* (Lima, Organo del Comité Local de "Amigos de la República Española"); *Excelsior* (Lima); *Garcilaso* (Lima); *El Heraldo* (Iquitos); *El Hombre de la Calle* (Lima); *Italia Nueva* (Lima); *El Liberal* (Lima); *La Luz* (Iquitos); *La Nación* (Lima); *La Noche* (Lima); *La Opinión Popular* (La Oroya); *Páginas Libres* (Lima); *Panoramas* (Lima); *El Perú* (Lima); *El Peru de Hoy* (Lima); *La Prensa* (Lima); *Reflejos* (Lima); *Revista de la Universidad Católica del Perú* (Lima); *Revista de los Colegios Raimondi* (Lima); *La Semana* (Lima); *Todo el Mundo* (Lima); *La Tribuna* (Lima); *El Universal* (Lima); *La Voz de España* (Lima).

57. Two examples are *Boletín del Comité Amigo de los Defensores de la República Española* (Lima) and *España Libre*, both of which are treated below.

58. *La Prensa*, January 9, 1936.

59. *La Prensa*, February 19, 1936. A few days earlier (February 8), the paper had called for the formation of an anti-Communist front of nations to combat Russia and her minions, stating that there was "positive proof of the existence of a formidable organization, in the heart of our Iberian America, pledged to throw us into the same state of chaos in which are found the great mass of enslaved Russian people."

60. *La Prensa*, April 17, 1936.

61. *La Prensa*, July 26, 1936. See also June 6, July 5, July 23, 1936.

62. *La Crónica,* August 3, 1936. See also August 6.

63. *La Crónica,* October 6, 1936.

64. For examples, see *La Crónica,* August 3, 17, 24, September 25, 27, and November 8, 1936. Greatly supportive of the paper's position was a huge, twenty-six-installment series of articles written by Gonzalo de Sandoval, entitled "A Short History of the Spanish Revolution (Notes of an Eyewitness)." Though decidedly pro-Franco, the articles had the appearance of presenting an objective analysis of the situation. The series ran during November 1–27, 1936.

65. *La Crónica,* April 14, 1937.

66. *La Crónica,* August 23, 1937. See also July 18, August 9, November 2, November 19, 1937.

67. One example is the January 30, 1937, issue, which carries not only a full-page picture of Hitler with a caption saluting him on his birthday but also a long article by Juan Tidow that praises Hitler and concludes: "The program for the first four years has been carried out brilliantly; there is no longer any unemployment in Germany, exports have risen, and the people have regained their faith in the future. There is not abundance, but everybody has what he needs." In addition there is a long interview with the Italian minister of foreign relations in which he emphasized racial purity and the family and claimed that the Russians and the Communists seek to destroy both. That they held to this line can be seen in a March 28, 1938, editorial that argued against accepting any refugees from either Germany or Spain because they were either Jews or Communists (or both) and thus represented a serious threat "to the political and social stability of each country." Finally, throughout 1936, Carlos Miró Quesada Laos (using the pseudonym "Garrotín") wrote long articles on fascism and national socialism.

68. See *El Comercio,* January 5, 17, 20, February 14, and July 17. In another issue (March 20, 1938), Peruvian intellectual Raúl Ferrero argued that liberalism was dead and that the corporate state of Mussolini's Italy was to be the new order.

69. *El Comercio,* March 30, 1939.

70. *El Universal,* July 19, 1936. See also February 24, June 20, July 31, and August 11.

71. *El Universal,* August 16, 1936.

72. *Las Derechas,* August 6, 1936.

73. On May 14, 1937, *Las Derechas,* in an editorial glorifying the Pope's encyclical against communism, equated APRA with the red Republicans in Spain and stated again that Western Christian civilization was locked in a death struggle with atheistic communism with no middle position possible. See also the following issues: July 28 and October 29, 1936, and June 11, 1937.

74. *El Amigo del Clero,* October, 1936, and July-August, 1937. See also letters from the Spanish episcopate and the archbishop of Toledo, outlining the horrible conditions in highly inflammatory language, which were published in September-October 1937, and two emotional articles, reprinted from *Cartas de Roma,* describing what had happened to the orphan children sent to Mexico by the pro-Republican Hijos de España (March 1938).

75. *El Amigo del Clero,* November, 1938. See also the articles that appeared in the issues of April, July, and September of 1938.

76. *La Noche,* September 23, 1931. For a penetrating analysis of Riva Agüero's political philosophy and how it adversely affected his scholarship see

Jorge Basadre, "Crónica Nacional: Riva Agüero," *Historia, Revista de Cultura* 8 (1944): 449–55. Earlier, Basadre had stated that Riva Agüero, since 1931, "has moved beyond the limits of strictly scientific scholarship and has become a militant politician." "La producción bibliográfica del Perú en 1937–38," *Boletín Bibliográfico de la Universidad Mayor de San Marcos* 3–4 (1938): 248–51.

77. "En el Centro de la Juventud Católica," in José de la Riva Agüero, *Por la verdad, la tradición y la patria (opúsculos)* 2 vols. (Lima, 1938), II, 128. Riva Agüero's writings on Mussolini and the rise of Italian fascism are far too extensive to be listed here, but the reader is directed to the following titles: *Dos estudios sobre Italia contemporánea* (Lima, 1937); introduction to Carlos Miró Quesada Laos, *Intorno agli scritti e discorse di Mussolini. Con introduzione de José de la Riva Agüero* (Milan, 1937); "La Italia moderna," in *Por la verdad*, I, 481–85; and a speech on communism and the need for a corporate state reprinted in *Las Derechas*, October 1, 1935. See also Luis Fabio Xammer, *Valores humanos en la obra de Leonidas Yerovi* (Lima, 1938), p. 73.

78. *Excelsior*, March 6, 1936. See also an article by Jorge Falcón that argued that the rightists had mounted a terror campaign designed to overthrow the Azaña government (March 19, 1936).

79. *Excelsior*, September 10, 1936.

80. *Excelsior*, February 1939.

81. It published three numbers: June 28, July 6, and July 17, 1937. *La Voz de España* was also badly mimeographed on cheap paper and circulated clandestinely. Only two numbers survive in the Peruvian National Library, and both of them concentrate almost exclusively on the world-wide maneuvering of Italy and Germany: no 2 (September 26, 1938) and no. 3 (October 8, 1938).

82. Jorge del Prado, *40 años de lucha: Partido Comunista Peruano, 1928–1968* (Lima, 1968), p. 20. There are several Communist party broadsides in the "volantes" file in the National Library in Lima. Two are entitled "Viva el Frente Popular Española" (dated July 23 and August 9, 1936) and are calls for all Peruvians to support the Spanish Republic against the Fascist militarism of Franco. In later years, the Communist party regularly pointed to Spain as an example of what could happen in Peru. Equating *hispanismo* with fascism and Haya de la Torre with Hitler and Franco, Communist writers such as Ricardo Martínez de la Torre argued that only a unified movement of workers and peasants, directed of course by the Peruvian Communist party, could prevent a Fascist take-over. See Martínez de la Torre, *Apuntes para una interpretación marxista de historia social del Perú*, 4 vols. (Lima, 1947–49), II, 35, 72–90, 171–72, 546–47.

83. Interview, November 3, 1976. In his memoirs, Sánchez makes no mention of the order, but he does state that "the Spanish civil war was decisive for those of us who were politically active in the period 1932–1940." He goes on to describe the impact on young Apristas of the struggle in Spain between Republicans and monarchists, liberals and conservatives. Sánchez's most important contribution, however, is his rather nostalgic reminiscence of the intellectual communities of Chile and Argentina and how they reacted to the war. *Testimonio personal: Memorias de un Peruano del siglo XX*, 4 vols. (Lima, 1969–76), II, 521–43.

84. This attitude is nowhere better reflected than in the party's official organ, *La Tribuna*. Although outlawed by the government, the paper published clandestine issues on a regular basis in the period 1935–1940. During that time,

Spain was mentioned only once, on August 10, 1936. Not until May 3, 1940, did the paper even refer to fascism or European affairs. See also May 17 and October 14, 1940.

85. Jeffrey L. Klaiber, *Religion and Revolution in Peru, 1824–1976* (Notre Dame, 1977), p. 122. For an important complementary piece see Fredrick B. Pike, "Religion, Collectivism, and Intrahistory: The Peruvian Ideal of Dependence," *Journal of Latin American Studies* 10 (1978): 239–62.

86. Rubén Vargas Ugarte, *¿Aprista o Católico?* (Lima, 1934). See also *Aprismo-Anticatolicismo* (Lima, 1934). Two pro-Aprista pamphlets arguing that Aprismo and Christianity were compatible are Luis Alberto Sánchez, *Aprismo y religión* (Lima, 1933), and [Carlos Rodríguez Pastor], *Catolicismo y Aprismo* (Lima: 1934).

87. No doubt as a part of the party's pragmatic neutrality, Apristas Luis Alberto Sánchez, Manuel Seoane, and Ciro Alegría all turned down invitations to attend the Congress of Anti-Fascist Writers held in Valencia in July 1937. *España Libre*, June 28, 1937, roundly condemned their refusal and noted in its next issue that "we have to conclude, painfully, that the enormous sympathy for Republican Spain that exists inside the Aprista party will not be represented in Valencia" (July 6, 1937).

88. The incredibly disparate and scattered materials on these volunteers have been carefully researched and compiled by Gerold Gino Baumann, and I am most grateful to him for allowing me to work with his manuscript, which has now been published as: *Extranjeros en la Guerra Civil Española: Los Peruanos* (Lima, 1979). One of the more fascinating cases was related to me by my father-in-law, General (r) José Monzón Linares, shortly before his death. Ceverino Llaque-Mori, godson of Aprista Manuel Seoane, was an officer in the Guardia Civil who won 10,000 *soles* in the Peruvian national rifle contest. He went on a tour of Europe, including a visit to Russia, and on entering Spain he was branded a Communist by the Peruvian embassy and forcibly retired from the Guardia Civil. Although never a Communist, Llaque-Mori found himself pushed to the left by Peruvian officials and did join the Republican army. After the war he returned to Lima and became a taxi driver. According to General Monzón, Llaque-Mori was highly intelligent and probably would have achieved the rank of general if his career had not been terminated for ideological reasons.

89. *Oiga* 41 (1978) and *España Libre* 2 (July 6, 1937). Interestingly, Falcón's Spanish-born first wife, Irene Levi-Rodríguez, has, since 1938, been the private secretary of Dolores Ibarruri, the legendary "La Pasionaria."

90. See Eudocio Ravines, *The Yenan Way* (New York, 1951), pp. 185–230, and *Oiga*, 41 (1978). Jorge del Prado, long-time leader of the Peruvian Communist party, asserts that Ravines was attached to the International Brigades but cowardly deserted. Since Ravines later became an extreme right-wing opponent of communism, del Prado's claim must be viewed with caution.

91. Space limitations preclude a fuller treatment of Vallejo and his work, but several major sources exist. By far the most sensitive and erudite is Jean Franco, *César Vallejo: The Dialectics of Poetry and Silence* (New York, 1976). See particularly chapter 9, which analyzes the impact of the Spanish Civil War. Clayton Eshleman and José Rubia Barca published a bi-lingual edition of *España, aparta de mí este cáliz* (New York, 1974). Other important sources include Armando Bazán (who himself fought in Spain), *César Vallejo: Dolor y poesía*

(Lima, n.d.); Ernesto More, *Vallejo, en la encrucijada del drama peruano* (Lima, 1968); Ángel Flores, ed., *Aproximaciones a César Vallejo,* 2 vols. (New York, 1971); and the impressive scholarly efforts of Vallejo's close friend Juan Larrera contained in the magazine *Aula Vallejo* (Córdoba, Argentina, 1969–76).

92. The best analysis of CAEM is Víctor Villanueva, *El CAEM y la revolución de la fuerza armada* (Lima, 1972). See also Loveman and Davies, *The Politics of Antipolitics,* particularly chapters 1, 5, and 6.

93. For a comprehensive, overly-optimistic view of the new military government see Abraham F. Lowenthal, ed., *The Peruvian Experiment: Continuity and Change Under Military Rule* (Princeton, 1975). See also Loveman and Davies, *The Politics of Antipolitics,* and Pike, *The United States and the Andean Republics,* pp. 339–81.

94. Quoted in *Anuario Político Español, 1969: Cambio social y modernización,* edited by Miguel Martínez Cuadrado (Madrid, 1970), p. 25.

Chile

Paul W. Drake

The bloody 1973 Chilean coup d'etat by General Augusto Pinochet Ugarte ushered in an authoritarian regime that evoked comparisons with the Spanish dictatorship imposed earlier by General Francisco Franco. Prior to Pinochet's military takeover, Chile had been politically unique in the hemisphere. From the 1930s to the 1970s, it had stood out as the only Latin American country to preserve an electoral democracy that included Marxist parties as the major leaders of the workers. Despite permissiveness toward reform movements, Chile maintained a far more limited and fundamentally conservative system of constitutional representative government than its partisans claimed. Beneath the rotation of political competitors, the country retained many social, economic, and cultural features in common with the rest of the Hispanic world. Political openness produced few socio-economic benefits for the Chilean masses until the sixties and seventies. Nevertheless, that multiparty system won the support of most of its citizens. It is within that unusual political-historical context that Chile's relationship and reaction to the Spanish civil war of the 1930s must be analyzed.

Introduction

It was primarily through that pluralistic electoral bargaining system that Chile reflected, deflected, and coped with the stresses of partial, delayed, and dependent "modernization." The aristocratic, parliamentary republic inherited from the nineteenth century broke down after World War

I. Constitutionalism cracked under spiraling pressures from the growing urban middle and working classes. Political stability eroded in the wake of plummeting nitrate sales, which had long been the mainstay of the export economy and state revenues. Legalistic liberal reforms begun by President Arturo Alessandri Palma in 1920 failed to reconcile traditional elites and new groups desiring more participation and modern urban, industrial advances. As a result, Chile experienced a crisis of authority similar to Spain's in the period. Temporary military solutions (1924–32) to the legitimacy vacuum opened up by the decline of exclusive upper-class rule collapsed with the Great Depression. That economic disaster and resulting political-military chaos during 1931–32 largely discredited the armed forces as a continuing governing option for the immediate future. Civilian elites renewed their determination to preserve constitutional order. An elected rightist government (1932–38) under the erstwhile reformer Alessandri restored political stability and economic growth. Alessandri's reconstruction, however, did not resolve the social problems of emergent urban sectors that had precipitated the crisis after World War I.

The integrationist solution that arose in the 1930s was the Popular Front. A populist variety of coalition politics, it united a few upper-class leaders along with most of the middle and working classes in the cities. They supported a gradual program of tandem industrialization and welfare reforms. Taking office peacefully, the Front (1938–41) and its successors through the 1940s incorporated the most articulated urban groups into the highly clientelistic state "spoils" system. This accommodation occurred without displacing established economic elites. Through the brokerage of the centrist Radical party, the Marxists (Communists and Socialists) and their followers were admitted into a subordinate role in the national electorate and bureaucracy; in exchange they accepted the democratic rules of the game and blunted their more militant demands. These political changes proved compatible with social and economic continuities under state capitalism.

Thus Chile, in contrast to Spain, postponed any showdown over the objectives and beneficiaries of twentieth-century urban and industrial changes. Chile was able to contain severe conflict over these issues partly because political participation remained very limited—less than 10 percent of the total population voted for presidential candidates until rapid electoral expansion began in the 1950s. During the era of Radical party presidents usually backed by Socialists and Communists (1938–52), the government restricted labor unions and reforms to a minority of workers in the mines and the mushrooming cities. These administrations made no frontal assaults on the roots of underdevelopment in the latifundia-dominated countryside or in the U.S.–dominated external sector. Economic growth remained slow, income distribution regressive, and inflation relentless. Nevertheless, protected import-substituting industrialization temporarily satisfied urban political actors. Most leaders of both the right and the left preferred shared but unequal participation through the expanding bureaucratic state to direct confrontation over sparse resources. Therefore Chile retained political stability as well as the most dynamic Marxist electoral movement in Latin America.

Although they exhibited significant similarities to their European counterparts, these Chilean movements obviously evolved their own rhythms and patterns. Logically, the civil war in Spain should have reverberated loudly in Chile. After all, the former colony had strengthening sentimental ties to the Mother Country, an upsurge in corporatist thought and movements in the wake of the Great Depression, and, above all, a comparable Popular Front. Although significant, the Spanish war's effect on Chileans was filtered and modulated by distinctive national conditions at the time. The ways in which they reacted to that tragedy in the *madre patria* shed valuable light on the character of Chilean society, culture, and politics in the 1930s. For example, Chile's Popular Front and its descendants in the 1940s became primarily dedicated to rallying the worker movement behind industrialization in order to catch up with the more affluent West. Compared to Fronts in Spain or France, they consequently placed less emphasis on working-class conquests. Chile's Front also won the support of that country's "Nazi" movement and the acquiescence of its Falange, both more reformist and moderate than their European namesakes. Moreover, the Chilean upper class, not unlike the British, repeatedly settled for cooptation or accommodation rather than coercion. The elites and the right could be intractable and repressive. Their distinguishing trait, however, was their sophisticated use of flexibility. This preserved more of their privileges than unbending resistance might have, at least in the short run. Although Chile grappled with similar problems of underdevelopment and similar ideological movements, it was not necessarily destined to repeat the Mother Country's horrendous experience during the interwar years.

By the 1960s and '70s, however, Chile's capacity to integrate and balance such diverse socio-economic and ideological interests declined. Rising population growth, snowballing urbanization, galloping inflation, and passage of the relatively easy stage of import-substituting industrialization left little surplus for assuaging competing demands. At the same time, an expanding electorate, an aroused rural work force, and increasingly strident bidding among competitive reform leaders pushed the country toward a zero-sum game. It proved ever more difficult to reconcile conflicting social-political claims. Populist coalitions among industrializers, the middle classes, and urban workers became less sustainable. Chile relied increasingly on a soaring foreign debt to try to keep the compromising but overloaded system afloat. Meanwhile, both the Marxists and their adversaries became more radical and rigid.

Following the 1970 election of President Salvador Allende Gossens by the Socialists, Communists, Radicals, and a handful of minor parties, an open social conflict raged over a limited supply of goods and power. The earlier Spanish struggle acquired increasing relevance as Chile swiftly polarized. In a more abundant and less politicized country, more demands and needs might have been met simultaneously. Instead, the Chilean reform system broke down. After forty years of restraint, the military seized office. They vowed to roll back social and political mobilization by eliminating the Marxists. By the early 1980s, Chile appeared to have delayed but ultimately not avoided the participation and distribution crises associated with modern change that had earlier destroyed Spain.

Just as Chilean democratic exceptionalism from the 1930s through the 1960s should not be blown out of proportion, neither should its authoritarian conservatism in the 1970s. Past movements with strong corporatist leanings fared quite poorly in Chile. Even the ultra-conservative and brutal Pinochet regime to date has implemented very few of its corporatist-Hispanist pronouncements. Important cultural-political corporatist thought has existed throughout twentieth-century Chile but usually only as a minor undercurrent. It is necessary to recognize paternalistic corporatist proclivities without exaggerating them.

Was there a long-run, vibrant, ingrained propensity for Chileans and other Spanish Americans to prefer dictatorial, patrimonial, hierarchical, Catholic, functionalist systems of thought and governance? If so, those sympathies and tendencies theoretically should have surfaced more intensely than they did in response to the Franco and Falange programs as models for Spain and the New World. More than an overt system of thought or political-social action, corporatism in Chile was normally more important as an implicit organizing principle for interest groups in their relationship with the state. Chilean thinkers and politicians in the 1930s and '40s gave Franco's *hispanidad* a lukewarm reception. This cautions against overstating the historic devotion of Chilean rightists to authoritarian Hispanic traditions. By the same token, it might well be a mistake to overestimate the appeal and longevity of Pinochet's tyranny and its ostensibly corporatist aspirations in the 1970s and '80s.

There are several reasons why the opposing sides in the Spanish civil war had fewer parallels with and influence on the Chilean right and left than might be expected. (1) In contrast to Peru and Mexico, *indigenismo* had little appeal in European-*mestizo* Chile; this reduced the attraction or ideological necessity of *indigenismo*'s conservative opposite, *hispanismo* or *hispanidad.* Chileans normally analyzed their national character as a cosmopolitan, Europeanized amalgam of ethnic types recast over time in a distinctive and hardy national mold. The weight of Spanish ingredients in that mixture, however, was always a debating point between the left and the right. (2) In addition, Chile lacked a romantic, glorious colonial period to hark back to. Instead, conservative and upper-class sectors typically identified with the aristocratic republican successes of the nineteenth century associated with Diego Portales. Leftist thinkers mainly looked to France or the United States for inspiration; they filled most of their pantheon of Chilean heroes with reformers from the later nineteenth century and the twentieth. Nevertheless, Spain became an increasingly important reference point for certain Chilean intellectuals at the time of civil war; this turned into a formative event most notably for poet Pablo Neruda. (3) Both rightist and leftist Chileans took pride in their much-touted difference from the rest of Latin America following independence from Spain. Patriotism embodied this reputed superiority in an unusually durable constitutional, representative government inherited from the nineteenth century and, at least according to national mythology, sustained by moderation and flexibility on all sides. (4) By Hispanic standards, the Chilean Roman Catholic church was relatively weak and progressive. (5) By those same standards, the Chilean military in the period appeared neither highly interventionist nor particularly conservative. The armed services usually preferred to exert influence from behind the scenes so long as civilian politicians did not upset the basic constitutional, economic, social, or military order. The armed forces' exceptional overt intrusions into politics from 1924 through 1932 resulted in reformist governments and burdened the military with the onus of the Great Depression and its accompanying disorders. This left most of the armed forces reluctant to march back into open politics. It also made the upper class wary of the officers' activism. (6) In contrast to Argentina, Chile had received very few Spanish immigrants. (7) Trade with Spain, even counting some nitrate sales vital to a heavily monocultural export economy, remained minuscule. (8) By the 1930s, nationalism had achieved such popularity in Chile that the Socialist party as well as rightist groups like the Nazis and the Falange denied close connections with any Eruopean brethren. During the 1938 electoral campaign, the most damaging salvos exchanged between the Chilean Popular Front of Pedro Aguirre Cerda and its conservative foes behind Gustavo Ross Santa María were charges of anti-nationalism. They accused each other of trying to import Spanish, French, Soviet, and Mexican revolutionary models on the one hand or Fascist ideas and U.S. imperialism on the other. Concomitantly, anti-foreignism prompted Chilean rightists and leftists to interpret their opposite numbers in Spain as handmaidens of external intruders. (9) At the same time, most Chileans welcomed expanded foreign trade and investment in the aftermath of the global depression. These economic desires drew Chile closer to the United States than to Spain. While preaching *hispanidad* as an alternative to Yankee penetration, the Mother Country could not supply the needed capital and industrial goods. The Good Neighbor Policy and World War II also rendered many Chileans less hesitant about closer relations with the United States. (10) Finally, progressive moderation of the Chilean Popular Front toward and after election day eased its opponents' fears. The Spanish Republic and its war with Franco helped shape the gradualist Popular Front strategy that guided the Chilean left from the 1930s on. The Chilean Front's domination by the traditional Radical party and a nominee from its right wing blurred polarization and helped avert a Spanish-style bloodletting.

No one of the above reasons in and of itself prevented the two sides in Spain's civil war from securing widespread and ardent followings in Chile. But, taken together, these factors help to explain why such followings were less numerous, fervent, and imitative than they might have been otherwise. Although both were more moderate than those on the peninsula, the Chilean right and left firmly supported their Spanish counterparts. Rather than an inspiration or a model to be emulated, the Spanish division mainly provided Chileans with an example to be avoided and to be manipulated to tarnish their local political opponents. Indeed, some Chileans argued that Spain should learn from them, rather than vice versa. Probably the main effect of the Mother Country's civil war was to reinforce the conviction of of most Chilean politicians that minimal concessions were normally preferable to unbridled conflict. Commentaries, contributions, volunteers, and political proximity indicate that the Spanish case probably aroused more attention and sympathy on the Chilean left than on the right, at least in the 1930s.

Social class and ideology largely determined Chilean attitudes toward Spain and events there. Hispanism, however, could cross those boundaries. It is necessary to distinguish among cultural, religious, economic, and political *hispanismo*. Some Chileans could be enthusiastic about Spanish language and letters without admiring the peninsular political system. They might advocate greater trade with the Mother

Country without wanting to import its avid Catholicism. The strongest correlation was between pro-clericalism and Hispanism, but that did not always translate into support for Iberian authoritarianism or corporatism. Although identification with Spain was often seen as the opposite pole from identification with the Anglo-Saxon United States, these were not totally incompatible positions. As Chile and Spain changed politically over the years, so did their postures toward each other.

Chronologically, Chile began its liberation from the Mother Country with heated anti-Spanish attitudes in the period of liberal ascendancy from 1817 to 1829. From the 1830s to the 1860s, attitudes toward Spain improved somewhat as conservative groups took charge in Santiago. The mid-century war with the former imperial master embittered relations from the 1860s to the 1880s. Closer, more friendly ties gradually developed from then until the 1930s. Chileans divided sharply during the Spanish civil war, when class and ideology more than ever fixed attitudes toward the *peninsulares.* During the 1940s, opinions of anti-democratic Spain were generally negative and remained little better into the 1960s. With the dramatic changes in both countries in the 1970s, Chilean orientations toward Spanish models once again, as in the 1930s, polarized into seemingly irreconcilable camps.

Improving Relations with Spain, 1880s–1930s

In the 1800s, Chile's prevailing external influences were France in intellectual matters, Britain in economic affairs, and the United States in political ideals. By the start of the twentieth century, relations with the Mother Country grew closer, partly because of the increase of Spanish residents in Chile. According to national censuses, these were the numbers of Spaniards living in Chile and the percentages they constituted of all foreigners residing in the country:

Census Year	Number of Spaniards	As a Percentage of All Foreign Residents
1854	915	5%
1865	1,150	5%
1875	1,072	4%
1885	2,508	3%
1895	8,494	11%
1907	18,755	14%
1920	25,962	22%
1930	23,439	22%

Still, resident Spaniards accounted for only .6 percent of the total Chilean population in 1907. By the twenties and thirties they had surpassed Peruvians, Bolivians, Italians, Germans, and French to become the largest single immigrant group in the country, but all foreigners still accounted for less than 3 percent of the total population. Most literate Chileans apparently saw Spanish arrivals as positive additions. One Chilean analyst of the country's ethnic makeup wrote in 1919: "The Spaniards have arrived at our shores not like foreigners in a strange land but rather like offspring from the same family who have the right to live in the common home."[1]

From the latter decades of the nineteenth century on, gradual strengthening of intellectual and cultural bonds made the *hispanista* sentiments of a minority of Chileans more widespread and acceptable. Numerous writers and politicians—usually associated with Chile's Conservative and Liberal parties—voiced Hispanist sympathies from World War I up to the Spanish civil war and beyond; these included Carlos Silva Vidósola, Julio Pérez Canto, Rafael Luis Gumucio, Rafael Maluenda, Tancredo Pinochet, Ernesto Barros Jarpa, Emilio Rodríguez Mendoza, Francisco Contreras, Pedro N. Cruz, Ricardo Latcham, Osvaldo Lira, Pedro Lira Urquieta, Héctor Rodríguez de la Sotta, Eugenio Orrego Vicuña, and Jaime Eyzaguirre. Many of these Chileans resisted U.S. influence from abroad and working-class ferment from beneath, and so they sought protection in traditional Spanish values. Despite growing closeness in the opening three decades of the twentieth century, most Chilean intellectuals still looked on Spain as a relatively laggard and unattractive source of national identity or inspiration.[2]

Spain vainly hoped that increased trade would pull Chile away from the United States and nearer to the Mother Country and her values. Nitrates accounted for roughly 90 percent of Chilean exports to Spain by the end of the 1920s. However, Spain never became one of Chile's primary nitrate customers, and copper began superseding that commodity as Chile's preeminent export by the 1930s. Maintaining a trade deficit with Chile, Spain mainly sold minor foodstuffs there, such as cooking oil and sardines. Total trade between Chile and Spain rose from 3.5 million Spanish pesetas in 1903 to 16.7 million in 1916 to 50.8 million at the peak in 1929, falling back to 15.9 million by 1934. Although this increase attracted more Chilean attention to Spain, neither country ever ranked among each other's top ten trading partners. By the late 1920s, Spain accounted for only about 1 percent of total Chilean external commerce. Meanwhile, the United States took roughly 60 percent of Chile's exports and supplied over 30 percent of her imports.

Nevertheless, out of Spain's total trade with Latin America in the twenties and thirties, Chile ranked third behind Argentina and Cuba.[3]

Significantly, Chile drew closest to Spain during the former's only sustained military-based dictatorship between the 1830s and the 1970s. Numerous conservative Chileans lauded and encouraged comparisons between the quasi-corporatist regimes of Carlos Ibáñez del Campo (1927–31) and Miguel Primo de Rivera (1923–30). Ibáñez signed a treaty of arbitration with Spain in 1927 and elevated their mutual diplomatic representatives to ambassadorial rank in 1928. Although flirting with Hispanism and corporatism, Ibáñez was no ideologue. He did not create a lasting functionalist system. When the global Great Depression toppled Primo and Ibáñez, Spain and Chile switched to republican forms of government, derailing at least for the moment their essays in semi-corporatist reform and reorganization.[4]

Improving relations with the Mother Country in recent decades had prepared Chileans to react with heightened interest to the Spanish civil war. It seemed unlikely, however, that most would feel a passionate, direct sense of commitment or imitation. Most Chileans saw themselves as superior to the Spaniards and as too cosmopolitan and deeply involved elsewhere to be consumed by Spain's conflicts. Nevertheless, the Chilean right and left instantly aligned with their Spanish counterparts and denounced their Spanish opposites. They did so in order to discredit their own Chilean opponents. Both the Chilean right and left mainly argued that their domestic adversaries might reproduce the horrible Spanish civil war, not that either the Spanish Nationalists or Republicans represented a model Chile should adopt unreservedly. With few exceptions, Chilean public opinion polarized around the conflict much as did groups in Spain. Therefore the following discussion will treat first the effect on the Chilean right, which held power during the war, and then on the Chilean left, which took over at the end.

Rightist Thought on the Spanish Civil War, 1936–39

For Chilean conservative groups and institutions, the advent of the civil war shifted the question of identification with Spanish traditions and patterns from the broad cultural-spiritual *hispanismo* that had been attracting more and more Chilean sympathizers to the increasingly ideologically rigid and controversial *hispanidad* of Franco.[5] Interest in Franquista *hispanidad* from 1936 on remained confined primarily to limited intellectual-political circles; even there, support was shallow.

Among conservative Chileans, almost all opposed the Spanish Loyalists; Franco's General Miguel Cabanellas appreciated the many expressions of support from Chile. Hatred for communism, socialism, and anarchism, however, did not necessarily translate into ardor for full-blown *franquismo* either afar in Spain or at home in Chile. Among rightists, some supported closer cultural or economic ties to the *madre patria,* some the Roman Catholic church, some an anti-liberal corporatist tradition, some Franco, some *hispanidad,* and some even fascism. But these were not necessarily synonymous positions. Nor did holding some of these opinions automatically rule out also being in favor of Chilean democracy, capitalism, social reform, and more intimate relations with the United States. In most cases, the Spanish armageddon was not a primary cause of Chilean attitudes on such issues. Rather, it constituted only one of several forces that reflected and, to a lesser extent, shaped those Chilean attitudes. Nevertheless, the intensity of that peninsular showdown made it an exceptionally revealing mirror of Chilean thought, politics, and development in the era. Most Chileans who applauded Franco apparently did so out of animosity toward his enemies, devotion to Catholicism, and/or fondness for the Spanish past. Only rarely was there any intense commitment to his perceived program as a solution for either Spain or Chile. Not surprisingly, mainly the wealthier middle and especially upper classes in Chile preferred the Nationalists.[6]

The leading voices of conservative opinion and *franquista* propaganda were the major establishment newspapers. They reflected upperclass views. The three prominent rightist dailies in Santiago were, in descending order of importance, *El Mercurio, El Diario Ilustrado,* and *El Imparcial.* All three gave the civil war slanted and extensive coverage, especially during its first two years. They credited the conflict with special salience for Chile because of its peninsular location. They blamed the hostilities on the Republic for having excessively raised mass expectations, for having served as the Trojan horse of Soviet communism, and for having committed countless atrocities. Since France had long been a more exalted inspiration for Chilean intellectuals than Spain, their editorial pages devoted almost as much space to alleged disasters caused by the Popular Front there. A common theme up to the election of 1938 was that the Chilean Front was bound to produce comparable social anarchy, economic disorder, fraternal bloodshed, and a hideous forced choice between leftist or rightist dictatorships.[7]

El Mercurio usually reflected attitudes similar to those of the Liberal party, the Alessandri administration, and the oligopolistic economic interests. Therefore its friendliness toward Franco and the Spanish heritage seldom rested on a defense of Catholicism or full-fledged Hispanidad. Rather, *El Mercurio* stressed the Nationalists' preservation of private property and economic stability, of the social hierarchy, and of law and "order" against the ravages of Marxism and anarchism. The newspaper hoped that Franco's awaited victory would restore the Spanish Republic, responsible democracy, and prudent "social justice," not the monarchy or fascism. For Chile, these columnists usually advocated coping with their own Popular Front by undercutting its appeal through cautious reforms, by defeating it at the polls, or by obstructing, mollifying, and coopting it once in office. The most fervently expressed desire was for salvation not through a military uprising but rather through avoiding the violence suffered in Spain. After all, the Chilean upper class had safeguarded its privileges and avoided social convulsions for decades through limited republican institutions far sturdier than those in Spain. Like Chilean leftists, these rightists argued that the Spanish civil war illustrated the danger of foreign elements intruding into national politics; *El Mercurio* hammered at the evils of Soviet communism in Spain and Chile. This nationalistic posture served as an effective weapon against domestic opponents. However, it left the Chilean right hard-pressed to propose that their country should follow the example of Franco in Spain, which of course was also foreign. Another approach used by *El Mercurio* was to distinguish between the Spanish Republicans' moderate leader Azaña and his more revolutionary allies, just as it differentiated between the temperate nominee of Chile's Popular Front (Pedro Aguirre Cerda, from the right wing of the centrist Radical party) and his Marxist backers. The newspaper intended to warn centrist groups—without alienating them from the right—that a heterogeneous coalition with Socialists and Communists would lead to dominance by the latter. Therefore, the Radicals and other middle-to-upper-class reformers were supposed to align with the right instead of the left to shield Chilean democracy from the destruction wrought in Spain.[8]

Inspired by ardent Catholicism, *El Diario Ilustrado* exuded even greater enthusiasm for Franco. This was expectable from a newspaper financed by the Archbishopric of Santiago and long associated with the pro-clerical Conservative party. More attracted than *El Mercurio* to the spiritual message of *hispanidad,* this daily generated more emotion over Spanish blood being spilled from "a race that is our own." However, at least in 1936, this newspaper denied that Franco's forces were monarchists or Fascists. Instead of drawing the lesson that Chile should follow Spain's example, these columnists concluded that Spain should follow Chile's. They saw their nation's love for republican institutions as also a Spanish tradition, and one that Chile should fortify and Franco should revive: "A type of Portalian Republic would be perhaps the most appropriate model for Spain." According to *El Diario Ilustrado,* the peninsular catastrophe taught wealthier, decent Chileans the importance of defeating their own country's Popular Front, but only through democratic means. The newspaper criticized some upper-class Chileans for overreacting to the Marxist threat illustrated by Spain and for leaping to the conclusion that an authoritarian government, especially one copied from foreign blueprints, could solve Chile's problems. To the contrary, the *Diario* pointed out, recent military upheavals and dictatorships in Chile had moved the nation and the right backward rather than forward. Although less eager than *El Mercurio* to court the anti-clerical Radical party, the *Diario* also worried that Aguirre Cerda would become "the Azaña of our country," meaning a stooge for Soviet communism. Comparing Aguirre Cerda to Azaña, this conservative publication warned: "He has no more talent and no better education than the Spaniard, and the elements that accompany him are even more audacious and less experienced than their peninsular counterparts." It advised Chilean workers, therefore, not to be deceived by a movement that was only a pretext to incite strikes, disorders, conflict, and tyranny: "Necessarily the government of a Popular Front (dictatorship without a program) is only the prelude to the dictatorship of the proletariat, or to the dictatorship of the military." Such fear of a Spanish-style confrontation could make rightists more intransigent and extremist or, as was mainly the case in Chile, more determined to preserve their constitutional, democratic defenses, controls, and stability, even if that required some concessions.[9]

Far less influential than the other two conservative dailies, *El Imparcial* imbided many more ideological components of *hispanidad.* This stemmed from its admiration for fascism. Outside the mainstream of right-wing opinion, *El Imparcial* supported not only Franco but also Hitler, Mussolini, and the Chilean "Nazis" (MNS, the National Socialist Movement). This newspaper placed more emphasis on defending the socio-economic order through fortifying corporatist-Hispanic traditions than on saving Catholicism. Hailing the Nationalists as the incarnation of past Spanish heroes, *El Imparcial* envisioned their restoring Spain ("our spiritual mother") to monarchical rule because republicanism was unsuited to Hispanic societies. Moderates such as Azaña and Aguirre Cerda were criticized almost as harshly as their Socialist allies.[10]

Among the minority of Chilean intellectuals on the conservative side, the most compelling arguments in favor of Franco normally consisted of cultural-linguistic affection for historic Spain, devotion to the Catholic church, and abhorrence of socialism and communism. Such leading Hispanists included Jaime Eyzaguirre, Roberto Peragallo, Osvoldo Lira, Francisco Contreras, and Pedro N. Cruz. Their perspective was reinforced by tours of *franquista* Spaniards through Chile during the civil war. One such visitor, Ramón Giner, concluded, however, that few Spanish Americans were likely to embrace the Nationalist program until the Mother Country caught up with more industrialized Western powers.[11]

Rightist Parties

Among Chilean political parties, corporatism had captivated many leaders in the wake of the economic and social disturbances generated by the Great Depression. A rash of tiny corporatist parties arose out of the depression years before the Spanish civil war began. None of these micro-parties was particularly Hispanist. All had dwindled in strength by the 1940s.[12]

The largest and most avowedly Fascist of these blatantly corporatist parties was the National Socialist Movement. Throughout the 1930s the MNS seldom mentioned Spain and explicitly rejected any connections with *hispanidad*. Its leaders not only shunned ties to Franco but also increasingly underscored their nationalism by shying away from their early affinity for Mussolini and Hitler. Instead, they emphasized resurrection of the golden age of Portales. Praise for Catholicism was tempered so as to keep the party open to anti-clericals. When asked about the Spanish civil war, party chief Jorge González von Marées said it showed that the Chilean right should not be so negative toward his movement. He compared Chile under Alessandri to Spain under Gil Robles before the advent of the Popular Front there made traditional rightists realize that only Fascists could save them from Marxists. During most of the 1938 electoral campaign, the MNS backed ex-dictator Ibáñez. They espoused a program of nationalism and social reform closer to that of the Popular Front than to that of the right. The National Socialists lambasted the Front as a mask for international communism. However, they argued that the best way to undercut surging Marxism in Chile was to steal the left's thunder with social reforms and spiritual renovation; they opposed the historic rightist parties and criticized them for engaging in merely counterproductive repressive measures against Marxists. In 1938 an abortive *putsch* by the MNS torpedoed the Ibáñez campaign. The Alessandri government's massacre of those Nazi rebels drove National Socialists and *ibañistas* to support the election of the Popular Front; this indicated their dissimilarity to the Franco forces and the perils of viewing Chilean politics through Spanish or European lenses. After helping assure inauguration of the Front, the MNS soon evaporated.[13]

The two leading rightist parties rarely cooperated politically with Chilean Fascists during 1936–38. Throughout the 1930s a few Conservatives advocated Catholic "corporatism" as the most viable alternative to populism and socialism. Even these ideologues, however, usually denied any "reactionary" intentions; they normally favored rather independent corporate groups, openly rejecting state fascism as perceived in Italy, Germany, and Spain. When the crises of the depression years faded, the party downplayed corporatist impulses. Instead, it forged an enduring alliance with the Liberals to pursue control of the government through electoral means. Since the constitutional separation of church and state in 1925, the nineteenth-century religious-clerical issues no longer kept the two upper-class parties apart. Nearly all Conservative leaders backed Franco. They did so mainly out of ardor for Catholicism and animosity for communism. Many, such as party right-wingers Pedro Lira Urquieta and Sergio Fernández Larraín, also extolled Spain as the spiritual-cultural citadel of Catholic, Western civilization. Most Conservatives wanted the Alessandri government, in which they served, to clamp down on the Chilean left before it reached Spanish proportions. However, they usually discounted the Spanish civil war "lesson" that the age forced them to choose between Fascist or Communist dictatorships. Some Conservative party Hispanists like Senator Rafael Luis Gumucio contended that the best way for Catholic forces to combat Marxism and fascism was to develop their own program of moderate, preemptive reforms. Within the Conservative camp, often the more reformist elements were most attracted to corporatism and syndicalism; some of them became leaders of the Falange. It formed within the Conservative party until breaking away at the end of 1938 to become a tiny, independent centrist alternative in the 1940s and the Christian Democratic party in the 1950s.[14]

Though never predominant, corporatist-Fascist influences on the Chilean Falange were most pronounced in the 1930s and subsided later. Some notable similarities existed between their program in the thirties and forties and that of the original Spanish Falange, which also had a minuscule separate branch in Chile. The indigenous Chilean Falange's call for a "communitarian society" to promote harmony between capital and labor integrated in functional organizations resembled José Antonio Primo de Rivera's notion of "national syndicalism." During the Spanish Republic many Chilean *falangistas* saw their peninsular namesakes as reformers reacting quite naturally to the excesses of that government.

In the 1930s, these Chileans endorsed "Christianity," "Hispanidad," and the "corporate state." Perhaps most attracted to *franquista* concepts among the top leaders was Manuel Garretón Walker. He dominated the young party until after World War II. Out of vehement opposition to Masons and Marxists, this devout Catholic lauded many of the actions and ideas of Mussolini as well as Franco. While rejecting fascism, Falange leaders Eduardo Frei Montalva and Bernardo Leighton Guzmán in the 1930s recommended autonomous corporatist intermediate bodies, especially for urban and rural laborers. Frei also gave a warmly-received speech to a rally of pro-Franco Spaniards resident in Santiago on the Día de la Raza, October 12, 1938. Spain's influence on the Chilean movement, however, was far overshadowed by that of reformist papal encyclicals and French philosopher Jacques Maritain. Emphasizing the humanistic social justice and pluralistic democratic facets of social Christian doctrines, Maritain shunned state corporatism. Moreover, he argued that the Spanish Nationalists were probably no better than the Republicans on the religious question. When the civil war caught fire, most Chilean *falangistas* apparently felt uncomfortable with both sides. The best evidence is that most of them shared little more than their party label, some mild notions of corporatism, and a broad commitment to Catholicism with their Spanish brethren. By the end of the 1930s, there was no doubt that they officially opposed Franco and fascism. They refused official support to their own right's nominee against the Popular Front in 1938 because they saw him as too reactionary. They also defended the Front's right to take office following its electoral victory. Thereafter, *falangistas* took an intermediate reformist position between the new administration and its conservative adversaries. When U.S. Ambassador Claude G. Bowers took up his post in Chile in 1939 after having served in Spain, he concluded that the Chilean Falange "had no remote resemblance to the party of the same name in Spain." In May 1939, Falange Vice-President Frei attended the second Ibero-American Congress of Catholic Students in Lima. Representatives from Franco's Spain also participated. The congress brimmed over with adulation for the Spanish and Catholic heritage in Latin America. Although it was a conservative conclave riddled with *hispanidad,* there is no evidence that this included enthusiasm for *franquista* fascism or that it reflected Frei's own views. During World War II the president of the Chilean Falange's university branch spoke for the party when he denounced *hispanidad* and Franco.[15]

The other major rightist party, the Liberals, also harbored a few advocates of corporatist political and social reorganization. It contained some avid Hispanists, including Raúl Marín Balmaceda, Ernesto Barros

Jarpa, and Agustín Edwards. Like *El Mercurio,* leading Liberals mainly saluted Franco for his defense of the socio-economic order rather than of Catholicism. During the 1938 campaign, the Liberals joined the Conservatives in defending Franco and warning that the Chilean Popular Front would repeat the Marxist carnage already visited upon Spain, France, and Russia; meanwhile, they portrayed themselves as more moderate than the Spanish right and therefore the surest guarantee of tranquility. Their minor party allies, the Democrats, took the same line. Most Liberals hoped to undermine the appeal of the Front through these scare tactics and through gradual welfare state and regional decentralization reforms within the framework of orderly representative democracy.[16]

The Alessandri Government's Relations with Spain, 1932–38

Like most administrations in Latin America, though to a lesser degree than many of the dictatorships, the Alessandri government favored Franco. The president reportedly told the Mexican ambassador to Chile that "everyone around me is in favor of the Spanish rebellion." Alessandri took no public personal position on the civil war. He justified, however, his use of extraordinary executive powers against domestic leftist and Fascist politicians and publications as necessary to prevent a government like the Spanish Popular Front from taking office and provoking similar fratricide; thus he blamed both leftist and rightist extremists for the Spanish holocaust.[17]

Chilean and Spanish leftists denounced the Alessandri government's preference for Franco and accused it of Fascist inclinations. Friction developed between Alessandri and the Spanish Republican Ambassador Rodrigo Soriano. Encouraging Chilean leftist campaigns for the Spanish Loyalists, Soriano repeatedly protested to Alessandri about slanders of the Republic in the establishment press. Alessandri probably avoided any closer identification with Franco so as not to lend credence to incessant Popular Front charges of crypto-fascism against the Chilean government and its 1938 presidential candidate, former Finance Minister Ross. More overt favoritism for the Nationalists would have further dimmed rightist hopes of courting centrist Radicals.[18]

In accord with its traditional reluctance to get enmeshed in European conflicts, Chile adopted an official policy of neutrality. Although clearly partial to Franco, the Alessandri administration spurned appeals from the rebels to recognize their belligerent status or their government at Burgos. As one United States observer noted: "Chile cannot afford an official rupture with the Barcelona government because of the number of refugees now receiving asylum in the Chilean Embassy in Spain. Such a rupture, moreover, would have an effect upon the presidential campaign now in progress here."[19]

Chile skirted not only formal recognition but also related mediation proposals. Trying to provide indirect recognition and assistance to the Franco forces, Uruguay proposed Pan American mediation of the conflict. Although they praised this effort, conservative Chileans saw it as premature in 1936. Their government also accepted parts of the proposal but lodged enough reservations to keep it shelved.[20]

It was the issue of refugees and asylum that most directly embroiled Chile in the Spanish conflict. At the time the civil war exploded, most Chilean officials concerned with Spain were Hispanophiles. These included Foreign Minister Miguel Cruchaga Tocornal, Ambassador Aurelio Núñez Morgado (1935–37), and the Second Secretary of the embassy in Madrid, the writer Edgardo Garrido Merino. At the start of the shooting, approximately two thousand pro-Franco Spaniards, many of them clergy or soldiers, poured into the Chilean embassy in Madrid.[21]

The ambassador and the Chilean government portrayed this extraordinary sheltering of *franquista* refugees as purely humanitarian. However, Núñez Morgado's fervent Catholicism and anti-communism made him openly friendly to the Nationalists and hostile to the Republicans. He provided a biased picture of the Spanish turmoil to the Alessandri administration, which warmly supported its embassy's defense of the refugees' right to asylum and safe passage from Spain. Chile then used this issue to apply political pressure against the Republic. It sought international support for its stand on asylum from the other Latin American countries, the United States, Great Britain, and the League of Nations.[22]

Hispanophile and Franco supporter Agustín Edwards spearheaded this international campaign against the Republic on the refugee issue. An affluent member of the Liberal party who had advocated corporatism during the Great Depression, Edwards served as Chile's ambassador to London. He also headed its delegation to the Assembly of the League of Nations. To the dismay of Chilean leftists, he opposed Republican attempts to have the League condemn the intrusion of foreigners in Franco's forces. In turn, the Republic rejected Chile's broad definition of the right to asylum. Therefore, Edwards opposed Spain's election to a nonpermanent seat on the Council of the League in 1937, which pleased the Nationalists; Spain blamed Chile for its nonelection, though it could not have won the seat in any case. This incident helped drag worsening relations between the two countries to their low point in 1938.[23]

In Spain, the Republican government resented the hostile Chilean ambassador and his hosting such an inordinate number of enemy refugees. Azaña's administration did not recognize any blanket right of asylum but only let a few leave the embassy and the country case by case. It believed the embassy refugees were conspiring against the Republic and trying to get out to join Franco's armies. In addition, the Spanish government reportedly feared that complete evacuation of the embassy would free Chile to recognize Franco immediately. Its displeasure with Núñez Morgado reached the point of considering asking for his removal. By contrast, of course, the Nationalists applauded Chile's position. Trying to offer proof that its stance was neutral and humanitarian, Chile pointed to its negotiations to attempt to convince Franco to exchange some of his prisoners of war for the liberation of those embassy refugees.[24]

In spite of persistent protests and appeals by Chile, it proved impossible to evacuate any of the refugees in 1936. As a result of painstaking negotiations, hundreds gradually came out during 1937–38; they fled to Chile, Belgium, France, and elsewhere, some slipping back to fight for Franco. If one adds other refugees from outside the embassy, some 450 persons—the vast majority Nationalists—were escorted out of Spain under Chilean diplomatic protection during the civil war. When Franco's troops took Madrid in 1939, the last 750 or so refugees exited the Chilean embassy. Then the situation was immediately reversed. Now Republican refugees flocked to the Chilean embassy, and a leftist government in Chile quarreled with a rightist regime in Spain over the same issue of asylum.[25]

The Alessandri government, the Liberals, and the Conservatives supported Gustavo Ross for the presidency in the 1938 campaign. Both major candidates promised to save Chilean democracy from the imputed totalitarian intentions of their opponents. Although favoring Ross and apparently Franco, there is no evidence that President Alessandri himself was captivated by *hispanidad.* On the contrary, he honored Chilean democratic traditions by grudgingly but peacefully transferring the presidential sash to Aguirre Cerda at the end of 1938.[26]

The Chilean Catholic Church

As Chile became more urban, industrial, literate, and secular, the Roman Catholic church ceased to be a leading partisan issue, political power, or champion of conservatism. By the end of the 1930s, some 98 percent of Chileans still baptized their children in the church, but barely 10 percent attended mass on Sundays and only some 50 percent got married in the church. It increasingly tried to revive its influence with the working classes by preaching material reforms as well as spiritual rewards.[27]

As in the rest of Spanish America, Chilean clergy and zealous lay Catholics constituted the most likely enthusiasts for Franco and his brand of *hispanidad.* Drawing terrifying analogies from Spain, many nuns and priests feared victory by the Chilean Popular Front. Clergy on the great estates and in the cities celebrated masses for Franco and sometimes for Ross.[28]

José Horacio Campillo, conservative archbishop of Santiago, shared the Nationalist sentiments of *El Diario Ilustrado.* He issued anti-Marxist pamphlets, conducted masses for the victims of Republican persecution, and hailed Franco's rebellion as a "movement of national salvation."[29] In October 1937, the annual conference of Chilean bishops reiterated and amplified their pro-Franco stand on the civil war. This bespoke firm fraternal support for the Spanish clergy. The Chilean manifesto, however, was not nearly so ardently *hispanista* or *franquista* as the outpourings from church officials in Argentina, Uruguay, Paraguay, and Mexico.[30] Among the Chilean clergy, perhaps the most notable long-standing Hispanist was Aníbal Carvajal, canon of the cathedral of Santiago. By the end of the civil war, however, his unflagging defense of Franco and of Spanish Catholicism neither embraced any clear political commitment to anti-democratic *hispanidad* nor attracted many Chileans.[31]

At the second Ibero-American Congress of Catholic Students in Lima in May 1939, on the heels of Franco's victory, the Chilean delegation took an intensely Hispanist position. They came out in favor of the noble Spanish past and its devotion to Catholicism. They proclaimed opposition to the French revolution, individualistic liberalism, materialism, the United States, Pan Americanism, and "romantic and Marxist Indianism." However, the Chileans, unlike some other Spanish American Catholic Hispanists, also condemned fascism and totalitarianism.[32]

The most striking aspect of the behavior of the Chilean church was not its predictable praise for the Hispanic Catholic heritage but rather its ability to avoid overdrawing the analogy from the Spanish civil war. Like so many other traditional groups and institutions in Chile, the church loathed the Popular Front in Spain but reached an accommodation with its namesake at home. On the announcement of the 1938 electoral results, Northern Bishop José María Caro immediately sent a congratulatory telegram to Aguirre Cerda; this helped legiti-mize the Front's narrow triumph and soften polarization. Afterward, Caro succeeded the reactionary Campillo as archbishop of Santiago to smooth relations with the Aguirre Cerda administration. In turn, the Popular Front government paid respect to the church and attacked neither its property nor its personnel. Caro also supported campaigns for Christian social reforms by younger priests as the best antidote to Marxism. By the start of the 1940s the Chilean church was not generally attracted to Franco; it achieved a reputation as probably the most pro-gressive in Latin America.[33]

The Chilean Military

The posture of the Chilean armed forces toward either the Spanish or Chilean Popular Fronts is difficult to establish. The officers said little publicly and apparently had a neutral or divided attitude toward both movements. From 1936 through 1939 the *Memorial del Ejército de Chile* contained only a handful of articles on the Spanish conflict; those were minor and technical, and were almost totally translations from foreign military journals, such as French analyses of infantry or aircraft deploy-ment in the peninsular battles. Indeed, this official journal of the Chil-ean army gave greater coverage to strife between China and Japan. The Navy's *Revista de Marina* also failed to lavish attention on the Spanish civil war.[34]

Most Chilean officers were unlikely to be inspired by or to imitate Franco's example in the 1930s. The military had a history of noninter-vention or of displeasure with the results of open political intrusion. Its deviation from the norm of political nonintervention during 1924–32 had left most of the armed forces reluctant to march back into the presidential palace. As a result of participation in the reformist govern-ments of Ibáñez (1927–31) and the Socialist Republic (1932), officers had incurred the distrust of the upper class and the stigma of the Great Depression. In the early 1930s the elites and the right chastized the armed services through the Alessandri government. Conservative groups also created civilian Republican Militias designed to curb the threat of both militarism and socialism. Meanwhile, former Commander of the Air Force Marmaduke Grove, who had led the ephemeral Socialist Republic, became the caudillo of the new Socialist party. It maintained friendly relations with segments of the armed forces. The Radical party and the Masons also had influence with the military, as did ex-dictator Ibáñez. He ultimately backed the election of the Popular Front when his own candidacy collapsed. The military was clearly anti-Communist and worried that victory by the Front might plunge Chile into Spanish-style bloodshed. It was not, however, committed to the right, the Church, or Hispanidad. The left opined that the right would fail in any attempts to replicate Franco's uprising because the Chilean army "is republican and leftist"; the Front also averred that Chilean workers would be ready to lash back like their comrades in Spain. On election eve, Gabriel González Videla, a leader of the Radical party and a future national president (1946–52), predicted that Chile's middle-class army would not take up arms like the Spanish in defense of the upper class. Both the Loyalists and the Nationalists recruited a few retired Chilean army and navy officers to fight in the civil war. Divided socially and ideologically, the Chilean armed forces rejected minor rightist pressures to intervene in the tense days between the balloting and the inauguration of the Popular Front in their own country.[35]

Because of the moderation of most of the Chilean Front and most of its opponents, the uneasy military took the preferred professional option of remaining in the barracks. The commanders-in-chief of the army and the carabineros declared that the Front had legitimately won its claim to the presidency. These officers said that they did not want to confront the kind of civil war that denying the left its victory would unleash. Thus the example of Spain helped the Chilean Front, however nonrevolutionary by comparison, to convince its potential adversaries that the costs of intervention would be too high. This decision by key sectors of the armed services convinced most civilian rightists to thenceforth combat the Front through the legal system, in which they still controlled the Congress, the judiciary, and much of the bureaucracy.[36] As Gumucio, a leader of the Conservatives and supporter of the Chilean Falange, observed: "For the conservatives, since we cannot count on either the masses or the armed forces, it suits us, even more than our adversaries, to maintain constitutional democracy."[37]

Other Rightist Groups

Throughout the 1938 campaign, the economic elites in the National Society for Agriculture, the Society for Factory Development, the National Society of Mining, the Central Chamber of Commerce, the Central Bank, and the all-encompassing Confederation of Production and Commerce locked arms with the rightist parties in an unprecedented public effort for Ross. Probably the most rightist and activist interest group was the National Society of Agriculture. Jaime Larraín García

Moreno headed both that landowners' association and the umbrella Confederation of Production and Commerce for all elite sectoral organizations. Pointing to disturbances caused by Popular Fronts in older, wealthier nations with deeper spiritual traditions (Spain and France), Larraín warned that damage in a younger, poorer, less integrated nation like Chile would be even worse. His agricultural society invited María de Maeztu, sister of deceased Hispanist Ramiro, to give a conference on *hispanidad* in February 1939; there the hope was expressed that Franco's victory would reawaken the historic spirit and majesty of Catholic Spain. Nevertheless, almost all these upper-class spokesmen arrived at a modus vivendi with the Chilean Front after it took office.[38]

At least as measured by contributions and volunteers, the Spanish war aroused more sympathy on the Chilean left than on the right. Out of an estimated forty-eight identifiable Chilean participants in the civil war arduously tracked down by Gerold Gino Baumann, only three fought for the Nationalists. Probably a few more untraceable Chileans, however, bore arms for one side or the other. Very few Latin Americans —perhaps three thousand at most—took part at all in the Spanish conflict; of those, approximately ten times as many enlisted with the Republicans as with the Nationalists. One of those Chileans taking up arms for Franco was Dr. Juan Francisco Jiménez. Loyalists executed him despite pleas for a commutation of sentence by the Chilean government. Heavily played up by rightist newspapers, this incident combined with disagreements over refugees to bring Chile to the brink of severing relations with Republican Spain in June 1938.[39]

Resident Spaniards in Chile avoided massive public displays of their sentiments. Nevertheless, they were "bitterly divided" over the civil war. The wealthier few, especially those in the clergy, tended to prefer Franco. Most Spanish merchants and manufacturers propagandized for the Nationalists, at times in league with German and Italian Fascists. These Spaniards mainly operated through the Circle of Spanish Action. Soon after Franco's 1939 victory, even ultra-rightist Spaniards in Chile grew lukewarm toward his cause; they did not want to invite local or international hostility during World War II. By 1942, both the Spanish Falange and the Circle of Spanish Action dissolved in Chile. They were ineffective, and they complicated foreign relations. Throughout the civil war, arguments of both rightists and leftist resident Spaniards were highly predictable, passionate, and correlated with their social class and their attitudes toward the Popular Front in Chile. Although it is impossible to know for sure, most observers concluded that a majority of Chile's Spaniards sided with both Popular Fronts or at least were unenthusiastic about Franco.[40]

Leftist Thought on the Spanish Civil War, 1936–39

Arriving in Santiago in 1939, U.S. Ambassador Bowers surmised that the vast majority of Chileans had favored the Spanish Republic. Both his Loyalist preferences and the timing of his arrival may have colored this assessment. Nevertheless, since the Chilean Popular Front did represent a majority of voters by 1938, Bowers may not have been far wrong.[41]

To an extent, the Front had been inspired by its Spanish counterpart, whose electoral victory in February 1936 had helped convince wavering Chileans to consolidate such a coalition. The Spanish struggle created a common rallying point for all the diverse Chilean Front parties. They cautioned their followers to heed the Spanish example and be prepared to defend their expected electoral victories. Front leaders introduced pro-Republican resolutions in Congress, where the conservative majority invariably defeated them. Leftists also raised money, sent volunteers, criticized Alessandri's Spanish policy, and organized huge rallies for the Loyalists.[42]

The arguments of the leftist press in Chile were unsurprising in their exuberance for the Loyalists and their distaste for the Nationalists. The Communist-dominated *Frente Popular* expressed the most vociferous support for both the Chilean and Spanish Fronts.[43] Socialist party papers also covered the war in expectable black-and-white terms.[44]

Close to the Socialists but independently leftist, *La Opinión* was the widest-circulation newspaper backing the Chilean and Spanish Popular Fronts. Like many rightists, this paper claimed to be Hispanist. According to *La Opinión,* the workers and common people had created Spain's past glories, conquered the New World, suffered like Chileans under the evil monarchy of the Black Legend, forged the Popular Front, and now bore arms to wreak their just vengeance on the aristocracy and the bourgeoisie, who had really betrayed Spain's proud ancestors. "For us, the Spanish Republic is something our own. Never have we felt more sons of Spain." Careful not to draw the analogy too tightly, *La Opinión* portrayed the Spanish right as far more similar than the left to its Chilean counterparts. It refuted rightist stories about Spanish Popular Front atrocities and denied even more vehemently that the Chilean version would produce parallel conflicts: "Our problems are different from those of other countries, but our creole rightists are the same as all the rightists of the earth, especially the royalists of Spain and France."[45]

The newspaper that reflected the views of the Radical party, *La Hora,* struck similar notes. It also compared the brutality of the Nationalists to past massacres of their subjects by Spanish monarchists, thus applying the Black Legend only to the Spanish right. Like the Radicals, *La Hora* said that the civil war taught Chileans the need for reforms to avoid revolution and for discipline and moderation on the part of reformers to avoid rightist rebellions.[46]

Intellectuals

Most Chilean intellectuals supported the Spanish Loyalists with gusto. Many of these professors, writers, and artists were Marxists, but most apparently acted out of admiration for democracy and abomination of fascism. They saw Franco's movement as destructive of international peace and culture.[47]

These anti-*franquista* intellectuals gathered in the Committee in Favor of Republican Spain. It enrolled non-Marxists (notable historians like committee head Luis Galdames, Eugenio Pereira, and Ricardo Donoso) as well as Marxists. Leading writers in the group included Ricardo Latcham, Valodia Teitelboim, Julio Alemparte, Ismael Valdés, and Mariano Latorre.[48]

A Hispanist from the left, Latcham cast the Republic's middle- and lower-class warriors as the bona fide descendants of all past heroic Spaniards. This essayist appealed to Chileans to aid the Loyalists because of primordial bonds "of race and culture." Latcham also saw the futures of the two countries as intimately entwined: "If the cause of the Spanish Republic perishes, with it will fall all our nascent democracies, and we will return to a torturous fascist Middle Ages."[49]

Alemparte advised Chilean leftists to scorn the name "Indo-America" and retain "Hispano-America." In his mind, the valiant struggle of the Loyalists ("the authentic Spain") meant that the former colonies should identify with the Mother Country. They should also once and for all discard the Black Legend.[50] The Society of Chilean Writers also ardently backed the Republican cause.[51]

The most famous Chilean intellectual partisans of the Spanish Republicans were poets. Focusing primarily on the intrinsic issues of the peninsular civil war, none of these writers drew many direct analogies to Chile. Their eloquence and fame helped generate support for the Popular Fronts in both countries; the Communist party's association with these efforts also facilitated its attraction of new recruits from the intelligentsia.[52]

Vicente Huidobro treated the war as a class struggle against fascism that the united workers and intellectuals were bound to win.

Journeying to Madrid, he served in the militias. Whereas Huidobro's Spanish commitment partly grew out of his affiliation with the Chilean Communist party, Pablo Neruda's commitment helped lead him to the Communists.[53]

The living symbol of Chilean, and to a certain extent Spanish American, intellectual-aesthetic dedication to the Spanish Republic was Neruda. The war there shifted him away from solitary artistic contemplation toward Communist activism, culminating in his official membership in the party by the 1940s. Like many Spanish Americans who took part in the war, Neruda happened to be in Spain at the outset. As consul there during 1934–36, he had befriended Federico García Lorca, whose murder by the Nationalists became a compelling issue for this Chilean poet. In 1936 in Madrid, Neruda began writing his classic *Spain in my Heart.* In those poems, Neruda excoriated the monarchy, the church, the military, the rich, and their foreign allies. He evinced some special Spanish American love for the Mother Country but did not indicate sharp parallels between her experiences and Chile's.[54]

In 1937 he championed the Republican cause at meetings of intellectuals in Paris. He also helped organize a congress of the Alliance of Antifascist Intellectuals that brought international literary luminaries to Spain. Returning thereafter to Latin America, Neruda explained his deep involvement in the Spanish war by saying that "the future of the spirit and culture of our race depends directly on the result of this struggle." Back home in 1938 Neruda edited the anti-Fascist weekly *Aurora de Chile* and campaigned for Aguirre Cerda.[55]

Following Franco's victory in 1939, Neruda devoted himself to the plight of Republican refugees. He hoped that the cause lost in Spain would now be carried on in the former colonies, expecially by the Popular Front in Chile. In his view, the Spanish Republicans had also died for the shared dreams of their offspring in the New World. Neruda implored all Spanish American countries to welcome Loyalist exiles under the slogan: "Spaniards to America, Spaniards to the lands they delivered to the world."[56]

Leftist Parties

All Chilean Popular Front parties, including minor supporters like the Democratics, unequivocally backed the Spanish Loyalists.[57] The moderate Radicals stood almost as steadfastly as the Marxists behind the Republicans. Radicals leery of the Marxists were partly convinced to join the Chilean Front in 1936 by victories of similar movements in

Spain, France, and China. They saw the coalition as a vehicle for solidarity against international fascism and imperialism, for unity of the middle and working classes, for preservation of democracy, and for advancement of their own employment and control in the bureaucratic state. More than their coalition allies, the Radicals also mentioned traditional anti-clericalism as a virtue of both their Front and Spain's. Within the Chilean movement, they saw themselves serving as a safety valve and a moderating influence over their socialist partners, thereby averting open class conflict as in Spain. By the same token, they advised conservative Chileans to accept evolutionary reforms. The Radicals argued that it was the unyielding blindness of the right in Spain that had provoked the mass upheaval.[58]

The Chilean Socialist party unswervingly favored the Spanish Republic but was divided over its lessons. The right wing of the party, close to Social Democratic thought, concluded that such alliances with moderate reformers were necessary to dissuade the middle class from fascism, to reach office, and to legislate reforms. The left wing, close to Communist or Trotskyist thought, concluded that Popular Fronts were too bourgeois to represent the workers, too timid to put through their programs (let alone Marxian revolution), and too fragile to resist fascism. Although these dissidents complained about the front throughout its campaign and tenure, the more pragmatic Socialists prevailed.[59]

Shocked by the Spanish example, most Socialist leaders in the late thirties and early forties became mesmerized by the threat of fascism (which was actually overstated in Chile). These Socialists toned down their early radical positions accordingly. They blamed capitalism and imperialism for the rise of *franquismo,* which made them ever more determined to promote and defend their own Popular Front. They expressed particular concern about the Spanish case because of their ancestral bonds. However, the Socialists, like other Chilean parties, always placed the greatest emphasis on nationalism and on the distinctive nature of local problems. They officially rejected European models and Internationals.[60]

The Communists were the most directly inspired by and committed to the Spanish civil war. The intensity of their involvement sprang not only from ideological predilections but also from membership in the Comintern. They formed and joined anti-Fascist committees to support the Loyalists; many Chileans attracted to these efforts were not themselves Communists, thus extending the party's reach. These committees later helped bring in Republican refugees during 1939–40. Partly motivated by the Spanish conflict, Chilean Communists, Socialists, and other Front supporters organized militias. These clashed with the MNS and other rightist paramilitary groups during the electoral campaign and stood ready to defend the Front once in office. The Spanish war buttressed the Communists' exaggerated claim that the Chilean election forced a choice between democracy and fascism. This argument swayed some moderate Chileans over to the Front. Along with directives from the Comintern, the agonies of their Spanish comrades also helped convince the Communists, like many Socialists, that immediate revolution was unlikely. Therefore reformist, modernizing coalitions appeared mandatory to avoid worse alternatives. To belie rightist propaganda against them and the Front, Chile's Communists from 1936 on increasingly emphasized nationalism over internationalism, welfare reforms for the middle class as well as workers, economic growth as much as redistribution, and electoral competition instead of class conflict. They welcomed support for the Front from idealistic Catholics, *ibañistas,* and the MNS. Pointing to reformist Chilean coups in 1924–25 and 1932, they praised the military as more progressive and democratic than Spain's armed forces. To disarm anti-Communist conspirators, the party took no cabinet posts in the Aguirre Cerda administration. This conciliatory approach brought the Communists mounting votes, members, unions, allies, respect, and influence. It also brought the Chilean Popular Front to the presidency without detonating a Spanish-style bloodbath.[61]

The Chilean Front's presidential nominating convention opened on April 14, 1938, to coincide with the seventh anniversary of the proclamation of the Spanish Republic. According to Communist leader Elías Lafertte, such symbolism aided recruitment by the Chilean Left, "if one considers that under the sign and banner of struggle to help Republican Spain in the war, the [Chilean] Popular Front had succeeded in winning the hearts of the popular masses." On the other hand, that peninsular conflict also forced Chilean leftists to plead that their election would not catalyze comparable vendettas over religion, morality, democracy, and property. By nominating Aguirre Cerda, a wealthy landowner and mild-mannered proponent of industrialization, the Front defused some rightist analogies with Spain, diluted its own militance, reduced polarization, and heightened its chances of victory.[62]

Middle and Working Classes

The Chilean middle classes were torn, but apparently most sided with the Popular Fronts at home as well as abroad. White-collar employees and teachers prominently backed the Radicals and Socialists. The Front also attracted intellectuals and professionals, though many in the latter category often sided with the upper class and the right. The Federation of Chilean Students, mainly middle class, endorsed the Spanish as well as the local Popular Front.[63]

Heavily influenced by French and Spanish examples, Chilean Masons were instrumental in creating and conducting the Popular Front. They represented many middle-class as well as anti-clerical elite elements. They wielded particular influence among Radicals and Socialists. Committed to evolutionary democratic reforms as an antidote to extremism from the left or the right, these Masons opposed conservatives in both Spain and Chile.[64]

Although peasant attitudes toward the Spanish Loyalists are impossible to discern, it appears that most tillers of the soil supported the right in the Chilean election. As for urban workers, they mainly backed both Popular Fronts, as even a Nationalist Spaniard visiting Chile during the civil war conceded. The new national Confederation of Chilean Workers (CTCH) formed as a byproduct of Front unification in 1936. Primarily incorporating and led by Socialist and Communist labor unions, it officially joined and supported the Front and its program. To facilitate compromises among the member parties and electoral success for Aguirre Cerda, the CTCH tempered worker demand and strikes. In response to appeals for solidarity from workers in Spain, the confederation and many individual trade unions also drummed up support for the Republicans. As late as the start of 1939, these Popular Front unions were promising the donation of a day's wage from their members to the Loyalist cause. Some workers also went to fight against Franco. For example, a handful of Chilean laborers formed the Club Obrero Chileno in New York and dispatched a few members to wage war against Iberian fascism; one of them signed up with the Abraham Lincoln Brigade.[65]

Some forty of fifty Chileans fought and propagandized in Spain for the Loyalists. Probably a large majority were Socialists and Communists, most of them workers and intellectuals. A couple came from remnants of the anarchosyndicalist movement. A few doctors, students, and retired military officers also pitched in. Though small, the number of Chilean participants ranked relatively high by South American standards. Several of these volunteers were sons of Spanish immigrants.[66]

Most resident Spaniards beneath the upper class apparently backed the Loyalists. A formerly apolitical and presumably representative "periodical of the Spanish colony of Chile," *Iberia*, landed on the Republican side as soon as the civil war began; it claimed to speak for most Spaniards in Chile.[67] Basques and Catalans seem to have been particularly adamant against the Nationalists. Anti-Franco Spaniards coordinated their efforts with Chilean intellectuals, labor unions, and leftist parties.[68]

Victory for the Popular Front in Chile

Following the 1938 balloting, the Chilean Popular Front celebrated its victory along with the second anniversary of the Loyalists' successful defense of Madrid, which was again under siege.[69] Despite some dissension, the Chilean Socialists joined the Aguirre Cerda administration; they did so to guard it against rightist plots, to check bourgeois attempts to emasculate its reformist content, and to provide sinecures and influence for their members. They did not want to underestimate the potential danger of fascism in Chile and then have to struggle against it later as in Europe. Some Socialists also criticized the Spanish and French Popular Fronts for being too tepidly reformist, for deceiving and sidetracking the worker movement, and for subordinating themselves to the influence of the Soviet Union. At the same time, the Socialists hoped that the Front's victory in Chile would hearten their Spanish comrades.[70]

The Communists reinforced those moderate Socialists who portrayed the coalition as merely a Chilean "New Deal." They scolded those who were pushing it toward bolder actions. They analyzed the victory as proof that the masses could triumph without violence. In the immediate aftermath of the balloting, the Communists vowed that "Chile will not be a second Spain. We will scotch fascism here before it can lift its head."[71]

The duty of reconciling nervous elites to the ascension of the Front mainly fell on the Radical party. Aguirre Cerda emphasized that expanding education and economic output, not redistributing power and property, constituted his highest priorities. The president-elect encouraged the view that his inauguration would pacify the left and the masses, thus guaranteeing more order than could rightist repression.[72]

For Aguirre Cerda's inauguration, the Spanish Republic sent Ambassadors Extraordinary Indalecio Prieto, Ángel Ossorio y Gallardo, and General Emilio Herrera. The right denounced their visit as an attempt to poison Chile as they had Spain. Prieto's speeches against Franco pleased the Front, which hoped that exposé would drive moderates away from the Chilean right. His discourses also prodded the Chilean Socialists to learn from the Spanish tragedy the need to muffle their radicalism, remain loyal to Aguirre Cerda, and preserve the unity of their party and coalition. Prieto, for example, suggested that even Socialists and Falangists in Spain should have sought more points in common instead of conflict.[73]

Prieto and Ambassador Soriano also persuaded the Aguirre Cerda government to investigate quietly the possibilities of reviving earlier Latin American proposals to mediate the Spanish war. The Alessandri administration had opposed such efforts in the past, as the virtually victorious Franco did now. Before the Chilean Popular Front could even formulate a public policy on the civil war, the lingering hopes of Republicans were dashed.[74]

Victory for Franco in Spain

When Franco consummated his victory, the Chilean government and public were absorbed with reconstruction after an extraordinary earthquake that had ripped the country at the end of January 1939. Therefore, comments on the final acts of the Spanish drama were scarcer than normal. Nevertheless, the definitive rout of the Loyalists obviously constituted a bitter pill for the Chilean leftists. Some voiced the feeble hope that the Republican collapse was "temporary."[75]

Chilean Communists were especially distressed by the loss in Spain. They blamed Popular Front failures there and in France on the Socialists. Conversely, they cast their party comrades as the indefatigable heroes of the Spanish Front, the civil war, and the subsequent underground resistance. Thus the Communists used these European experiences to try to convert Chilean workers from the Socialists to themselves. They also interpreted the Spanish calamity as further proof of the wisdom of gradualism on the part of the Chilean Front.[76]

In its precarious opening months the Popular Front wanted to normalize all international relations but not alienate its supporters. Therefore it anguished over recognizing Franco. As throughout his administration, however, Aguirre Cerda ultimately opted for a more pragmatic course than the one preferred by Socialists and Communists. Chile looked for "moral" support for its intended recognition of the new Spanish regime. It tried to get the pro-Republican governments of Colombia and Mexico to join in the act, but Colombia refused to wait and Mexico refused to recognize. To the right's consternation, Chile abstained during February and March. To the left's dismay, it finally became the last country in South America to establish relations with Spain on April 5, 1939. The United States embassy reported that "the Chilean Government is so obviously out of sympathy with the Franco Government that it was only with a visible swallowing of pride that it forced itself to recognize the Franco Government."[77]

The Popular Front's friction with Spain formed part of its intrinsic poor relations with all Fascist countries. In contrast to Alessandri, the Front also initially experienced difficulties with Germany and Italy. Despite inevitable tensions, Aguirre Cerda's government always sought cordial relations with Franco and retained "affection for Spain as a nation."[78]

The desire by both countries for expanded trade dampened ideological antagonisms. Although commercial relations still theoretically rested on most-favored-nation treatment, there had been very little exchange of any kind during the civil war. Therefore the Chilean Front began exploring ways to reactivate that commerce as soon as it assumed office. Nitrate exporters pressured the government to reopen normal relations with Spain. In 1940 the two countries agreed on amounts and means of payment for the nitrate trade, which gradually revived even during World War II. At times, however, Chilean dockworker strikes against any exchange with Franco interrupted these nitrate shipments. This presented another instance in which Popular Front labor and leftist groups clashed with their administration, which seldom let ideology override economic practicality. The Front refused to extend most-favored-nation status to Spanish wines that competed with Chilean production; this became a perennial source of discord because Spain normally sustained an unfavorable balance of payments with Chile. All trade between the two remained small, and therefore rarely determined diplomatic relations.[79]

Another sore point involved repeated Spanish complaints to the Popular Front government about slanders of Franco in newspapers, speeches, and demonstrations. Aguirre Cerda's administration always replied that, however much they might regret such attacks on the Nationalist regime, there was no way to prevent it in a democratic system. This dispute revealed the ability of ideological considerations to disrupt economic concerns; negotiations to amplify trade between the two countries had to be suspended when Spain broke off diplomatic relations in July 1940 over the insults of the Popular Front. That break came because the official radio broadcast anti-Franco statements by non-government Front leaders during a rally at the presidential palace attended by Aguirre Cerda and other high officials. Spain also severed relations because it was already angry at the Chilean embassy in Madrid for hosting Republican refugees. Furthermore, Franco apparently hoped to isolate Chile, along with Mexico, from their rightist Latin American neighbors. He thus sought to advance Spain's claim to leadership of the conservative camp in the Hispanic world. Some Chileans even interpreted this diplomatic rupture as an attempt to topple Aguirre Cerda. Franco's government exceeded the bounds of international decorum in the note breaking off relations: Spain charged that such anarchic behavior was typical of Popular Fronts everywhere and recommended that the suffering Chileans deserved a better government. The Chilean right, especially *El Mercurio,* joined the left in reacting very negatively to this interference in internal affairs. The Popular Front also won the support of the other Latin American nations in this inflated feud with Spain. Since he had harmed the cause of *hispanidad,* Franco swiftly restored relations in October 1940.[80]

Another faux pas by Franco in 1940 also evidenced the disinclination of most of the Chilean right to follow his lead. Spain urged Chile not to allow U.S. bases on its territory and praised the Front's minister of national defense for opposing such concessions. Though remaining sympathetic to the Nationalists, *El Mercurio* again seconded the leftist press in taking umbrage at this intrusion into national questions.[81]

As under Alessandri, the most thorny issue faced by Aguirre Cerda was Spain's denial of the right of asylum to refugees in the Chilean embassy. Seventeen Republican students, intellectuals, and professionals took refuge in the embassy in March 1939. Although the Nationalist government decorated former Ambassador Núñez Morgado, it refused to grant Chile's new representative the right of the Loyalist refugees to leave the embassy and Spain. Franco also declined to exchange ambassadors with Chile as long as the refugee question remained unresolved. At least on this issue, Chileans became united and consistent. Except for a few extreme rightists, virtually all shades of opinion—including *La Nación, La Hora, El Siglo, El Mercurio, El Diario Ilustrado,* and *El Imparcial*—endorsed this position of the Popular Front. The press pointed out their embassy's previous protection of Nationalist refugees and Franco's previous criticism of Azaña for not letting them go. The other Latin American nations also took Chile's side on this asylum issue. Consequently, Spain set the refugees free as it renewed relations with Chile in October 1940, and ambassadors were finally exchanged. However much some Nationalists relished a quarrel with the Chilean Popular Front, they scarcely wanted bad relations with the rest of the hemisphere as well.[82]

Spanish Exiles

The other major official involvement of the Chilean Front government with the Spanish question concerned Republican exiles from Europe. The Popular Front parties waxed enthusiastic about bringing refugees to Chile. But the administration, as always, did not want to press too far an issue that might enrage the right. Despite Aguirre Cerda's caution, Chile did far more for Spanish refugees than did most of Latin America, with the exception of Mexico. The Chilean government, however, decided against mass immigration. Instead, it wanted to take the refugees case-by-case. It expressed a preference for farmers and workers rather than intellectuals, politicians, and professionals. A principal reason for keeping the number of refugees small was existing problems with earthquake reconstruction and unemployment. At the same time, the Popular Front let some Jewish families enter freely from Germany. Not only his coalition partners but also Eduardo Frei criticized Aguirre Cerda for being too intimidated by rightist resistance to welcome thousands more Spanish exiles whose skills could have benefited the economy. The administration calmed conservative critics by announcing that the number of Spanish entrants would be held under two thousand (skilled workers plus their families); it also promised that the nearly eight thousand European Jews who had come to Chile under the Popular Front would not be allowed to become street peddlers but instead would be employed in established businesses. The government carried through on this limited program by meeting the arriving Spaniards and helping them resettle. The Chilean and Mexican legations in Paris also continued aiding Republican refugees there. Such assistance to Loyalists outside Spain was one further irritant underlying Franco's 1940 break in relations with Chile.[83]

The Chilean Front sent Pablo Neruda as consul general to organize the refugee movement from Paris. From the government's point of view, the poet did his job too well. It ordered him to stop rounding up so many refugees. Neruda also got involved in the never-ending feud among the disparate members of the Spanish Republican coalition. Apparently he favored the Communists. They reportedly constituted the largest group of refugees embarking for Chile. Anarchists accounted for less than 1 percent. The Republican government-in-exile in Paris purchased a ship, the *Winnipeg,* to transport these refugees. In spite of some last-minute hesitation by Aguirre Cerda's government, the ship sailed in August 1939. It reached Chile in September with its cargo of slightly over two thousand Spaniards. Maybe a hundred more arrived later by other means.[84]

Chilean leftists heaped praise on this enterprise by Neruda and the Front. To counter rightist charges that these refugees would cost Chilean workers jobs, the ideologically loyal CTCH led a rally in favor of transporting and receiving the Spaniards fraternally. Local Republican Spanish organizations cooperated with the Aguirre Cerda government in integrating the newcomers economically and socially.[85]

The most outspoken opponent of the Spanish influx was *El Diario Ilustrado*. It still supported Franco and Hispanic Catholicism. *El Mercurio* and *El Imparcial* echoed its charges that these Spaniards ("agitators" and "adventurers") would import radical ideas, capture Chilean jobs, and hinder ongoing earthquake rehabilitation efforts to house and employ displaced Chileans. They also accused Front government officials of exacting bribes from the refugees. Since many of the voyagers aboard the *Winnipeg* had served in the Spanish Loyalist army, the right feared they would enroll in the local Socialist Militia. Some conservatives also protested the admission of Jews. By the time the *Winnipeg* docked in Chile, the establishment press remained inhospitable but was turning its attention to the rush of bellicose events in Europe.[86]

Among the Spanish refugees coming to Latin America, the Chilean contingent proved unusually working-class. Apparently their social composition was as proletarian as their ideology. Once again, social class served as a distinctive factor affecting the Spanish question in Chile. Bringing very few liberal professionals, the *Winnipeg* unloaded numerous fishermen, farm laborers, metal workers, sailors, carpenters, chauffeurs, clerks, draftsmen, mechanics, nurses, cabinet makers, bakers, electricians, painters, and shoemakers.[87]

Chile absorbed these immigrants rapidly. At least half of them quickly found jobs. Although most were workers, some were merchants, doctors, architects, engineers, scientists, intellectuals, and professors. A few of the refugees boasted significant political backgrounds, and some joined the Chilean Popular Front parties. For example, Spanish refugees started the Chilean Socialist Party newspaper *La Crítica* (1939–42). A handful of former officers from the Spanish Republican army enlisted in the Socialist Militia. Within the Communist party, Spanish comrades almost at once entered and took part in decision-making. They became particularly militant members, arguing for discipline, rectitude, and dedication to radical social change. Receiving information from Franco's Spanish embassy in Chile, Conservative Sergio Fernández Larraín charged that former peninsular Communists now with the Chilean party were serving as Stalin's agents in South America. He accused them of trying to infiltrate the army, writing propaganda for newspapers and magazines, and meddling subversively in Chilean politics. This continuing rightist animosity toward leftist Spaniards finally bore fruit during the presidency of Radical González Videla at the end of the 1940s. Partly because of Cold War pressure from the United States, he turned against his Communist and labor union allies. Previously González Videla had been prominent on Chilean national committees to help Spanish Loyalist refugees. But now he ordered several more politically-active refugees jailed along with numerous Chilean Communists and trade union leaders. Thus the effect of the Spanish left on Chile stayed alive as an issue well after the civil war. These former refugees apparently were later divided like all Chileans about the governments of Socialist Salvador Allende and his successor General Augusto Pinochet in the 1970s. At least one Spanish Republican who took up residence in Chile, Salvador Téllez, suffered persecution under Pinochet for his support of Allende and so, ironically, returned to Spain under the protection of the Mother Country's embassy.[88]

Chile's Popular Front in Office, 1939–41

Chilean rightist parties and publications vehemently opposed the Popular Front throughout its tenure but usually not to the point of trying to overthrow it. They charged that the Front was anti-national for trying to impose revolutionary models from Spain, Mexico, or Russia. Naturally the Front replied in kind. It dismissed such opponents as servants of foreign capitalism, imperialism, and fascism. Rightists continued to warn leftists that being too harsh with their adversaries could trigger explosions like the Spanish tragedy.[89]

Attracting scant followings, a few extremist groups and publications advocating Franco-style fascism did crop up. Learning from Spain's experience, Aguirre Cerda replaced nearly all questionable military and police officers. The closest Chile came to an armed uprising comparable to Franco's was the 1939 "pronouncement" by General Ariosto Herrera Ramírez. An admirer of Mussolini and his anti-communism, Herrera proposed a corporatist state, but his coup was nipped in the bud by the loyal military, backed up by leftist unions, parties, and militias. His unsuccessful revolt helped convince both right and left to be compromising enough to stay a safe distance from open conflict.[90]

The Chilean Popular Front did not go farther in its support for or imitation of the Spanish Republic, so as to avoid similar assaults from the local right. The Front did not try to alter power or property relationships to the same extent as had its Spanish and French predecessors. Chile lacked comparable anarchist groups, agrarian upheaval, or regionalist movements on the left. By the same token, the Chilean right contained few comparable monarchists, ultramontanes, or Fascists. The Front did not take office until the Spanish civil war was virtually over. World War II then loomed as a far more engrossing international issue. That global conflict constrained resources available for reforms (as did the earthquake). It also increased the incentives to cooperate with all domestic and international democratic forces against the Axis. An increasing alignment with and economic dependence on the United States dampened the Front's enthusiasm for structural measures to distribute a part of the income of foreign and domestic capitalists to the poor. Aguirre Cerda and his successors in the 1940s believed that Chile had to catch up with the more industrialized West. Therefore they concentrated on raising and modernizing production more than on improving the standard of living of the lower classes. Marxists held their demands and followers in check so as not to disturb the industrialization campaign and so as not to make the government vulnerable to destablization by the right. As a result, the Front proved much more cautious in office than it had been on the hustings; it achieved a record of reform well above that of past administrations but well beneath its campaign promises. Moreover, those reforms were confined to the urban middle class and organized labor in order to pacify agrarian elites.[91]

U. S. Ambassador Bowers contrasted Chilean politicians and their Front with what he had witnessed in Spain. He found the former more tolerant, dispassionate, compromising, democratic, and cosmopolitan. In his view, although Chileans took pride in their Hispanic ethnic and cultural heritage, "Chile today is no more Spanish, except for language, than the United States is English. The political thinking of the Chileans today is no more Spanish than it was when they declared their independence from Spain."[92]

Legacies of the Spanish Civil War

Ironically, the Spanish civil war and the issues associated with it had more relevance for and parallels with Chile four decades after it had convulsed the peninsula. For years following that Spanish conflict, postures toward it remained one dividing line, albeit often unspoken, between the Chilean right and left. The strength of the Marxists and their coalition movements persisted in Chile. Therefore, lively and apprehensive discussion resurfaced from time to time as to whether the Mother Country's rending experience might someday be reenacted by its offspring. From the 1940s into the 1960s, minuscule neo-Fascist movements and Hispanist intellectuals made sporadic appearances without any great political or cultural resonance. Some neo-corporatist reformers vainly hoped that the governments of Ibáñez (1952–58) or Frei (1964–70) would implement more of their functionalist ideas. Then the election of Socialist President Allende in 1970 electrified ideological fervor on both the right and the left. Fears of a Spanish-style conflagration rose to a peak.[93]

The attempt by Allende's Popular Unity government to move Chile toward socialism through democratic means became far more radical than the program of the earlier Popular Front of Aguirre Cerda. The Popular Unity actually began transferring property and power away from the privileged foreign and domestic elites. Now social change also included peasants and rural laborers. This rendered it impossible for urban reformers and organized workers to reap benefits for themselves while consoling the upper class by maintaining the rural status quo. Peasant and working-class seizures of the means of production outstripped even government expectations. Mass mobilization appeared out of control to the frightened middle and upper classes. Such outbursts of class conflict made the maintenance of political pluralism and representative democracy increasingly precarious, especially in an inflation-ridden economy of scarcity dependent on hostile foreign capital. Some rightist Chileans fled to Spain under Allende, as some leftists would after his death. Both sides swapped charges of illegality, immorality, antinationalism, and illegitimacy. Consensus broke down over what it meant to be a Chilean, a national identity increasingly defined by class and ideology. Small paramilitary groups on both sides began arming, though not on the scale of the militias of the 1930s. As the rhetoric and organizations of the opposition assumed more and more corporatist features, Communists revived the slogans of the Spanish civil war; they warned and marched against confrontation and fascism. However, the very specter of fratricide that had previously deterred military interventions in Chile might now be used to justify one. Ambassador to France Pablo Neruda worried that the United States and emergent "Fascists" in Chile would recreate the horrors he had witnessed in Spain. As polarization intensified, centrist groups—notably the Christian Democrats—increasingly locked arms with the right against the left. Both sides pressured the armed forces to play a larger role as arbiters. Then the Popular Unity stunned its foreign and domestic opponents by raising its 36 percent support in 1970 to 44 percent in the 1973 congressional elections; like the electoral victory of the Spanish Popular Front decades before, these balloting results provided the prelude to a military uprising. On September 11, 1973, President Allende died defending his coalition government against one of the most savage coup d'etats in Latin American history.[94]

The takeover by Army General Augusto Pinochet produced a slaughter, not a Spanish-style civil war. The left proved unprepared to do battle with the armed forces, which did not divide as had been predicted. Instead, the military murdered, jailed, tortured, and exiled tens of thousands of Chileans. Just as Franco's rise to power began with the death of a renowned poet, García Lorca, so did Pinochet's; on September 23, Pablo Neruda, winner of the Nobel prize, died of natural causes. Pinochet's junta promised aristocratic "Catholic and Hispanic" nationalism, anti-Marxism, "authoritarian" efficiency, "organic" social "harmony", functionalism, depoliticization, neo-orthodox capitalism, and more than one generation of military rule to reconstruct the nation. At least on paper, Chile's dictators suggested a corporatist state inspired by the Hispanic heritage and modeled along *franquista* lines. They enshrined Portales as the supreme national hero. They blamed all the political developments of the last forty years for Chile's problems. The junta dismantled every mechanism of democracy and autonomous working-class mobilization. All facets of national life fell under military supervision. The historic Chilean pattern of welcoming refugees from tyranny was reversed, as hundreds of thousands escaped the country. In the opening days of the Pinochet regime, when Chile came close to the level of civil strife that had engulfed Spain earlier, the military violated the right of asylum in foreign embassies—the same right Chile had previously defended so ardently against the Spanish Republicans and Nationalists. Mexico immediately became the most receptive Latin American nation to Chilean exiles, as it had been before to Spaniards. In 1975, Pinochet stood out as the only Latin American chief executive to visit Spain for Franco's funeral, marking the formal transfer of power to Juan Carlos. As Spain liberalized thereafter, the two Hispanic countries, at least temporarily, once again headed in seemingly opposite political directions.[95]

At the beginning of the 1980s, it remained unclear how close Pinochet's policies would come to Franco's. Critical differences remained, such as the paucity of church support for the less institutionalized Chilean regime. Those Chileans desirous of a return to democracy hoped that the smooth transition to political freedom in Spain would provide a tempting example to the internationally ostracized junta. On the other hand, the vigor of the peninsular left, after forty years of repression, must have given pause to the Chilean military, which had vowed to extirpate Marxism for all time.[96] Despite the divergent tracks taken by the two countries from the mid-1970s onward, it could not be assumed that either the Spanish right or the Chilean left were defeated for long. Nor could it be taken for granted that similar responses by Spain and Chile to the crises of underdevelopment and capitalist modernization might not arise again.

Notes

1. Luis Thayer Ojeda, *Elementos étnicos que han intervenido en la población de Chile* (Santiago, 1919), pp. 44–47, 111, 157–61; Carl Solberg, *Immigration and Nationalism, Argentina and Chile, 1890–1914* (Austin, 1970), pp. 20, 38–39, 68–69, 99; Clarence H. Haring, *South America Looks at the United States* (New York, 1928), pp. 169, 218–20; Roberto Peragallo, *Por España* (Santiago, 1941), p. 38; Javier Fernández Pesquero, *España ante el concepto americano* (Madrid, 1922), pp. 69, 151, 192–93, 200–322; Fredrick B. Pike, *Hispanismo, 1898–1936* (Notre Dame, 1971), pp. 232–41, 246, 410, 439; United States, Department of State Archives, Record Group 59, 1930–39, from Santiago, August 29, 1934, 825.-55/19, 2–5; Madrid, August 14, 1934, 852.55/13, 30–47.

2. Fredrick B. Pike, *Chile and the United States, 1880–1962* (*Notre Dame,* 1962), pp. 418–19; Jaime Eyzaguirre, *Fisonomía histórica de Chile* (Mexico City, 1948); *Hispanoamérica del dolor* (Santiago, 1969); Emilio Rodríquez Mendoza, *La España que ví y viví* (Santiago, 1948) and *En España* (Santiago, 1932); Osvaldo Lira, *Hispanidad y mestizaje y otros ensayos* (Madrid, 1952); Juan Bardina, *Leyenda perjudicial* (Santiago, 1932); Rafael Luis Gumucio, *El deber político* (Santiago, 1933); Haring, p. 219; Fernández Pesquero, pp. 20–21, 91–92, 150–51, 167–68; Peragallo, pp. 7–15.

3. Vicente Torrente and Gabriel Mañueco, *Las relaciones económicas de España con Hispanoamérica* (Madrid, 1953), pp. 64–65, 205–7, 399, 433; Pike, *Hispanismo,* 233–35, 214–15, 221–22, 304; Aníbal Jara Letelier and Manuel G. Muirhead, *Chile en Sevilla* (Santiago, 1929), pp. 137–40; Carlos Badía Malagrida, *El factor geográfico en la política sudamericana,* 2nd ed. (Madrid, 1946), pp. 194–202.

4. Paul W. Drake, "Corporatism and Functionalism in Modern Chilean Politics," *Journal of Latin American Studies* 10, no. 1 (May 1978): 83–116; H. E. Bicheno, "Anti-Parliamentary Themes in Chilean History: 1920–70," *Government and Opposition* 7, no. 3 (Summer 1972): 351–88; Guillermo Viviani Contreras, *Sociología chilena* (Santiago, 1926); Pike, *Chile,* pp. 191–95, and *Hispanismo,* pp. 196–97, 436; Rodríguez Mendoza, *La España,* pp. 6, 159, 160, 210, 211, and *En España;* Fernández Pesquero, pp. 156–57, 192–93.

5. William B. Bristol, "Hispanidad in South America, 1936–1945," Ph.D. dissertation, University of Pennsylvania, 1947, pp. 215–19, 325, 589; Pike, *Hispanismo,* pp. 320–24, and *Chile,* pp. 418–19.

6. Bristol, pp. 254–55, 314–24, 590–97; Claude G. Bowers, *Chile through Embassy Windows: 1939–1953* (New York, 1958), p. 144; Carlos Vela Monsalve, *España después del 18 de julio* (n.p., n.d.), p. 45; Ramón Giner, *Nuestra guerra civil ante el mundo* (Santiago, 1937), pp. 74–76, 89–90.

7. Marta Infante Barros, *Testigos del treinta y ocho* (Santiago, 1972), especially, pp. 61, 67, 80; *España Nueva,* May 8, 1937.

8. *El Mercurio,* July 1936–April 1939; in particular see July 21, 24, 25, 28, August 5, 7, 9, 14, 1936, March 6, 1937, September-October, 1938 (for similar points of view, also consult the official government newspaper *La Nación,* for example April-October 1938); Bristol, pp. 264–68, 344; Infante Barros, especially pp. 78, 83; U.S., D. of State, Santiago, April 20, 1938, 825.00/1026, 2–4.

9. *El Diario Ilustrado,* July 1936–April 1939—in particular see July 20–23, 26, 1936, March 2, 5–8, 1937, September, October 8, 15, 23, 25, November 13, 15, 1938, and February 20, 1939. For comparable commentary, also see the periodical *Mañana* (my thanks to William Sater for providing these citations),

June and August 1938. Infante Barros, particularly pp. 11, 49; Haring, p. 220. Diego Portales forged Chile's conservative constitutional republic in the 1830s; it became a model of stable civilian government under strict upper-class control.

10. *El Imparcial,* especially July 21–27, August 11, 18, 1936.

11. Bristol, pp. 215–19, 320–24; Giner, especially pp. 74–79, 89–92; U.S., D. of State, Santiago, June 4, 1938, 725.52/3; Alberto Martín Artajo, *Hacia la comunidad hispánica de naciones* (Madrid, 1956), p. 8; Henri Massis and Robert Brasillach, *Los cadetes del Alcázar* (Santiago, 1937).

12. Drake, "Corporatism"; Oscar Álvarez Andrews, *Bases para una constitución funcional* (Santiago, 1932); Frente Funcional Socialista, *Manifiesto* (Santiago, 1934); Partido Agrario, *Declaración de principios y programa* (Temuco, 1934), *¿Qué es el Partido Agrario?* (Talca, 1935), and *Acción corporativa* (Chillán, 1941); Unión Republicana, *Declaraciones de sus juntas generales de directorios* (Santiago, 1936?); Acción Nacionalista de Chile, *Ideología* (Santiago, 1932); Acción Republicana, *Programa y estatutos* (Santiago, 1937); Guillermo Izquierdo Araya, *La racionalización de la democracia* (Santiago, 1934); Diego Guillén Santa Ana, *Política económica-sociología corporativismo* (Santiago, 1940); George W. Grayson, Jr., *El Partido Demócrata Cristiano Chileno* (Buenos Aires, 1968), pp. 90–112.

13. Pike, *Chile,* pp. 204–8; Vela Monsalve, p. 108. Bicheno, pp. 373–81; Ricardo Donoso, *Alessandri, agitador y demoledor,* 2 vols. (Mexico City and Buenos Aires, 1952, 1954), II, 193; Ricardo Boizard, *Historia de una derrota* (Santiago, 1941), p. 74, *El Movimiento Nacional-Socialista de Chile* (Santiago, 1932); *El Movimiento Nacional-Socialista de Chile* (Santiago, 1933); Jorge González von Marées, *La concepción nacista del estado* (Santiago, 1934), especially, pp. 19–49, also *La mentira democrática* (Santiago, 1936), *La hora de la decisión* (Santiago, 1937), and *El mal de Chile* (Santiago, 1940); Wilfredo Mayorga, "La fugaz violencia del nacismo," *Ercilla* 1611 (April 20, 1966): 18–19, and "Jorge González von Marées," *Ercilla* 1740 (October 23–29, 1968): 41–42.

14. Vela Monsalve, pp. 106–11; Donoso, *Alessandri,* II, 193, 194; Peragallo, pp. 10–11; Marcial Sanfuentes Carrión, *El Partido Conservador* (Santiago, 1957), especially pp. 57–102; Partido Conservador, *Programa y estatutos* (Santiago, 1933); Bartolomé Palacios M., *El Partido Conservador y la democracia cristiana* (Santiago, 1933); Pedro Lira Urquieta, *El futuro del país y el Partido Conservador* (Santiago, 1934); Rafael Luis Gumucio, *No más* (Santiago, 1932); *El deber;* Sergio Fernández Larraín, *El Partido Conservador en la vida nacional* (Santiago, 1940); *33 meses de gobierno de Frente Popular* (Santiago, 1941); *España . . .¿zona de peste?* (Santiago, 1945).

15. Grayson, pp. 64–173; Pike, *Hispanismo,* pp. 291, 298–99, 457–58; Halperin, pp. 182–90; Bowers, *Chile,* p. 40; Drake, "Corporatism"; Bristol, pp. 242, 262, 293; Donoso, *Alessandri,* II, 206; *El Mercurio,* October 13, 1938; *El Diario Ilustrado,* December 16, 1935, and July 25, 1936; U.S., D. of State, Santiago, March 29, 1939, 825.00/1136, 1–4, and Lima, May 31, 1939, 823.43 Ibero-American students/1; Lot Files, Western Hemisphere II, Office of Intelligence Research, Division of Research for the American Republics, Box No. 15, Confidential Book File, Falange, "Falange in the Other American Republics," 2/21/42, "Chile," 3, and Box No. 16, Confidential Book File, Falange, "Falange Universitaria, Chile," MA No. 7137 IG "154 9/4/44"; Eduardo Frei Montalva, *Chile desconocido* (Santiago, 1937), especially pp. 18, 138, 141–46, 162–65; *Aún es tiempo* (Santiago, 1942); Alberto Edwards Vives and Eduardo Frei Montalva, *Historia de los partidos políticos chilenos* (Santiago, 1949), pp. 242–43; Ricardo

Boizard, *La democracia cristiana en Chile* (Santiago, 1963), pp. 36–37, 107–79, 200–2, and *Historia*, pp. 67–68, 143–51; Wilfredo Mayorga, "El camino a la Moneda," *Ercilla* 1588 (October 27, 1965): 14–15; Luis Vitale, *Esencia y apariencia de la democracia cristiana* (Santiago, 1964), pp. 59–72; Jaime Castillo Velasco, *Las fuentes de la democracia cristiana*, 2nd ed. (Santiago, 1963), especially pp. 107–77; Federico G. Gil, *The Political System of Chile* (Boston, 1966), pp. 266–68; John Gunther, *Inside Latin America* (New York, 1941), p. 252.

16. Infante Barros, pp. 36–38; *El Diario Ilustrado*, October 18, 1938; *El Mercurio*, July 1936–October 1938, especially October 8, 1938; *La Nación* (Santiago), April–October, 1938; Agustín Edwards, *Las corporaciones y la doctrina liberal* (Santiago, 1934); Partido Liberal, *Programa y estatuto* (Santiago, 1934); Edgardo Garrido Merino, *Espíritu y acción del liberalismo* (Santiago, 1934), and *Las fuerzas productoras ante la elección presidencial* (Santiago, 1938); José Maza, *Liberalismo constructivo* (Santiago, 1942); Víctor M. Villagra, *Discurso del presidente del Partido Liberal de Bulnes* (Chillán, 1938); Raúl Marín and Manuel Vega, *La futura presidencia de la república* (Santiago, 1938); Raúl Marín, *Chile y la intervención en España* (Santiago, 1938); *Luis Mandujano Tobar, candidato a senador por Cautín y Bío-Bío* (Santiago, 1936?).

17. Mexico, Archivo de la Secretaría de Relaciones Exteriores, from Santiago, September 8, 1936, III/510 (46) "36" /1, III–767–7, and Valencia, April 2, 1937, III/516 (46–0)/2, III–1246–6 (I am grateful to Thomas G. Powell for these citations from the Mexican archives); Bristol, pp. 47, 90, 222, 277–78; Bowers, *Chile*, p. 144; Vela Monsalve, pp. 104–6; Donoso, *Alessandri*, II, 198–99.

18. Mexico, Archivo, Santiago, September 2, 1936, III/146 (46)/1, III–1325–5; U.S., D. of State, Santiago, June 4, 1938, 725.52/3; *La Opinión*, July 27, 1936; *España Nueva*, April 24, 1937.

19. U.S., D. of State, Santiago, June 28, 1938, 725.52/4, 3; Bristol, p. 222.

20. Donoso, *Alessandri*, II, 344–47; *El Imparcial*, August 18, 1936; Chile, *Memoria del Ministerio de Relaciones Exteriores y Comercio correspondiente al año 1936* (Santiago, 1937), p. 417; Donald M. Dozer, *Are We Good Neighbors?* (Gainesville, Florida, 1959), p. 40–44; Richard P. Traina, *American Diplomacy and the Spanish Civil War* (Bloomington, Indiana, 1968), pp. 146–51, 275.

21. Chile, *Memoria . . . 1936*, pp. 563–67, 577, and *Memoria . . . 1938*, pp. 437–38; Aurelio Núñez Morgado, *Los sucesos de España vistos por un diplomático* (Buenos Aires, 1941), especially pp. 254–71.

22. Chile, *Memoria . . . 1936*, pp. 415–21, 570–76, and *Memoria . . . 1938*, pp. 422–38; Mexico, Archivo, Madrid, October 4, 1936, III/510 (46) "37"/1, III–764–1, Part 1, and Valencia, April 2, 1937, III/516 (46–0)/2, III–1246–6; Núñez Morgado, particularly p. 273; Traina, pp. 148–49, 275.

23. Edwards, *Las corporaciones;* Donoso, *Alessandri*, II; 342–48; U.S., D. of State, Geneva, October 5, 1937, 352.0022/52, 1–4; Chile, *Memoria del Ministerio de Relaciones Exteriores y Comercio correspondiente al año 1937* (Santiago, 1938), pp. 268–70.

24. Chile, *Memoria . . . 1936*, pp. 570–79, *Memoria . . . 1937*, 261–78, and *Memoria . . . 1938*, pp. 428–29, 437–38; Mexico, Archivo, Madrid, July 25, 1936, III/510 (46) "37"/1, III–764–1, Part 1; U.S., D. of State, Madrid, October 13, 1936, 352.0022/6, Geneva, October 5, 1937, 352.0022/52, 2, and Santiago, June 4, 1938, 725.52/3.

25. Chile, *Memoria . . . 1936*, p. 576, *Memoria . . . 1937*, pp. 262–68, and *Memoria . . . 1938*, pp. 422–37; Mario Barros van Buren, *Historia diplomática de*

Chile, 1541–1938 (Barcelona, 1970), pp. 740–44; Carlos Morla Lynch, *Misión en España* (Santiago, 1940).

26. Unfortunately, Alessandri does not elaborate on the Spanish issue in his memoirs. Arturo Alessandri Palma, *Recuerdos de gobierno,* 3 vols. (Santiago, 1952); *Doctrina rossiana* (Santiago, 1938); Edecio Torreblanca, *Ante la próxima elección presidencial* (Santiago, 1938); *El Diario Ilustrado,* October 18, 1938; *La Nación,* April-October, 1938; U.S., D. of State, Santiago, July 30, 1937, 825.00/1004, 1–3, April 26, 1938, 825.00/1030, June 23, 1938, 825.00/1035—1/2, June 28, 1938, 825.00/1042, October 18, 1938, 825.00/1078, and October 29, 1938, 825.00/1085.

27. Bristol, p. 259; Gumucio, *El deber,* pp. 1–19; Fidel Araneda Bravo, *El Arzobispo Errázuriz y la evolución política y social de Chile* (Santiago, 1956), pp. 25–31, 152–54, 181–229.

28. Gaston Nerval, "Europe vs. the United States in Latin America," *Foreign Affairs* 15, no. 4 (July 1937): 636–45; Grayson, pp. 64–71; Bristol, pp. 350–51, 594; Vela Monsalve, pp. 104–5; Mexico, Archivo, Santiago, September 8, 1936, III/510 (46) "36"/1, III–767–7; U.S., D. of State, Santiago, August 26, 1938, 825.00/1050, October 29, 1938, 825.00/1085, Lot Files, Box No. 14, "Reports Prepared by the Special Section of the Division of American Republics," Vol. III, February 1942 to February 1943, 27, and Box No. 15, "Totalitarian Activities—Spanish Falange in the Western Hemisphere Today," December, 1943, 266.

29. *El Diario Ilustrado,* July 25, 1936; El Amigo del Pueblo, *El socialismo y el comunismo ante el sentido común* (Santiago, 1939); Bristol, 257.

30. Centro de Información Católica Internacional, *El mundo católico y la carta colectiva del episcopado español* (Burgos, 1938), especially pp. 132–49.

31. Bristol, pp. 198–99, 349–50; U.S., D. of State, Lot Files, Box No. 15, "Falange," 2/21/42, "Chile," 2.

32. U.S., D. of State, Lima, May 31, 1939, 823.43 Ibero-American Students/1; Bristol, pp. 352–53.

33. Wilfredo Mayorga, "Cuatro cartas de triunfo para don Pedro," *Ercilla* 1622 (July 6, 1966): 23–25; Hubert Herring, *Good Neighbors* (New Haven, 1941), pp. 219–20; José María Caro, *La iglesia está con el pueblo* (Valparaíso, 1940); U.S., D. of State, Santiago, October 29, 1938, 825.00/1085; Ángel Ossorio y Gallardo, *Agua pasada* (Santiago, 1938), especially chapter 3; Carlos Contreras Labarca, *Unidad para defender la victoria* (Santiago, 1938), pp. 31–32; Bristol, pp. 350–53.

34. Chile, *Memorial del Ejército de Chile* XXIX (Santiago, 1936), XXX (Santiago, 1937), XXXI (Santiago, 1938); and XXXII (Santiago, 1939); I am indebted to William Sater for information concerning the *Revista de Marina.*

35. Paul W. Drake, *Socialism and Populism in Chile, 1932–52* (Urbana, 1978), pp. 120, 129–30, 193–94, 209–10; Gerold Gino Baumann—to whom I am deeply thankful for his gracious generosity with his research results—"La participación extranjera en la guerra civil española: Los latinoamericanos," unpublished manuscript (Lima, 1977); Mario Bravo Lavín, *Chile frente al socialismo y al comunismo* (Santiago, 1934), particularly pp. 24–68; *El Diario Ilustrado,* July 23, 1936; *La Opinión,* July 24, 1936; U.S., D. of State, Santiago, July 23, 1937, 825.00/1003, 3–4; Mayorga, "Cuatro," 23–25; Infante Barros, p. 79.

36. Wilfredo Mayorga, "Las intrigas electorales de 1938," *Ercilla* 1619 (June 15, 1966): 18–19, "Cuando el ejército 'dio pase' a don Pedro," *Ercilla* 1687 (October 4, 1967): 15, and "Cuatro," pp. 23–25; Leonidas Bravo Ríos, *Lo que supo*

un auditor de guerra (Santiago, 1955), pp. 92–95; *El Mercurio,* November 14–16, 1938; *El Diario Ilustrado,* November 13–15, 1938; U.S., D. of State, Santiago, November 2, 1938, 825.00/1086, 35, November 13, 1938, 825.00/1091, 1–2, November 14, 1938, 825.00/1095, November 16, 1938, 825.00/1096, 2–6, and November 23, 1938, 825.00/1097, 6–9.

37. Rafael Luis Gumucio, *Me defiendo* (Santiago, 1939), p. 65.

38. *Las fuerzas;* Giner, p. 89; Drake, *Socialism,* pp. 190–2, 220–25; La Sociedad Nacional de Agricultura, *El Campesino* (1938–39); *El Mercurio,* October 12, 1938; *El Diario Ilustrado,* October 12, 18, 1938, February 23, 1939; *España Nueva,* May 8, 1937.

39. Baumann; Barros, p. 744; Sergio Fernández Larraín, *[¡Tración!]* (Santiago, 1941), pp. 203, 204; Chile, *Memoria . . .1938,* p. 438; U.S., D. of State, Santiago, June 28, 1938, 725.52/4, 2–3.

40. Bristol, pp. 225–26, 237–47; Baumann; Giner, pp. 89–90; Peragallo, p. 238; Pike, *Hispanismo,* pp. 241, 246; *España y Chile,* October 1938; *Iberia,* 1935–39; *El Diario Ilustrado,* July 25, 1936, and October 12, 1938; U.S., D. of State, Santiago, April 12, 1939, 725.52/5, Lot Files, Box No. 15, "Totalitarian," "Falange," 2/21/42, "Chile," 1–2; La Confederación de Trabajadores de Chile, *La C.T.C.H. y el proletariado de América latina* (Santiago, 1939), pp. 43–45.

41. Bowers, *Chile,* p. 144.

42. *Iberia,* August 2, 1936; *La Opinión,* July 22, 25, 27, 1936; *España Nueva,* April 17, 1937; U.S., D. of State, Santiago, June 16, 1937, 825.00/997, 3; Bristol, p. 252; Drake, *Socialism,* pp. 173–81; Eudocio Ravines, *La gran estafa,* 10th ed. (n.p., 1974), pp. 288–89; E. Gil, "Repercussions of the Spanish Crisis in Latin America," *Foreign Affairs,* 15, no. 3 (April 1937): 547–53.

43. *Frente Popular,* 1936–39. Also see *España Republicana* 1, no. 1 (September 1936).

44. *Consigna,* 1936–37; *Claridad,* 1937–38; *La Crítica,* 1939–41.

45. *La Opinión,* 1936-39, especially July 19–24, 1936, and November 2, 1938; Infante Barros, p. 92.

46. *La Hora,* July 20–22, 1936, and 1937; Infante Barros, p. 33.

47. Raúl González-Tuñón, *Las puertas del fuego* (Santiago, 1938); E. N. Dzelepy, *El complot español* (Santiago, 1937); Fernando Solano Palacio, *Entre dos fascismos* (Valparaíso, 1940); José Miguel Varas, *Chacón* (Santiago, 1968), p. 107; Giner, p. 89; U.S., D. of State, Santiago, June 4, 1938, 725.52/3.

48. *España Nueva,* March 27, April 17, June 5, 1937; FOARE Mexicana, *Boletín* no. 11 (n.d.).

49. *España Nueva,* December 5, 1936, and March 27, 1937.

50. *España Nueva,* January 9, 1937.

51. Bristol, p. 252; Alberto Romero, *España está un poco mal* (Santiago, 1938), especially pp. 3, 68–73, 194–95; another young writer stirred by the Spanish civil war was Fernando Alegría, *Mañana los guerreros* (Santiago, 1964).

52. Vicente Huidobro et al., *Madre España* (Santiago, 1937), particularly pp. 3–4, 13–14, 17, 38–39; Marta Vergara, *Memorias de una mujer irreverente* (Santiago, 1961), pp. 134–45.

53. Huidobro et al; *La Opinión,* July 21, 1936; René de Costa, *Vicente Huidobro y el creacionismo* (Madrid, 1975).

54. Pablo Neruda, *Memoirs,* trans. Hardie St. Martin (New York, 1976), pp. 64, 122–30, 135–39, 149, 355–57, *España en el corazón,* 2nd ed. (Santiago, 1938), and *Presencia de García Lorca* (Mexico City, 1943); Huidobro et al.

288   THE SPANISH CIVIL WAR: AMERICAN HEMISPHERIC PERSPECTIVES

55. Neruda, *Memoirs*, pp. 126–39, 356; Rogelio García Lupo, *Los que fueron a España* (Buenos Aires, 1973), pp. 105–7.

56. Emilio Oribe, Juan Marinello, and Pablo Neruda, *Neruda entre nosotros* (Montevideo, 1939), pp. 9, 13, 33–51.

57. *La Opinión*, July 25, 1936.

58. Partido Radical, *Convención extraordinaria del Partido Radical* (Santiago, 1937); Héctor Arancibia Laso, *La doctrina radical* (Santiago, 1937); *La Hora*, July 20–22, 1936; *El Diario Ilustrado*, July 21, 1936; *La Opinión*, July 25–27, 1936; *Hoy* 278 (March 18, 1937): 10; U.S., D. of State, Santiago, November 9, 1938, 825.-00/1093; John Reese Stevenson, *The Chilean Popular Front* (Philadelphia, 1942), pp. 65–69; Infante Barros, pp. 33, 79.

59. Alejandro Chelén Rojas, *Trayectoria del socialismo* (Buenos Aires, 1967), pp. 88–95; Luis Zúñiga, *El Partido Socialista en la política chilena* (Santiago, 1938), pp. 15–27; Humberto Mendoza Bañados *¿Y ahora?* (Santiago, 1942), pp. 179–82; Fernando Casanueva Valencia and Manuel Fernández Canque, *El Partido Socialista y la lucha de clases en Chile* (Santiago, 1973); *Consigna*, March 14, November 14, 1936.

60. As early as the 1937 congressional contests, a few of the Chilean Socialist party's candidates were recently-nationalized Spaniards. Drake, *Socialism*, pp. 176–77, 182, 212; *Rumbos* (1939–40); *España Nueva*, December 26, 1936; *España*, January 7, 1939; Partido Socialista, *Homenaje del Partido Socialista a España republicana* (Santiago, 1938); Julio César Jobet, *El Partido Socialista de Chile*, 2 vols. (Santiago, 1971), pp. 141–42.

61. Infante Barros, p. 75; Partido Socialista, *Tesis política* (Santiago, 1939), p. 12; Luis Cruz Salas, *Historia social de Chile: 1931–1945. Los partidos populares: 1931–1941* (Santiago, 1969), pp. 32, 40, 80, 109, 110, 235–41, 265–97; Galo González Díaz, *El congreso de la victoria* (Santiago, 1938); Elías Lafertte and Carlos Contreras Labarca, *Los comunistas, el Frente Popular, y la independencia nacional* (Santiago, 1937); Carlos Contreras Labarca, *América latina invadida por el fascismo* (Santiago, 1938), and *Unidad*.

62. Elías Lafertte, *Vida de un comunista* (Santiago, 1957), pp. 305, 310; U.S., D. of State, Santiago, October 29, 1938, 825.00/1085; *Alegría*, p. 270; Drake, *Socialism*, pp. 186–87, 201–3, 308–13; Stevenson, pp. 71–85; Boizard, *Historia*, pp. 35–37, 97–151.

63. *España Nueva*, April 17, May 29, 1937; *La Opinión*, July 25, 1936; *Claridad*, October 23, 1938; Stevenson, p. 128; Drake, *Socialism*, pp. 192–93, 201; Alberto Cabero, *Recuerdos de don Pedro Aguirre Cerda* (Santiago, 1948), pp. 170–77.

64. Giner, p. 90; Alejandro Bravo G., *Cincuenta años de vida masónica en Chile* (Santiago, 1951); Fernando Pinto Lagarrigue, *La masonería: su influencia en Chile*, 3rd ed. (Santiago, 1966); Gran Logia de Chile, *Tercera conferencia dada por el serenísimo gran maestro el 12 de octubre de 1935 en el valle de Talca* (Santiago, 1935?), and *Cuarta conferencia dada por el serenísimo gran maestro el 4 de diciembre de 1935* (Santiago, 1935?), especially pp. 10–14.

65. *Claridad*, April 10, 15, 1938; *La Opinión*, July 25, 1936, and August 23, 1938; *Iberia*, August 2, 1936; *España Nueva*, April 17, 1937; La Confederación de Trabajadores de Chile, *Treinta meses de acción en favor del proletariado de Chile* (Santiago, 1939), p. 38; Baumann; Giner, p. 89; Infante Barros, p. 61; Stevenson, pp. 71–75; Fernández Larraín, *Traición*, p. 206; Alan Angell, *Politics and the Labour Movement in Chile* (London, 1972), pp. 7–8, 40–42, 108–22.

66. See Baumann for additional information; Mexico, Archivo, Bar-

celona, June 13, 1938, III/510 (46) "37"/1, III–769–3, Part 2; *España Nueva,* March 13, 1937; *Frente Popular,* 1937–39; Cruz Salas, p. 238; Barros, p. 744.

67. *Iberia,* 1935–39; see especially August 18, 1935, and June 28, July 19, August 2, 1936; *España Nueva,* November 28, 1936, and April 24, 1937; *El Diario Ilustrado,* July 25, 1936; Giner, pp. 89–90; Bristol, pp. 225–26, 237–47.

68. *El Diario Ilustrado,* July 25, 1936; *España Nueva,* 1936–37; *España,* 1937–39; *La Opinión,* July 20, 1936; U.S., D. of State, Box No. 15, "Totalitarian," 270.

69. U.S., D. of State, Santiago, October 29, 1938, 825.00/1085, November 9, 1938, 825.00/1092, and December 6, 1938, 825.00/1102.

70. Partido Socialista, *Tesis,* especially pp. 5–13; *Significado de la República Socialista del 4 de junio* (Santiago, 1939), especially pp. 4–29; *El Partido Socialista y su 6to congreso ordinario* (Santiago, 1940), p. 6; *Claridad,* October 28, 1938; Cruz Salas, pp. 79, 80, 270, 271.

71. U.S., D. of State, Santiago, October 29, 1938, 825.00/1085; Carlos Contreras Labarca, *Por la paz, por nuevas victorias del Frente Popular* (Santiago, 1939), p. 27, and *Unidad,* pp. 20–40; Lafertte and Contreras, pp. 7–21.

72. U.S., D. of State, Santiago, October 29, 1938, 825.00/1085, November 9, 1938, 825.00/1092, November 23, 1938, 825.00/1097, and January 17, 1939, 825.00/1118.

73. Indalecio Prieto, *Palabras de ayer y de hoy* (Santiago, 1938), and *La tragedia de España* (Buenos Aires, 1939); Indalecio Prieto and Ángel Ossorio y Gallardo, *En defensa de la república española* (Santiago, 1938); Ángel Ossorio y Gallardo, *La verdad sobre España* (Santiago, 1938), and *Agua;* Infante Barros, pp. 113–14; Boizard, *Historia,* pp. 159–60; Fernández Larraín, *Traición,* pp. 201–18.

74. *La Opinión,* March 13, 1939; Claude G. Bowers, *My Mission to Spain* (New York, 1954), pp. 380–81.

75. U.S., D. of State, Santiago, April 12, 1939, 725.52/5; Mexico, Archivo, Santiago, April 1, 1939, III/510 (46) "36"/1, III–767–7; *La Hora,* February 9, 1939; *La Opinión,* January-March, 1939, especially February 23, 1939; Infante Barros, pp. 138, 147.

76. Carlos Contreras Labarca, *El programa del Frente Popular debe ser realizado* (Santiago, 1940), pp. 20–22; Marcos Chamudes, *Chile, una advertencia americana* (Santiago?, 1972?), p. 54.

77. U.S., D. of State, Santiago, April 12, 1939, 725.52/5, and June 2, 1939, 725.00/13; Mexico, Archivo, Santiago, February 18, 1939, III/510 (46) "36"/1, III–767–7, March 8, 1939, III/510 (46)"36"/1, III–767–7, and April 1, 1939, III/510 (46) "36"/1, III–767–7; *La Opinión,* February 23, 1929; *El Diario Ilustrado,* February 21, 27, 1939; Bristol, pp. 281–82.

78. *La Opinión,* March 13, 1939; U.S., D. of State, Santiago, June 2, 1939, 725.00/13; Bristol, pp. 347–49.

79. Chile, *Memoria del Ministerio de Relaciones Exteriores y Comercio correspondiente al año 1939* (Santiago, 1941), p. 345, and *Memoria del Ministerio de Relaciones Exteriores y Comercio correspondiente al año 1940* (Santiago, 1943), p. 539; Mexico, Archivo, Santiago, March 8, 1939, III/510 (46) "36"/1, III–767–7; Torrente and Mañueco, pp. 67–68, 88, 178–79.

80. Chile, *Memoria . . .1939,* pp. 202–10, and *Memoria . . . 1940,* pp. 352–59, 431–39; Bristol, pp. 204–8; Bowers, *Chile,* pp. 70–71; Thomas J. Hamilton, *Appeasement's Child: The Franco Regime in Spain* (New York, 1943), pp. 258–59.

81. Bristol, pp. 151, 285–86.

82. Chile, *Memoria . . .1939,* pp. 248–62, and *Memoria . . .1940,* pp. 355–59, 433–39; U.S., D. of State, Santiago, May 17, 1939, 352.0022/57, June 17, 1939, 352.0022/62, August 17, 1939, 352.0022/81, and October 16, 1939, 352.-0022/85; *Rumbos* (August 1939): 49–51; Barros, pp. 744–45.

83. Ravines, p. 416; Frei, *Aún,* p. 46; David Wingeate Pike, *Vae victis!* (Paris, 1969), pp. 105, 108–9; *La Opinión,* March 27, 1939; Mexico, Archivo, Santiago, April 3, 1939, III/510 (46) "36"/1, III–767–7; U.S., D. of State, Santiago, July 5, 1939, 825.00/1157, July 7, 1939, 825.5552/2, and September 12, 1939, 825.5552/3.

84. D. W. Pike, *Vae,* p. 86; Neruda, *Memoirs,* pp. 140–50; Fernando Solano Palacio, *El éxodo: Por un refugiado español* (Valparaíso, 1939).

85. *España,* June 21, August 12, 26, 1939; U.S., D. of State, Santiago, September 12, 1939, 825.5552/3, and 1940–44, Santiago, June 26, 1940, 825.-55/42.

86. Fernández Larraín, *Traición,* p. 187; Neruda, *Memoirs,* pp. 143–44; *El Diario Ilustrado,* February 25, 1939; *España,* July 8, 1939, and August 12, 1939; U.S., D. of State, Santiago, July 7, 1939, 825.5552/2, September 7, 1939, 825.55552/3, September 12, 1939, 825.5552/3, and 1940–44, Santiago, June 26, 1940, 825.55/42.

87. Vicente Llorens, *La emigración republicana de 1939* (Madrid, 1976), pp. 159–60; U.S., D. of State, Santiago, July 7, 1939, 825.5552/2, and September 7, 1939, 825.5552/4.

88. Llorens, pp. 160–62; Chamudes, pp. 102–3; Vergara, p. 168; Fernández Larraín, *Traición,* pp. 36–37, 45–46; Partido Socialista, *Homenaje,* p. 54; Pablo Neruda, *Pablo Neruda acusa* (Montevideo, 1948), pp. 30, 58, 64–65; Vicente Salas Viu, *Las primeras jornadas y otras narraciones de la guerra española* (Santiago, 1940).

89. Florencio Durán Bernales, *El Partido Radical* (Santiago, 1958), pp. 54–59, 98–100, 140–41, 198–207; Fernández Larraín, *Traición,* pp. 38–39, 136–37; Bristol, p. 282; Drake, *Socialism,* pp. 220–25, 232, 234; *El Diario Ilustrado,* February 28, 1939.

90. U.S., D. of State, Santiago, March 3, 1939, 825.917/5, July 11, 1939, 825.00/1159, August 24, 1939, 825.00B/61, August 26, 1939, 825.00/1170, 1–4, and 1940–44, September 26, 1940, 825.00/1253; Wilfredo Mayorga, "El golpe de estado de 1939," *Ercilla* 1701 (January 24, 1968): 15, and "Cuatro," pp. 23–25; Bravo Ríos, pp. 123–41; Stevenson, p. 96.

91. Drake, *Socialism,* pp. 214–66; Durán, pp. 174–90.

92. Bowers, *Chile,* p. 22.

93. Drake, "Corporatism"; F. B. Pike, *Chile,* pp. 414–15.

94. Pablo Neruda, *Incitación al Nixonicidio y alabanza de la revolución chilena* (Lima, 1973), pp. 8, 45–46, and *Memoirs,* pp. 338–49; Ian Roxborough et al., *Chile: The State and Revolution* (New York, 1977); Drake, *Socialism,* pp. 314–36.

95. Chile, La Junta de Gobierno, *Declaración de principios del gobierno de Chile* (Santiago, 1974); Chile, Secretaría General de Gobierno, *Libro blanco del cambio de gobierno en Chile,* 2nd ed. (Santiago, 1973); Drake, "Corporatism"; Thomas G. Sanders, "Chile: The 'New Institutionality' and the 'Consultation,'" *American Universities Field Staff Reports,* No. 5, South America (1978); Neruda, *Memoirs,* pp. 349–50, 364.

96. *El Mercurio,* July 15, 1977; Sanders.

Argentina

Mark Falcoff

The Hispano-Argentine Connection

When Spain's internal conflicts exploded into civil war in midsummer 1936, few foreign countries—certainly few outside of Western Europe —had greater reason for concern than the Argentine Republic. For, despite enormous geographical distances, the latter had many claims to being the principal expression of Spain Overseas. This primacy was founded, above all, on Argentina's role as the repository of an enormous peninsular diaspora, in 1936 variously estimated at between 1.5 and 2 million persons,[1] roughly 15 percent of the nation's population,[2] greater in proportion to the whole than in any Spanish American republic except Cuba. And although the once-vital economic relationship had long been superseded by more substantial links with Northern Europe and, latterly, the United States, it remained important for both countries, though in somewhat unexpected and even unconventional ways.

Economic indicators of themselves revealed little: measured by value, Argentine purchases from the peninsula amounted to slightly less than 3 percent of her acquisitions abroad in 1935, and Argentine sales to the Mother Country the same year exceeded slightly more than 1 percent of all exports.[3] Yet, even so, Argentina was one of the very few countries with which Spain consistently maintained a favorable balance of trade.[4] Commerce understood merely as the transfer of funds, however, would probably establish an even larger deficit in favor of the peninsula, for millions of Argentine pesos were remitted by the immigrants to their families back home during the five or six decades preceding 1936; what the Spanish monarchy, plagued by domestic disorder and colonial wars, would have done throughout the late nineteenth and early twentieth centuries without this sure source of foreign exchange is difficult to imagine.

Further, if Spanish industry had relatively little to offer Argentina, Spaniards themselves played a vital role in that part of the economy with which most Argentines were familiar—retail commerce. Denied, like other immigrants, meaningful access to land ownership, they settled in cities; in time they acquired sufficient means to found their own banks and mutual aid societies, and to impress their demands for specialized consumer goods on the marketplace as a whole. By the outbreak of the civil war, as one writer has recounted, Argentines "cooked with Spanish olive oil, bathed with Spanish soap, ate Spanish ham." Spanish, too, were the "sardines, the cognac, the bacalao, the olives, . . . the garbanzo beans, the lentils, the chorizo sausages." In addition, whereas most of the important foreign investment in the country was British, American, or German, there were "very important Spanish enterprises in every branch of economic activity, veritable commercial networks that extended throughout the country. The Plaza Mayo–Palermo subway line had been built by a Spanish consortium; the interests of Spanish banks and navigation companies overlapped." A Spanish concern provided the prinicipal source of electricity for metropolitan Buenos Aires. Spaniards virtually dominated the hotel, grocery, and restaurant fields. Argentina in 1936, he concludes, "was inconceivable without its Spanish grocers, streetcar conductors, cafe waiters, taxi drivers, and female domestics."[5]

In cultural life the Spanish impress on Argentina was likewise very strong. The glittering theatrical life of Buenos Aires was dominated by Spanish actresses Lola Membrives and Margarita Xirgú, the latter famous for her representations of the works of Alejandro Casona and Federico García Lorca. The Sunday supplements of the capital's two great newspapers, La Prensa and La Nación, carried frequent contributions by Spain's greatest writers. The Institución Cultural Española, founded in 1912, established chairs of Spanish culture in several Argentine universities, and from 1916 sponsored annual lecture tours by leading Spanish intellectuals, beginning with philosopher José Ortega y Gasset.

The Spanish book trade reflected a similar vigor. Until the end of the civil war there were few Argentine publishing houses, and peninsular firms did a big business, particularly in school texts. This was particularly true of those Spanish publishers, like Espasa-Calpe, that had established Argentine branches. By 1925 Argentina had come to constitute the principal export market for Spanish books, followed at a considerable distance by Cuba and Mexico.[6] Although the Argentine elite, much as in other South American countries, demonstrated a decided preference for British and French culture and fashions, for the vast majority of Argentines the meaningful foreign influences on their lives were Italian and Spanish.

Far more difficult to document, but no less worthy of mention, were the thousands of informal contacts between the two countries. There were, to begin with, many bi-national families residing on both sides of the Atlantic; prior to 1930 neither government gave much thought to the legal niceties involved, and there was a free and more or less uninterrupted movement of persons back and forth. Some Spaniards, notably merchant sailors and commercial travelers, may indeed have maintained families in both countries. Leading Spanish businessmen and politicians dabbled in Argentine investments; even novelist Vicente Blasco Ibáñez at one time owned Argentine cattle ranches. Some wealthy Argentines acquired property in Spain, and at least one obtained for himself a patent of nobility by rescuing the perennially bankrupt Spanish monarchy. In 1936 the Spanish community in Argentina included several grandees; virtually every Spanish political party had an Argentine branch, including the Falange; royalists were represented by both the Alfonsine and Carlist persuasions. The line between what was "Spanish" and what was "Argentine" had never clearly been drawn, a fact that generated serious problems once the Mother Country split in half, and persons on both sides of the ocean found themselves caught in the midst of extremely tangled legal and political conflicts.

The Spanish Image in Argentina

Historically, Argentina has managed to avoid sharp divisions of opinion over the meaning of her Spanish heritage and the colonial past. This stands in vivid contrast to many Spanish American republics where history, the search for national identity, and religious, social, and racial conflict have overlapped and intersected to the benefit or detriment of the Mother Country. Unlike Mexico or Peru, Argentina possessed no large, settled Indian populations prior to the Spanish conquest. The few indigenes who survived into the national period were nomadic tribes who either confined themselves to inaccessible areas or periodically raided villages on the frontier. Perhaps, indeed, there should be a literature of self-rebuke in connection with the subjugation and final extermination of these natives, but Argentines have not thought so. More to the point, the marginal effect of an Indian population on the country as a whole has meant that, for the most of her history, racial divisions within the country have not been politically significant. Again, the contrast with Meso-America and the Andean republics is illuminating here: whereas, in the latter, the Spanish heritage was regarded, quite properly, as the cultural expression of a "white" landowning class, which through a variety of devices exploited an Indian and mestizo peasant mass, in Argentina such racial gradations as existed to the 1860s cut across cultural and political lines. After that date, they became even less important, as the result of a massive "whitening" of the Argentine population through European immigration. The fact that—by the end of the great immigrant flood (1880–1930)—Argentina had incorporated slightly more newcomers from Italy than from Spain itself rendered still more ambiguous the significance of the nation's peninsular origins.

Further, the Argentine struggle for independence from Spain was a relatively brief affair; when it ended in 1816 it left few scars or grievances. Spanish recognition of the new republic had to wait nearly an additional half-century, but in the intervening period there were no peninsular attempts, as elsewhere, to mount destructive counter-revolutionary expeditions. The ritual expression of anti-Spanish sentiments that dominated the intellectual life of most of the American republics in the nineteenth century had a sporadic and rather tepid life in Argentina. After the establishment of formal diplomatic relations in the late 1850s, and until the outbreak of the civil war in the mid-1930s, there were few occasions for serious friction.

The Spanish image in Argentina has thus been rendered in a far wider range of tones than elsewhere in Latin America; at the same time, identification with Spanish values and traditions has served a striking diversity of political and social purposes. Some elements of the Argentine right, to be sure, have regarded Spain as the authentic base of a conservative faith and of a national identity; an entire school of writers expanded on this theme in the decade prior to 1914, when the social consequences of massive immigration and economic modernization were making themselves felt with a particular virulence. Yet until 1936 most well-to-do Argentines continued to identify Spain as the source of an immigrant proletariat rather than an aristocratic tradition. In matters political as well as cultural, France exercised unquestioned hegemony. This included even right-wing doctrines and ideologies: although Spanish conservatism was well-represented in the person of Ambassador Ramiro de Maeztu in the twenties, the principal foreign influence on the right remained Charles Maurras.[7] It was only when the Spanish right demonstrated its vitality on the field of battle that the peninsula suddenly became a principal focus of Argentine conservative interest.

By way of contrast, for many years Argentine liberals had found much in Spain that accorded with their own values and aspirations. The Spanish proclivity for dealing with the tensions generated by urbanization and social change through paternalism and clientelistic patronage networks (*caciquismo*) was fully congruent with many strands of Argentine reformism, particularly that represented by the majoritarian Radical party. And even those further to the left could appreciate the social legislation that Eduardo Dato had piloted through the Spanish Cortes in 1900. Also, frequent contact, by mail and in person, between Spanish and Argentine labor leaders and Socialist politicians resulted in an active interchange of ideas and practices. Further, in the twenties the most representative figures of Spanish culture brought to Argentina by the Institución Cultural Española were not theologians, poets, or other exponents of "spirituality" but scientists and reformers.[8] Although the monarchy and the dictatorship of General Miguel Primo de Rivera (1923–30) were regarded as anachronisms by many Argentines, this did not prevent the establishment of extremely cordial relations between Madrid and the popularly-elected governments of Hipólito Yrigoyen (1916–22, 1928–30) and Marcelo T. de Alvear (1922–8). Many Argentines doubtless regarded Spain as a backward country but, with characteristic positivist presumption, conceived it to be a nation whose development was proceeding in much the same direction as their own, although, burdened by the weight of history, at a much slower pace. The notion of two Spains—one monarchist, clerical, and reactionary, the other Republican, reformist, and anti-clerical—had to await the polarization of opinion in both countries after 1930–31.

The richness and complexity of the Spanish image in Argentina meant that, once the civil war began, it was extremely difficult for advocates of the Nationalist cause to credibly lay claim to exclusive representation of the "authentic" Mother Country; at the same time, it made it possible for pro-Loyalist elements to draw on deep reserves of genuine revolutionary patriotism in the Spanish community and to attract wide support from like-minded Argentine liberal and labor groups. Both of these factors may well have influenced the decision of two successive Argentine administrations to persist in recognizing the Spanish Republic until almost the moment of its collapse.

The Argentine Crisis of 1930 and Its Aftermath

The year 1930 saw the almost simultaneous collapse of the political and economic conditions that had shaped Argentina's development for the previous fifty years. The main lines of that development were export-led economic growth, through the production of foodstuffs and raw materials for Western Europe, and the steady importation of skilled manpower, technology, and capital from the North Atlantic area. Such an arrangement presupposed not only a generally-agreed-on international division of labor but the relatively unobstructed movement of goods and persons across national frontiers, conditions that ceased to exist for most countries after 1914. Argentina escaped some of the sharper consequences of the shrinking liberality of the international economic order in the twenties—rising tariffs, trade and currency blocs, moves toward agricultural self-sufficiency—largely through the accident that her principal trading partner, Great Britain, had not fully discarded her pre-war economic conceptions and practices.

The continued presence of the British market, and a final boom in the prices for agricultural raw materials in the mid-twenties, extended the glow of euphoria to the very end of the decade. The coming of the world crisis of 1929–30, however, brought an end both to these conditions and to the prospects they afforded. As a result of the collapse of North Atlantic markets, Argentina experienced a precipitous drop in the prices of her exports, with a concomitant increase in the burden of her foreign debt and massive unemployment. And then, at the very moment when the Argentine economy had hit bottom, Great Britain announced, in July 1932, an economic conference in Ottawa in which she and her dominions would discuss, among other topics, imperial preferences. It was generally recognized by mid-1932 that an era had come to an end, but no one was certain precisely what configuration the new economic order would assume.[9]

The downward curve of economic indicators was accompanied by a similar movement in politics. Up to 1930 Argentina's reputation as the leading South American republic was based not only on her unrivaled wealth but also on her political stability and her impressive progress toward constitutional democracy. As the result of a universal manhood suffrage law sponsored by President Roque Saenz Peña in 1912, the road was opened four years hence for the accession to power of the Radical Civic Union (UCR), or Radical party, a coalition of urban and provincial interests broadly representative of Argentina's large if somewhat amorphous middle class.

By the late twenties, however, Argentine politics was approaching a dead end. The Radicals had exhausted what few ideas they had brought with them to government fourteen years before. Corruption, jobbery, incompetence, and nepotism were rife (it was a very large party, with many friends to satisfy). The Radical movement itself split in 1924 between Yrigoyen ("Personalist") and Alvear ("Anti-Personalist") wings. And Yrigoyen himself, though then approaching his eightieth birthday, insisted on returning to power in 1928. When the world crisis closed in on Argentina two years later, it was clear to all but the most inflexible Personalist that the aged chief executive had outlived his usefulness and would have to go.

When Lieutenant-General José F. Uriburu, retired Inspector-General of the Army, deposed the government in a military coup on September 6, 1930, all of the country's major political forces, including many Radicals, cheered him on, fully expecting that, once conditions returned to normal, the provisional government would convene an election in which Argentines would be able to vote, for the first time in years, free of the specter of Yrigoyen. As it happened, however, General Uriburu contemplated far-reaching institutional changes for his country's political system. Advised by poet Leopoldo Lugones and a group of young right-wing intellectuals around the newspaper *La Nueva República,* Uriburu saw the September Revolution as the virtual turning point in the country's constitutional development. Henceforth, he believed, Argentina would best be served by a nationalist approach in economic development and a corporate system of representation somewhat along the lines of Mussolini's Italy. The Conservatives and the high command of the army were not anxious to see the Radicals return, but neither did they wish to seriously alter the economic system or the external forms of parliamentary democracy. In the end a compromise was reached: the provisional president stepped down, and his corporatist plans were scrapped, but the Radicals were permanently relegated to the political wilderness by means of the systematic application of electoral fraud. Under the new rules, General Agustín P. Justo, a former Radical friendly to the Argentine Conservative party, was "elected" president of Argentina in November 1931 for a six-year term and inaugurated in February 1932.

There remained the economic half of the equation. When the Ottawa Conference announced shortly after General Justo's assumption of power that an agreement had been reached to gradually replace British purchases of Argentine beef with shipments from the Dominions, a high-level mission headed by Vice-President Julio A. Roca, Jr., was dispatched to London. After months of negotiations with Board of Trade President Walter Runciman, the Argentine mission reached an agreement (the so-called Roca-Runciman Pact) that established that in economic matters Argentina would be treated essentially as a "sixth dominion" of the British Empire. (The words did not figure in the treaty itself, but were used by Roca in public statements in England.) In exchange for continued British purchases of Argentine meat, Great Britain would be accorded a series of trade and tariff concessions intended to stem the American and German competition in Argentina that had slowly been threatening to overtake English exporters there for more than a decade. At the same time, it seemed to ward off the threat of import-substitution in what was still one of Britain's important overseas markets.

By mid-1933, then, it appeared as if Argentina had weathered the world crisis and managed to reassemble the shattered pieces of her economic and political life. Appearances to the contrary, however, it proved impossible to restore the previous period in all of its details. The forms of constitutional government had been saved, but only by sacrificing their democratic content, however imperfect. Argentine politics during the depression decade were characterized by growing disillusionment, cynicism, despair. In economic matters, too, things were never quite the same again. The Anglo-Argentine connection had been preserved, but at a cost that many outside the privileged circle of the elite (and some within it) found excessive. A rising tide of nationalism in the thirties increasingly impugned Argentina's subordinate role in the international division of labor, and summoned up feelings of hostility to the "Anglo-Saxon" world that had lain long-dormant in the country's Hispanic past.

The Argentine Right in the Thirties

The Revolution of 1930 restored to Argentina's National Democratic, or Conservative, party (PDN) the power it had lost with the advent of suffrage reform in 1916. What that movement could not do, however, was to paper over growing differences within the ranks of the PDN and between it and its allies in the military, church, press, business community, and intelligentsia as to what Argentine conservatism had come to mean and how best (and by which agencies and persons) its goals could be accomplished. Officially the regime hid its differences behind a mask that one historian has aptly called "the myth of September," namely, the claim that the policies of General Justo "were the natural outgrowth of the Uriburu ideologies of corporativism and authoritarianism."[10] Nobody recognized the hollowness of this claim, however, more than Uriburu's abandoned followers, who behind the scenes complained bitterly at the way the Conservative politicos had used and later discarded them.[11]

The Conservative restoration of the thirties took the form of a nominal coalition (the Concordancia) between the PDN and the Anti-Personalist wing of the Radical party. Under the terms of their alliance, the Anti-Personalists were to provide the presidential candidate and the "popular" following,[12] the Conservatives the running mate, the finances, and their matchless expertise in the falsification of election returns. When Alvear refused to lend himself to this scheme, the Concordancia was left with part of the Radical name and some Anti-Personalist leaders, but in all other matters was understood to be a Conservative operation. Although its policies were not uniformly regressive, the language used to advance them often was, and persons brought into the government to execute them were men with deep roots in the old order: lawyers for important foreign economic concerns, cereal exporters and cattlemen, and Conservative party wheelhorses. For those who believed that the Revolution of 1930 had been made to effect a clean sweep of government offices, replacing machine politicians with military men, technocrats, and intellectuals above party, the advent of the Concordancia was an acute disappointment.

Although to some extent the division between September revolutionaries and establishment Conservatives was generational, it was also founded on serious differences of world view. As elsewhere in the Latin world in the thirties, in Argentina the right found its allegiance torn between an essentially Anglo-French model of national development and the more ancient corporatist conceptions inherited from Spain and Rome, now surfacing in some modified form as fascism. For the fifty years prior to 1930, it was the former that had shaped and dominated Argentine life: "conservatism" meant British parliamentary institutions tempered by some form of limited suffrage, the Napoleonic code and French modes of government organization, free trade, a minimum of government interference in economic life, and a virtual separation of church and state, manifested principally through the civil register and the absence of religious instruction in the public schools. Freedom of speech, press, and assembly had always been honored sporadically at best, but on an ideological level their desirability had never been denied.

This view of politics rested on certain assumptions about the international order and on economic and political corollaries derived therefrom. Traditionally, Argentine Conservatives regarded the British Empire as little less than eternal and saw their nation's evolution in terms of it and of liberal international institutions. From the fact of British hegemony, they derived not only political values but an economic model that established for Argentina a primarily pastoral role in world trade. Thus for many decades Argentine Conservatives tended to oppose industrialization on the grounds that "we cannot sell without buying from those who buy from us."[13] For the fortunate few who owned the principal centers of agro-pastoral production, this argument was a transparent expression of class interest, but before 1930 it was shared quite disinterestedly by many of their fellow citizens, who were convinced that it represented the best response to what was, for them, in the final analysis inevitable.

In reality, the "new" Argentine conservatism of the thirties was not all that new; many of its themes, in a somewhat embryonic form, could be found in earlier periods of the nation's history. In particular, xenophobic, clerical authoritarianism was characteristic of both the colonial period and, after independence, the regime of Juan Manuel de Rosas (1829–52). With the triumph of liberalism in the Constitution of 1853, these reactionary ghosts were thought to have been laid to rest. Their reappearance, at least in the form they assumed in the thirties, owed much to the emergence of a "social question" in Argentina shortly before the First World War. The development of a trade union movement under anarchist (later, anarcho-syndicalist) leadership in the early years of this century was an unpleasant surprise to many Argentine public men, who had long told themselves that as a land of opportunity theirs would escape the crucible of class and social conflict. Labor protest was treated as a police problem prior to Yrigoyen's first presidency, and even beyond it, as was evidenced by the response to the General Strike of 1919, also (and appropriately) known as the Tragic Week.

But even before the 1920s, the Catholic church and certain Conservative politicians were beginning to question the strict economic directives of laissez faire. Catholic trade unions and such benevolent associations as the Asociación de Trabajo attempted to meet the social question half way with charity; the other half was met with armed force, through such quasi-military organizations as the Liga Patriótica Argentina, whose civilian members were trained in strike-breaking techniques by Argentine officers on military bases.

The emergence of Mussolini's Italy in the early twenties, the Lateran Pact of 1929, and several papal encyclicals dealing with the social question all led Argentina's new right to argue that the interests of order and property could no longer be secured by the institutions of the past. They therefore advocated an authoritarian state in which corporate interests would supplant party politics and individual suffrage, balanced by a full range of social laws and benefits for workers, vigorous intervention to promote economic development, and the reintroduction of Catholic religious influence in national life. Implicit in this agenda was the recognition that bourgeois liberalism had always been something of a hothouse plant in Argentina, artificially cultivated in an environment lacking the economic substructure (and the true middle class) of the Northern European societies in which that ideology had originated. The parallels between this view and that held by the Spanish right of the same era hardly need to be emphasized.

Perhaps the most striking difference between Argentina's "old" right and "new" was the latter's acceptance of industrialization. It was not so much a question of welcoming what was recognized as a potentially wrenching change as of admitting its inevitability and desiring to move early enough to meet and control its social consequences. The new right in the twenties and thirties saw, as the old right often did not, that the world economic order dominated by Great Britain was in sharp decline and that Argentina would have to make some adjustment to meet this harsh reality. This was all the more evident by the mid-thirties, when the United States's vigorous farm lobby successfully blocked Argentine attempts to find in North America a replacement for her shrinking British market.[14] Members of the new right often professed to believe in the rising star of Fascist Italy, and later, National Socialist Germany, but it should be emphasized that their views on the need to realign Argentina's foreign policy were inspired not only by the harsher terms of the Anglo-Argentine (and Argentine-American) relationship, or the need to find new overseas markets, but also by a historic quest for coherence in the fit between Argentine domestic institutions and the nation's international policies.

The conflict between old right and new was tempered not only by assiduous cultivation of the "myth of September" but also by the careful division of revolutionary spoils. Although those agencies that determined the actual direction of Argentine life throughout the thirties—the executive power, and the ministries of Foreign Relations, Agriculture, and Finance—remained firmly in the hands of traditional Conservatives, the new right was allowed to tamper with the country's political and social fabric through more or less continuous control of the ministries of Interior and Justice (which included Public Instruction), as well as strong representation in the Senate and in key provincial government houses. The result was a political and economic system that displayed many of the characteristic vices of nineteenth-century liberalism but increasingly few of its virtues.

Spain and Argentina, 1931–36: Divergent Paths

The collapse of the monarchy and the advent of the Second Republic in Spain in April 1931 opened the way for a frontal attack on an entire series of national ills whose nature had been the subject of informed public discussion for more than a hundred years. By decree, and later by legislative fiat, during its first months the Republican government attempted to resolve problems of land reform, the size of the army officer corps, the rights of the agricultural proletariat, the question of regional and ethnic autonomies, and, most controversial of all, the relationship between church and state. Under the Constitution of 1931 Spain was declared to have no official religion, and divorce was legalized in 1932. State support for the secular clergy was to be eliminated within two years, and the religious orders were directed to divest themselves of their very considerable real estate holdings and to submit to the normal tax laws.

The troubled history of what followed is rich in irony. The unenviable reputation for reddest radicalism that the Second Republic enjoyed in conservative and Catholic circles abroad stemmed from reforms that for the most part remained unrealized. Many ambitious projects, such as a rural school construction program, had to be abandoned for lack of funds. Others, such as the complicated provision for land reform, waited on the myriad subterfuges afforded by a baroque judicial system. For twenty-seven months, nearly half the life-span of the regime, power reposed in the hands of a center-right coalition, Republican in name but, "exception made for certain nuances, . . . unabashedly reactionary."[15] Many of the innovations of the 1931 charter, particularly those pertaining to church-state relations, were not markedly different from the norms that prevailed in many Catholic countries, including Spanish-American republics like Argentina, since at least the end of the nineteenth century. Why, then, did so many Argentine conservatives, old style or new, regard the Republic as such a disjunction, so radical a departure from what they regarded as a common cultural and historic patrimony?

On the Spanish side, the answer can be found partly in a mind-set, partly in the tone and direction of political life. Historians who can agree on little else universally concede that the Second Spanish Republic was born in a burst of optimism and hope peculiar to its time. To many, the fall of the monarchy was the signal for the release of pent-up energies and forces, through whose actions Spain would presumably telescope in a few brief moments the centuries of European history that had passed her by since the Counter Reformation. This attitude assumed a diversity of forms, some of which, viewed from a distance, at least, seemed less inspired by a vision of renewal than by an atavistic impulse to destruction, a wholesale repudiation of the past. For one thing, the proclamation of the Republic was followed by an almost uninterrupted succession of challenges to public order. In Madrid and other cities, convents and other religious buildings were attacked and burned, and there was a rash of political strikes as the labor movement sought to exercise new-found faculties. Even after a period of consolidation set in sometime in 1932 or 1933, the country's fragile political peace was continually interrupted by violent incidents, the last of which finally succeeded in igniting the civil war.

At the same time, Spain appeared to be passing through what in later years would be called a cultural revolution. Education was secularized. Exiles returned. New periodicals appeared, preaching exotic doctrines including vegetarianism, spiritism, and free love. The bookstores of Barcelona, Madrid, and the university towns began to display cheap, paper-covered editions of the works of Marx, Engels, Lenin, and Bakunin, as well as bad translations of German and French pornographic novels. Upper-class Argentines were familiar with this sort of thing in Paris (in fact, for them it was one of that city's special charms), but it was one thing to find it draped across the bosom of one's mistress, quite another across that of one's mother. Finally, extravagant statements proclaiming the imminent settlement of age-old social grievances by left-wing politicians, journalists, and labor leaders were taken at face value by friends and enemies alike, belying the true strength of anti-Republican elements in the army, the civil service, and society generally.

The millenarian flavor of Spanish political life in the early thirties was partly an expression of certain national peculiarities, but it also responded to the strong anarchist and anarcho-syndicalist presence in the trade union movement, particularly in Catalonia. Further, the Spanish Socialist party, though formally affiliated with the Second International, stood considerably to the left of its Northern European counterparts, and its trade union central, the Unión General de Trabajadores (UGT), played a role in Republican politics hardly less revolutionary than that of its anarcho-syndicalist rival, the Confederación Nacional de Trabajo (CNT).[16] This much was demonstrated by Socialist leadership of the Asturian miners' uprising in October 1934, the most serious left-wing challenge to the regime and the high point of trade union radicalism prior to the outbreak of the civil war. Although it was possible for Argentine conservatives to derive some comfort from the effective military suppression of the Asturian movement and the generally rightward course of the Republican government in 1935, these hopeful auguries were abruptly terminated by the victory of the Popular Front in the 1936 elections. The prospect of a Spanish government uniting not only Socialists and Communists but (unofficially) anarchists and anarcho-syndicalists with bourgeois Republicans seemed to dem-

onstrate once and for all that the fortunes of Spain had fallen irretriev-
ably into the hands of a revolutionary labor movement and
intelligentsia.

It would be difficult to imagine a more dramatic contrast to the
expansive vistas of Spanish republicanism, however befogged by the
mists of utopia, than the contemporaneous Argentine perspective. The
crisis of 1930 left Argentines with an acute sense of shrinking possibilities, not merely as the result of the Roca-Runciman Pact and the declining international standing it symbolized, but the ultimate arrival, all the
more shattering for its tardiness, of the post-war cultural pessimism that
the country had avoided during the boom years of the 1920s.[17] Like
Americans, Argentines were accustomed to thinking themselves im-
mune to history. The events of 1930 appeared to demonstrate that the
forces their forefathers had left in Europe had followed them across the
seas, and inspired a healthy respect (indeed, probably too healthy) for
the past and its supposed lessons.

This backward look out of the crisis inspired a growing wave of
historical revisionism, whose principal theme was that the liberal, secu-
larizing forces that had opened Argentina to foreign immigration, investment, and influence after 1853 had not only destroyed a distinctive
way of life but had also aborted the possibilities of economic independence. Works such as Julio and Rodolfo Irazusta's *La Argentina y el
imperialismo británico* (1934) and José María Rosa's *Defensa y pérdida de
nuestra independencia económica* (1943) advanced the view that the opening of Argentina to unrestricted British trade in the 1860s had destroyed
the country's cottage industries.[18] Thus, the argument continued, a
unique historic opportunity to effect a transition to self-sustained industrial development (and, by implication, to avoid present humilia-
tions and difficulties) had been lost. To many, the same line of reasoning
suggested, by indirection at least, that immigrants were an unnecessary
(and presumably undesirable element) in Argentine life, and that post-
Hispanic cultural influences were destructive not only of national identity and public order but even of physical survival.

A revisionist mood could not be restricted to history books. If
nothing could be done on an international level to redress grievances,
at least some scores at home could be settled, and from 1930 onwards
a xenophobic strain could be discerned throughout Argentine life. In
1932 new immigration laws reversed a long-standing policy of unrestricted welcome to newcomers. Foreign workers who participated in
strikes were summarily deported.[19] The government even arbitrarily
banned from the mails apolitical foreign-language periodicals.[20]

In an apparent search to recover the authentic roots of national identity, some Argentines turned to the church, and the country experienced a virulent epidemic of clericalism. The principal target of attack was the nation's public school system, where religious instruction had been forbidden since 1888. Desecularization on a national level was forestalled by combined Radical-Socialist forces in Congress until that body was dissolved by the military in 1943, but obligatory catechism classes were reintroduced by provincial ministries in Santa Fe (1936), Catamarca (1936), and Buenos Aires (1937). Particularly in the latter, the line between religion and patriotism in schools became increasingly indistinct. At the same time, the Argentine army reintroduced open-air masses for conscripts. Church authorities openly attacked founders of the Argentine laicist tradition, notably the venerated President D. F. Sarmiento (1868–74). And visible manifestations of anti-Semitism increased. Among other things, Argentina's most popular Catholic novelist achieved enormous financial success with a two-volume novel based on *The Protocols of the Elders of Zion*.[21]

The resurgence of clericalism was but one symptom of a general decline of liberal values in depression-decade Argentina. In March 1932, and then again in September 1936, restrictions were placed on the right of public assembly. The responsible dependencies of the Ministry of Interior frequently refused radio time to opposition politicians and arbitrarily withdrew mailing privileges from Socialist and liberal periodicals.[22] Several academics of known left-wing sympathies were separated from their chairs in the national university system for no apparent cause. And in November 1936, after weeks of impassioned debate, the Argentine Senate passed a bill, for the ostensible repression of communism, that defined its object so broadly that virtually any expression of liberal opinion could become a matter of criminal justice.[23]

In contrast to Spain during the same period, liberal and left-wing forces in national politics were disorganized and demoralized, utterly unable to mount a joint offensive against the Conservative restoration. Much of the problem resided in the Radical party, which represented 70 percent of the vote and without which no Popular Front was possible. Apart from a traditional distaste for coalitions, the Radicals were reluctant to enter into an alliance with other opposition parties because they already possessed a theoretical majority, which led them to concentrate their energies on the elimination of electoral fraud. The Conservatives understood this fact and turned it to their benefit; under both Presidents Justo (1932–38) and Ortiz (1938–40), a series of understandings were reached with Marcelo de Alvear that, though falling short of facilitating a full Radical return, held out sufficient stimulus to keep the party divided from other democratic forces and options.

In the eventuality of free and honest elections, no other party could hope to come to power on its own. The Progressive Democrats, the most "liberal" (in the Spanish sense of the term) of Argentine groups, was small and confined to a regional base in the provinces of Sante Fe and Entre Ríos. The Argentine Socialist party was somewhat larger in membership but also geographically restricted—its following was overwhelmingly concentrated in Greater Buenos Aires and some of the larger towns of the capital province. Although also intertwined with the labor movement, the Argentine party, unlike its Spanish counterpart, had a strong, social-democratic tradition. It also possessed deep roots in Argentine history and culture, so that from many points of view it was a truly "nationalist" party in the most constructive sense of that word. This meant that for both ideological and patriotic reasons it was not attracted to invitations to coalition tendered by the Argentine Communists. In any event, the latter were ill-equipped to play a meaningful role in the building of a Popular Front, since, outlawed in late 1930, they spent much of the subsequent decade either underground or under severe harassment by the police.

Ironically, much of the energy that the democratic forces of the center and left might have expended in their own interest had to be focused on strengthening the hand of the more traditional Conservatives within the governing coalition. Whatever their differences, Radicals and Socialists shared with the old right a stated commitment to constitutional government. It was well understood that the increasingly authoritarian and clerical turn that national politics assumed during the second half of the thirties was due to the presence of the new right in key ministries and government offices. It was also a matter of common knowledge that the gap between the two branches of the Conservative party was widening, particularly when Roberto M. Ortiz, one of Alvear's former ministers, assumed the presidency in 1938. As a matter of fact, when Ortiz was forced to take a medical leave in 1940, his principal supporters in the struggle for power with his new right vice-president turned out to be the Radicals and the Socialists, not the Anti-Personalists to whom he nominally belonged.

Argentina and Spain on the eve of the civil war thus presented a peculiar and even paradoxical contrast. The Mother Country, whose physical poverty and moral exhaustion had induced so many of her best sons and daughters to emigrate, appeared somehow to have been galvanized into action and to vigorous historic redress. On the other hand, Argentina, to whom millions of Spaniards had fled for the wider perspectives and opportunities denied them in their native land, appeared to have lost faith in the future, to have withdrawn its secular promise.

The wonder of it is that, in spite of these diverging paths, relations between Argentina and Republican Spain were reasonably cordial up to the war. Of course, for much of the time before the victory of the Popular Front in the Spanish elections of February 1936, there was some reason to think that the conservative, Catholic CEDA would dominate Republican politics—as in fact it very nearly did in 1934 and 1935. And many Spanish issues, though familiar to Argentines, had not yet been internationalized. That is, until the summer of 1936, nothing was thought to hinge on the outcome of Spanish politics but the future of Spain itself. When the matter was restated in terms of a conflict between systems or historic options, Argentines could easily recognize the local import of Spanish questions and draw implications for action.

A Question of Diplomatic Privilege: Asylum

During the first weeks of the war, the Argentine embassy in Madrid was faced with problems of diplomatic responsibility that unexpectedly broadened to become difficult political questions. The first of these turned on the evacuation of several thousand Argentine nationals; the second concerned the use of the embassy's chancery buildings as a place of refuge for Nationalist sympathizers. Both issues, but particularly the latter, brought the two republics to the brink of severing relations, even before a rival regime was solidly established in Burgos.

Normally there would be no reason to expect the evacuation of foreign nationals from a war-torn country to provoke any degree of diplomatic controversy. But circumstances in Spain in the weeks following the outbreak of the war were far from normal. For the first six months of the war, as Gabriel Jackson has written, "the most profound social revolution since the fifteenth century took place in the territory remaining in the hands of the Popular Front," the major characteristics of which were "a passion for equality and the affirmation of local and collective authority." [24] In many cities, police and government authority evaporated, to be replaced by party militias and armed workers' committees. Factories were taken over by labor delegations; foreign enterprises were confiscated; in both city and countryside, left-wing elements of the Popular Front, sometimes seconded by common criminals and teen-age gangs, carried out a blood purge of political enemies, real and imagined. In spite of repeated efforts by responsible elements within the government to reassert duly-constituted authority, the wave of terror was not easily contained. By the time some degree of order had been restored in late fall, some five or six thousand monks and priests had been killed, along with scores of known right-wing politicians, military men, and professional and well-to-do people whose political sympathies were assumed to lie on the Insurgent side.

The problem this wave of terror presented to the Argentine mission in Spain was twofold. First, the majority of Argentina's peninsular residents were solidly bourgeois at a time when the wearing of a felt hat and a a tie in certain areas was regarded as a concrete political statement. Individuals were roughed up by street patrols, and several palatial homes belonging to Argentine nationals were attacked and denuded of furniture, jewels, and works of art.[25] During the early days of the war, embassy officials in Madrid found it necessary to make frequent trips to the city's jails to determine if Argentine nationals were among those confined by revolutionary committees. Eventually some six hundred Argentines and their families were successfully evacuated from the Spanish capital, but between July and October a half-dozen Argentines died violently, four under mysterious circumstances, two at the hands of militiamen. The fact that one Argentine was shot even after the embassy made repeated representations on his behalf to the authorities lent credit to the frequent charge by the Republic's enemies in both countries that the Madrid government was unable to control its own dependencies.[26]

Second, the constant nocturnal activities of the execution squads, particularly in Madrid, led many Spaniards to seek asylum in embassies and legations. The Argentine mission sheltered some fifteen hundred at various points in the war, to accommodate which it rented additional buildings. A great number of these were ultimately evacuated from Republican territory aboard the Argentine cruiser 25 de Mayo.[27] The fact that many aislados (asylees) were members of the nobility and upper bourgeoisie, often with important Insurgent connections—among them, General Franco's brother-in-law Ramón Serrano Suñer[28]—and the fact, too, that by their "repatriation" on Argentine ships, many were able subsequently to join the rebel forces, led many partisans of the Republic to regard Argentine diplomatic hospitality as a calculated act of subversion.

The granting of diplomatic asylum in embassy buildings was a widely accepted practice in Latin America, embodied in a number of hemispheric agreements to which Argentina was a party. Although Spain had not subscribed to these instruments, and had never explicitly recognized the right of diplomatic asylum, at the outset the Republican government had no desire to antagonize foreign countries, particularly Spanish-speaking nations, by refusing to honor it in actual practice.[29] However, as Gabriel Jackson has pointed out, "the right of asylum as practiced in Latin America was understood to apply to leaders of governments overturned by revolutions, or to prominent personalities belonging to persecuted political parties.[30] Relatively few of the *aislados* in Madrid were leaders of anti-government parties, and none could be said to be functionaries of an overturned regime—quite the contrary, in fact: most sought refuge precisely because the existing government had *not* been successfully overthrown.

Much of the acrimony this issue provoked between Buenos Aires and Madrid was due to a studious Argentine refusal to recognize this anomaly. But the matter went even further: during the first weeks of the war, Insurgent troops were expected to fall on the city at any time, and Minister of State Julio Alvarez del Vayo claimed to have "absolute proof," as he later told U.S. Ambassador William Bullitt in Paris, "that arms had been smuggled into missions harboring refugees, and detailed plans worked out for these refugees to make a sortie and fall on the Government troops from behind when they were being attacked severely by Franco's forces."[31]

By mid-September, in the wake of documented abuses of the right of asylum by the Cuban, Finnish, and Peruvian legations,[32] Alvarez del Vayo attempted to tighten restrictions. In a circular letter to all embassies and legations, the minister of state accepted the unlimited right of women and children to seek safety in diplomatic compounds, but sought to establish a "clear distinction" between "considerations evidently of a humanitarian order, and well-known abuses" by those who "utilize[d] hospitality to continue their subversive activities."[33] The Republican government could accept the granting of asylum to persons who had played a prominent role in the insurgency, but only if they ceased all political activity on entering the diplomatic compound and, even then, only if their hosts were prepared to submit their names to the Ministry of State within twenty-four hours of their arrival.[34]

In an unusually rapid cabled response, the Argentine Foreign Ministry abruptly rejected all of Alvarez del Vayo's requests. Not a single instance of the "well-known abuses" had occurred under Argentine auspices, it reminded him, and for this reason "the Argentine government rests assured that the absolute guarantees offered by Your Excellency [for the safety of embassy buildings, personnel, and guests] will be maintained." It closed with the scarcely-veiled threat that "any alteration in the exercise of [the] right of asylum thus consented to [by your government] could influence the diplomatic relations of this government with Spain."[35] No lists of names were in fact ever provided.

The Argentine government was no less unyielding in the matter of the physical evacuation of the *aislados.* When the Republican government tried to argue that the guests lost whatever diplomatic protection they might have acquired once they left diplomatic precincts, the Foreign Ministry announced that under such circumstances the Argentine mission would lodge them indefinitely.[36] Here, too, the Republic backed down. The first *aislados* left the Madrid compound for Mediterranean ports in the company of the Argentine chargé d'affaires in early November; by mid-February, 1937, the embassy chancery was devoid of its unusual guests. That as intransigent a figure as Alvarez del Vayo yielded so readily to the Argentines on both occasions speaks not only for the courage and energy of their diplomats but also for the determination of the Republican government not to allow its irritation with foreign missions generally to endanger its relations with the leading Spanish-speaking republic of South America.

The refugee episode was, however, an unfortunate beginning for wartime relations. For, at the very moment when the Republic needed most to affirm its legitimacy, the Argentine Foreign Ministry was receiving a steady stream of horror stories that lost nothing in the telling, particularly in late August and in September and October, when armed committees of militiamen were knocking on legation doors to demand the surrender of *aislados* to revolutionary justice. When the precincts of the Venezuelan mission were violated on September 24, ministry officials in Buenos Aires learned of the event in these terms: "The government," normally moderate chargé d'affaires Edgardo Pérez Quesada cabled home, "is powerless to impose authority, and [is] dominated not only by workers' associations, but by roving bands of common criminals. . . . It is entirely impossible to obtain guarantees in spite of the desires of those in power."[37]

The image of a Republican government essentially at the mercy of radical labor unions and armed mobs—for which there was some limited evidence in the early weeks of the war—thus conveyed across the South Atlantic cable became permanently fixed in the minds of Argentine policy makers and, by extension, of important segments of the press and public. In spite of repeated attempts in subsequent months by Republican diplomats and spokesmen (and their Argentine friends) to clarify and explain, those first dispatches continued to influence Argentine deliberations on the war long after they ceased to accurately portray life in the Popular Front zone.

While these events were unfolding in Madrid, another drama of equal significance for Hispano-Argentine relations was taking place in the Basque province of Guipúzcoa, where Argentine Ambassador (and dean of the diplomatic corps) Daniel García Mansilla stumbled into an unexpected contretemps with local authorities of the Popular Front. On

July 18, the ambassador and his family had left Madrid for San Sebastián, former summer residence of the monarch, still observed as the
official seasonal retreat of the diplomatic corps. At the precise moment
of the uprising, he and his party had reached Zarauz, a small village
several kilometers from their ultimate destination. Temporarily cut off
from communication with Madrid and Buenos Aires, García Mansilla
settled down in a hotel for what turned out to be a stay of several weeks'
duration.

Within a few days, the ambassador began to experience serious
inconvenience. His salary and operating expenses, which he had depos-
ited in a nearby bank, were frozen, as were all such assets throughout
the Popular Front zone during the early days of the war. When contact
was reestablished with Buenos Aires (at first through Paris), he complained that the confidentiality of his messages was being violated. And,
most important, he reported to the Argentine Foreign Ministry that
guarantees for his personal safety and freedom of movement were
"steadily eroding."[38]

The crux of the problem, in Zarauz as it had been in Madrid, was
the question of diplomatic asylum. When García Mansilla's presence in
the area became known to two conservative Spanish politicians, they
sought and obtained refuge with him;[39] their number was eventually
augmented by more than a dozen. What the ambassador later referred
to in an extremely damaging interview with the Argentine press as "the
Soviet authority installed in Zarauz" eventually surrounded his hotel
and demanded the surrender of his guests. In the event of non-compli-
ance, he reported, these left-wing elements threatened to dynamite the
building. A frantic telephone call to the civil governor in San Sebastián
led to the dispatch of twenty soldiers and militiamen to protect the
ambassador and his party, until the arrival of the German warship
Albatross in mid-August made it possible for the entire group to be
evacuated to St. Jean de Luz. A strongly-worded diplomatic note
handed to the Ministry of State by the Argentine chargé on August 7
sufficed to release the frozen funds and put an end to further harassment
of his peripatetic chief. The experience, however, was clearly an unset-
tling one for a man whose life up to then had been notable largely for
its lack of discomforts. García Mansilla himself remembered the "siege
of Zarauz" as "the ten most anguished days of my diplomatic career."[40]
After a period in France presiding over the Madrid diplomatic corps-in-
exile, first at St. Jean de Luz, then in Hendaye, finally in Cibourne, in
the Lower Pyrenees, the ambassador returned to Buenos Aires. Both in
France, however, and later in Argentina, where he continued technically
to be ambassador to Spain until his retirement form the foreign service

in March 1939, he used what influence he could to undermine the Republican cause.

Early Wartime Relations between Argentina and the Republic, 1936–38

Quite apart from the apocalyptic vision of events in Spain retailed by her diplomats, the Argentine Republic could not be expected to embrace the cause of the Popular Front. Here, after all, was a country many of whose leaders were highly receptive to the prevailing currents of European reaction and—what is perhaps more to the point—whose government owed its existence to a military coup of its own. However, in spite of early soundings by the Insurgent junta,[41] seconded by the Peruvian government,[42] leading personalities of the Argentine Conservative party,[43] and the Roman Catholic hierarchy, the Argentine government held back from openly recognizing Burgos. There was some informal communication between the two governments through Lisbon, but it appears to have been strictly limited to matters relating to the evacuation of *aislados* and to an occasional appeal for clemency on behalf of Argentine nationals in the Insurgent zone or condemned Spaniards with relatives in Argentina.[44] Beyond this, Buenos Aires did not go, even at the cost of forfeiting the opportunity to protest the impressment of Argentine nationals into the rebel army.[45]

This position—which the Argentine government maintained, despite all, almost to the final days of the war—was inspired by a complex mix of international and domestic political considerations. In the first weeks, the most pressing reason to continue relations with the Republic was that it still controlled the greater part of Spanish territory and all but one of the principal cities. Then, too, a special obligation weighed on the Argentines after September 22, when Uruguay broke relations with the Republic over the shooting of three sisters of its vice-consul in Madrid. The tiny Platine republic (once an Argentine province) had asked Argentina to take over representation of its interests in the Loyalist zone, and for historical reasons Argentina could not refuse. On the other hand, this created an additional obligation to remain on correct terms with the Republican government, even after its territory began to shrink. The continued recognition of the Popular Front government through 1938 by Great Britain, France, and the United States also had its effect.

Insofar as domestic political considerations were concerned, the Concordancia in Argentina was dominated by traditional Conservatives with a distaste for military governments. Although these people had no compunctions about using the Argentine army to topple the Radicals in a moment of crisis, once the deed was done they preferred to see the troops return to their barracks. The experience of General Uriburu in 1930 and 1931 had taught them, among other things, that politicians in uniform developed undesirable ambitions of their own. (The selection of General Justo to head the official electoral slate in 1931 was due precisely to his greater willingness to exchange his uniform for civilian clothes, and more than in just a sartorial sense.) In contrast, new right elements in Argentina—whether in the press, the legislatures, or provincial government houses—openly avowed that the Burgos junta, and later the Franco dictatorship, were complete models of what ought to replace their own country's civilian, constitutional regime, however empty of democratic content it might actually have been.

Finally, there was Argentine public sentiment to take into account. Although elections were largely fraudulent, and public opinion presumably a cipher, the pro-Republican views of a large section, probably the majority, of the Argentine people could not be totally ignored, if for no other reason than to avoid untoward demonstrations and disorder. Moreover, there was no reason to recognize Burgos when an equal amount of damage could be inflicted on the Spanish Republic more conveniently, at a lower domestic political cost, by continuing to work through the existing framework of normal diplomatic relations.

Argentina's fundamental policy towards the war was thus established very early: correct if not always cordial relations with the embattled Republican government, balanced to some degree by a steadfast refusal to recognize its rival in Burgos. Between these two poles there remained, of course, a wide latitude for options of various shadings, a situation that allowed for continuing conflict within the Argentine Conservative establishment and a quiet but persistent guerrilla war waged against Loyalist Spain by certain diplomats and key Foreign Ministry functionaries.

The first of these was Ambassador García Mansilla himself, who during the first days of the war attempted to exploit the political possibilities of his position as dean of the diplomatic corps. During August and September, he convened regular meetings of the chiefs of mission accredited to Madrid at his mountaintop residence in Cibourne. The purpose of these gatherings, as U.S. Ambassador Claude Bowers indignantly recalled, was to advance—under cover of attempts at "mediation," and in clear violation of neutrality—the international status of the Insurgents.[46] When Bowers and his British colleague pointedly absented themselves from these gatherings, the Argentine ambassador was forced to abandon his plans and pack his bags for home.

In Buenos Aires, the Republic fared little better at the hands of García Mansilla's chief, Foreign Minister Carlos Saavedra Lamas. When his Uruguayan counterpart proposed joint mediation of the war by the American hemispheric chancelleries in mid-August,[47] Saavedra Lamas enthusiastically took up the project,[48] until the U. S. chargé d'affaires pointedly reminded him that "in the mediation suggested [by the Uruguayans], the very act of communicating with the rebels might . . . be tantamount to recognizing them as belligerents." Thus confronted, the Argentine precipitously withdrew his sponsorship, and the proposal quietly died.[49]

Saavedra Lamas's equivocal role in the Spanish war continued, however, in Europe itself, where he journeyed at the end of August to preside over the General Assembly of the League of Nations. Debarking in Cherbourg, after a brief stay in Paris, he proceeded to Geneva, where he found himself face-to-face with Spanish Minister of State Julio Alvarez del Vayo, who had made the journey from Madrid to present evidence of Italian, German, and Portuguese intervention in the affairs of his country.

Even before Saavedra Lamas's arrival, Alvarez del Vayo had experienced serious difficulties presenting his information to the proper League bodies (he found no satisfaction at the first meeting of the Non-Intervention Committee on September 9). In desperation he planned to turn to the General Assembly, but once again met with unexpected difficulty—this time in getting the subject placed on the agenda. The arrival of the new Assembly president did not improve Spanish prospects. A few hours before Alvarez del Vayo was scheduled to speak, Saavedra Lamas summoned him to his private chamber; after several hours' discussion he managed to persuade the Spaniard to confine his remarks to "general considerations," omitting any specific charges against the intervening powers.[50] The Spaniards had to content themselves with the publication of a White Book, while Saavedra Lamas basked in the warm appreciation of his Geneva colleagues.

While the Argentine foreign minister was in Europe, Republican Spain had to contend with the wiles of his replacement, Interior Minister Ramón S. Castillo, seconded by Undersecretary Oscar Ibarra García. Ibarra García was a career diplomat, but Castillo was an important political personality in his own right, of whom much more was to be heard; perhaps most important in this context, he was a traditional Conservative who after 1930 switched his loyalties to the new right. It was during these weeks of Castillo's temporary stewardship at the Foreign Ministry that a curious story appeared in the Buenos Aires press, alleging—on the credit of "unofficial sources"—that "the government of Madrid" had "lost control of the situation" to "certain extremist elements" and that the highest government officials in the Spanish capital were negotiating an Argentine asylum for themselves and their families.[51] The story created an instant sensation, so much so, in fact, that Ibarra García found it necessary to disavow the rumor within twenty-four hours of its publication. A few weeks later, in private conversation with Mexican Ambassador Alfonso Reyes, the undersecretary committed the rare indiscretion of admitting that the story had been "planted" in the Argentine press by Castillo.[52]

The Spanish ambassador in Argentina, Enrique Diez-Canedo, was a poet and literary critic of minor distinction, utterly unprepared to deal with the wave of duplicity and cynical maneuvering that the civil war occasioned at the Argentine Foreign Ministry. His task was rendered no easier when virtually his entire embassy staff and more than half the Spanish consular corps in Argentina resigned between July and September 1936 to support the Nationalist uprising. It was several months before a new staff could be named and dispatched; in the meanwhile, Diez-Canedo was forced to face matters alone. In February 1937 he found himself unable to continue, and quietly resigned.

With Diez-Canedo gone, Republican affairs devolved into the hands of the new first secretary, Felipe Jiménez de Asúa, who had arrived in January. Several days after Diez-Canedo's resignation, the Argentines granted diplomatic approval to Professor Julián Besteiro, president of the Cortes, who subsequently refused the job.[53] That is where matters rested for more than a year, until the Republic was finally able to obtain approval for Angel Ossorio y Gallardo, who arrived in June 1938. During most of 1937 and half of 1938, then, the Republic remained underrepresented in Argentina, while a Nationalist "delegate" moved about performing what amounted to unofficial ambassadorial duties.

In Spain itself, Argentina remained without an ambassador *in situ* after García Mansilla quit the country in August 1936. His second-in-command, chargé d'affaires Enrique Pérez Quesada, was transferred to Lisbon in February 1937; what remained of the Argentine mission was moved to Valencia, then Barcelona, where it remained in the hands of second- and third-rank officials, largely drawn from the consular service. The Argentine embassy was not reestablished in Madrid—complete with a plenipotentiary—until after the victory of the Nationalists in 1939.

Pro-Republican Parties and Personalities

In Argentina, as elsewhere in much of the Western world, both liberal and left-wing parties and movements adopted the Loyalist cause as their own. The Radical party was unambiguously sympathetic to the Republic, seeing in the Nationalist uprising much the same kind of assault on civilian rule and political democracy as had unseated President Yrigoyen in 1930. The Radicals tended to downplay the revolutionary social content of some Republican forces in Spain, partly for reasons of convenience, partly by way of overreaction to the exaggerated imputations to which *they* in turn had been subject in 1929 and 1930 by Argentine Conservatives. The support of the Radicals was the strongest card in the Republic's Argentine deck, not only because this party was the largest political force in the country (however disenfranchised at the moment) but because its commitment to bourgeois social values was never seriously in question. In contrast to the Spanish and the French, the Argentine Radicals even lacked an anti-clerical tradition; in fact, many Radical leaders were devout Catholics, and some Radical friends of Loyalist Spain were figures of enormous social prestige, starting with former President Marcelo T. de Alvear.

The Republic could also count on the active assistance of the Argentine Socialist party and its brilliant team of orators and parliamentarians, led by the colorful Senator Alfredo Palacios. Perhaps even more important was the collaboration of the Socialist-controlled Confederación General de Trabajo (CGT), the largest labor organization in the country. The leader of the small Progressive Democratic party, Lisandro de la Torre, was a public figure of unimpeachable integrity and commanding presence, worth a division in himself.

These groups represented for the Republic not merely a base from which to raise funds or recruit combat volunteers, but skilled and experienced lawyers to come to the defense of Republican Spaniards and pro-Loyalist Argentines who fell afoul of the Ministry of Interior, the Directorate-General of Immigration, or Governor Manuel Fresco's openly pro-Insurgent regime in nearby La Plata, capital of the province of Buenos Aires. To these same organizations fell the ultimate, tragic task of attempting to pry open firmly-shut Argentine doors to Republican exiles, once the contest in the peninsula had been decided.

Argentine Aid to the Loyalists

The base of the pro-Republican sentiment referred to above was centered in Argentina's Spanish community, where Basques, Catalans, and

Galicians were represented in somewhat greater proportion than in the Mother Country itself, and (with a few exceptions) in the more than three hundred Spanish fraternal and mutual aid organizations that existed in Argentina in 1936. In addition, dozens of ad hoc agencies were created within the Spanish community specifically to raise money for the Republican war effort. One such group, the Junta Central Pro-Socorro y Reconstrucción de España in Rosario, managed to sell 30 million pesos' worth (U.S. $91,000) of unofficial war bonds to pay for shipments of food, clothing, and medicines to the Republican war front.[54] The Asociación Patriótica Española, which originally tried to maintain a neutral stance in the war,[55] raised more that 400,000 pesetas for the Spanish Red Cross in the fall of 1936, but by mid–1937 that organization had clearly come out for the Insurgents,[56] and the Spanish Red Cross had become suspect to the Nationalists and their Argentine sympathizers.[57] Efforts to unify all Spanish war charities met with failure. Nonetheless, the conflict galvanized Argentina's Spanish community, and for nearly three years kept it continually in the news; its widely-advertised pro-Republican stance continually undermined the claims of the Burgos representation.

The pro-Loyalist sentiment of liberal Argentina congealed into sixteen specific Republican aid organizations. Here, too, attempts to consolidate all of these into one umbrella organization, the Federación de Organismos de Ayuda a la República Española (FOARE) were frustrated; on the other hand, by the end of 1937 FOARE had become a major cause in itself, with a hundred and twenty chapters throughout the country and twenty-nine supporting committees. Apart from the FOARE and from specifically Spanish groups such as the Rosario junta, there were single-purpose groups like the Junta Argentina Médica de Ayuda Sanitaria a España Republicana (JAMSER), which raised enough money to purchase thirty-nine ambulances and two field hospitals, as well as miscellaneous medical and surgical supplies, for the Republican Army.[58]

Among these organizations, the Socialist party, and the labor movement (CGT), by the end of 1937 friends of Loyalist Spain had collected something in excess of two million Argentine pesos (U.S. $610,000), and just short of a million more (U.S. $290,000) by the end of 1938. Doubtless these figures are very conservative, since they merely consolidate sums announced in the daily press; of themselves, however, they are impressive, given the depressed economic conditions of the time, the limited resources of individual contributors, and the many obstacles placed in the way of Loyalist fund-raising activities, to which we shall refer shortly.

Argentine aid to the Republic included combat volunteers, although this episode is still beclouded by official reticence on the Spanish side, incomplete (or destroyed) Republican archives, and some confusion over the actual nationality of the personalities concerned. Although Loyalist Spain did little to discourage this form of assistance elsewhere, in Argentina inquiries to the Spanish embassy from potential volunteers in 1936 and 1937 were sharply turned aside.[59] Presumably Republican relations with the Justo government were shaky enough without having to explain recruitment activities that—apart from being in technical violation of local conscription laws—revived an ancient dispute over notions of sovereignty and citizenship.

In spite of this, many Argentines (or Argentine residents) went off to fight in Spain, although the figures for volunteers vary to a disconcerting degree—from a low of two hundred to a high of five hundred. It is known that Argentine volunteers fought in both the Republican Army and the International Brigades. Two sources claim that the commander of the 24th Brigade of the Republican Army was an Argentine;[60] another asserts that eighty-nine Argentines in the International Brigades fought in the critical battle of Brunete, in July 1937.[61]

As was the case in many countries, Argentine volunteers included young men of apparent political promise, drawn principally from the parties of the left. The Radicals contributed Dr. Gregorio Topolevsky; the Socialists, Angel Ortelli, general secretary of the syndicate of building trades workers. Independent Marxist physician and professor Gregorio Bermann served in the Sanitary Services of the International Brigades, and founded (in Spain) the Comité de Relaciones Hispano-Latinoamericanas.[62] The Communists dispatched career functionaries Juan José Real and José Belloqui; their most important figure, however, Vittorio Codovilla, proceeded to Spain via Chile, whence he had taken refuge after official proscription of the party in 1930. Reputedly "one of the Latin American leaders closest to Stalin," Codovilla operated in the peninsula as Comintern agent "Medina," and as such was instrumental in effecting the fusion of Spain's Communist and Socialist youth organizations. One highly regarded student of the period asserts that "during the first year of the Civil War, [Codovilla] was the real head of the Spanish Communist party."[63]

Alongside these easily-identifiable figures stood the bulk of Argentina's contribution to the fighting forces of Loyalist Spain—hundreds of anonymous young men with no previous (or subsequent) political experience. If surnames alone are any guide, the vast majority were Spanish residents of Argentina or Argentine-born children of Spaniards.[64] Some may have returned to the Mother Country to render service to what they regarded as its legitimate government; others sought adventure and an escape from the routine of working-class life; still others were presumably motivated by the political ideals that were the announced purpose of the International Brigades.[65]

These efforts to aid Republican Spain had to negotiate past repeated obstacles placed in their way by the Ministry of Interior, on one hand, and that of Justice and Public Instruction on the other. In their treatment of Loyalist sympathizers, both ministries clearly reflected the increasingly restrictive view of the right of assembly that Argentine law had been taking even before the war. Specifically, a regulation promulgated on March 16, 1932, granted police authorities broad discretion in the definition of "public order" and the considerations governing parade and meeting permits. In September 1936, a new decree from the chief of police of the Federal Capital prohibited political gatherings in the open (as opposed to meeting halls) and required sponsoring organizations to apply for permission at least four days in advance even for the more limited form of assembly.[66] In November 1937, new police regulations restricted still further even those functions held in closed quarters.[67]

Although of doubtful constitutionality, none of these legal innovations was successfully challenged in the Argentine courts, and Interior Minister Castillo and Justice Minister Jorge de la Torre applied them with vigor and enthusiasm. During the three years of the Spanish war, the pro-Republican press reported twenty-seven different incidents abridging the right of Loyalists or their friends to assemble: twelve meetings, including a giant rally sponsored by the CGT in Luna Park, were denied permits; eight were forcibly dispersed by the police authorities after having obtained the necessary permission; seven were broken up by fascist thugs—some in the uniform of quasi-military "shock sections" of right-wing movements—with the open connivance or benevolent neutrality of the police. The most egregious case was the refusal of a permit to a congress of Republican aid organizations that would have been held in August 1937.

Other methods of obstruction included arresting young ladies collecting money for the Republic on streets and subways for violating municipal ordinances against vagrancy, prostitution, or mendacity,[68] cashiering conspicuously pro-Loyalist professors in the national university system for "dissolvent propaganda in conjunction with well-known social agitators and Communists,"[69] and refusal of mailing permits to pro-Republican publications or, periodically, to aid shipments destined to the Peninsula.[70] The dependency of the Ministry of Interior that controlled the airwaves occasionally refused Loyalist elements access to radio time.[71] The pro-Republican press repeatedly complained about these irregularities,[72] and parliamentary deputations from the Radical and Socialist blocs regularly called at the Interior Ministry to present their complaints, with results that at best could be called disappointing.

The Nationalist "Crusade" in Argentina

Almost from the beginning of the war, the Insurgent leadership recognized the importance of Argentina and made a conscious effort to win aid and recognition—if not from its government, then from as broad a spectrum of society as possible. For this purpose, Juan Pablo de Lojendio, a 34-year-old career diplomat, was appointed Nationalist "delegate" to Argentina, arriving in Buenos Aires on New Year's Day, 1937. Through some Argentine Conservative leaders who made no secret of their Insurgent sympathies, as well as through Francisco de Amat, who had stayed on in the country after resigning as first secretary of the Loyalist embassy in August 1936, he was in a position to make contact with many of the most influential figures in Argentine society. Although Lojendio was not formally received by Argentine officials until the end of the war, it is not likely that he was meeting them for the first time in March or April 1939.

As representative of the Burgos state, Lojendio enjoyed a particular advantage of non-recognition: he could not be called to account for any discrepancies of view between the two governments or for outstanding claims—unlike the situation that often confronted Republican envoys. Also, whereas the Republic had to bear the political inconvenience (as it was) of public support from the Argentine Communist party, Lojendio saw no reason to be embarrassed by the solidarity expressed by local Carlists, Alfonsine monarchists, Falangists, members of the Argentine "nationalist" new right, even White Russian refugees! His efforts to get significant numbers of Spaniards in Argentina to recognized his legitimate representation of national interests were not successful, but since he was playing principally to a select group of Argentine policy-makers, this did not really matter. With Loyalist diplomacy in Argentina, just about the opposite was the case: having failed to impress the government to which it was accredited, the Republic had no choice but to make muted appeals over its head to its people.

Lojendio's principal links to the Argentine political establishment were Senators Matías Sánchez Sorondo and Benjamín Villafañe, as well as Dr. Manuel Fresco, governor of the province of Buenos Aires. All three were among the most strident right-wing voices during the Concordancia period. Sánchez Sorondo had been interior minister during the provisional government of General Uriburu, and as such had presided over a nearly unprecedented period of police brutality and political repression. A public advocate of the repeal of the Saenz Peña law, Sánchez Sorondo was immensely unpopular; his Senate seat had clearly been arranged to get rid of him, and he knew it. Even then, he continued to embarrass the dominant Anglophile wing of the Conservative party with his fulsome praise of Hitler and Mussolini; he was an honored guest of the last two and of General Franco on a visit to Europe in October 1937.[73]

Villafañe was a former Radical who had quarreled with President Yrigoyen during the latter's first term, and whose contempt for democracy had grown a bit too pronounced even for the tastes of the PDN, which he supported but to which he never formally belonged. Villafañe repeatedly insisted that the chaos afflicting Loyalist Spain in the summer of 1936 was but a foretaste of the "social war" Argentines could anticipate if Radicalism were ever allowed to return to power.[74] Both men managed to round up nearly a dozen senatorial colleagues to sign a telegram of support to Burgos in the early days of the war,[75] but apart from this and from repeated threats to introduce a resolution calling for the recognition of the Nationalist regime, they were forced to manifest their pro-Insurgent sympathies outside the normal framework of Conservative party politics.[76]

Governor Fresco was a far greater prize for Nationalist Spain: younger and more dynamic than Sánchez Sorondo or Villafañe, he was also more charismatic and even innovative. Further, since he harbored presidential ambitions, he was reluctant to sever his links to mainstream Conservatism, in whose councils he figured importantly until his forcible expulsion from office in 1940. The Fresco regime in Buenos Aires province (1936–40) was unquestionably right-wing—the intromission of the church in public education was unequaled; police authorities relentlessly hounded alleged leftist causes, organizations, and personalities. Fresco even sponsored a private paramilitary force (the "Legión Avance") to spy on and harass his political opponents.

Yet, unlike Sánchez Sorondo, Fresco was (by his lights) a genuine reformer. He clearly understood that a new order in Argentina had to be built on something more than mere repression. He was particularly sensitive to the fact that 90 percent of the country's growing industrial plant was located within his provincial boundaries, and he deliberately sought to wean the workers from their traditional political commitments through what one of his biographers has aptly termed "oligarchical populism."[77] This was a local blend of the social encyclicals of the Roman Catholic church, the corporatist notions of Fascist Italy, and the personalist techniques of machine politics as they had always been practiced in Argentina.

Under Fresco's rule, the provincial labor code was completely rewritten to provide for compulsory arbitration in labor-management disputes, at a time in Argentina when in many parts of the country the labor movement itself lacked legal personality. A vast public works program endowed the province with dozens of schools and the best all-weather roads in the country. A modest agrarian reform envisioned acquisitions of public lands by colonizers on a system of deferred payments. Fresco's approach to public housing, school construction, and public works generally was far in advance of anything else in Argentina, indeed in all South America. All of this was done within the framework of an overarching paternalism and a strongly authoritarian political environment, equally offensive to traditional members of the PDN (who resented Fresco's economic and social activism) and to liberal and left-wing parties (who felt the brunt of the governor's dictatorial practices while at the same time fearing that he might undercut their hold on their traditional constituencies). This attempt to shape a non-Socialist but post-capitalist economic order—in the face of combined opposition from liberals, democratic Socialists, revolutionary Marxists, and stodgy Conservatives—allowed Fresco (and others) to perceive a certain congruity between his own regime and that which the Falangists claimed to be establishing in Spain.

Apart from idiosyncratic figures such as these, most Argentine Conservatives preferred to curse the Spanish Republic in private while in public following the "correct" diplomatic posturings of Foreign Minister Saavedra Lamas. The most conspicuous organizational support for General Franco came from Argentine "nationalist" bodies like the Legión Cívica Argentina, Catholic student federations, or special purpose groups created specifically to raise funds for the Insurgents. The most important of these was the Legionarios Cívicos de Franco, founded in April 1937 by Soledad Alonso de Drysdale, one of the wealthiest society ladies in Argentina. By the end of the year, eight thousand people had answered the call, and a budget of 211,000 pesos ($64,000) had been raised to fund future activities.

Since pro-Insurgent elements in Argentina were far less inclined to submit their accounts to public scrutiny, the exact financial measure of their success cannot be known. Their principal fund-raising activity was the one-dish meal, followed by a harangue by Lojendio or one of his deputies, or, very occasionally, a "typical chocolate." These functions, which were extremely common, involved as many as a thousand persons at a time. Notwithstanding, it is very possible that a few individuals, such as Señora Alonso de Drysdale, carried a disproportionate share of the financial burden. In October 1936 she made the Burgos Junta an outright gift of 20,000 pounds sterling and 20,000 wool jackets for its army,[78] and in January 1937 she followed this donation up with another—400,000 cans of Argentine corned beef for the troops.[79] The following year she presented General Franco with an automobile completely equipped with two field radios.[80] Her reiterated interest was the founding of an orphanage in Spain, an emotional issue because of the Republican government's highly controversial decision to send some children to the Soviet Union. In February 1937, conceivably with her financial support, the Argentine branch of the Spanish Falange offered to place a thousand war orphans in Catholic homes throughout the country.[81] It is known that she offered to pay the passage of any Spaniard in Argentina who desired to return home to fight for Franco, and about three dozen young men responded.[82]

The Argentine Church and the Spanish War

The principal asset of the Nationalist "crusade" world-wide was the unambiguous support of the Roman Catholic church; in all Catholic countries (and in many that were not) the local hierarchy spoke up— sometimes with astounding vehemence—in favor of the Insurgent cause. The Argentine church did not stray from this general pattern, but the impact of its pronouncements was somewhat muted and even counteracted by a long-standing suspicion of clerical intromission into national politics and by the church's growing attack on secular values held even by many Argentine conservatives.

In 1936, Argentina was indisputably one of the major Catholic nations, in the sense that the Roman communion was the confessed or attributed affiliation of some 95 percent of its population. But the meaning of that identification was quite different than in Spain, Ireland, Colombia, or many other predominantly Catholic societies. In Argentina, French cultural influences operative on the nation's elite, a proletarian anti-clericalism that constituted an important part of Italian and Spanish immigrant life, and a vigorous Masonic movement among ranking military and professional men all converged to sharply circumscribe the prerogatives of the episcopacy. Religious instruction had been formally banned in the nation's school system in 1888; a regalist conception of episcopal appointments in effect subordinated church to state; a system of state financial patronage effectively removed the church from politics while assuring it a predictable source of income.[83]

For more than half a century, the Argentine hierarchy had reconciled itself to a situation that was less than ideal. In an environment
dominated (at least in certain areas) by North Atlantic values and the
worship of progress, little choice remained to it in any case. When the
national mood changed dramatically atter 1930, the church perceived a
drastic improvement of its prospects. The International Eucharistic
Congress, held in Buenos Aires in 1934, occasioned an unexpected outpouring of Catholic piety from high government officials and ordinary
citizens alike.[84] And, from 1931, as indicated above, a strongly clerical
wave was evident in Argentine politics.

The principal argument of Argentine clericals was that secularization laws and practices not only worked against the ultimate spiritual
values that ought to be the proper concern of any citizen but also,
questions of theology apart, were subversive of political and social
order. In this context, events in Spain were made to order, and the
Catholic daily *Pueblo* and the influential Catholic intellectual weekly
Criterio made the most of disturbances that shook the Republic in 1931
and after. To some degree, of course, the Argentine church was merely
following the lead of the Vatican, which had condemned the new Spanish Constitution and continually quarreled with Republican authorities;
but it was also playing a game of its own—holding up Spain's chaotic
political environment as a kind of mirror of the future to Argentine
conservatives who persisted in excluding the church from a role in
national politics.[85]

No member of the hierarchy was more energetic in this task than
Monsignor Gustavo Franceschi, editor of *Criterio*. A brilliant polemicist
and no mean intellectual himself, Franceschi saw the outbreak of the
Spanish war as the confirmation of his direst predictions, and he repeatedly pointed to the holocaust in the peninsula to call errant Argentine
Catholics—and conservatives—to order.[86] During the latter part of 1936
and all of 1937 the back pages of *Criterio* were crammed with accounts
of sanguinary events purportedly occurring in Republican areas. At the
same time, Franceschi threw himself wholeheartedly into pro-Insurgent
activities. With the support of the wife of President Justo,[87] he initiated
a collection of church vestments, chalices, holy pictures, and other sac-
ramental paraphernalia to replace what had reportedly been destroyed
by the "Reds" during the early days of the war. In March 1937 he set
off for the peninsula to deliver personally twenty-seven crates of these
religious objects to the Spanish episcopacy.

The monsignor's journey lasted three months—twelve critical
weeks that bracketed two events in Spain that profoundly shook the
conscience of the Argentine Catholic community. The first was the
bombing of the Basque village of Guernica, presumably by the German

Condor Legion, on April 24. Apart from the horrific impression it was bound to make on civilian populations the world over, this event had an especial effect on Argentina, where a large Basque population was conspicuous for its industry, frugality, and Catholic piety. Moreover, the fact that the attack was the work of German planes gave the lie to the purely "Nationalist" nature of Franco's crusade and raised the disturbing question of whether foreign influence on the Insurgent side might not match—or even exceed—the Soviet domination that Argentine Catholics had long been told prevailed in the Republican zone.

The second explosion that occurred in Franceschi's absence was purely metaphorical but no less devastating—the publication of an article denying some of the principal ideological claims of the Spanish Insurgents by French Catholic philosopher Jacques Maritain, first in the *Nouvelle Revue Française* in June, and in Spanish translation in the distinguished Argentine literary journal *Sur* in August. Maritain's principal point was that, although anti-clerical excesses by Spanish Republicans or their supporters were "infinitely deplorable," these events in themselves were "not sufficient to transform [the Spanish conflict] into a holy war, or rather . . . into a war elevated to the same level and consecrated by God."[88] Let the Spanish Insurgents wage war "in the name of social order, or that of the nation," if they must, he continued, "but let them not kill in the name of Christ the King, who is not a military chieftain but a king of grace and charity who died for all men, and whose kingdom is not of this world."[89] To claim that "the right in the Spanish war lies only on one side" was an argument that Maritain could grudgingly allow to a "conservative atheist" whose values were political rather than religious. But those who used the doctrines of the church to support what amounted to a struggle for social and economic power were committing "a sacrilege in the strictest sense of the term."[90]

As a result of the bombing of Guernica, by the time Monsignor Franceschi returned from his triumphal progress in the Nationalist zone much of the propaganda value extracted from the church burnings of 1936 had been spent and his own moral credit locally was becoming overdrawn. Unflappable as ever, however, the prelate launched a counterattack. On the authority of his recent visit to Spain, he demanded Catholic acceptance of General Franco's version of events in Guernica (e.g., that the city had been burned by retreating Basque forces themselves), and he added that he himself had visited the town (or rather, what remained of it) and found the signs of destruction by arson, rather than bombing, unmistakable.[91] To silence the doubts raised by the obvious presence of Axis "volunteers" in Nationalist Spain, *Criterio* countered that these amounted to no more than 31 percent (including Spanish African levies), whereas the foreigners fighting on the Republican side amounted to nearly 50 percent of effectives, including, needless to say, the ubiquitous Russians![92]

The broadside by Maritain was an even more formidable challenge, since, only twelve months before, the French philosopher had visited Buenos Aires to give a series of lectures—under the auspices of the metropolitan archdiocese. At first Franceschi pleaded with Maritain in a dramatic public letter to recognize that in the Spanish war there could be but two sides—"one, truly demonic, that synthesizes everything that is hatred of Christ; another that, in spite of the shortcomings that exist everywhere in the best of human works, serves God and allows hearts to be lifted up unto Him."[93]

In an equally public reply to Franceschi, Maritain cautioned the Argentines against the "tragic misunderstanding" that the Spanish rebellion would permanently introduce between the church and the working class,[94] and insisted that "if one wishes to avoid the fate that has befallen Spain, then one must avoid the [social and economic] errors that have generated them."[95] Ironically, this was not very far from the monsignor's own political views, of which more below. At the moment, however, it was more important to discount Maritain's views on the morality of the war than to elucidate its causes. Thus, in his final exchange of letters with his French colleague, Franceschi rather unchivalrously suggested that his opponent's views on Spain were inspired less by matters of conscience than by an understandable French "patriotic concern" that the victory of Franco would increase German influence in Western Europe. However regrettable this eventuality might be, the prelate added, it was wholly extraneous to the fundamental spiritual and moral questions raised by the Spanish war.[96]

Franceschi and his associates reiterated these arguments in late 1937 and 1938, to refute the subsequently-published views of French Catholic writers François Mauric[97] and Georges Bernanos[98] on the Spanish war, as well as to denounce the attempts of Spanish Catholics exiled in France to reach a compromise peace.[99] The official Argentine Catholic position thus placed in sharp relief the "Spanish" character of this branch of the church, which retained much of the militant, triumphalist, socially-conservative quality of its progenitor. At the same time, it demarcated the line at which, as late as 1938, French cultural influences in Argentine elite circles abruptly stopped. Perhaps to some degree the uncompromising tone of the Argentine Catholic discussion of the Spanish war reflected an unspoken fear on the part of the hierarchy that this one, final redoubt of peninsular influence in Argentina might at last fall to the godless French. To judge by subsequent history, this fear, if it existed, was not without foundation.

Although the Church remained firm in its position to the very end of the war, even to the point of opposing immigrant visas for Republican refugees, in the final analysis it was forced to content itself with the support of those Catholics whose religious commitment shaded into some version of authoritarian traditionalism. Most Argentines, though nominally Catholic, had no difficulty in reconciling their faith with their more generally liberal political views. Nor was Monsignor Franceschi as successful as he might have wished in teaching traditional Argentine Conservatives what he regarded as the lessons of the Spanish war. For him the Burgos state not merely pointed to a desirable reordering of church-state relations in countries such as Argentina, but was a model for a corporatist, post-liberal economic and social system.[100] When not attempting to score points at the expense of opponents like Maritain, Franceschi could be just as unsparing in his criticism of Spain's pre-war social order, and merciless in his castigation of the Argentine *señoritos* who, he wrote, were committing the same errors as their Spanish counterparts and thus preparing the day when "they will be hostages to social hatred ... the logical and inevitable consequence of vice and injustice."[101] Nor did the prelate excuse the older members of the Argentine establishment, whose persistent "liberalism" in religious matters (and in some areas of domestic and foreign policy) he referred to bitterly as a "leftism of omission" (*izquierdismo de complacencia*), fed by an exclusive concern with "decadent pleasures" while the barbarians were massing at the very gates.[102] This was strong medicine for the habitués of the Jockey Club and the pleasure domes of the Calle Florida, many of whom would have preferred an Insurgent victory in Spain at a far lower ideological cost. Small wonder, indeed, that at the end of the Spanish war pro-Insurgent clericals had advanced no closer to the Mainstream of Argentine politics.

The Media and the Literary Establishment

During the years of the Spanish war, Buenos Aires possessed an extremely vigorous journalistic life—more than a dozen major dailies, scores of weeklies, and many magazines. Although the most prestigious newspapers were subtly (or not so subtly) pro-Insurgent, the Republic enjoyed the support of *Crítica,* a tabloid that in 1936 had the largest circulation of any Spanish-language daily in the world. The Socialist daily *La Vanguardia* made up in enthusiasm what it lacked in design and circulation: its coverage of the war was so heavily slanted toward the Loyalist side that General Franco's victory in 1939 would have come as a total surprise to anyone who read nothing else. *La Vanguardia* developed the theme that eventually underpinned all Loyalist appeals in Argentina—that the war was a clear-cut conflict between two contending nations: one "of privilege, parasitic, reactionary, and retrograde . . . the other, the Spain of the people: virgin Spain, the Spain of honest labor, the altruistic Spain, of elevated mentality and morality."[103] *La Vanguardia* also made it a point to continuously publish photographs illustrating the elaborate efforts of Republican authorities to respect and protect artistic and religious artifacts, not so much to reassure its own readers as to meet the pro-Insurgent public and press on one of its most frequently-chosen fields of battle. A somewhat attenuated version of *La Vanguardia's* treatment of the war appeared in the pro-Radical daily *Noticias Gráficas.* Some of the smaller papers—*El Diario, Italia del Popolo, Argentinisches Tageblatt,* and the *Buenos Aires Herald*—were also favorable to the Republic.

The journals often referred to as the "serious press," *La Nación, La Razón,* and *La Prensa,* were all in greater or lesser degree hostile to the Republic, if not always outspokenly pro-Insurgent. In this they faithfully reflected the views of the Argentine Foreign Ministry and the Argentine Conservative establishment generally. *La Nación,* property of the powerful Mitre family, struck a pose of objectivity by maintaining correspondents in both zones, but its editorial pages were dominated by pro-Insurgent commentators. After 1937 *La Razón* maintained only one reporter in the peninsula—Francisco Casares, a right-wing journalist who had escaped death in the desperate late-summer days of 1936 only by holing up in the Argentine embassy, and who subsequently used his position to settle scores with his former persecutors.[104]

The case of *La Prensa,* most respected of Argentine dailies, was somewhat more interesting. Like *La Nación,* it posted journalists to both camps, and it never specifically declared for either side. Expressing the views of Argentina's traditional Conservatives, it pointedly regretted the conflict and the political polarization that had led to it. The problem in Republican Spain, one editorial stated with characteristic reference to the British system, was the failure to "cushion" popular opinion through indirect representation; what had been wanting there had been "measure and restraint."[105] "What in our opinion has created the painful situation in Spain," it editorialized in mid-1937, "is the unexpected result of the preaching of class struggle."[106] This it deplored in the peninsula and elsewhere. When more moderate elements in the Republican coalition seemed to prevail later that year, *La Prensa* expressed firm satisfaction.[107] In any case, it repeatedly insisted, whichever side won the war, Spain would continue to be Spain—it would never tolerate the imposition of foreign ideologies or totalitarian political systems.

On the other hand, *La Prensa's* coverage of the war was dominated by dispatches from the Nationalist zone drafted by its effusively pro-Insurgent correspondent, Ricardo Sáenz Hayes. A remarkably prolific journalist, during late 1936 and 1937 Sáenz Hayes fed his paper a steady stream of stories emphasizing the Russian role in the Popular Front zone[108] (which he did not take the trouble to visit) while ruthlessly minimizing the German and Italian contribution to the forces of his hosts.[109] At the same time, he repeatedly emphasized the contrast to be found between the "chaos" of Loyalist Spain,[110] which, he told his readers, lived continually under the threat of a "workers' dictatorship of the Muscovite type,"[111] and the "near-normality" that allegedly prevailed in the Nationalist areas.[112] In one particularly memorable dispatch, Sáenz Hayes all but lost control in a lyrical description of the Burgos state: "Order, tranquility, discipline, optimism, . . . schools that function normally, public dining halls for children of soldiers and for orphans, hospital beds for the sick"—in other words, no beggars on the streets. Such was the "fruit of an irresistible moral force" that *La Prensa's* correspondent perceived in Nationalist Spain.[113] There were lessons here for Argentines, he gamely suggested. The most important was that "in order to save itself from impending collapse, liberal democracy must demonstrate that [it] is conceivable within the framework of order."[114]

The most outspoken support for Franco in the Argentine press came from papers that represented ideological extremes and therefore were quite possibly less useful—Catholic periodicals like *Pueblo* and *Criterio,* as well as the "nationalist" papers *Crisol, La Fronda,* and *Clarinada,* which were already at war with Argentina's own republican regime. Although most of the Spanish community in Argentina was pro-Republican, the Insurgents were supported by the *Correo de Galicia* and the *Diario Español,* both of which reflected the views of the expatriate business community.

To deal adequately with the Spanish war and the Argentine literary establishment would require a chapter apart. In general, however, it can be said that, with very few exceptions, discrepancies of view were generational: younger writers supported the Republic. Pro-Loyalist literary figures included writers Alfonsina Storni, Jorge Luis Borges, Eduardo Mallea, and Alberto Gerchunoff, editors Victoria Ocampo *(Sur)* and Roberto Guisti *(Nosotros),* playwright Samuel Eichelbaum, philosophers Alejandro Korn, Saul Taborda, Luis Reissig, Francisco Romero, and Aníbal Ponce, and historians Emilio Ravignani and Ricardo Rojas.[115] Of these only Ponce was a Marxist.

The Argentine delegation to the Congress of Anti-Fascist Writers held in Valencia in July 1937 was decidedly left-wing, as might be expected, given the problematic nature of the journey and the environment in which the congress itself was held. The Argentine representation included Pablo Rojas Paz, Raúl González Tuñón, and Cayetano Córdova Iturburu. González Tuñón had already touched on Spanish issues in *La rosa blindada* (1936), a poetic celebration of the 1934 rising of the Asturian miners. Córdova Iturburu, a Communist militant as well as a poet, subsequently characterized his stay as a brief vision of the future in *España bajo el mando del pueblo* (1938), a testimonial written in the breathless prose style common to the leftist journalism of the period.[116] What is surprising about the Argentine literary involvement in the Spanish war is that—considering the general level of Argentine letters and the achievements the war inspired elsewhere—it generated so little in the way of enduring work. The sole exception is the wartime poetry of González Tuñón, *La muerte en Madrid* (1939), which even so does not approach the level of Neruda or Vallejo.

Nationalist Spain also enjoyed the support of many figures in Argentina's literary world: novelists Manuel Gálvez and Leopoldo Marechal, poets Leopoldo Lugones, Delfina Bunge de Gálvez, Olegario Andrade, and Carlos Obligado, historians Alberto Ezcurra Medrano, Rómulo Carbía, Vicente Sierra, Ismael Bucich Escobar and Carlos Ibarguren, and essayists Ramón Doll, Juan F. Ramos, Ignacio Anzóategui, and Federico Ibarguren. Most of these writers were members of the so-called "Generation of 1900," which had been vaguely anarchist in its day but had settled down later to a conspicuous Catholic piety and a comfortable berth in the state's extensive cultural apparatus. One exception was a young writer, as yet unknown, who would emerge as an international literary gadfly of the fashionable left in the 1960s—Julio *("Yo soy el hijo del Che Guevara")* Cortázar.[117] Shortly after the outbreak of the war, these authors organized the Socorro Blanco Argentino pro-Reconstrucción de España to gather funds to help Nationalist Spain confront "the diabolic forces of Communism." The Argentine branch of the International Congress of PEN Clubs, headed by Carlos Ibarguren, also petitioned the Republican government to spare the life of José Antonio Primo de Rivera,[118] and the Academy of Letters made a similar gesture on behalf of Ramiro de Maeztu, who met death at about the same time as the founder of the Falange.[119]

The principal task of pro-Burgos writers in 1936 and 1937 was not fund-raising or amnesties, however, but cushioning the devastating effect on the Argentine literary public of the wanton murder of Federico García Lorca by Nationalist minions in the first hours of the war. The young Granadine writer had made a triumphal tour of the country in 1933 and 1934 and was still vividly remembered in the Argentine capital for his enormous personal charm, his undeniable talent, and his dramatic works, which met with success on *porteño* boards before they were fully appreciated in the author's home country.[120] Further, Lorca's stay in Argentina was extended enough to convince all who met him, including many writers hostile to the Republic, that he was essentially apolitical.

The death of Lorca was a propaganda challenge that Burgos's literary friends in Argentina bungled almost as badly as their counterparts in the peninsula.[121] At first they claimed ignorance of the circumstances surrounding the poet's death. Then they denied Insurgent responsibility for it, citing the authority of a remarkable interview that General Franco gave Ricardo Sáenz Hayes in November 1937.[122] Finally, when neither claim could withstand further scrutiny, they tried to downgrade Lorca's literary achievement.[123] At the 1937 PEN Club meeting in Paris, Argentine representative Sáenz Hayes managed to force delegates to tone down the text of a memorial resolution,[124] but in the end Argentine enemies of the Republic were forced to join their peninsular colleagues in admitting that Lorca's murder was a costly and stupid political error, as well as a human and artistic tragedy of monumental proportions.[125]

A Change of Guard at the Casa Rosada

On February 20, 1938, President Justo surrendered the seals of office to his hand-picked successor, Roberto M. Ortiz. A former minister in Alvear's government during the twenties, Ortiz was an Anti-Personalist Radical who had joined with Conservatives in creating the Concordancia in 1932. His ultimate reward was its presidential nomination in the 1937 elections, in which he "defeated" his former chief, Alvear, who had returned to national politics as the Radical standard-bearer. In the earlier part of the decade, Ortiz had served both in Justo's cabinet and as the lawyer for several British railroads in Argentina. With his excellent business and political connections, he was an agreeable choice for the traditional wing of the PDN, but his moderate political views and his links to foreign capital were highly displeasing to the new right. Apart from this, both Sánchez Sorondo and Fresco harbored presidential ambitions. Frustrated once again by the preponderant weight of the traditional Conservatives in the Concordancia, they and their followers had to content themselves with symbolic victories at its 1937 convention—passage of a resolution expressing hopes for an Insurgent victory in Spain,[126] and the addition of Interior Minister Ramón S. Castillo to the ticket as vice-presidential candidate.

The men who had selected Ortiz for the presidency expected him to continue the system perfected under General Justo, a curious mixture of legality and fraud, lubricated by patronage. In this they were quickly disappointed. Ortiz indicated shortly after his inauguration that the electoral irregularities that had characterized Argentine politics since 1931 were about to end, by federal intervention in the offending provinces, if necessary. In time this decision provoked a serious crisis within the regime, for it held out the prospect of a return to power of the Radical party six years hence—even sooner in some provinces and in the Congress. Worse still, it implied the end of efforts within the Argentine right to utilize the Conservative restoration to reshape the political system in an authoritarian and corporatist mould.

The full effect of Ortiz's decision on domestic politics was not felt immediately, but its implications for foreign policy were rapidly apparent in the appointing in early 1938 of José María Cantilo to replace Saavedra Lamas at the Foreign Ministry. A career diplomat and a former Radical like Ortiz, Cantilo was identified with the Anglophile wing of the PDN and its liberal traditions in international affairs. At the time of his appointment he was serving as Argentine ambassador to Rome. Italian Foreign Minister Count Galeazzo Ciano, who knew him well, regarded Cantilo as "a disagreeable man and no friend of ours . . . a democrat, a League man, a fathead—in fact, a League man because he is a fathead."[127] The German ambassador in Buenos Aires, Count Edouard von Thermann, concurred. Cantilo, he reported to Berlin, was not merely "an anti-Fascist [but] quite ready to defend the usual liberal democratic ideals together with President Roosevelt." A less desirable replacement for Saavedra Lamas could hardly be imagined.[128]

The Axis diplomats were not mistaken in their judgement of Cantilo. Shortly after he returned to Argentina to take up new duties in April 1938, Argentine missions abroad received a circular letter reaffirming their government's neutrality toward "the political problems now being debated throughout the world." At the same time, however, Cantilo pointed out that traditional Argentine hospitality could no longer be abused by "foreign immigrant communities" in order to introduce into the country "exotic problems of race, religion, or politics, which are completely alien to [our] ideals and interests."[129] Two executive decrees, dated April 27 and April 29, 1938, prohibited the display of foreign flags in public meetings or the broadcast of foreign anthems (except on designated national holidays). "In no case," the second decree read, "may radio stations transmit hymns, marches, or foreign songs that may be taken to symbolize, represent, or display particular social and political tendencies, whatever may be their meaning in their countries of origin."[130] Foreign uniforms and symbols were banned, as were all meetings and public acts bearing on overseas political events.[131] Although this last was apparently inspired by parliamentary revelations of the activities of the Argentine branch of the German National Socialist party, all of these measures implied a desire to proscribe the activities of the local branch of the Spanish Falange as well.

As far as Spanish issues were concerned, however, the change in foreign ministers was most evident in the sudden approval granted on April 22 to Angel Ossorio y Gallardo to be the new Republican ambassador to Argentina. Coming at a time when Chile and Uruguay had but recently appointed "diplomatic agents" to Burgos, and when Peru had broken off relations with the Loyalist government in Barcelona,[132] the willingness of Argentina to receive a new, fully accredited Republican representative was an overt political declaration, all the more so since the envoy-designate had deeply offended Saavedra Lamas's outsized vanity less than twelve months before, when the latter had attempted to launch an international convention on asylum that would have taken as its precedent the Argentine use of its diplomatic precincts in 1936 Madrid.[133]

Nominated by the Republican government in December 1937, Ossorio y Gallardo's appointment had reportedly left Foreign Ministry officials in Buenos Aires "amazed and stupified;"[134] they shuffled and reshuffled the papers relating to the appointment until Cantilo returned home and forced through its approval. The new Spanish ambassador arrived in late June. Having already experienced the diplomatic chill of Brussels and later Paris, Ossorio y Gallardo was prepared for the worst in Buenos Aires, but the change of climate was striking. "Here," he later recalled, "for the first time I was well-received."[135]

The Immigration Question

The new Spanish ambassador was hardly settled in before he discovered that his most serious task would be to deal with Argentine immigration authorities—about Republican Spaniards already in Argentina and, indirectly, on behalf of the thousands who wished to emigrate. By mid-1938 it was becoming increasingly obvious that the Republic was going to lose the war and that the already large Spanish refugee population crowded into French concentration camps would have to be resettled elsewhere. Matters in France had become so difficult, in fact, that the Basque government-in-exile there had dispatched a special mission to Argentina (as well as to Uruguay and Chile) to study the possibilities of relocating large numbers of its people in South America.[136] As time went on, the number of "political" refugees, as opposed to persons merely wishing to escape the destruction of war, threatened to become very large indeed.

In earlier years, Argentina would have been the natural reception point for this diaspora, as indeed it had been for earlier waves of Spaniards fleeing the collapse of the First Republic, the Carlist wars, or the pronunciamiento of General Miguel Primo de Rivera. But—apart from the vastly greater numbers involved—times had changed. Between the overthrow of Yrigoyen and the outbreak of the Spanish civil war, Argentina's traditionally liberal immigration laws had undergone three stringent revisions (1930, 1932, 1936), ostensibly, at least, in response to the world economic crisis. In addition, after 1938 Republican Spaniards found themselves clamoring for asylum alongside unexpected competitors—Jews from Germany and Austria who flocked to the South American consulates of Berlin and Vienna, knowing nothing of the countries to which they sought to emigrate except that they represented the possibility of physical survival.

As early as 1937 Argentine authorities had publicly expressed doubts about the political reliability of this new wave of Spanish immigration;[137] now, an ugly "racial" element was added. (Without belaboring the point, it is indisputable that the Argentine government was no more anxious than that of the United States to become a safe haven for Central European Jewry.) Thus, on July 28, 1938, the Argentine government published a new immigration decree that further restricted entry by foreigners, whatever their origins. The new law established that as of October 1, Argentine consuls abroad would be forbidden to issue visas until the prospective traveler could present a "debarkation permit." These could be obtained only from a committee composed of representatives of the ministries of Interior, Agriculture, and Foreign Relations, who had the right to inquire as to the applicant's motives, skills, and so forth. The idea behind the law, the foreign minister explained at its first reading to the press, was to apply "a more discriminating criterion of selection, in accordance with the country's economic, social, and cultural necessities."[138] Its effect, however, was to drastically reduce the number of immigrants entering the country. By July, 1939, the figure had dropped by nearly fifteen thousand as compared to the same twelve-month period preceding July of the year before. [139] Between the end of the Spanish conflict in April and the opening of the Second World War in September, the numbers fell still further.

In the final days of the Spanish war, friends of the Republic initiated a campaign to except Spanish orphans, or to lift the restrictions insofar as they applied to scientists, intellectuals, and artists "of known moral conditions and reputation." Lojendio publicly warned the Argentine government against relaxing its vigilance against his Republican countrymen—they were of "dissolvent character," he declared, and Argentina would do well to steer clear of them.[140] A full-scale parliamentary debate on the question would have to wait until the end of the war, but the basic framework of Spanish immigration had been laid, presumably at least, for years to come.

The End of the War

In spite of the darkening prospects for the Republic, the Ortiz administration put off recognition of the Insurgents until almost the very end. On January 26, 1939, however, Barcelona fell to the Insurgents, and on February 7 President Azaña fled to France. The same day, the Argentine Foreign Ministry announced that the Republican government in Spain had become "provisionally non-existent" (which was not far from the truth) and ordered the Argentine chargé d'affaires to close his offices and move to France.[141] While the Argentines postponed further action, on February 15 Peru, which had broken relations with the Republic in March 1938, became the first South American government to recognize Franco.[142] Uruguay followed two days later;[143] Venezuela, a week after that.[144] It was rumored (correctly) that Britain and France were about to do the same, and on February 25 Cantilo called a press conference to announce his government's intention of exchanging ambassadors with Nationalist Spain. On February 27, a telegram inviting the opening of formal relations arrived at the Insurgent headquarters in Burgos.[145] In order to make Ossorio y Gallardo's melancholy task of evacuating the embassy buildings in Buenos Aires a bit easier, two Argentine Foreign Ministry officials allowed him to deliver the chancellery compound and its contents to them rather than directly to Lojendio and Francisco de Amat, who came to take possession a few hours later.[146]

The end of the war in April posed two immediate problems for Argentine policy-makers. One was the repatriation of combat volunteers; the other, the continuing controversy over the admission of Spanish Republicans, now as refugees. In January 1939, five months prior to the resolution of the conflict, more than 200 Argentine ex-combatants had been identified in French concentration camps.[147] By July, investigations by Argentine consular officials had raised the figure to 268.[148] Some had already petitioned the Argentine embassy in Paris for financial assistance in returning home, since the Republican bills with which they had been mustered out had since become worthless.[149] Others, however, preferred to avoid their country's representatives for reasons of their own. In late February, Cantilo had ordered Argentine diplomatic officials in France to study each case carefully before issuing funds and papers for return.[150] Shortly thereafter, Ambassador Miguel Angel Cárcano reported from Paris that a number of former members of the International Brigades who had indicated that they did not wish to return to Argentina had disappeared. Others, when visited in concentration camps by consular representatives, had spurned the forms they were handed. "In general," he consoled the Foreign Ministry, "these are Argentines without roots in the country *(sin mayor arraigo)*, with police records *(malos antecedentes)*, and with incomplete, deficient, or false documentation."[151]

Before September 1939, the Argentine government had approved the repatriation of 157 volunteers.[152] In late August, however, the Foreign Ministry suspended its repatriation activities, as Europe became enveloped in a general conflagration. Argentine consular officials found themselves overwhelmed by the clamor for repatriation of their more fortunately placed compatriots. Some ex-combatants who remained in France eventually fought in the Resistance during the German occupation; others, an Argentine dispersion of indetermined size, were swallowed up by French cities and towns and never heard from again. In Argentina itself, the heroes of Brunete and Teruel received a mixed reception. None with police records or serious political problems were allowed repatriation, so that most of these could expect a minimum of harassment. However, a group of thirty young men whose number had been called in the national conscription lottery while they were away fighting in Spain were brought to justice for violation of the Argentine law of military service.[153] The rest were left to look for work, which, like volunteers in the United States, they did not readily find,[154] or to receive the scattered tributes of the Loyalist community and its friends. In time, most of them were reintegrated into the basically non-political environment from which they had come.

The other problem—that of opening the doors to Republican refugees—was not resolved so neatly nor so quickly. A popular campaign to lift existing immigration restrictions, sponsored by the Socialist and Radical parties, was initiated in July, 1939,[155] but in spite of the support of such unimpeachably respectable figures as Marcelo de Alvear and (even) Carlos Saavedra Lamas it met with no success. A full-scale parliamentary discussion in August on the subject of immigration legislation in general, featuring interpellations in the Chamber of Deputies of Cantilo and Agriculture Minister José Padilla, established only that the government was determined to hew to its previously-announced policy of "selective immigration," symbolized by the debarkation permit.[156] On that occasion, Foreign Minister Cantilo frankly avowed that, Argentine tradition notwithstanding, there was such a thing as "bad immigration," although he tactfully abstained from fixing the charge on any one nationality.[157]

Eventually, friends of the expired Spanish Republic in Argentina were compelled to channel their energies and funds toward the resettlement of refugees in more hospitable lands. FOARE raised sufficient funds to sustain for six months the two thousand refugees admitted to Chile in July, and 40,000 pesos (U. S. $12,000) were raised by the Argentine syndicate of taxi drivers to underwrite the settlement of Republicans in Mexico.[158] The Comisión Argentina de Ayuda a los Intelectuales Españoles collected a considerable sum to aid Spanish colleagues in French concentration camps,[159] many of whom ultimately found safe haven in Mexico, Cuba, or the United States.

While government officials in Argentina cloaked restrictive immigration practices behind norms of economic expediency, some anti-Loyalist elements in the country were quite frank about their opposition to the specific admission of Spanish Republicans. For example, the Catholic journal *Criterio* commented editorially that, even if one could forgive such people for the cause for which they fought, "no one can deny that they would bring to our land their problems, their hatreds, their desires for vengeance, and would attempt—as have all political emigrés of every age—to turn our people against the authorities of their own country, . . . to renew from [Argentina the Spanish civil war], and even to provoke a similar struggle among us."[160] To this kind of argument Socialist deputy Juan Antonio Solari, a leader in the fight to obtain visas for Republican refugees, eloquently replied: "We need to abandon the absurd, and I would say even suicidal, policy of closing the doors to foreign immigration under the supposed rubrics of 'extremists' and 'Jews.' These Spaniards who wish to live with us—I affirm it categorically—are worthy of sharing our land." Could Argentines allow themselves, he asked, "to be less generous and hospitable than other sister nations of America?"[161]

The answer, apparently, was yes. With the exception of two special exemptions dated January 20 and July 18, 1940, which opened the doors to Basques from both Spain and France,[162] by 1941 or 1942—apart from the difficulties inherent in wartime shipping—only those Spaniards with excellent Argentine connections and unassailable political records could easily negotiate the barrier. Prototypically, these were celebrities like General Vicente Rojo, former President Niceto Alcalá-

Zamora, former Minister of State Augusto Barcía Trelles, philosopher José Ortega y Gasset, penalist and diplomat Luis Jiménez de Asúa, and historian-diplomat Claudio Sánchez-Albórnoz. One Spaniard who probably could have entered the country without much difficulty, but (perhaps understandably) chose Mexico instead, was former Spanish Ambassador Enrique Diez-Canedo.

The Aftermath

For a time the victory of Nationalist arms in the peninsula seemed the only good news for Franco's Argentine admirers. For, during the late months of 1938 and all of 1939, President Ortiz moved decisively to restore honest electoral practices in a half-dozen Argentine provinces, including Catamarca, home of Vice-President Castillo. Then, in February 1940, in the wake of an unusually fraudulent and violent election in the province of Buenos Aires, the president sent in federal authorities to depose Governor Manuel Fresco. After the outbreak of the European war in September, Ortiz's democratic sympathies were evident in a policy of friendly neutrality toward the Allies, along with decisive measures to curtail pro-Axis activities at home.[163]

Events suddenly shifted course in June 1940 when Ortiz was compelled for reasons of health to take a leave of absence from office. Power was surrendered to Vice-President Castillo, and federal intromission into electoral practices came to an abrupt halt. At the same time, Cantilo was cashiered at the Foreign Ministry and replaced for a brief time by Julio A. Roca, Jr. However, in March 1941 Roca was asked to leave and was replaced by Enrique Ruiz-Guiñazú, ambassador to the Holy See, whose connections with the Axis were a matter of acute speculation and whose affinities for Nationalist Spain were a matter of record.[164] Once established at the Foreign Ministry, Ruiz-Guiñazú convinced Castillo to suppress a report of the Damonte Taborda committee of the Argentine Congress, purportedly exposing, among other things, the activities of Spanish Ambassador José Coll Mirambell in the illegal importation of Falangist propaganda materials.[165]

The appointment of Ruiz-Guiñazú coincided with an increasing coolness toward the Allies, leading many traditional Conservatives to join with Radicals and Socialists in forming Acción Argentina, a popular organization that reaffirmed the country's historic ties with Britain and France. The new international drift of the Castillo government led Ortiz to attempt protest from his sickbed, in which effort he was joined by former foreign ministers Saavedra Lamas, Cantilo, and Roca. Partly on the basis of a difference in foreign policy views, former President Justo began discussions with the Radical party as a possible presidential nominee in 1944.

The division between old right and new was never tested at the ballot box. Instead, on June 4, 1943, the Argentine Army deposed the Castillo government and unleashed a process that unsettled the entire foundations of Argentine politics. The chief beneficiary of this change —in some ways, its progenitor and chief protagonist—was a hitherto unknown officer, Colonel Juan D. Perón, whose name would forever after be linked with Argentina's in the remotest corners of the earth.

The Perón regime (1946–55) was a source of both encouragement and frustration for the Franco government in Spain. During these years Argentina pointedly refused to join in a post-war diplomatic quarantine of the peninsula urged on it by the victorious Allies, particularly Great Britain and the United States. In 1948, Perón went even further and signed a commercial accord that provided the exhausted peninsula with credits for the massive purchase of foodstuffs and agricultural raw materials. Some believed at the time (and others persist in believing today) that this last assured Franco's survival at the most critical juncture of his career since 1936.

On the other hand, in spite of superficial resemblances, there were as many points of conflict as similarity between the two regimes. Franco's first post-war ambassador in Argentina understood as much; in his memoirs he has defined the government to which he was accredited as "an extremely complex union . . . comprehending factions and groups sharply opposed to one another." Insofar as Spain was concerned, he wrote, "there existed elements [within the Perón government] irreconcilably hostile to the Spanish regime, who under various pretexts sabotaged as much as they could" the flow of goods to the peninsula.[166] Though the ambassador offered no names, one needed to search no further than Foreign Minister Juan Antonio Bramuglia and Interior Minister Angel Borlenghi, both of whom were veterans of the Argentine labor movement and conspicuous in the Loyalist aid organizations of the period. And then there was the president's wife, Eva Duarte de Perón, who had made a ceremonial visit to Spain in 1947 and thereafter conceived—in the words of her husband—a dislike for "the abrupt contrast [she found there] between the luxury of the few and the poverty of the many."[167] For his part, General Franco privately complained in 1954 that he could never understand "why that woman conceived such a hatred of Spain after the enormous galas [*agasajos*] that were staged here when she visited us as a state guest—at her own invitation, be it noted. One would have thought that they were giving us the wheat free of charge." And then the caudillo added thoughtfully, "Perhaps, indeed, that is still what many ignorant Spaniards believe."[168]

The fact was that the Argentines were *not* giving the Spaniards wheat "free of charge." In exchange, Spain was obligated to manufacture and deliver a series of merchant bottoms and provide a large schedule of specialized imports—from sherry to olive oil. When the economic situation in Argentina deteriorated in the early '50s, Perón turned to demanding payment of Spain's still outstanding debt in dollar values rather than in pesos or pesetas as provided for in the existing accords. When the Franco government balked, twenty Spanish merchant ships that had gone to Argentina to pick up the latest foodstuffs were sent back empty—at the command of Eva Perón herself, if the Spanish dictator was correctly informed.[169] In 1954 and 1955, Perón's quarrel with the church and the introduction of a divorce law estranged him from Franco, who was already unhappy with the demagogic measures used by the Argentine leader to win over his own working class and with the evident presence in his government of "Masons, Jews, and irreligious Italian immigrants." He ultimately came to regard Perón as "a weak man who in the first instance allowed himself to be dominated by his wife . . . and now [April, 1955] allows himself to be dominated by the [Masonic] lodges."[170] There were no tears shed in Madrid's Pardo Palace when the Perón regime collapsed in September 1955.

One of the legacies Perón had bequeathed to Argentina was a vastly enlarged Spanish Republican community, for, after a long period of tight restrictions, in 1947 Argentina opened its doors once again to massive Spanish immigration, and during this period it provided hospitality to thousands of Republicans, many of whom came to make substantial contributions to Argentine life.[171] In particular, the infant Argentine book-publishing industry received an enormous boost from this immigrant wave, as did banking, education, hosteling, and food processing, as well as light manufacturing. Of course, many of the Spaniards who entered Argentina during these years could not be regarded as "Republican refugees" in the strictest sense; if they came directly from the peninsula, their motives were more often economic than political. But unlike the situation during the last Conservative governments, under Perón no attempt was made to exclude potential entrants on the basis of past Spanish politics. For his part, Perón's relations with the exiled Republican community were always excellent.

If Argentina failed to live up to Franco's expectations, so, too, did the regime in Spain survive to disappoint its Argentine admirers. In spite of the shell of a Fascist movement established under the banner of the Falange, Franco's regime never bothered to breathe life into the thousands of "organic" bodies it created on paper. And far from superseding collectivism and capitalism with a new economic system ("national syndicalism"), Franco presided over a capitalist revolution in Spain that utterly disrupted the semi-feudal institutions on whose behalf he had ostensibly fought. Then, in the 1950s, by signing a defense treaty with the United States that permitted American military bases on Spanish territory, the regime forfeited whatever claim it might once have had to representing for right-wing Argentines a political standard to which they might readily repair. Worst of all, by restoring the monarchy, Franco made possible a peaceful transition to the very institution so abhorred by his Argentine admirers—parliamentary democracy. By 1970, in fact, it was *Spain* that now had a large middle class, a growing industrial base, a literate proletariat, an increasingly up-to-date economic infrastructure, and a precariously moderate political climate. In the meanwhile, Argentina had become afflicted with negative economic growth, outdated railroads and communications, a divided labor movement, a politically hyperactive military, and an intelligentsia given over either to apocalyptic visions or to emigration. The divisions of the 1930s had not been resolved, and a few new ones had been added. For, in addition to the conflict between industry and agriculture, an entirely new element was added to the equation—a working class loyal to the exiled dictator and, after his return in 1973 and death in 1974, to his legend. To many, Argentina seemed ready for a civil war of its own; in fact, by the mid-70s it was already under way—by installments, through the terrorist activities of the left and the right. Insofar as comparisons with the peninsula had any relevance forty years after the close of the Spanish war, it would seem as if Argentina had come out with the worst of both worlds: neither the political peace nor the economic modernization so dearly purchased by her peninsular cousins, at a price that in the end might prove nearly as high. If there were Argentine lessons to be learned from the Spanish experience, it appeared that the most valuable ones of all were precisely the ones that were being missed.

Notes

1. The precise number of Spanish residents in Argentina is extremely difficult to establish, partly because of inadequate census data, partly because of differing legal criteria for determining citizenship. It has been fairly well established that between 1910 and 1935 more than a million Spaniards emigrated to Argentina; since their Argentine-born children were regarded as Span-

iards by the government in Madrid, and since at least a quarter of those immigrants already resident in the country by 1910 can be assumed to have survived to 1936, the figure two million does not seem excessive. "Población de la República Argentina," *Revista de Economía Argentina* 25, nos. 214–16 (1936): 45. A "high Argentine official" in discussion with German Ambassador Count Edouard von Thermann in May 1938 also set the figure at two million. U. S. Department of State, *Documents on German Foreign Policy, 1914–1945*, Series D (1937–45), vol 5, p. 851. (Hereinafter referred to as *DGFP*, with the corresponding volume number.)

2. The 1936 population of Argentina was estimated at 12.4 million. *The Statesman's Yearbook, 1937* (London, 1937), p. 690.

3. "Comercio exterior argentino por paises," *Revista de Economía Argentina* 20, no. 241 (1938): 193.

4. Indalecio Prieto, "Cooperación de las Américas para Reconstruir a España," speech to the Centro Asturiano of Buenos Aires, January 11, 1939, in *La tragedia de España: Discursos pronunciados en América del sur* (Buenos Aires, 1939), pp. 69–70. See also Fredrick B. Pike, *Hispanismo: Spanish Liberals and Conservatives and their Relations with Spanish America, 1898–1936* (Notre Dame, 1971), pp. 221–23, 228.

5. Enrique Pereira, "La guerra civil española en la Argentina," *Todo Es Historia* 10, no. 110 (1976): 7.

6. In that year Argentina purchased 882,000 volumes, twice the number consumed by Cuba. Leopoldo Calvo Sotelo, *El libro español en América* (Madrid, 1927), p. 13.

7. This is the repeated testimony of many witnesses, most notably Julio Irazusta, *Memorias* (Buenos Aires, 1974).

8. See the reports published by Institución Cultural Española, Buenos Aires, *Anales* [1912–1930], vols. 1–3 (Buenos Aires, 1947–53).

9. Here I am following closely the account of Javier Villanueva, "Economic Development," in Mark Falcoff and Ronald H. Dolkart, eds., *Prologue to Perón: Argentina in Depression and War, 1930–43* (Berkeley and Los Angeles, 1975), pp. 57–65.

10. Ronald H. Dolkart, "Manuel Fresco, Governor of the Province of Buenos Aires, 1936–40: A Study of the Argentine Right and its Response to Economic and Social Change" (Ph.D. dissertation, University of California, Los Angeles, 1969), p. 38.

11. Irazusta, *Memorias*, esp. pp. 196–230.

12. In 1928 the Anti-Personalist presidential candidate Leopoldo Melo polled slightly more than 30 percent of the popular vote.

13. Carlos Alberto Pueyrredón, quoted by Mark Falcoff in "Intellectual Currents," *Prologue to Perón*, p. 134. Not all Argentine Conservatives opposed industrialization, but those who did preferred this particular argument.

14. Joseph Tulchin, "Foreign Policy," in ibid., pp. 101–109.

15. Gabriel Jackson, *The Spanish Republic and the Civil War, 1931–1939* (Princeton, N. J., 1965), p. 173.

16. Ibid., pp. 17–18.

17. See Carlos Ibarguren, "The World Spiritual Moment in Literature," *XIV International Congress of the PEN Clubs* [Buenos Aires], *September 5–15, 1936, Speeches and Discussions* trans. Arturo Orzábal Quintana (Buenos Aires, 1936), pp. 15–19.

18. Clifton Kroeber, "Rosas and the Revision of Argentine History, 1880–1955," *Revista Interamericana de Bibliografía* 11, no. 1 (1960).

19. During a building trades strike in 1937 massive numbers of anti-Fascist Italian laborers were forcibly repatriated to their native land and to certain imprisonment, despite efforts of the Argentine labor movement to arrange for a more politically agreeable destination. *La Vanguardia* (Buenos Aires), November 1, 23, 1937.

20. Ibid., September 26, 1938.

21. The same man, Gustavo Martínez Zuviría (pen name "Hugo Wast"), an ardent friend of Nationalist Spain, as Minister of Public Instruction signed the decree-law restoring church influence in public education throughout Argentina in 1943.

22. "Censura postal inadmisible" (editorial), *La Vanguardia,* July 23, 1936. When Interior Minister Ramón S. Castillo was questioned about this censorship in the Chamber of Deputies on September 23, 1936, he abruptly left the Chamber rather than respond. Ibid., September 24, 1936.

23. Enrique Gil, "Repercussions of the Spanish Crisis in Latin America," *Foreign Affairs* 15, no. 3 (1937): 549, 551.

24. *Spanish Republic and Civil War,* p. 277.

25. Adrián C. Escobar, *Diálogo íntimo con España: Memorias de un embajador durante la tempestad europea* (Buenos Aires, 1950), pp. 320–327.

26. *La Vanguardia,* August 11, 1936; *La Prensa* (Buenos Aires), September 17, 1936; República Argentina, Ministerio de Relaciones Exteriores y Culto, *Memoria presentada al honorable Congreso Nacional correspondiente al período 1936–37* (Buenos Aires, 1938), I, 28–38, 63–64, 75. Hereinafter referred to as MREC, *Memoria,* with the corresponding dates and volume number.)

27. *La Prensa,* February 24, 1937.

28. Ramón Serrano Suñer, *Entre Hendaya y Gibraltar* (Barcelona, 1973), pp. 37–45.

29. Julio Álvarez del Vayo, *Freedom's Battle,* trans. Eileen E. Brooke (New York, 1940), p. 240.

30. *Spanish Republic and Civil War,* p. 436.

31. Bullitt (Paris) to Secretary of State, January 30, 1937, U. S. Department of State, *Foreign Relations of the United States, 1937* (Washington, 1964), I, 237. (Hereinafter referred to as *FRUS,* with the corresponding date and volume number.)

32. *Spanish Republic and Civil War,* p. 438; Claude Bowers, *My Mission to Spain* (New York, 1954), pp. 299–302.

33. Text in MREC, *Memoria, 1936–37,* I, 78.

34. Álvarez del Vayo, *Freedom's Battle,* p. 240.

35. Text (dated October 21, 1936) in *La Vanguardia,* November 6, 1936 and MREC, *Memoria, 1936–37,* I, 73–74.

36. *La Prensa,* October 20, 1936.

37. MREC, *Memoria, 1936–37,* I, 46–47.

38. Ibid., I, 24.

39. Ibid., I, 13.

40. Ricardo Sáenz Hayes, "Concepto del Embajador Argentino en España acerca de su actuación en Zarauz," *La Prensa,* August 19, 1936.

41. *El Mercurio* (Santiago de Chile), July 30, 1936.

42. The Mexican ambassador to Peru reported that both Argentina and

Chile had been quietly approached by Lima on (1) recognition of Burgos or, failing that, (2) granting the Nationalist regime belligerency status. Sáenz (Lima) to Minister of Foreign Relations, August 11, 1936, Archivo de la Secretaría de Relaciones Exteriores (Mexico), III/510/(46) "36"/1, III-768-8, hereinafter referred to as ASRE with corresponding folio numbers. I owe this and other citations from the same source to my colleague T. G. Powell.

43. *La Prensa,* August 29, 1936; *La Vanguardia,* August 27, 31, 1936.

44. *La Prensa,* July 26, 1937.

45. One pro-Republican source claimed "on good authority" that some 200 Argentine citizens of Spanish parentage resident in Andalusia had been obligated to serve in the rebel army. *La Vanguardia,* February 10, 1939. The majority of those impressed were progeny of Spanish fathers who after their birth in Argentina brought them back to the peninsula. "Argentinos en la zona rebelde" (editorial), *La Vanguardia,* July 15, 1938.

46. *My Mission to Spain.* p. 291.

47. Lay (Montevideo) to Secretary of State, August 17, 1936, *FRUS, 1936* (Washington, 1954), II, 489.

48. *La Prensa,* August 20, 1936.

49. Cox (Buenos Aires) to Secretary of State, August 18, 1936, *FRUS, 1936,* II, 494.

50. *La Prensa,* September 25, 29, 1936.

51. Ibid., September 26, 1936.

52. *La Vanguardia,* September 26, 27, 1936; Reyes (Buenos Aires) to Minister of Foreign Relations, November 4, 1936. ASRE, III/510/(46) "36"/1. III-776-3.

53. *La Prensa,* February 13, 21, 1936.

54. Ibid., September 7, 29, 1936.

55. Ibid., July 28, 39, 1936.

56. *La Vanguardia,* October 8, 1937.

57. *La Prensa,* September 12, 1936.

58. *La Vanguardia,* June 22, 1939.

59. *La Prensa,* August 5, 1936; *La Vanguardia,* March 5, 1938.

60. Academy of Sciences of the USSR and Soviet War Veterans' Committee, *International Solidarity with the Spanish Republic, 1936–1939* (Moscow, 1975), p. 38; see also Cayetano Córdova Iturburu, *España bajo el mando del pueblo* (Buenos Aires, 1938).

61. Andreu Castells, *Las brigadas internacionales de la guerra de España* (Barcelona, 1974), pp. 377–83.

62. *International Solidarity with the Spanish Republic,* loc. cit.; see also Gregorio Bermann, *Conciencia de nuestro tiempo* (Buenos Aires, 1971).

63. On Codovilla's career and connections, see Robert J. Alexander, *Communism in Latin America* (New Brunswick, N. J., 1957), pp. 73–79; Rollie Poppino, *International Communism in Latin America: A History of the Movement, 1917–1963* (New York and London, 1964), pp. 59, 111–113, 124, 153. His activities in Spain are specifically treated in Burnett Bolloten, *The Grand Camouflage: The Spanish Civil War and Revolution, 1936–1939* (New York, 1968), pp. 115–116, 304. Bolloten is the authority cited at the end of the passage.

64. This conclusion is based on a collation of the manifests of ships bearing home former Argentine volunteers; see especially *La Vanguardia,* June 25, July 23, 1939, and Ministerio de Relaciones Exteriores y Culto, *Informaciones Argentinas* (July, 1939), p. 64.

65. Vincent Brome, *The International Brigades* (London, 1965), dissects the complex motivations of volunteers.

66. *La Vanguardia,* September 20, 1936.

67. Ibid., November 21, 1937.

68. Ibid., July 19, 1936, July 2, 1939.

69. *La Prensa,* December 18, 1936; see also *La Vanguardia,* December 18, 1936, and Bermann, *Conciencia de nuestro tiempo,* pp. 49–56. For the case of Ponce, see *La Vanguardia,* October 28, December 4, 10, 1936.

70. *La Vanguardia,* November 4, 17, 1936.

71. Ibid., February 1, 1938.

72. "Prohibiciones policiales: esencia reaccionaria del gobierno" (editorial), *La Vanguardia,* April 15, 1938; on the same subject, see ibid., April 21, May 8, 1937, and February 13, 1938.

73. Ibid., October 14, 1937.

74. Ibid., August 22, 1936.

75. Ibid., September 2, 1936. Twelve senators put their name to this document, three short of an absolute majority in the upper chamber.

76. Although officials of national cabinet rank stayed away from public meetings on the Spanish war, this was not always the case in the provinces. See the complaints of "Funcionarios oficiales en un acto de española nacionalista" (editorial), *La Vanguardia,* October 5, 1937.

77. Dolkart, "Manuel Fresco," pp. 104–105.

78. *La Vanguardia,* October 22, 1936.

79. *La Prensa,* January 8, 14, 1937.

80. Ibid., December 16, 1936.

81. Ibid., February 21, 1937.

82. *La Vanguardia,* October 22, 1936; *La Prensa,* August 26, September 18, 22, October 31, 1936.

83. For a very cogent discussion of this complicated matter, see John J. Kennedy, *Catholicism, Nationalism, and Democracy in Argentina* (Notre Dame, 1958), pp. 17–23.

84. On this congress see the excellent description of Noreen Stack, "Avoiding the Lesser Evil: The Response of the Argentine Catholic Church to Juan Perón, 1943–55" (Ph.D. dissertation, Rutgers University, 1976), pp. 73–78. A novelistic treatment of the event, excellent from the point of view of social reportage, for all of its melodramatic qualities, is Manuel Gálvez, *La noche toca su fin* (Buenos Aires, 1934).

85. See *Criterio,* passim, 1931–34.

86. "Mártires, rehenes, y verdugos," ibid. 9, no. 461 (December 31, 1936): 413-416.

87. "La cruzada pro iglesias devastadas de España," ibid. 9, no. 456 (November 26, 1936): 309.

88. Jacques Maritain, "Sobre la guerra santa," *Sur* 7, no. 35 (1937): 101.

89. Ibid., pp. 107–108.

90. Ibid., p. 108.

91. "El eclipse de la moral," *Criterio* 10, no. 482 (May 27, 1937): 77–79.

92. "Voluntarios extranjeros en España," ibid. 10, no. 476 (April 15, 1937): 345.

93. "Posiciones," ibid. 10, no. 493 (August 12, 1937): 350.

94. "Puntualizaciones," in ibid. 10, no. 498 (September 16, 1937): 53.

95. Ibid., p. 54.

96. Ibid., p. 55.

97. "La imparcialidad de Sr. Mauriac," ibid. 10, no. 520 (February 17, 1938): 153–54.

98. "La guerra española y los católicos franceses," ibid 10, no. 547 (August 25, 1938): 416–17.

99. "En torno a la guerra de España," ibid. 10, no. 506 (November 11, 1937).

100. "El Jefe," ibid. 10, no. 485 (June 17, 1937): 149–51, allowed Franceschi to describe General Franco as "infused with a desire for social justice, desirous of constructing a *new state* that will be the bridge between Spanish traditions and modern conditions" (p. 149).

101. "Mártires, rehenes, y verdugos."

102. "Demencia," ibid. 10, no. 451 (October 22, 1936): 174.

103. *La Vanguardia,* January 1, 1939.

104. His *Azaña y ellos* (Granada, 1938), published after his return to Spain, contains references to Republican figures that skirt the pornographic.

105. "La libertad y el orden" (editorial), *La Prensa,* January 25, 1937.

106. "El drama de España" (editorial), ibid., July 17, 1937.

107. "Ni fascismo ni comunismo, dicen también en España" (editorial), ibid., October 6, 1937.

108. Ibid., October 24, 29, 1936.

109. "Procúrase desvirtuar la realidad sobre la intervención extranjera en España," ibid., November 13, 1937.

110. Ibid., September 29, 1936, February 13, 1937.

111. "Es evidente que la República Española se debate entre la vida y la muerte," ibid, July 22, 1936.

112. Ibid., October 1, 1936.

113. "La guerra española, tanto o más que una tragedia política, es una conmoción social de consecuencias," ibid., November 17, 1937.

114. "Los tradicionalistas españoles son antiliberales y antidemocráticos como los comunistas y fascistas," ibid., October 10, 1937.

115. Ibid., August 1, 1936; *La Vanguardia,* August 2, 19, 1936; Pereira, "La guerra civil," pp. 16–18.

116. *La Prensa,* July 3, 1937; *La Vanguardia,* July 5, 1937.

117. "Socorro Elanco Argentino pro-Reconstrucción de España," *Criterio* 10, no. 459 (December 17, 1936); see also *La Prensa,* August 15, 1936.

118. *La Prensa,* October 13, 1936.

119. Ibid., October 17, 1936.

120. For an excellent account of Lorca's stay in Buenos Aires, see Mildred Adams, *García Lorca: Playwright and Poet* (New York, 1977), pp. 154–66.

121. For some interesting parallels, see Ian Gibson, *The Death of Lorca* (Chicago, 1977), pp. 136–45.

122. "Para 'La Prensa' El Gral. Franco hizo importantes declaraciones," *La Prensa,* November 26, 1937.

123. See, for example, two articles by José E. Assaf, "Pemán y García [Lorca]," *Criterio* 10, no. 477 (April 22, 1937) and "Sobre la muerte de F. García Lorca," ibid. 10, no. 509 (December 2, 1937).

124. *La Prensa,* June 22, 24, 25, 1937.

125. Gibson, *Death of Lorca,* pp. 145–146, discusses some second thoughts on the part of Spanish Nationalist personalities. I have heard similar ideas

expressed in Argentina by right-wing nationalist intellectuals who lived through this period.

126. *La Prensa,* June 26, 1937.

127. *Ciano's Diary, 1937–38,* ed. and trans. Andreas Mayor (London, 1952), pp. 75, 93–94.

128. Thermann (Buenos Aires) to Foreign Minister, May 18, 1938, *DGFP,* V, 849.

129. Text of this letter, dated June 21, 1938, in MREC, *Memoria, 1938–39* (Buenos Aires, 1939), I, 57–58.

130. MREC, *Informaciones Argentinas* (June, 1938), mimeo., unpaginated.

131. Dolkart, "Manuel Fresco," pp. 129–30.

132. *La Prensa,* February 17, 1938 (Chile), and March 7, 1938 (Uruguay); March 19, 1938.

133. The text of the draft of this convention is in Norman J. Padelford, *International Law and Diplomacy in the Spanish Civil Strife* (New York, 1939), pp. 639–45; Ossorio y Gallardo's brief against the proposal, insisting that it was instigated at the time "solely to aid the fascists," is in *La Prensa,* August 6, 7, 1937.

134. *La Prensa,* January 5, 1938.

135. Angel Ossorio y Gallardo, *Mis memorias* (Buenos Aires, 1946), p. 243.

136. *La Prensa,* October 7, 1937.

137. MREC, *Memoria, 1936–37,* I, 48–50.

138. *La Prensa,* July 29, 1938.

139. *La Vanguardia,* September 1, 1939.

140. *La Prensa,* February 23, 1939.

141. Ibid., February 8, 1939.

142. Ibid., February 16, 1939.

143. Ibid., February 18, 1939.

144. Ibid., February 26, 1939.

145. Ibid., February 26, 38, 1939; MREC, *Memoria, 1938–39,* I, 173–75.

146. Pereira, "La guerra civil española," p. 30; MREC, *Memoria, 1938–39,* I, 179–84; see also *La Prensa,* March 1, 1939, and Ossorio y Gallardo, *La España de mi vida* (Buenos Aires, 1949); p. 179.

147. María de Villarino, "El éxodo español," *Sur* 9, no. 58 (1939): 61–68.

148. *La Prensa,* May 16, 1939; MREC, Informaciones Argentinas (July, 1939), p. 64.

149. *La Prensa,* February 9, 1939.

150. *La Vanguardia,* February 23, 25, 1939.

151. *La Prensa,* March 1, 15, 1939.

152. *La Vanguardia,* March 27, May 14, 22, June 25, July 16, August 23, 1939.

153. Ibid., June 27, 1939.

154. Ibid., July 1, 1939.

155. Ibid., July 11, 1939.

156. República Argentina, Cámara de Diputados, *Diario de Sesiones, Año 1939,* (Buenos Aires, 1939), II, 836–909.

157. Ibid., p. 853.

158. *La Vanguardia,* June 11, 1939; *La Prensa,* July 6, 7, 1939; *International Solidarity with the Spanish Republic,* p. 37.

159. *La Vanguardia,* May 21, 1939.

160. "Intelectuales españoles refugiados en Francia," *Criterio* 12, no. 581 (1939): 369–70.

161. "La radicación de familias españolas en la Argentina," *La Vanguardia,* April 22, 1939.

162. MREC, *Informaciones Argentinas* (August 1940), p. 79.

163. In his address to the opening of the 1939 legislative session of the Argentine Congress, the president deplored the growth of what he called "ideological fronts" based on developments abroad, and called for a "cleansing" of Argentine politics of "ideologies and regimes repugnant to our civic institutions and our psychology." *CD/DS, 1939,* vol. 1, p. 16. Less than a week later, probably in response to the findings of a parliamentary committee investigating the activities of the Third Reich in Argentina, a new executive decree forbade the organization of foreign political parties on Argentine soil. *La Vanguardia,* May 11, 15, 16, 1939.

164. On Ruiz-Guiñazú's general foreign policy views, see Michael Francis, *The Limits of Hegemony: United States Relations with Argentina and Chile during World War II* (Notre Dame, 1977), pp. 175–77. As Argentine minister in Geneva during the 1930s, Ruiz-Guiñazú was well remembered for his pro-Insurgent sympathies, manifested in his conduct as a member of the League of Nations delegation. On his way back to Argentina from Rome in 1942 he stopped in Madrid to pour effusive praise on the Franco regime.

165. Allen Chase, *Falange: The Axis Secret Army of the Americas* (New York, 1943), p. 187. In general I have used this source as it should be used—with extreme care.

166. José María de Areilza, *Así los he visto* (Barcelona, 1974), p. 196.

167. Torcuato Luca de Tena et al., *Yo, Juan Domingo Perón* (Barcelona, 1976), p. 174.

168. Francisco Franco Salgado-Araujo, *Mis conversaciones privadas con Franco* (Barcelona, 1976), p. 17.

169. Ibid., loc. cit.

170. Ibid., p. 95.

171. For a complete list of the better-known Republicans who settled in Argentina, see Vicente Llorens, *La emigración republicana de 1939* (Madrid, 1976), pp. 163–169.

The Contributors

DAVID BUSHNELL is Professor of Latin American History at the University of Florida. His books include *The Santander Regime in Gran Colombia* (1954), *Eduardo Santos and the Good Neighbor, 1938–42* (1967), and *Bolívar: Man and Image* (1970).

THOMAS M. DAVIES, JR., is Professor of Latin American History at San Diego State University and author of *Indian Integration in Peru: A Half-Century of Experience, 1900–1948* (1974). He has edited (with Brian Loveman) *The Politics of Antipolitics: The Military in Latin America* (1978) and (with Víctor Villanueva) *300 documentos para la historia del APRA* (1978).

PAUL W. DRAKE is Associate Professor of History and Director of the Center for Latin American Studies, University of Illinois. His *Socialism and Populism in Chile, 1932–52* (1978) was awarded the Bolton Prize of the American Historical Association.

MARK FALCOFF is Resident Fellow at the American Enterprise Institute and co-editor (with Ronald H. Dolkart) of *Prologue to Perón: Argentina in Depression and War, 1930–1943* (1975).

ALISTAIR HENNESSY is Professor of Latin American History and Director of the Joint School of Comparative American Studies at the University of Warwick. He is the author of *The Federal Republic in Spain* (1962) and *The Frontier in Latin American History* (1978).

FREDRICK B. PIKE is Professor of Latin American History at the University of Notre Dame. His many books include *Chile and the United States, 1880–1962* (1963), *The Modern History of Peru* (1965), *Hispanismo: 1898–1936: Spanish Liberals and Conservatives and Their Relations with*

Spanish America (1971), and *The United States and the Andean Republics* (1977).

T. G. POWELL is Associate Professor of History at the State University College of Arts and Sciences, Buffalo, N.Y., and author of *El liberalismo y el campesinado en el centro de México* (1974) and of *Mexico and the Spanish Civil War* (1981).

Index